CHINA'S RISE

Development-Oriented Finance and Sustainable Development

CHINA'S RISE

Development-Oriented Finance and Sustainable Development

Lixing Zou

China Development Bank Research Institute, China

World Scientific

NEW JERSEY • LONDON • SINGAPORE • BEIJING • SHANGHAI • HONG KONG • TAIPEI • CHENNAI

Published by

World Scientific Publishing Co. Pte. Ltd.
5 Toh Tuck Link, Singapore 596224
USA office: 27 Warren Street, Suite 401-402, Hackensack, NJ 07601
UK office: 57 Shelton Street, Covent Garden, London WC2H 9HE

Library of Congress Cataloging-in-Publication Data
Zou, Lixing.
China's rise : development-oriented finance and sustainable development / by Lixing Zou (China Development Bank Research Institute, China).
pages cm
Includes bibliographical references and index.
ISBN 978-9814596664 (hardcover : alk. paper)
1. China--Economic conditions--2000– 2. Sustainable development--China. 3. Banks and banking--China. 4. China--Foreign economic relations. 5. China--Politics and government--2002– I. Title.
HC427.95.Z6798 2014
332.10951--dc23

2014011430

British Library Cataloguing-in-Publication Data
A catalogue record for this book is available from the British Library.

Typeset by Stallion Press
Email: enquiries@stallionpress.com

Printed in Singapore by B & Jo Enterprise Pte Ltd

Contents

Foreword

It is justified for China to enjoy rapid development. China Development Bank (CDB), regarded as the only development-oriented finance institution of Chinese government, has combined the world's advanced financial theories with China's realistic situations, thus forming the theory and practice of development-oriented finance through removing economic barriers of financing, enhancing the establishment of market credit system, and supporting the smooth and rapid development of economy and society. All of the above reflect some vital characteristics of China's socialist market economy.

Since its founding, CDB has seriously performed its functions and carried out some effective work to accelerate the balanced development among regions, guarantee national economic security, strengthen national economic competitiveness, and promote the development of public welfare undertakings, thus playing an important role in promoting the implementation of major national strategies. For example, CDB greatly supported the extension of emergency loans such as the earthquake relief, the "going global" strategy performed by enterprises on energy resources, the strategies of Western Development, revitalization of northeast old industrial bases, and rise of Central China implemented by the State, as well as construction of rural infrastructure, growth of small and medium enterprises (SMEs), housing for low and medium income families, and financial aid to students and trainings for migrant work. In a word, CDB always devotes itself to the steady and rapid economic development either in adversities or favorable situations. Therefore, it has become an important means for the government to regulate and control the economy.

The reform and growth of CDB have been closely connected with the reform, opening up, and economic development of China, which have been full of explorations, practices, and difficulties. Lots of bottleneck restrictions are imposed on the market system, infrastructure, and social development in China as a transitional economy. In these years, CDB has actively explored and developed the theories and practices on development-oriented finance with Chinese characteristics to tackle bottleneck problems in the economic development, hence achieving outstanding results. By combining government targets with market mechanism, development-oriented finance has been proved to be an important tool to solve such bottleneck problems and quicken the development in China. In the meantime, it is also an important means for China to follow up a road to characteristic socialism market economy. The targets of theories and practices of development-oriented finance are to seek an effective way to combine finance and government, finance and society, finance and economy, and finance and market, and to boost the overall progress and coordinated development of economy and society by means of mechanism, system, and market construction. The cores lie in system building, institutional improvement, market construction, and credit construction. The basic features of development-oriented finance theories are innovation, development, and finance. Such theories and practices not only aim to deal with the financing problem in the medium and long-term construction, more importantly, they would also speed up the construction of system, market, and credit, bring more energy into market, and create conditions for achieving national strategic objectives. In addition, the comrades of CDB seriously summarize the experiences and laws in the practices and explorations, draw wisdom and strength from practices and explorations, and constantly learn, practice, and explore again and again in the changing situations, which is of much significance.

Due to the severe situations brought about by international financial crisis and economic downside, the unfavorable and uncertain factors of external environments are increasing. As a big developing country, China has been staying in the primary stage of socialism for a long time, with a large population, shortage in resources, and unbalanced development. The next period is critical for China to realize industrialization, urbanization, and modernization of national economy. Therefore, we must intensify and improve macroeconomic control in a practical manner, apply a market economy development mode under the leading of the government, and attach great importance to the position and role of development-oriented finance in new situations. For a long period in the future, infrastructure, basic construction, strategic industry, environmental protection, poverty reduction, disease control, and rural development will be the concerns of China's government and the long-term objectives of CDB as a national development-oriented finance institution. Anyway, the role of development-oriented finance is quite important and irreplaceable. The future development of CDB should focus on the medium and long-term policy-related businesses, follow a development route different from that of commercial banks, maximize favorable factors and minimize unfavorable ones, and combine banking characteristics such as commercial transformation and medium and long-term bonds with national development strategies, to continuously improve the market operation mechanism for development-oriented finance, and fulfil differential development of commercial banks. Besides, differential regulatory policies, incentive mechanism, and legal support for development-oriented finance should be prepared based on the improvement of commercial banking form to provide legal guarantee for the long-term sustainable development of CDB.

13 September, 2010
Professor Jiang Zhenghua
Former Vice Chairman of the Standing Committee of the National
People's Congress

Preface

Compared to its worldwide counterparts, China started modernization relatively late and encountered enormous difficulties. Since the Revolution of 1911 initiated by Sun Yat-sen and many others with lofty ideals that ushered in modern industrial civilization, the country has come to embrace industrial technology, modern finance and international credit. The first generation of revolutionaries led by Comrade Mao Zedong brought the Chinese people together to form the People's Republic of China after overthrowing imperialism, feudalism and bureaucrat-capitalism, which weighed like three big mountains on the backs of people before liberation. This event is unquestionably a milestone in China's modernization course. Thereupon, Chinese people become their own masters and have real control of their own destiny. Under the guidance of the second generation of central collective leadership with Deng Xiaoping as the core and the subsequent central leaderships with Jiang Zemin and Hu Jintao successively as General Secretary of the CPC Central Committee, China's unprecedented reform and opening up have brought about remarkable economic and social achievements across the country. Since then, China has embarked on the new era of accelerating socialist modernization and advancing into a moderately prosperous society in an all-round way. Today, China is standing rock-firm in the family of nations as one of the most influential countries in the world. Nonetheless, we are clearly aware that China is still in the primary stage of socialism and needs further development; in other words, while advanced countries have entered the era of knowledge economy, China still busies itself with industrial and economic development. Despite its economic achievements, China is in face of plentiful contradictions and problems, such as: the large population; limited resources; unbalanced development; the wide gap between urban and rural areas, between eastern and western regions and between the rich and poor; the defective and backward market system; the insufficient capacity for independent industrial innovation; the large production capacity but with only a few well-known brands; and the underdeveloped capital market despite the large number of foreign exchange reserves. In the coming 30 years, with around 500 million farmers moving from rural areas to cities and towns, the level of urbanization will escalate from the current 46% to 75%, bringing extremely arduous tasks of the construction and maintenance of urban infrastructure, the renewal of old industrial bases and the transformation of urban regions deplete of resources. In the 21st century, to develop into a moderately prosperous country and accomplish the most spectacular social change in the history of mankind, China needs to overcome a series of bottlenecks and constraints, among which a fundamental problem is how to accelerate financial development and build an efficient market credit system to raise the tremendous medium- and long-term development funds in support of modernization.

China's financial development model is a government-led one in terms of market-oriented finance. The government-let financial development requires planning, regulation, and services, which is conducive to maximizing the organizational function of the government, well handling of relations in a mixed economy, integrating resources and accelerating the development. The market-oriented financial sector requires market players to carry out financial activities by making full use of market-based instruments. This is also a vital factor for improving the financial efficiency and avoiding market risks and is in compliance with the requirements of the law of economic and financial activities. China's financial development model has integrated both sectors into one. As an important form and reflection of government-led market-oriented financial reform, China Development Bank (CDB) has actively quested for development financial theory and practice with Chinese characteristics. With national development goals as its own mission, CDB has improved the macroeconomic operational status through market-based operations, overcome the obstacles of long-term construction financing to provide strong support for the development of national infrastructure, basic industries, strategic industries and social progress, actively participated in global economic governance and regional cooperation, promoted the leapfrog development of industrialization and urbanization, and stepped up the process of modernization.

CDB has always adopted a factual and realistic work style in its exploratory activities. As China's problems arising from its development have no ready resolutions and can never be solved by drawing on foreign experience, CDB strives to ensure the financing source of national key projects based on careful studies of the problems. In particular, since CDB set up the new party committee in 1998, the Bank has conscientiously summed up the lessons of the Asian financial crisis and the global financial crisis, profoundly analyzed the changes in domestic and international economic and social situations, and actively explored new ways of reform and development in strict line with the country's long- and mid-term development strategy. Concentrating on the principal contradiction, CDB has endeavored to realize the government's goals by relying on market-oriented operations and has persistently abided by the standards of first-class international banks. During its operation, it always combines modern civilization with good traditions, draws on international experience based on China's reality, focuses on economic efficiency without neglecting social responsibility, and energetically supports economic and social development while guarding against financial risks; it simplifies complex problems, systemizes simple issues and clearly recognizes its own advantages and disadvantages. Through these efforts, it not only provides financing support to overcome the material obstacles, but also unwaveringly aspires to be the vanguard of the market credit system development. By now, CDB has transformed from a "cashier" of the government in its early years of establishment in 1994 into a development financial institution with significant influence both at home and abroad. It has developed the operational mode and theoretical framework of development-oriented finance with Chinese characteristics, helped achieve national strategies through market-oriented means, effectively implemented the national macroeconomic policies, bolstered infrastructure construction and the development of other key areas, promoted the cooperation of grassroots financial institutions with international giants, and sped up China's urbanization and industrialization. CDB ranks first in terms of market share in RMB bond market and long-term loans (excluding personal consumption loans), and serves as the main bank to provide financing for infrastructure construction, market development and institution building, greatly boosting the fast development of China.

In response to the international financial crisis, by actively implementing the central government's policy of "securing growth, expanding domestic demand and adjusting structure" and taking full advantage of prior planning, sufficient project reserves and sound credit development and preparations, CDB has rationalized the direction and rhythm of extending loans to vigorously support the affordable housing projects, livelihood undertakings, infrastructure construction, environmental protection, post-disaster reconstruction and independent innovation, given full play to the role of development-oriented finance in stabilizing the economic fluctuations, and helped steer the economy toward the direction which the macro regulation and control expects.

Amidst the general trend of the accelerating global economic integration, CDB has actively implemented the "Go Global" strategy and dispatched working groups to over 150 countries to conduct in-depth research on local investment and financing market, seek worldwide business opportunities and vigorously develop international business. At the end of 2011, CDB reported a balance of foreign exchange loans of more than US$200 billion, expanded its business to 113 countries, and became China's largest outbound investment and financing bank. In particular, under the guidance of the central government and the State Council, CDB has delicately operated a number of foreign exchange lending projects like China–Russia Oil Pipeline Project, China–Venezuela Fund and China–Africa Fund, which have great strategic significance and are vital to the national economic security.

As China is at the primary stage of socialism, CDB has played and will continue to play its special role in accelerating China's modernization process. After years of efforts, CDB has formed distinctive development-oriented finance theory through practice, and has proved and will continue to prove with practical results that: planning is a core competitiveness; in the market economy, unique competitive advantages can be obtained by adhering to the inherent law of planning-led development, discarding the irrational part of planned economy and inheriting and carrying forward the rational ones, and consciously regarding prioritized planning as business philosophy; market credit system building is an important drive for economic development and credit enhancement, and can speed up the market institutional building; bond financing based on national credit can be a good source of funding for the medium- and long-term development; building a risk management mechanism jointly with social forces and giving full play to financing portfolio can better guard against financial risks; and by developing the bank though party building, making full use of political and organizational advantages and nurturing a credit culture with Chinese characteristics, efforts can be concentrated on major projects. Moreover, by adhering to the working principles that feature government priority, timely help, prior planning, credit building, and financing promotion and by establishing a business model featuring government entry, financial incubation and market exit, we can link government targets to market mechanisms and promote institutional building, market development and credit building through financing, thereby not only able to solve the difficulty of medium- and long-term construction financing, but also enhance market players' function to lay a foundation for the realization of national strategic goals. Development-oriented finance is an important means in compliance with the needs of national development and the requirement of financial system reform to mitigate the constraints and address development issues, an important manifestation of the socialist market economy with Chinese characteristics; it reflects the advanced productive forces, advanced culture and the fundamental interests of the overwhelming majority; and it is also a key demonstration of the scientific outlook on development and an essential force of the modernization drive.

In recent years, under the leadership of the State Council and relevant departments, CDB has endeavored to forge ahead on the basis of summing up experience and has ushered in a new stage of development. According to the CDB Reform Program of the State Council, CDB will be transformed from a policy financial institution into a commercial bank. After the reform, it will support significant long- and mid-term development strategies of the economy by providing financial services such as long- and mid-term credit loans and investments. In other words, the foremost focus in long- and mid-term businesses which CDB should persist in after its transformation will distinguish it from other commercial banks. In the meantime, the Reform Program further clarifies that CDB will become a multi-purpose bank with credit and investment functions. Thus, it can be seen that the reform of CDB is very different from that of other state-owned banks including ICBC, ABC, BOC and CCB. Aiming to establish a development financial institution that takes shape of a commercial bank, the reform of CDB is a new exploration in China's financial system reform and also an energetic initiative of accelerating the modernization process.

The reform and development of CDB is an important component of China's long- and mid-term development strategy. Considering the complex domestic and international situations and the tasks China is facing, the reform and development of CDB need to concentrate on serving the national development strategy, reflect the requirements of financial ecological diversity and further take full advantage of development-oriented finance to stand out in international competition. CDB will persist in the reform and development, improve the financial model, adhere to market-based operations, combine the fund management strength of development-oriented finance with the organizational advantage of the government, improve development financing mechanisms, and boost the healthy development of credit entities, investment and financing platform. In line with the overall layout of economic and social development, CBD will continuously give full play to the strengths and role of medium- and long-term investment and financing, adhere to the direction of medium- and long-term business and uphold the position of medium- and long-term bond bank to promote the building of credit system, support the development of basic facilities, basic industries and pillar industries, grassroots financing and international cooperation. It will further improve corporate governance, business process, and incentive mechanisms in accordance with the requirements of modern financial enterprise, stimulate the innovation of business model, enhance competitive edge and maximize comprehensive income; and it will further strengthen overall risk management, promote the implementation of the new Basel Accord, and improve social supervision mechanism to achieve first-class performance. Furthermore, CDB will vigorously shore up the financial cooperation with Latin America, Africa, and neighboring countries of Asia and speed up the implementation of the "Go Global" strategy to support the sound and rapid social and economic development and promote the modernization process.

China's modernization is a significant initiative to rejuvenate the Chinese nation and an important chapter in the development history of world civilization. Characterized by the coexistence of both advanced and backward facets and the intertwining of both old and new contractions, the present-day modernization is facing many unprecedented opportunities and challenges. With a high sense of mission and responsibility, under the guidance of the scientific outlook on development, all members of CDB have joined forces with people from all walks of the society to energetically explore the theory and practice of development-oriented finance with Chinese characteristics and do their bit to accomplish the country's all-round modernization as soon as possible.

Written in the setting of great history, great change and great challenge, this book is suitable for economic workers, college teachers and students as it contains a systematic study of the theory and practice of development-oriented finance that has evolved along with China's reform and opening up, and an in-depth analysis of the ideological basis, theoretical contents, operating principles and innovative development of Chinese-style development-oriented finance. Hopefully, the publication of this book will promote further discussions and researches on China's modern economic and financial systems and in turn the sustainable development of the Chinese economy and the world economy at large.

Introduction: Reflection on Development-Oriented Finance in China

One

China has developed so quickly in the recent 30 years, which is a big surprise to many people around the world. We are so proud of such great achievement, reflecting our people's great efforts. As a witness of these great events, I am responsible to record my experience through those changes in order to share with more people. As a participant of this reform, I should reflect on the theory and practices of this reform for making some contributions to our next generation. As a person working in the economic field, I aspire after knowledge, especially after the road which my country has followed to achieve economic success. With the opportunity to work in China Development Bank (CDB) and to participate in the building of theories and practices of development-oriented finance under the leadership of Chen Yuan, I will present some of my opinions of development-oriented finance. Development-oriented finance, as a special financial movement, has the task of policy making, but does not rely on fiscal policy subsidies; has a market function, but does not pursue profit; and has the nature of financial enterprises, but more to reflect the government's intention. This financial market-oriented means is utilized to achieve national development goals, especially playing a special role in support of national infrastructure, strategic industries, livelihood projects, and country building. This kind of theory is combined with China's reform and opening up policy to attain growth and progress despite the difficulties it faces. Acting as a government development-oriented financial institute, CDB actively explores the socialist market economy with Chinese characteristics, promotes the project construction and credit institution building, and breaks the bottleneck of financing to support social and economic development, forming the theory and practices of development-oriented finance. Studying and concluding this theory and practice, I deeply feel that it is the crystallization of advanced theory and Chinese reality, an innovation of mechanisms of development, and a real record of financial services and national long-term development strategy. It contains China's reform and development experience, reflects the way of social construction with Chinese characteristics, and demonstrates the spirit of the times of great changes; it has certain positive influence on China's sustainable development. China's development has surpassed that of developing countries and is synchronized with the international economy.

Two

The book contains 4 parts and 20 chapters. I have concentrated on four parts, namely, (i) the logical basis of development-oriented finance, (ii) the theoretical contents of development-oriented finance, (iii) the operation mechanism of development-oriented finance, and (iv) the reform of development-oriented financial institute. I hope that this study will contribute to the research of China's modern financial institution, serving China for better development.

There are five chapters in Part 1, which discusses the logic foundation of development-oriented finance. It includes the following:

(1) China should seize the main contradiction, especially the main contradiction in the mid- and long-term economic development. In the initial stage of socialism in China, the economy developed under the background of resource restrictions where social demand exceeded the total demand without proper limits. This kind of development is on the stage of tight economic operation. The deepest and most central reason of tight macroeconomic operation is defective and backward of the credit system. The lagged credit system cannot meet China's huge demand of industrialization and urbanization, rapid progress in infrastructure construction, the upgrading of the

industrial structure and consumption structure, environmental protection, ecological construction, and social undertakings.

(2) China should explore the solution to the problem in a realistic way. In the process of economic development, the government plays an important role in the allocation of resource through financial transfers and public goods supply but we should not rely only on government finances, instead of that, we need to make full play of the market credit, business credit, and personal credit. As important financial institutions, commercial banks are essential for the modern credit system construction, but the governance structure of commercial banks, the way to prevent the risks, and their goal of seeking profits determine that they are unable to provide long-term loan. As a result of that, it is difficult to meet some basic financing demand of certain industries and to support the field which needs financing services but lacks credit. Moreover, it is difficult to balance regional economic development. Although international experience is worth learning, it cannot solve China's own problems. China's problems require the solutions provided by development-oriented finance. CDB looks for truth from facts depicting national conditions. It always makes creative work, explores the development-oriented finance with Chinese characteristics, and actively solves the contradiction between the enormous financial demand and the lagged financial market development.

(3) In the process of solving the conflicts, we should develop Marxist dialectical theory of credit. Credit activities have common attributes with construction projects and other social activities, while there are some unique properties for it, such as social, moral, and subjective. As the basis for social activities, credit activities not only reflect the reality of existence but also continue to create a new existence. **Credit is able to be built and credit construction can be driven.** Development-oriented finance finds an internal conversion condition between the lack of credit and existence of credit, which can speed up the construction of credit system.

(4) We should inherit and carry forward our fine traditional culture and political organizational advantages, and speed up market credit

institution building. Traditional Chinese culture is the ideological source of development-oriented finance. Development-oriented finance attaches great importance to the development of the financial responsibility of the modern credit. On the one hand, it makes full use of historical resources to speed up the construction of the modern credit system. On the other hand, it enriches our culture by constantly thinking of modern credit and financial knowledge, which lays a fundamental basis for consolidating long-term development.

(5) We should judge the basic direction and motivation of sustainable development under the conditions of international competition. There are two kinds of globalization in the modern world. One is based on the US as the driving force of globalization, forming the consumption engine for global economic development. The other is the globalization driven by China's urbanization, namely, China's urban infrastructure construction and industrialization are the engines of this kind of globalization. Development-oriented finance is based on global strategic thoughts. On the one hand, it attaches great importance to the US-led financial consumption power, while avoiding the emergence of China's "new fetishism of commodities" and abuse of consumer credit. On the other hand, it firmly grasps the huge market and opportunities brought by urbanization. In economic globalization, China's urbanization is the world's largest modern movement and the enormous demand that comes along with urbanization provides new opportunities and incentives for improving the modern credit structure. Development-oriented finance adheres to "credit will be around the whole world". Like the revolution of credit to provide adequate funding for the consumer in the United States during the 20th century, development-oriented finance provides adequate credit support for urbanization, acting as the engine power for increasing urbanization in China.

There are five chapters in Part 2, which is concerned about the theoretical contents of development-oriented finance. It mainly contains the following:

(1) Planning is the core competence. Scientific planning should reflect the strategy of economic and social development, comprehensive, balanced, and innovative requirements. We can support development and avoid risks by prioritizing planning, grasping the key points, integrating government, financial and market forces from the upper side, finding major projects, identifying resourcing potential, giving full play of the forces of multifarious fields, scientifically predicting strategic credit space, reasonably using existing resources and future resources, making overall arrangements for medium and long-term infrastructure funding and funding in the key and relatively weak field, whilst considering the balance of cash flow and profits balance, and jointly promoting the credit building, institution building, and market development.

(2) Credit building of the market is the key propulsion of economic development. In developing countries, credit building of the market can be a priority to integrate the different forces of society, especially integrating the relating elements of market credit with institutions, including planning, political advantages, and traditional culture. We should give full play of every part of the market in order to promote the development of the market credit and guarantee the operation of the society and market, which is a must to ensure the long-term sustainable development.

(3) Efforts should be taken to transfer the forces of market with the forces of government so as to accelerate the construction of credit system. Development-oriented finance brings to light the government's organizational advantage in imperfect financial markets, creatively builds the financing mechanism coordinated by the government, simultaneously meeting the national conditions to promote the building of credit system. We can better address the financing needs of urban infrastructure construction, major projects and hot issues, speeding up the infrastructure construction and livelihood financial development.

(4) We should play the advantage of financing in a combined way, which is not only able to prevent the risk but also support our construction. Financing in a combined way is a financing mechanism of integrating resources, arranging funds properly, hedging risks, and

coordinating development, which is reflecting the "using ideas of combination to guide the development, while using the wholesale way to carry out risk management". This kind of idea expands on the extension of the Western portfolio investment theory, helping to extend the financing business model of developing the urban infrastructure and in other areas. It not only leads to support economic and social development by better utilization of social capital, alleviates the bottleneck in economic and social development and the relatively weak part so as to promote the formation of diversified investment and financing system, but also improves the asset structure of financial institutions, asset quality and risk prevention capacity, and overall business efficiency.

(5) The socialization of finance is closely connected with the mid- and long-term development. Through the social organization and management of credit resources to establish a social-based, systematic, and standardized credit system, we will be able to allocate profits and risks in a social way, which will be done in a "fair, integrated, and transparent" manner so as to make everyone enjoy their privilege of financing, meet people's immediate needs, and support the construction of harmonious society. **Moreover,** it adheres to the party building, banking operation, consolidating the micro-political foundation of long-term development. The Chinese Communist Party uses its strong advantage of political organization to enable China to achieve success. CDB actively explores the development of grassroots party organizations, adheres to the combination of traditional Chinese culture with the party's mission, the combination of political party building with business building and the combination of political party's ideology advantage, political advantage, organization, and coordination strengths with the advantages of bank financing. We should utilize party construction to promote the development of the bank and use the development of the bank to test the party construction, making party building and bank building integrate in goals and measures so as to strengthen the function of grassroots party organizations.

There are four chapters in Part 3, which explores the key factors of development-oriented finance operation, mainly including the funding resource, operation mechanism, and governance structure and management style. Development-oriented finance raises the fund for mid- and long-term construction and livelihood matters, depending on the government's credit to issue financial bonds. This kind of funding mechanism expands the credit of government and strengthens government's monetary credit. We should utilize government's credit correctly; transfer the short-term and socialized fund of commercial bank to long-term and big amount of money so as to effectively arrange the social funds to support the mid- and long-term infrastructure construction and development of social affairs. Concurrently, it cuts the connection of mid- and long-term construction with basic money from the sources, lowering the systematic risks of financial industry. Development-oriented finance insists on the principle of operation as "government entrance, financial support, and market exit". **Government entrance is that development-oriented finance actively sheds light on the area where market function is not working well, and gives play of the government's organization advantages. Financial support is to implement the idea of development-oriented finance, raise capital to promote credit construction, improve the construction of the legal system, cash flow, credit, and project, and at last form mature projects and market institutions which meet the regulation of commercial operation and the requirements of financial risk management. Market exit is that development-oriented finance adjusts its strategy according to the change of situations.** It mainly reflects in the area that giving away some shares of loans, introducing market funds; leaving a part of the traditional markets, opening up the field of blue sea; leaving some part of the developed regions, developing the backward areas; leaving some part of the large-scale projects, fostering SME projects; and leaving some part of domestic business, expanding international markets. The basic operation structure of development-oriented finance is one center, three main lines, four features, and an opening structure.

(1) *One center*: we focus on customer-oriented feature, enhance customer relationship management, improve bank governance, and consolidate the basis for financial development.
(2) *Three main lines*: we set up our business, risk control, and support systems to protect three types of departments.
(3) *Four major features*: the internal organizational structure reflects the characteristics of "flat, flexibility, specialization, and integration".
(4) *Opening structure*: We focus on the business-oriented feature and establish the structure based on the open-matrix structure. With the help from all sectors of society, we build organizational structure based on "four platforms and one association" (government finance platform, financing platform, security platform, supervision platform, and credit association), extend the root nets and form the open structure. Development-oriented finance adheres to the management style of "diversified service, marketed operation, and regulated management". We implement financial activities in a large-scale and deep manner; integrate domestic and foreign resources; scientifically use credit, investment, investment banking, and other various financial instruments; improve operational efficiency; and strengthen the core competitiveness to serve for major and long-term economic development strategy and social development.

Part 4 includes 5 chapters from Chapters 16 to 20, which discuss some profound problems of financial reform in the global background of great history, great reform, and great challenges.

(1) Commercialization of CDB is different from the reform in commercial banks. Since the commercialization of CDB, we need to continue our financial business in mid- and long-term credit and investment, serving for significant mid- and long-term strategy of national economy. China's urbanization has entered a new climax, which needs CDB to provide more mid- and long-term capital for urban construction. CDB's policy tasks are harder and heavier. Despite continuing support for infrastructure, basic industries, and pillar industries, CDB gives support to grassroots finance, "going

out" policy, new and high technology, and industrial updating. There is an increased awareness to maintain quantity as well as quality of the policy tasks. According to international norm, serving for long-term national strategy needs the government to ensure long-term and all-round policy support, especially national credit support. Therefore, CDB's reform requires analyzing problems realistically and sticking to "practice, cognition, and then practice".

(2) Second, the imbalanced development of China determines China's diversified finance. It is vital to actively explore development-oriented financial institutes with characteristics of commercial banks.

(3) Third, China's finance confronts with opportunities and challenges in the global reform. We should make our goal, task, and measures clear in China's stable economy and mid- and long-term development.

(4) Fourth, financial diplomacy is a great event of China. With the development of globalization, international financial relationship has become an important part of international relations. The focus of the giant countries is not the cooperation and competition in the fields of military, but the priority to make the financial regulations. In order to be a great country in the world, we need a brilliant strategy for diplomatic relationship with other countries. From the overall situation of China's strategy and the regulations and features of financial work, development-oriented finance adheres to "goodness priority" to build long-term credit relationship; adheres to "give more and ask for less" to build sincere credit relationship; adheres to "resource exchange" to build mutual helping credit relationship; adheres to "diversified service" to build flexible credit relationship; and adheres to "focus on key points" to develop credit relationship with countries from the third world, mainly emphasizing on cooperation with Asian, Latin American, and African countries.

(5) China needs to handle the following four relationships to ensure that our economy develops in a stable and fast way: (i) the relationship between domestic market and international market; (ii) the relationship between real economy and virtual economy; (iii) the relationship between financial innovation and regulation; and

(iv) the relationship between financial reform and development. To confront with the financial crisis and the imbalance and unsustainable development of China's economy, we should conclude from our history lesson and build a long-term system to prevent financial risks.

Three

We emphasize the giant impact advanced theory has had on construction and development. As a development-oriented financial department of the government, CDB adheres to the combination of epistemology and practice, looks for the credit conversion conditions between immature and mature credit, promotes the market of credit system construction in the basic socioeconomic areas and relatively weak areas, and vigorously forms a number of important ideas of development, improving and enriching itself in practice.

(1) *The ideas of development*: the market can be developed and market development can be promoted. Market development must be people-oriented and based on institutions as the main body. Away from the financing main body with creativity and good credit structure, all financial activities will lack their source. Development-oriented finance attaches great emphasis on strengthening the development of financial market, giving full play of people's creativity, developing people's inherent potential, developing government departments' organizational advantages and various resources, and adhering to rearing the blood-making function of main credit body so as to make them have a long vitality.
(2) *The idea of planning ahead*: planning is a kind of thought of development. Scientific development planning is a combination of knowledge and practice: "Science" is the theory of knowledge which is mainly reflected on the relationship between man and awareness of nature, awareness of country's actual conditions, and the understanding of its own path to achieve success by economically lagged countries. "Development" is the practice theory, mainly reflected in the application of science and technology, not

only recognize and obey the law of science and technology and socioeconomic development but also use the law to speed up development. Scientific development planning in developing countries is the foundation for regaining the initiative, avoiding detours, speeding up development, and an important prerequisite for scientific development. Development-oriented finance insists that planning should be put in the first position and committed to give full play of planning as the core of competitiveness so as to effectively adjust the overall situation.

(3) *The idea of strategic option*: strategic option is a combination of epistemology and practice. Strategy is epistemology and is the understanding and planning for the future; option is practice and is an application of financial technology. Strategic option is an important technical and ideal support for the scientific development planning. In the process of planning the development of a region or a sector, we should take full account of the actual and potential strengths of the region and rationally use its credit support demanded by large-scale construction so as to attain the goal of avoiding risks and speeding up development. Development-oriented finance uses strategic options to achieve the profit and loss in the overall balance in the process of support for the local and major industrial development, while in the meantime using the continuous financial arrangements to resolve the problem of the realization of a sustainable long-term investment returns and profits in order to support economic and social sustainable development.

(4) *The idea of credit by organization*: rely on the advantages of governmental organizations, use the basic role of government credit, improve linkage with fiscal financing, and promote the healthy business, healthy finance, and healthy coordinated economic development. Development-oriented finance adheres to combine their own financial advantage with the advantage of government organizations, combines the nature of quasi-debt funds with financial assets management, improves the development of financing mechanisms, promotes government, business, and market mechanisms to be combined into the main body of credit and financing platform so as to transfer the state credit,

bank credit, and the local government into business credit. On the one hand, we can guarantee the security of assets and on the other hand, we can support the economy to develop in an overall, coordinated, and sustainable development.

(5) *The idea of creativity*: creativity includes creative thinking, system innovation, and technological innovation, all of which aim at overcoming the difficulties in the process of development and reducing contract costs. Creative thinking is the people's interaction and a human revolution to overcome its own difficulties, which is helpful to reduce system cost; system innovation is the interaction between people and is the system's development, which is helpful to reduce the cost of the technological revolution; technological innovation is the interaction between man and nature and is the human act to transform nature and protect the environment, which is helpful to reduce production costs. Development-oriented finance adheres to theoretical innovation, institutional innovation, policy innovation, product innovation, and establishing financial theory with Chinese characteristics. We should establish modern credit system from the optimization of microeconomic behavior, in order to explore new ideas for economic development.

Four

To facilitate understanding, we hereby provide the following explanations on some new concepts.

In this book, "**Development-oriented finance**" refers to a financial entity that aims to realize government objectives and promote the sound, rapid, and sustainable development of the economy and the society. As CDB is the innovator and practitioner of such financial entity, we treat development-oriented finance as an animate subject and sometimes make no special distinction between it and CDB during our narration.

The development of market credit system is an integral part of the socialist market economy of China, and also a major focus of the book. To simplify narration, "market development" and "credit system building" as mentioned in the book both refer to **"the development of market credit system"**. To accelerate the development of market credit system is imperative for developing countries to achieve rapid, healthy, and sustainable development. This is a basic idea of development-oriented finance.

The concept of **"credit capital"** mentioned in the book reflects the close relationship between the efficiency of capital use and the development degree of market credit system. A sound credit system will increase the capital mobility and significantly improve the efficiency of capital investment.

All in all, development-oriented finance plays initiative function under the guidance of the scientific development concept, adheres to dialectical thinking, innovation, correctly handles the relationship between internal reasons and external reasons, between the government market and enterprises so as to build an effective macro-policy and market adjustment transmission mechanism and break the credit bottlenecks, provide financial services and promote economic and social sustainable development. The theory and practice of development-oriented finance is not only good to CDB's work but also good to other kind of work, not only beneficial to China's economic development but also beneficial to the international community, particularly to developing countries. The theory and practice of development-oriented finance will continue to deepen and develop, while this study will be carried forward.

Part I

The Logical Basis of Development-Oriented Finance

Development-oriented finance is the outcome of the reform and opening-up policy, which is a system built to deal with the bottleneck of the development. This kind of finance undertakes policy-related tasks, but does not depend on funding from fiscal policy; it has the function of market, but does not aims only at pursuing market profits; and it has the characteristics of financial enterprises, but represents the intention of the central government. As the development-oriented financial institute of the government, CDB actively explores and improves socialism market economy with China's characteristics, breaks the bottleneck of fund raising, and promotes the construction of market credit system so as to support China's booming economy. Moreover, CDB has formed the theory and practices of development-oriented finance. From studying and comparing the theory and practices of development-oriented finance, it is not hard to find that China's development-oriented finance links with China's special problems, solutions, thoughts, and culture and also has a close relationship with our international environment. In this part, we analyze the logical basis of the theory and practices of development-oriented finance, making efforts to answer the question of "how to produce". There are five aspects that are addressed: (i) seize the main contradictions, especially seizing the key contradiction between mid- and long-term development; (ii) find the solutions to problems realistically, actively working out the contradiction between economic development which calls for a great demand for finance, and the lagging of the financial market development; (iii) modernize the theory of credit and find an inner condition for transferring from lack of credit to existence of credit; (iv) inherit and carry forward the fine traditional culture and the advantage of political organization, escalating the development of market credit system so as to consolidate the basics for mid- and long-term development; and (v) judge scientifically the basic direction of sustainable development and impetus for urbanization under the conditions of international competition, and promote the development of urbanization and the development of consuming finance market.

Chapter 1

Seizing the Major Contradiction in Development

China stays in a period of strategic opportunities characterized by its adjustment toward global patterns, development of urban areas, and transformation of mode of production. As a result of China's basic conditions, there are lots of contradictions existing in its economic and social development, in which, from the point of economy and finance, the most prominent one is the contradiction between huge financial demands and the laggard development of its financial market. As finance is the core of socioeconomic development, the causes and solutions of all development problems can be traced from finance. China Development Bank (CDB), as a development-oriented finance institution of the government, combines advanced international theories with China's actual situation, adheres to the theories and practices of development-oriented finance, concentrates on the principal contradictions occurring in the tight operation of its macroeconomy, and discusses the acceleration of medium and long-term infrastructure construction and sustainable development mechanism of the economy and the society.

1.1 China's market credit mechanism cannot meet the needs of smooth and rapid economic development

The founding of the People's Republic of China, in particular, the 30 years of reform and opening up to the outside world have profoundly changed the destiny of an old nation. Economic development, social progress, improvement in people's livelihood, and building comprehensive national strength are some of the factors that have brought in tremendous changes in this great land that constitute the remarkable achievements of China. However, China generally lies in a middle stage of industrialization, with many deep problems and formidable medium and long-term construction tasks. A series of challenges would appear in the course of economic globalization, including the following aspects. First, the development of urban and rural areas remains imbalanced, and income gap should be further narrowed. Among the 1.3 billion people in China, 44% of them live in urban areas while the remaining 56% live in rural areas. The spending by rural people is about one-third that of urban ones, that is, three peasants equal one urban resident in terms of purchasing power. Second, industrial structure is unsound, agricultural foundation is fragile, industry is extensive but not strong, and service industry lags. In the economic structure, structures of production, resource, market, technology, and business organization present strategic defects, and such defects are becoming more and more manifest and acute. Third, independent innovative capacity is not powerful enough because of the lack of independent intellectual property rights, core technologies, and global well-known brands. Among the 49 major countries in the world, China takes the middle and low place with respect to innovative capacity in science and technology and is inferior to developed countries and even developing countries such as Brazil and India, respectively. China's dependence on foreign technologies reaches over 60%, while that of developed countries is less than 30%, in which, that of USA and Japan is only below 5%. If such a situation cannot be altered soon, China will be regarded as a low-tech and low value-added country in the international division of labor on a long-term basis. China is confronted with a significant strategic choice in her economic development to enhance her independent innovative capacity in an all-round manner. Fourth, economic development entails huge costs on resources, environment, and society. The economic growth in China still presents low efficiency and quality, and the extensive mode of growth, i.e., high input, high consumption, heavy pollution, uncoordinated development, and low benefit, has not been changed fundamentally. Fifth, social development lags behind economic development, showing an uneven state, and resulting in big pressures on employment and social security. It will be hard to meet the needs of the people for the development of social public welfare undertakings if it only relies on the market-based allocation of resources. Thus, we still have a long way to go in building a harmonious society. Many new subjects have been brought forward in terms of further deepening of system reform as well as adjustment of economic structure, social structure, and interest pattern. China's actual situation is that its advantages and disadvantages exist together, new contradictions and old contradictions make the situation more complicated. A variety of problems in connection with its economy and society indicate that China's macroeconomy stays in a state of "tight operation".

1.2 China's macroeconomy will be in a state of tight operation for a long time

In the primary stage of socialism, on the one hand, China's economic development is restricted by natural resources, human capital and managerial competence, innovative capacity, technological conditions, development environment, and other economic resources; on the other hand, various changing demands of social members push forward the over-expansion of aggregate demand. For the purpose of utilizing limited economic resources to a maximum extent and meeting various demands of social members, it is inevitable to generate a state of tight economic operation represented by excessive growth of demands and restriction by resources. The basic features of such a tight operation include the following: (i) despite the over-supply in some aspects in a certain period, aggregate demand is more than aggregate supply by and large; (ii) severe structural imbalance exists due to excessive growth of aggregate demand; and (iii) tight allocation of macroeconomic resources and sluggish allocation of microeconomic resources coexist during the allocation of social and economic resources. The dynamic mechanism of tight operation lies in the following: first, defects are inevitable in the national economy of China, which could be related to both products and sectors, resulting in a state of shortage. In a market economy, it is difficult to regulate quantum and major structural relationship in the national economy by means of market price mechanism, thus it is hard to overcome the problem of shortage. As China is a country with an undeveloped market economy, it will face great difficulties if it attempts to reach economic balance by market regulation. Though administrative interference by the government may release some pressures, the shortage dominates the market explicitly or implicitly. Under such circumstances, aggregate demand will show a trend of over expansion, bringing about the exhaustion of some important resources and eventually result in economic imbalance. If macroeconomic planning is not ready, China will overly meet middle-economic (region) and microeconomic (enterprise) demands for investment and consumption, and excessive importance would be attached to the control of quantum by value balance in terms of the relationship between value balance and physical balance, where non-price defects may give rise to economic shocks. And then macroeconomic retrenchment and structural adjustment will ensue. Second, there are six influential interest bodies in the operation of China's national economy, i.e., (i) country, (ii) central ministries and commissions (line status), (iii) local governments (square status), (iv) enterprises, (v) social organizations, and (vi) families (residents). Different interest bodies have different pursuits, and big discrepancies exist between communities. In particular, central ministries, commissions, and local governments shoulder diverse economic and social responsibilities, which often scramble for investment and role in the national economy, exacerbating the shortage economy. Presently, China's mechanism to operate its economy comprises both the unity and the discrepancy among different economic bodies. Ideally, the community of interests would constitute the foundation of an economy's harmonious operation. Therefore, any discrepancy in interests is the root cause of economic shocks. Third, the tight operation in China is determined by historical characteristics in the primary stage of socialism, and it is an inevitable outcome from the mode of production and operational rules in such stage. Some mechanisms need to be further improved to aid the development process, for example, the balance mechanism on demand and supply, and self-motivation and self-discipline mechanism of economic bodies in respect of production and consumption. Currently, China's systems cannot effectively restrain the growing demands. Particularly, the lack of a demand restraint mechanism at the microeconomic level makes the asymmetry between social demand and supply graver. The stronger the economy surpasses the growing demand levels blindly, the more difficult the effective and synchronous growth of supply is. Consequently, it is hard to restrain the excessive growth of social aggregate demand, making tight economic operation become a basic feature in the primary stage of socialism. About 20 years ago, Mr. Chen Yuan made such judgment,[1] which has been proved by nearly 20 years of development. In the current and next periods, the above contradictions and challenges appearing in the economic development of China are not related to the above-mentioned feature, and China's decisions and choices on reform and development have taken the above-mentioned feature into consideration. Overall, in the primary stage of socialism, China's economy is always stays in a state of "tight operation", which is the basic national condition of China.

1.3 The underlying reason of tight operation of macroeconomy lies in the laggard market credit system

The underlying core reason for the tight operation of China's macroeconomy is due to its defective and laggard credit system, that is, the backward financial system. Funds are essential in construction and development. Shortage could be summarized as shortage of funds. Scrambling for investment and resources is just for the

[1] Chen Yuan: *Economic Research*, Issue 8, 1987, "Tight Operation: A Basic Feature of Economic Operation in the Primary Stage of Socialism in China", p. 17.

dominance of funds. Why do social aggregate demand and supply show a state of imbalance? Why is it hard to regulate the quantum and major structural relationship in the national economy by means of price mechanism? We may attribute the reasons to China's defective and laggard credit system. A strong credit system is the basic system and fundamental pattern for the allocation of resources in the country. **An advanced credit system mobilizes credit resources from various sources, promotes the development of productive force, reduces currency flows, accelerates capital turnover, and facilitates the establishment and development of modern enterprise system.** Conversely, a laggard credit system will severely hamper credit information flow and credit transactions in the whole society, and lead to the segmentation of economic resources and high trading costs as well as restrict social and economic development. According to the relationship of economic interest, Karl Marx once analyzed the capitalist credit system in a dynamic manner and elaborated the position of the credit system on a profound basis. He said, credit system accelerated the material development of productive force and the formation of world market. Marx developed the material basis for a new form of production to a relatively high degree.[2] As a result of a laggard credit system, credit defect is grave comparatively, which could extend to other areas of the economy and severely affect the harmonious development of economy and society. This is not a simple economic problem, but the problem of a state's basic system, because behind the credit system is the creditworthiness of a country and the government. It is also one of the important perspectives in Marx's credit theories.[3] Problems in a credit system cannot be solved only by reliance on the market. Its construction could be treated as a social system project, covering economy, culture, education, and politics, which will be affected by both tradition and the outside

[2] Karl Marx: *Das Kapital*, Volume 2 [M], People's Publishing House, 1st Edition in June 1975, pp. 499–501.

[3] Karl Marx: *Das Kapital*, Volume 3 [M], People's Publishing House, 1st Edition in June 1975, pp. 455–457.

world. In addition to the government credit system, the credit system also includes market credit system, corporate credit system, and personal credit system, that is, some micro-credit systems exist in the society (the micro-credit system has several forms, which can be a person, a family, a company, a department, or even a region). An advanced credit system will be necessary to connect such numerous micro-credit systems, to develop into a sustainable credit system for the entire society. The key here is to establish an advanced credit system. A system is the guarantee of a framework. In the case of lack of the credit system, it would be impossible to build a "bridge" for the development of the capital market, sustain the financing system for economic development, and develop standardized credit and securities financing. Besides, the contradiction between huge financing demands for urban infrastructure and short supply will not be perfectly tackled. At present, China's economy, system, and market are developing, loans are provided by banks in an energetic manner to support China's economic growth, and the role of financial system in national economy keeps improving. Nevertheless, the arrangements of the Chinese financial system, to a large extent, fall behind the requirements of economic reform and development, with the bank's low efficiency in extending credit. Structural distortion is found in the allocation of credit resources, and financial development fails to keep up with social and economic development, thus becoming a bottleneck and a weak link in the country's socioeconomic development. Financial development involves a series of deep problems and long-term contradictions, reflecting periodic characteristics in the economic development and special problems in the transitional period. Beside the historic problems and new situations brought about by all-round opening up, the fundamental problem lies in the laggard modern credit system of China. For that reason, China's financing system reform should aim to strengthen the construction of a modern credit system, build a social credit system, construct and maintain an efficient market, and bring high efficiency in finance into full play. In order to resolve financing difficulties and credit bottlenecks, the root of problem must be thoroughly dealt with (Figure 1.1).

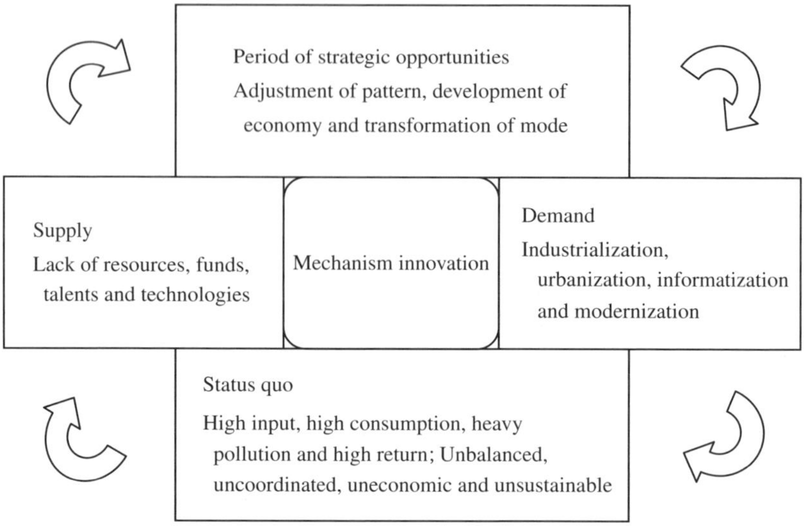

Figure 1.1: China's economic forms.

1.4 Summary

The contradiction between huge demands for rapid economic growth and the presence of a backward credit system is the principal contradiction in the economic development of China. The laggard credit system is far from meeting the stupendous demands from the rapid development of industrialization and urbanization in China, such as the demand for infrastructure construction, upgrade of industrial and consumption structures, environmental protection, ecological construction, and development of social undertakings. At present, China faces the major problem of defective credit arrangement, represented by low recognition to credit, much importance to material construction, and contempt to credit construction and financing system construction. These are the key reasons for the laggard financial reform and backward economic development in China, and are also a major "bottleneck" in economic development, especially in market system construction. As a basic economic system within the scope of history, a credit system emerges and develops due to the needs of economic development, and changes with the development of the productive force. In a market-oriented economic development, the general credit level of the society reflects an equilibrium point between the supply of and demand for resources, while the status of market credit system suggests the development level, development environment, and development conditions of a country or region. Countries with a developed market economy usually have a sound credit system. And China, a country staying in the primary stage of socialist market economy, particularly needs the support from a credit system. It is hard to believe that the transformation of economic system and economic development can go smoothly in a country which has a weak credit foundation. Hence, the construction of a credit system is a core component of China's socialist market economic system. As a development-oriented finance institution of the government, CDB targets at transforming credit construction into its core competitiveness and a controllable mechanism. Fundamentally, China lacks no funds, but it lacks an effective mechanism to mobilize and allocate funds. Also, the Chinese are short of an effective mechanism to arouse the credit of the whole society, not credit elements. As pointed out in the Decision on Improving Socialist Market Economic System issued at the Third Plenary Session of the Sixteenth Central Committee of the Communist Party of China, it is of significance to expedite the construction of a social credit system.

Chapter 2

Realistically Exploring the Solution to Problems

We should adhere to the principle of being pragmatic and realistic toward development-oriented finance based on national conditions and have the courage to innovate, explore an effective approach, and address the principal contradiction in a tight macroeconomic operation.

Such principal contradiction lies between rapid economic growth and backward credit system. Development-based ideas and approaches are necessary to explore an effective mechanism that arouses and activates the entire society's credit and establish a modern credit system. The following factors are essential requirements in addressing problems in economic development: (i) summarizing experiences, (ii) studying the problems, (iii) analyzing the contradictions, and (iv) proposing ideas based on the principle of being pragmatic and realistic. In implementing sustainable development, the key is to research and identify the problems to be solved, and to establish advantages and disadvantages. This way, great efforts should be made to explore a basic long-effective mechanism by taking into consideration people's fundamental and long-term interests.

2.1 Traditional approach cannot tackle the problem of backward credit system in China

Without doubt, the government's financial support plays an important role in the construction of a modern credit system. However, it is far from enough. The role of market credit, corporate credit, and personal credit must be brought into play. In the meantime, a transmission mechanism for macroeconomic policies and market regulation should be established between the following: (i) government credit and market credit, (ii) market credit and corporate credit, and (iii) corporate credit and personal credit. In the course of economic development, the government plays an important role in the allocation of resources by means of financial transfer and supply of public goods. Under a modern market economy, finance serves as an inherent automatic stabilizer. Nevertheless, during economic fluctuations, it is not enough to handle the problem only by relying upon the government's financial support. First, the effect of the government's fiscal policies, more or less, is subject to the government's financial strength. Relative to the development of market economy, financial strength is limited, thereby restricting the impact of fiscal policies. Furthermore, in terms of financial expenditure, there are two parts: one is the non-production and construction expenditures, which are rigid without much room for adjustment. The other is the production and construction expenditures, which mainly include investment expenses. The increase or decrease in such expenditures will obviously affect social aggregate demand to a certain degree. The budgetary investment of the State is mainly used for key construction projects complying with national economy and with the need to enhance people's livelihood to ensure a reasonable economic structure. As a result, when social aggregate demand is more than aggregate supply, the demand retrenchment cannot rely only on the reduction of budgetary investment. If it does so, the economic structure of the country will worsen.

Second, the effect of fiscal policies on the adjustment of imbalance between social aggregate demand and supply is not satisfactory. When social aggregate supply exceeds aggregate demand, expansionary fiscal policies should be adopted to increase the demand and curb supply. Here, the expansion of government's expenditure has a certain "crowding-out effect" on personal consumption and social investment. When social investment is excluded from the government's investment, changing demand bottleneck by means of financial expenditure will show less effect. If social aggregate demand is greater than aggregate supply, tightening fiscal policies will be taken to curb demand and increase supply. In this case, the available means include increasing taxes, issuing bonds, reducing subsidies and balancing the budget. However, these means are not different with respect to the effect imposed on social aggregate demand and supply, i.e., restricting production and controlling aggregate demand.

Third, China's fiscal policies sometimes are subject to monetary policies without flexibility. For example, a bond issue is the most commonly used fiscal policy means by the government. In a market economy, bonds should be issued by the central bank, in general. Issue of bonds is a major part of fiscal policies, but bonds controlled by the central bank constitute a part of monetary policies and become an important instrument to regulate financial markets. Consequently, the central bank has the initiative to control social aggregate demand by means of bonds, which depends on the targeted needs of monetary policies.

Fourth, fiscal policies have little connection with the market mechanism. Instead, such policies are more connected with the planning mechanism, which may lead to the phenomena of laggard policies. And the decision to adopt financial interventions or not is likely to generate laggard judgment, selection, implementation, and correction. With the deepening of market economy and opening up to the outside world, the frequent and long-term use of fiscal policies will jeopardize the normal and healthy development of socialist market economic system.

Needless to say, as important financial institutions, commercial banks play a certain role in policy transmission and resource allocation between the government and the market as well as between the market and the enterprise, which is an essential element in the construction of modern credit system. Nevertheless, the corporate governance structure, methods of risk prevention, and motives in seeking interests in the commercial banks signify that it is hard for them to provide long-term loans, meet financing demands of some basic industries, offer financing service to SMEs, and balance regional economic development.

For a long time, China boasted no genuine commercial banks. Influenced by the former Soviet Union, China adopted a planned economy after founding and established a financing system focused on fiscal financing. The government then took measures to control economic resources which were essential for the development of the country. The State made savings mandatory from partial incomes of urban and rural residents by means of industrial and agriculture price scissors and low salaries. Funds were centralized by forcing state-owned enterprises to turn in their profits, so as to allocate funds to the industries and areas that needed investment. This helped to develop a nationwide system of "unified receipt and payment". Under such a system, investment activities were decided by government plans, and investment resources were allocated by the government in full amount, which played a certain role in controlling limited resources, and quickening industrialization and capital construction. Banks had been established during this period. However, they were not functioning as financing institutions but as a cashier. The credit activities of banks exerted almost nil influence on social financing and financing decisions. After the reform and opening up in 1978, China's planned economy system was transformed to a market economy system step-by-step, wherein the national income distribution pattern changed profoundly, residents' saving levels rose, and the proportion of government's financial revenues in national income declined. Therefore, financial funds were insufficient to sustain the growth of the economy. In 1985, China began to transform the financing system focusing on "loans converted from allocated funds" and "financial allocations" to a system focusing on "bank financing". Banks in different areas gradually regained their functions as a bank, changing the role as a cashier of government. Commercial banks started to grant loans to enterprises, but mainly to the state-owned enterprises designated by the government. Thus, government's financial allocations decreased. Enterprises, the main body of market economy, gradually restored their decision-making power. However, the rigid dependence of state-owned enterprises on financial allocations remained unchanged. As the market was underdeveloped, the rigid demands for long-term funds in economic development made state-owned commercial banks become a major financing tool of the government to provide public and policy financing services.

This way, the pressure on capital turnover and distortion of supply exacerbated. Under the control of the government, commercial banks, bearing huge reform costs brought about by economic transformation, were more like a department of the government instead of an enterprise. Some state-owned enterprises occupied credit funds of banks on a long-term basis. Mergers, divisions, acquisitions, bankruptcies, other forms of evasion of bank debts, high non-performing loans (NPLs) ratio, and low efficiency brought commercial banks into trouble. Despite the monopoly position in the financial system covered by the sustained growth of savings, the problems of commercial banks were hard to see on the surface, but actually the difficulties were quite severe. After China's entry into the World Trade Organization (WTO), commercial banks and enterprises carried out joint stock reform in a positive manner. The former was engaged in the stripping of non-performing assets and more importance was attached to modern commercial banking system and modern enterprise system. As important financial institutions, commercial banks played an essential role in the construction of modern credit system, with some significant advantages, such as: commercial banks boasted comparatively complete branch networks which could supervise loan projects in different areas at any time and send feedback on important information in a timely manner; commercial banks could provide deposit and loan services to enterprises and residents with stable funding sources; commercial banks could provide abundant financial products including deposits, loans, and fee-based services to customers along with customized financial services. Of course, they also had some disadvantages, including decentralized funding sources, short-term deposits, inability to independently undertake large construction projects, "maturity mismatch" brought about by long-term loans and short-term deposits. In addition, the lack of personnel in carrying out professional assessment of projects under review rendered projects without being assessed for stability and risk factors. In particular, the corporate governance structure, their instinct for risk prevention, and motives in seeking interests of commercial banks indicated that they could only operate in a mature market environment. For immature and underdeveloped markets, it was obviously beyond commercial banks. This is why medium and long-term financing in China has become a bottleneck in social and economic development, and businesses in counties and small and medium enterprises (SMEs) always have troubles in securing loans.

According to international experiences, a development-oriented finance institution backed by the government will fulfill the government's objectives in the form of market operation, which will help to accelerate the construction of a modern credit system. In response to an international financial crisis, fully exerting the functions of development-oriented finance is an important approach for the government to regulate market and maintain the healthy development of the economy and the financial structure. China can draw upon international experiences, but such learning cannot solve the problems of China. Development-oriented finance with Chinese characteristics should be evolved to deal with such problems.

Earlier, development-oriented finance was adopted by developed countries to evolve special macroeconomic and managerial measures. The Great Depression that occurred in 1929 forced the American government to interfere with its economic operations, in which one of the measures it adopted was to establish a development-oriented finance institution. At that time, to ease the tough situation brought about by the Great Depression, investment activities were recovered. The Hoover Administration, which was in pursuit of free market, set up the Reconstruction Finance Corporation (RFC), a financial company affiliated to the federal government. The main purpose of establishing the company was to prevent the failure of national credit machine. During the period of Roosevelt, RFC's functions and sphere of activities were expanded considerably. The federal government often let it handle some activities which were hard to be authorized by the Congress such as purchase of gold and foreign trade credit. In this way, RFC quickly extended its scope of loans to almost all economic areas, acting as an important leverage for the American economy to develop into a state monopoly capitalism. After World War II, most countries embarked on the objectives of resuming production and rebuilding their economies. A great amount of funds were mobilized by countries to develop or reconstruct industrial enterprises. To realize such objectives in a fast manner, many countries adopted the strategy of relying on government force, thus development-oriented finance gained rapid development. The United States established professional development-oriented financial institutes including Freddie Mac and Fannie Mae; Germany set up the KfW Bank and the Industrial Bank of Berlin; and Japan established the Renaissance Financial Corporation, Japan Development Bank, and regional development-oriented financial institutes such as Japan Finance Corporation in Eastern Hokkaido and Industrial Revitalization Corporation in Okinawa. In particular, it should be pointed out that according to the Marshall Plan, America proposed to establish International Bank for Reconstruction and Development (IBRD), i.e., World Bank. The initial purpose was to raise funds for economic reconstruction after the war. Later, financial aid was provided to developing countries through the World Bank. In fact, the economic position of the United States gave it absolute control over these institutions. The true purpose of providing aid to foreign countries was to strengthen its special economic and political benefits. The international community also established other international development-oriented financial institutions to provide long-term capital and financing service for the reconstruction and economic development after war. In 1970s and 1980s, economic globalization and financial liberalization emerged gradually. Both developed countries and developing countries carried out financial reforms one after the other to reorganize financial institutions. Under the impact of such a wave, development-oriented financial institutions in various countries made corresponding adjustments. Some were closed, some were transformed, and the remaining policy banks adjusted their businesses to adapt to the new situation. The financial downturn and world economic recession brought about by the Asian financial crisis in 1997 and the US sub-prime mortgage crisis in 2008 enabled people to rediscover and rethink the importance of development-oriented finance. Faced with the failure of commercial banks, credit damage, increasing bad debts, bankruptcy of enterprises, and rising unemployment rate, governments of the countries affected by the crisis again requested development-oriented financial institutions to exert their important functions to reconstruct their economies. It has been proved in practice that development-oriented financial institutions could play a significant role in helping affected countries to resume production and reconstruct their economies in a rapid manner. Besides, they have become an integral part of a country's financial system. By its nature, development-oriented finance, as a means of the government to regulate economy, is usually adopted by governments during some special periods or development stages. Especially when the country's financial system is not very sound or in the event of a crisis, development-oriented finance has proved to be effective. Besides providing loan assistance, technical aid is offered and support is given to train personnel and introduce advanced technologies to help regions affected by the crisis to recover and sustain long-term development. Making a comprehensive view of international development-oriented financial institutions in both developed and developing countries, the basic functions of development-oriented finance are to provide assistance in the process of economic development, support the determination of key industries, and propel the development of local economy. Functioning as an important tool for state interference and economic regulation, development-oriented financial institutions supplement the limitations of market mechanism and contribute to the rapid development of the economy. Currently, there are 550 development-oriented financial institutions in the world — their strategic positions and irreplaceable functions are becoming more and more manifest. As required by national macroeconomic and financial development strategies, development-oriented financial institutions can be broken down into much more professional development-oriented finances, such as development-oriented finance for SMEs, for agriculture, for import and export, and for social security and insurance. In terms of implementation and realization of national macroeconomic and financial development strategies, development-oriented financial institutions are more powerful, effective, and direct compared with commercial finance. With changing economic and financial environments, development-oriented financial institutions in various countries dynamically adjust specific business areas according to changing environments and degree of industrialization. As international and domestic climates vary, the development orientation, business model, mechanism and organization, and business areas of development-oriented financial institutions show great variance. The successful experiences of countries in development-oriented finance are based on local social and economic situations. Due to varied financial environments and economic situations, it is irrational for China to imitate the financial systems of developed western countries. China's characteristic socialist politics and economic system as well as its background of social and economic development require China to choose a route of economic construction and financial development with Chinese characteristics. Moreover, the core competitiveness of financial sector cannot be drawn upon — China's financial system, financial development strategies, and financial culture must be rooted in China. With respect to reform and sustainable development, Chinese policy banks, on the one hand, should learn and meet the reform and development trends of international policy banks, to advance with the times. On the other hand, the actualities of China and its financial ecological environment should be taken into consideration, so as to explore a sustainable development road with Chinese characteristics for policy banks. It could be said that development-oriented finance is the major orientation in the reform and development of Chinese policy banks.

2.2 CDB explores a development route for development-oriented finance in a positive manner

In a modern society, it is critical for a country to maintain long-term stable economic development and establish a sound, effective, and coordinated financing mechanism. Making a comprehensive view of different countries, a variety of financing methods including fiscal financing, policy financing, credit financing, and securities financing, are essential for economic and social development. Based on national credit and fiscal resources, fiscal financing is a primary form of direct financing to carry out the government's functions, which is necessary for the development of national public welfare undertakings and the maintenance of social justice. Policy financing, as an extension of national finance, makes up for market energy by means of fiscal means such as subsidy to achieve the targets of the government. This financing method is also indispensable as it guarantees reasonable allocation of social resources and helps in recovery from market failures. Credit financing, taking commercial banks as financing agency, requires the security of assets and flow-back of funds under the laggard restriction by the public and the market. As an indirect financing method in the market economy, it is a basic way to satisfy social capital needs. Securities financing is extensively restricted by the public and market risks. It can be directly participated by the public, but needs the support of a highly developed social credit system. This kind of financing method is strongly based on the society and the market with low costs and high efficiency. These four financing methods have diverse functions and operational rules. Under different market environments and economic development stages, their functions and contributions vary, but with long-term coexistence.

China still focuses on large-scale credit finance with numerous non-performing assets. As the financial system and its rules are fairly fragile, the effect of coordinated development of multiple financing modes cannot be brought into full play. To achieve that, the scale should be matched and functions should be supplemented, except the growth of financing numbers, financing concepts, methods, and systems are required to be innovated. Hence, we should accelerate the construction of financial infrastructure and micro-systems. On the one hand, the leading role of credit financing should be fully exerted; on the other hand, the macro-control effect of fiscal and monetary policies should also be brought into play. The focus on government financing should be shifted to the combination of government financing and market financing. Capital market should be cultivated in an accelerated manner to integrate credit market, bond market with stock market, and ensure that they promote each other and develop in a coordinated way. Now the question is: How to quicken the construction of financial infrastructure and micro-systems to support the above focusing field?

According to international and domestic experiences, as an important transmission mechanism between macroeconomy and micro-enterprises as well as a major bridge between government and market, development-oriented finance is a significant promoter and leverage to accelerate the construction of a modern credit system. It not only helps to exert the advantages of various financing methods but also helps to establish an effective financing mechanism with coordinated development. The China Development Bank (CDB) aims to achieve the social and economic development objectives of the country and governments at various levels and build an effective and coordinated investment and financing mechanism to form a developed financial market system. In addition, by combining advanced international financial theories with China's actualities, CDB actively explores the theories and practices of development-oriented finance with Chinese characteristics, so as to set up a development-oriented finance mode which adapts to national conditions (Table 2.1).

Table 2.1: Formation of development-oriented finance theories.

Stage	Time	Features
Stage of exploration	March 1994 to August 1998	Basically operate according to traditional policy banking mode
Stage of initial creation	August 1998 to November 2000	Sign financial cooperation agreements with local governments; create bundled loan mode
Stage of formation	November 2000 to March 2003	Design of credit structure Evaluation system for credit development degree
Stage of improvement	March 2003 to November 2008	Focus on credit management: propose portfolio risk management; Determine the positioning of development-oriented finance institution; expand grassroots businesses in the counties and carry out "going global" business
Stage of deepening	November 2008 to 2013	Explore the development of development-oriented finance institution in the form of business

Until now, CDB has gone through five stages including (i) exploration, (ii) initial creation, (iii) formation, (iv) improvement, and (v) transformation (deepening). Development-oriented finance theories are continuously tested and improved in practice, laying a sound ideological foundation for the reform and development of the CDB. An advanced banking operation mechanism in accordance with international practices has been established in the Bank, making operating results continuously reach new highs. Outside the Bank, the construction of a market credit system is promoted, and system defects and market failures are remedied to facilitate economic development.

The period from March 1994 to August 1998 concentrated on the preliminary exploration of development-oriented finance when the CDB basically operated and managed development-oriented finance according to the traditional policy banking mode. In March 1994, the CDB was established with the approval of the State Council. Due to shortage of funds in the country, CDB undertook two aspects of responsibilities including guaranteeing the fund needs of national key projects and preventing inflation arising from blind expansion of capital construction to solve the problem of arrears in the key projects. Affected by the macroeconomic system and the existing stage of economic development, the working systems in the initial period of CDB were the extension of fiscal financing by and large, without strong market awareness and concepts. CDB operated the banking business by following the concepts and ideas of administration, allocation, and subsidy. Projects were designated by government departments, bonds were issued according to administrative plans, and loans were granted under the entrustment of commercial banks. Basically, CDB could be regarded as a "cashier" bank. Its lending risks continuously accumulated as commercial banks. At the end of 1997, the Bank's NPLs reached RMB170 billion, with the NPL ratio of 42.7%, bringing CDB into a difficult state. In this case, it was hard for the Bank to act as a development bank in the country's economic development. During this initial period, almost everything depended on the government, and the Bank ran its operations without considering the banking law.

The period from August 1998 to November 2000 marked the stage of initial creation of CDB's credit construction theories. It was also the stage of basic construction of theories on development-oriented finance. In August 1998, CDB signed a financial cooperation agreement with Anhui Provincial People's government, symbolizing that CDB had started to create credit construction instruments and construct a new type of financing mechanism by taking advantage of the government organization. The Asian financial crisis in 1997 alarmed China's financial sector. The astronomical NPLs and defect risk had become great hidden dangers to national economic development. Financial sector, as a subsidiary of governmental finance, has failed to meet the requirements of new situation. The contradiction between the defect in the financial system and market, and the requirements of rapid economic development were becoming more and more apparent. Internally, CDB was also confronted with huge NPLs and downside operating pressures. The recovered interests declined year by year (from 91.4% in 1994 to 85.5% in 1997, in which more than 95% was deducted from the interests on construction in process), and NPL ratio hovered at a high level (32.63% in 1997). Five industries suffered losses including coal, military industry, chemical fertilizer, non-ferrous metal, and forest industry, and showed precarious asset status, severe evasion of debts and obvious moral hazard. Faced with such a situation, CDB, led by President Chen Yuan, proposed to cooperate with local governments to transform the advantage of being a government organization into a credit advantage. Financial cooperation agreements were signed with provincial governments, the mode of packing loans was designed in a creative way, the credit resources of government were utilized on a comprehensive basis, and local non-performing assets were reduced by adopting the approach of "three links" in order to contain the moral hazard. In the meantime, a series of credit construction instruments and measures were worked out in a creative manner, a financing platform for urban infrastructure construction was successfully set up by taking the advantage of government organization, and a financing mechanism for infrastructure construction that met national conditions was launched, which provided a practical foundation for the improvement of development-oriented finance theories.

The period from November 2000 to March 2003 was the stage of formation of CDB's credit construction theories. It was also the stage of formation of theories on development-oriented finance. In 2000, the Bank's operational indicators turned better in an all-round manner, with the balance of loans increasing to RMB662.3 billion from RMB513.1 billion in 1998, NPLs dropping to RMB58.2 billion from RMB 167.4 billion, and NPL ratio declining to 8.78% from 32.63% in 1998. At the same time, faced with the challenges brought by China's entry into the WTO and financial globalization as well as the competitive situations at home and abroad, the new objectives of CDB were to accelerate development based on a new starting point and height, and integrate with the international financial sector. Consequently, the Bank put forward the credit structure theories in a creative manner, proposed to establish risk diversification and sharing mechanism by use of the principles and approaches for capital market, and took the design and improvement of credit structure as the fundamental tasks for project review. With respect to approaches, the Bank brought forward to apply "open negotiation" and change the process of review to processes of coordination and negotiation, credit structure improvement, and credit construction. Meanwhile, some internal management systems were set up, including measures and systems for the review of credit construction and quality, and measures for the analysis of loans risks. In November 2002, CDB proposed theories and evaluation systems for the degree of credit development. From then on, the focus of credit construction was shifted to a systematic and purposeful business instrument with quantitative analysis with fragmented, separate, and qualitative risk prevention measures. Based on the analysis for periodic features, dynamic development features, and saltatory features of credit construction, the entire bank was required to "transform credit construction, to its core competitiveness, and general operating principles throughout the businesses of CDB", thereby, the theories on development-oriented finance basically took shape.

The period from March 2003 to November 2008 was the stage of improvement of CDB's credit construction theories. It was also the stage of improvement of theories on development-oriented finance. In March 2003, CDB realized two transformations in the whole bank, that is, from "focusing on debt management" to "focusing on credit management", and from "debt review first" to "credit review first". Based on credit review as the basis and credit cooperation agreement as the link, the bank closely combined the credit advantages of government, departments, and industries with credit funds of CDB, and preliminarily established a development platform for development-oriented finance. The concept of portfolio risk management was put forward systematically along with standards, procedures, and management measures for effective allocation of credit resources among industries, regions, customers, and products. Credit review was performed in an all-round manner, regional credit lines, industrial concentration control targets, and quota management standards were established, and a bidirectional and comprehensive credit management system was evolved to improve the working systems of the credit rating committee of the bank, and to propel the construction of the credit review system. Besides, credit construction, as the core competitiveness of CDB, was brought into full play, CDB was formally positioned as a development-oriented finance institution, and research on strategic credit place was commenced. In addition, loans to counties, loans to SMEs, loans for peasants, rural areas, and agriculture, loans for revitalizing north east old industrial base, and loans for other central issues of government were given on a comprehensive basis, signifying that CDB had taken sound steps toward a first-class international bank. In this way, the theories on development-oriented finance were further ameliorated.

The period from December 2008 to 2013 has witnessed CDB's exploration and progress in commercial transformation. And it is also the stage of deepening of theories on credit construction and development-oriented finance. On December 16, 2008, under the leading of the State Council and relevant authorities, China Development Bank Corporation was founded, signifying CDB's transformation into a new stage after reform. At the same time, the theories and practices on development-oriented finance also stepped into a new stage of development. With regard to CDB's reform program, the State Council pointed out the objective of "transforming CDB from a policy financial institution to a commercial bank. After the reform, CDB should serve major medium and long-term development strategies for the national economy by means of financial businesses such as medium and long-term loans and investments". It was suggested that the Bank must stick to its current work characteristics after reform and transformation, carry out medium and long-term businesses, and serve major medium and long-term development strategies for the national economy, which would be different from that of a commercial bank. In the meantime, CDB's reform program further defined that the Bank must transform from a policy-level financial institution to a commercial bank and act as a multifunctional bank with credit and investment functions. All these indicated that CDB's reform was greatly different from that of the state-owned banks including ICBC, ABC, BOC, and CCB. Its reform objective was to establish a development-oriented finance institution in the form of commercial bank, or to carry out medium and long-term businesses within the framework of a commercial bank, which would be formidable. Just as pointed out by Vice Premier Wang Qishan in the survey of CDB on December 12, 2008, the reform of CDB was a new practice and exploration for the reform and development in China's financial system. It was a great transformation, which was filled with a great deal of explorations, practices, and difficulties.

CDB's reform and transformation would be a process of arduous exploration. No experience could be drawn on when transforming a policy bank into a commercial bank focusing on medium and long-term businesses. Thereby, we should emancipate our minds, advance with times, and explore in a continuous manner. Once exploration was successful, a road of successful transformation to policy bank under Chinese conditions would be created; if not, CDB would fall into a second- or third-class bank and step-off from the stage of history gradually with decreasing size of assets. Thus, CDB must continue developing theories and practices on development-oriented finance, exert its advantages in medium and long-term investments and financing, and in the function of stabilizing business cycle fluctuation which would endeavor CDB to develop into a commercial bank serving medium and long-term construction needs based on financial bonds, instead of a traditional commercial bank based on savings. According to national conditions, medium and long-term investment and financing served as the force to sustain the development of the construction stage. As a bank engaging in medium and long-term businesses mainly, CDB should adapt to the needs of long-term construction stage in the country and play a positive role in accelerating the process of urbanization, which could not be altered owing to transformation to commercial bank. Only if CDB could integrate its own development with China's medium and long-term construction and urbanization, it would be possible for it to maintain a permanent vitality. Otherwise, pure pursuit of self-development without taking into account economic and social development would lead to loss of direction, and eventually we would fall behind. In addition, CDB's features and advantages lie in medium and long-term investment and financing. In the past years, by means of medium and long-term bond financing, the Bank realized the transformation from short term and scattered savings to long term and large deposits, which solved the problem of maturity risk that was reflected by development loans, and provided long-term, stable, sustainable, and quick financial support for areas including infrastructure construction. More importantly, the features of business counter-cycle and reverse regulation represented in the medium and long-term investment and financing were brought into play by CDB, so that the bank could devote itself to economic development either in favorable situations or adversities. Market shares were transferred in the period of economic upswing, creating conditions for other commercial banks to enter the market. In the event of economic downturn, the bank took the lead to inject funds into priority development areas, so as to strengthen market confidence. Seldom have financial institutions worldwide successfully carried out medium and long-term businesses like CDB on a large-scale and on a centralized basis. It could be regarded that the practices and experiences of CDB provide reference and basis for relevant Chinese authorities to prepare risk evaluation, control, and regulation standards on medium and long-term investment and financing. In the future, CDB will still be a bank focusing on bond financing and medium and long-term loans and follow a development road different from that of traditional commercial banks.

2.3 Main features of development-oriented finance

After summarizing and studying the development course of development-oriented finance in CDB, the following important features could be found preliminarily:

(1) Development-oriented finance is based on national credit, with market performance as its pillar. This is the fundamental feature of development-oriented finance, and also reflects the deepening and development of policy finance. Both policy and development-oriented finance are the products of practice. The former is generated from fiscal financing, while the latter is the result of market construction. Breakeven was the goal of policy finance for the purpose of implementation of national policies. It emerged as the basic practice and principle of policy finance before market results were available. In fact, such practice was to transfer interests to enterprises, which could be treated as the extension of financial subsidy. However, many projects under the support of policy finance fell into NPLs and led to moral hazard, indicating that breakeven was at the cost of asset quality and credit construction, without strong capability in sustainable development. Instead, development-oriented finance emphasizes on market performance. While shoring up project construction by means of fund raising with national credit, it pushes forward institutional improvement and market construction in an active manner to achieve development objectives of the government. In the past 10 years, CDB neither depended on subsidy and national discount, nor simply distributed national credit. Instead, by relying on national credit, it continuously applied and augmented the role of

national credit in market construction and institutional improvement in order to allocate limited financial resources to capital projects in compliance with national industrial policies. It has been proved in practice that development-oriented finance could be used to deal with most problems that policy finance failed to tackle, the capability and potentiality of which were greater than that of the latter. With functions increasing gradually, the two approaches are complementary to each other and could be used simultaneously in some stages.

(2) Development-oriented finance realizes economic and social development objectives of the government by relying on the market. In contrast to commercial finance, development-oriented finance could utilize and rely on national credit in a positive way, construct market in a place without market, and make full use of and improve the market. In the process of operation, development-oriented finance does not directly enter commercial areas which have been highly mature; instead, it sets out in an immature market. As international and domestic experiences suggest, areas with market defect are usually the key and difficult areas that the government is concerned with. Commercial institutions are reluctant to enter these areas, while development-oriented financial institutes have such responsibility. In these areas, development-oriented finance starts from the realization of national strategic objectives, adheres to market construction, takes financing to leverage, makes use of the advantages of government organization, and guides capital orientation toward the industries encouraged by national policies. In response to market gap and credit defect, institutional improvement, market construction, and credit construction are included in the financing work to construct micro-market basis and transmission mechanism for commercial and financial operations. In this way, areas that require development and are without finance, market, and credit can be developed and accessed by financial institutions, various markets, and commercial banks, which thus become an integral part of the market economy. Taking government credit as cohesion and bonder, development-oriented finance combines various financial market elements, applies different kinds of financial instruments on a comprehensive basis, and starts from building a basic system for market entities to incubate, evaluate,

cultivate, and improve the legal system in an energetic manner, as well as hatch out enterprise credit from development bank credit and local government credit. Besides, we should not only construct projects but also build systems, markets, and credit to reduce own credit risk and promote local economic development.

(3) Development-oriented finance takes organizational credit enhancement as its basic method and means. Organizational credit enhancement is a kind of cooperation between CDB and the government in which the two sides jointly construct the credit system and the institutional system to prevent risks, thus embodying a relationship of consensus, common construction, coordination, and cooperation. By means of it, development-oriented finance institution can fully exert the organizational advantages of the government and effectively make up the defects of existing financial systems. In a financing system completely based on market, the government does not directly participate in the market's operations. Nevertheless, in the current situation in China, the government has multiple identities, including management, regulation, provision of system framework, and participation in economic operation, which is a basic characteristic of the economic system in the primary stages of socialism. In the development-oriented finance, organizational credit enhancement is applied to construct credit structure and risk sharing mechanism, effectively control credit risks, optimize the allocation of credit resources, and enhance market performance and core competitiveness.

(4) Development-oriented finance sticks to the combination of financial bonds and financial assets management, which is helpful to achieve breakeven. In 1994, the state contributed RMB50 billion to CDB as capital and vested the bank with quasi-sovereignty government credit and corresponding legal positions, which constituted the basis for CDB's market operation and performance. With respect to fund sources, CDB enjoys a charted right to issue financial bonds in the market. According to international practice, development financial bonds, treated as government agency bonds, are managed in a way different from treasury bonds. The funds of treasury bonds are not managed in the form of financial budget, without breakeven requirements and the task of undertaking institutional improvements.

The financing areas of CDB are between treasury bonds and commercial finance, which need overall institutional improvement and market construction, so as to intensify the management of financial assets, improve asset quality and return on capital, and persist in the recovery of principal and interests to achieve breakeven. In the meantime, considering the projects with insufficient prior earnings that development-oriented financial institutions are confronted with, CDB actively explores a way to ensure earnings by means of strategic options. Some options are developed, including those that could be realized before project growth prospect is achieved, to lock up the risks arising in the development, propel the construction of a credit system in a continuous manner, and fulfill breakeven after smooth withdrawal. By utilizing various means, including coordination with the government, land reserves, and non-budgetary funds, CDB tracks cash flows of all the projects and combines cash flows of original projects with issue of new bonds and repayment of old bonds. CDB also develops the ability in overall cycling to form a sufficient operational space, props up the withdrawal of development-oriented finance, and ensures the quality of assets. When the earnings of development-oriented finance institution cannot cover the payment of principal and interests of bonds in the revolving bond issue, liquidity would be maintained by means of issue of new bonds and repayment of old bonds. It is an important feature of development-oriented finance where the liquidity equilibrium ability is greater than the breakeven ability. In summary, development-oriented finance boosts project construction, corporate construction, credit construction, and market construction to achieve breakeven eventually.

Case Study 1: Financing to Border Areas — Supporting the Development of Corps with Development-Oriented Finance

I. *Background*

"Xinjiang's stability determines the State's stability". Xinjiang Production and Construction Corps (the "Corps") shoulders the divine mission of "developing and protecting border areas and maintaining stability". It is a special "production team, task force, and fighting team" combining government, army, and enterprises. At the turn of the century, while maintaining stability in the border areas and supporting border development, the Corps faces the problem of how to survive and develop in the tense competition brought about by market economy. Due to relatively slow economic growth, irrational industrial structure, and lagging development of social structure, health care, and other undertakings, many social contradictions are more manifest and intensified, which may harm the social stability in Xinjiang. Such issues also affect the historic mission of the Corps, i.e., "stabilizing and rejuvenating Xinjiang, making people rich, and stabilizing border areas". According to the needs of the Corps, CDB conscientiously implements national strategic guidelines and actively tackles the problems occurred in the development of the Corps.

II. *Cause*

There are many reasons for the lagging development of the Corps. From the perspective of finance, the most important reason lies in the following "four shortages" structure in the financing system of the Corps.

(1) *Shortage of financial resources*: As the Corps is specifically designated in the State's plan, it belongs to a primary budgetary unit under the Central Government without tax revenues. Restricted by its accumulated assets, it is hard for the Corps to raise a large amount of funds in a short period of time for the construction of medium and long-term projects.
(2) *Shortage of bank loans*: Affected by some factors in recent years, lots of funds of Xinjiang flow to developed provinces and areas by means of commercial financial institutions, showing a weakening trend with respect to financial support. The special nature of the Division as the main economic entity of the Corps in the legal qualification for loans and guarantee also restricts the access to loans. Thus, financing bottleneck has remained for a long time in economic development.

(3) *Shortage of capital market*: Most listed companies under the Corps have a comparatively small size of capital stock with ordinary operating results. Hence, it is difficult for them to acquire refinancing opportunities in the inefficient capital market.
(4) *Shortage of enterprise accumulation*: Due to prominent contradictions in the industrial structure, agriculture instead of industry is paid more attention in the Corps, and only few outstanding enterprises can be found in Xinjiang. The aforementioned shortages actually reflect the special credit resources and backward financing system of the Corps. It is a government, but it does not collect taxes. It is an army, but it has no outlays. It is an enterprise, but it also runs social undertakings. Financial institutions know little about credit resources of the Corps, so it is hard for it to raise necessary development funds under the market economy. In addition, the backward financing system fails to provide sufficient capital for the medium and long-term construction of the Corps. Consequently, the shortage of funds restricts its economic development and threatens its mission of stabilizing border areas.

III. *Solution*

In response to these problems, CDB actively explores new thoughts that are suitable for the development of the Corps.

(1) CDB combines its culture with that of the Corps to commonly build the credit of the Corps in the western border areas. CDB's culture is represented by "exploration and enterprising", while that of the Corps highlights "diligent efforts". By combining these two cultures, support is given to the Corps to establish an advanced financing mechanism. In addition, the Corps has its own independent system, including police, procuratorate and court as well as institutions for urban construction, scientific research, culture, and medical care with complete social functions. Therefore, it could be considered as a special government. Known as "China Xinjiang Group" to the public, the Corps has the qualification of a corporate as an independent accounting unit, which is one of the important economic pillars in Xinjiang.

About one-third arable lands in Xinjiang have been reclaimed by the Corps, thus it has been one of the major grain and cotton production base in the country. To fully excavate and utilize the special credit resources of the Corps, CDB has entered into a partnership agreement on development-oriented finance with the Corps for four times in order to deepen the cooperation in the areas of planning, financing, and financial innovation. Besides, according to the principle of marketization, assistance has been provided to the Corps to establish investment-limited liability company and shore up its construction and development.

(2) CDB combines its mission with that of the Corps to help the Corps grow bigger and stronger through financing. CDB shoulders the mission of "strengthening national strength and improving people's livelihood", which is closely connected with that of the Corps. For that reason, CDB made great efforts to support the development of the Corps. First, acting as a counselor of Corps, assistance is provided to the Corps to improve its development programs and strategies. CDB actively carries out preparatory works of major projects, urging the Corps to make plans in advance. Second, as an assistant to the Corps, the process of new type of industrialization is expedited in the Corps. Targeting at listed and strong enterprises such as Xinjiang Tianye, Tianfu Thermoelectric, and Hongji Coking, support is given to the development of leading enterprises under the Corps. Third, as a good partner of the Corps, CDB actively pushes forward the agricultural industrialization development of the Corps. The cotton output of the Corps represents one-sixth of total cotton output in the country, while cotton picking is the most onerous physical labor for employees of the Corps. In 2005, CDB completed the review of mechanical cotton pocking project of the Corps and disbursed loans within one month, which ensured the timely placement of 100 imported cotton pickers and solved the development problem that had worried the Corps for almost half a century. Fourth, as a close friend of the Corps, the undertakings of the Corps related to people's livelihood are boosted under the assistance of CDB. Great importance is attached to the development of such undertakings, and

energetic support is contributed to the construction of infrastructure and social undertakings such as medical care, education, SMEs, economically affordable housing, and environmental protection, so as to raise the living standards of the Corps (Figure 2.1).

(3) CDB attaches importance to the strategic idea of "financing to border areas" and explores the new thought on long-term governance in the northwest border areas. CDB persists in the

Figure 2.1: Top: The no. 1 plough in the world — employees of the Corps plough the field manually instead of using domestic animals. Bottom: Mechanical cotton picking — CDB gives financial support to the agricultural industrialization project of the Corps.

combination of advantage of financial institutions in financing with that of the Corps in organization, so as to boost the construction of corporate governance structure, construction of fund flow, and credit construction for the Corps. An advanced financing mechanism containing "project entry selected by the Corps, incubation by development-oriented finance, and market access" has been set up to maintain efficient operation of funds of the Corps and financial institutions, strengthen market competitiveness of the Corps, realize its economic and social development objectives through the market path, and consolidate the northwest frontier areas. Specific measures include the following: (i) great support has been given to the urbanization construction of the Corps so that more people could remain there; (ii) great support has been given to the development of modern agriculture and emerging industry of the Corps in order to speed up adjustment of industrial structure; (iii) great support has been given to the integration of the Corps and the autonomous region to achieve common development. By applying the portfolio financing theory in the development-oriented finance, the Corps and the autonomous region are urged to break through administrative boundaries and remove the concept of segmentation, so as to establish a new regional economic pattern with market as the bond based on free combination of interested parties. Furthermore, the new economic pattern should target rational distribution of productive forces and optimiz allocation of resources to effect interest combination, complementary advantages, sharing on an affordable basis, and rapid development; and (iv) active assistance is provided to relevant ministries and commissions of the State to formulate more effective economic policies for the sustainable development of the Corps, so that the Corps can be developed and strengthened in a continuous manner.

IV. *Comments*

"The stability of Xinjiang depends on a strong Corps". A strong Corps will be helpful for the local government to maintain social stability, its development will be conducive to national unity in the border areas, and its prosperity will contribute to the accelerated economic development of Xinjiang. The traditional ideas for developing and protecting border areas aim to solve the food problem first, which suggests that only if the Corps exists, can homeland security be safeguarded. The basic idea of "financing to border areas" targets at the development in new situations. That is to say, only if the Corps develops, can the border areas be defended solidly. In other words, the idea of "financing to border areas" could be regarded as the inheritance and extension of traditional idea for developing and protecting border areas, which is a positive exploration under the market economy for the long-term peace and stability of western border areas. CDB persists in supporting the development of the Corps through development-oriented finance and insists on helping the Corps establish an effective financing mechanism by all possible financial means to substantially enhance the position of the Corps' economy in the medium and long-term development strategies, which will be of strategic significance for China to achieve modernization and national rejuvenation.

2.4 Summary

In this chapter, we have discussed the practical basis of development-oriented financial theory. If we analyze the formation of the theory and practice of development-oriented finance from the perspective of practice, we can safely conclude that development-oriented finance is a product of seeking truth from facts (Figure 2.2). As an important development financial institution of China, CDB proceeds from reality, adheres to international advanced financial principles based on domestic conditions, persists in combining the government's organizational advantages with CDB's edge in mid- and long-term financing and combining market-oriented operations under the premise of serving national strategy, gives priority to planning and focuses on promoting project construction, legal construction, credit building, and market building through financing. Therefore, it has opened up a path suitable for China's specific conditions and has progressively

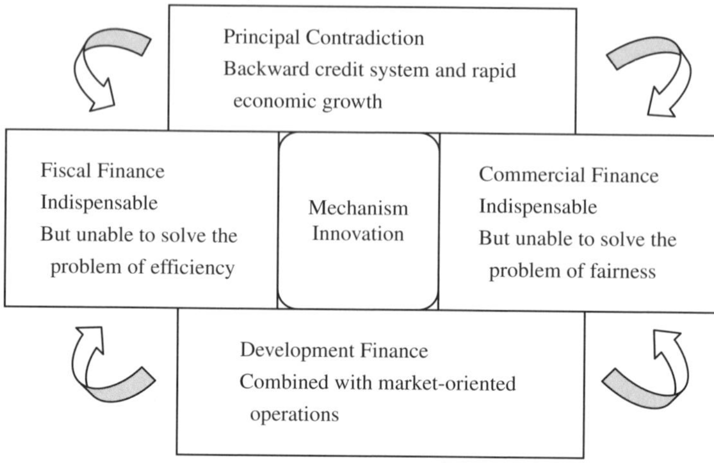

Figure 2.2: Seeking truth from facts is a rational resolution to the contradiction.

established distinctive theory and practice of development-oriented finance. Based on government credit, development-oriented finance makes use of development options and combines a variety of market elements to promote institutional building, actively develop the non-commercial profitability and achieve breakeven amidst long-term large-amount concentration risks, which is a major distinction between development-oriented finance and commercial finance. While giving priority to development and concentrating on delivering quality financing services based on national strategy, development-oriented finance has also achieved fundamental changes and rapid development in their own performance, reporting RMB5 trillion of good assets in December 2011, compared to RMB50 billion of capital in its infancy. Through active exploration and fruitful operations of "developing the Bank and supporting development", development-oriented finance has justified its applicability to national conditions and its function of promoting development.

Chapter 3

Cultural Foundation of Development-Oriented Finance

3.1 Introduction

In this chapter, we will expound on the cultural foundation of development-oriented finance based on the understanding that the theory and practice of development-oriented finance introduced by the China Development Bank (CDB) draw on and promote China's fine cultural tradition and the Chinese government's great organizational capacity. China is a creditworthy nation with rich thoughts about credit. Its traditional concepts of integrity and honesty, mutual help as well as joint security constitute the cultural foundation for the theory and practice of development-oriented finance. Highly organized and disciplined, the Chinese government recently plays an important part in advocating the principal role of the market force, facilitating the growth of the credit market, and ensuring the sustainability of socioeconomic development in China. In drawing on and promoting traditional Chinese culture and the Chinese government's organizational strength, development-oriented finance has enriched the financial thinking with distinctive Chinese features, representing an important showcase for the socialist market economy with Chinese characteristics.

3.2 China's excellent traditional culture is the ideological source of development-oriented finance

China has advocated honesty and morality since ancient times, and establishing credibility and personality is always a basic principle of social activities. Ancient Chinese people recognized the special role of credit very early and kept bringing into full play the role to promote social progress. Many great minds in ancient China have left us with enormous wealth in humanities, philosophy, economic ethics, monetary ideas, and financial activities, which have influenced the undertakings, thinking, and ideology of later generations.

(1) *The people-oriented economic thought of "respecting virtue and protecting the people"*. As early as in the Zhou Dynasty, the Spring and Autumn Period, and the Warring States Period (1066BC–221BC), Zhou Gong, the founder of the Zhou Dynasty, and other wise ancients had already realized the role of virtue in reflecting on the fall of the Shang Dynasty. Zhou Gong warned his offspring in Shang Shu·Zhao Hao (《尚书·召诰》), "I should learn something from the fall of the Xia Dynasty and that of the Shang Dynasty", so rule of virtue must be practiced. Xiao Jing (《孝经》 Doctrine of Dutifulness) says "humans are the most valuable under heaven and on earth". Xun Zi(荀子) put forward the thought that "the upper class will be poor if the lower class is poor, and the upper class will be rich if the lower class is rich"; "The monarch is the boat, and the common people are water. Water can carry the boat, and also overthrow the boat"; and concluded, "To maintain social stability, no other method is better than to implement rule of virtue and love the people" (Fu Guo, 《富国》 Enriching the State). Mencius (孟子) argued, "People are the most valuable, the country is medium, and the monarch is the least important". From the perspective of benevolence, Confucius (孔子) acknowledged "the welfare of people", the "gain of foods", and the "profit" obtained in the normal way, and on this basis, came up with the governing ideology of "enriching the state, enriching the people", and the principle of "equilibration is peace" in the rule of virtue. Therefore, the concept that people are the foundation of the state and a firm foundation makes a peaceful state has been deeply rooted in the heart of Chinese people. Development-oriented finance focuses on the people, highlights the role of the people as major social

players, and recognizes the purpose of developing a harmonious society as serving the people. It respects, understands, cares, and relies on the people, delivers what they want, works for their well-being, inspires their creativity, keeps the social nature of finance, and holds that everybody has the right of finance and everybody also has the financial responsibility, which raises money for the well-being projects — all these are just the inheritance and development of the people-oriented thought of the Chinese civilization.

(2) *The value of naturalism — oneness of man and nature*. In traditional Chinese culture, either Confucianism or Taoism advocates the "oneness of man and nature". Mencius (孟子) said, "He who uses his heart to the full understands his very nature and thus Mother Nature." It is the full use of heart that enables a person to know his nature and Mother Nature, because man and nature are integrated as one. Lao Zi (老子) claimed, "Human observes the earth, the earth observes the heaven, the heaven observes the rule, and the rule observes nature"; Zhuang Zi (庄子) stressed, "Heaven and earth live together with us, and all the creatures are unified with me", Zhong Yong (《中庸》, The Doctrine of Balance) says, "Striking a balance between two extremes is the root of heaven, and harmony is the ultimate rule of heaven. If balance is achieved, heaven and earth will be in the right place, and all things are fostered", and so on. All these credos pursue the "oneness of man and nature" as the ultimate realm. The human body is just like heaven and earth, and gets the rule and essence of heaven and earth; so between heaven and earth, it is the rule and also the essence of heaven and earth to seek survival. Traditional Chinese culture not only highlights the harmony between people as well as between people and the society but also stands for the harmony between man and nature — this is the thought of "oneness of man and nature". In response to that, man's spiritual development must pursue the "oneness of knowledge and action". What man thinks and does must be rational. To that end, we should start with education. Where education leads, a country leads; developed education makes a developed

country. It was education that had enabled the Chinese feudal society to achieve the topmost prosperity. It is also education that has created America's extraordinary economic and financial strength. To promote China's modernization with the development-oriented finance, we should do well in assisting student in poverty, protecting the environment, and developing a harmonious society.

(3) *The dialectic thinking about universe and life on the whole.* Traditional Chinese culture advocates a sense of balance. This is true with Confucianism. For example, the Analects of Confucius (《论语》) says "hold both ends, and use the middle to treat people". Taoism also upholds balance. Lao Zi (老子) stressed that things should not develop to the extremity, which is also a kind of balance. Such a notion — "no excess, no inadequacy", moderateness and compliance with normal standard, and objection to using extreme methods to handle problems — has always influenced what Chinese people think and do. Development-oriented finance adheres to the dialectic thinking, facilitates the transition from passiveness to activeness, from lack of credit to credibility, and from an immature market to a mature one, and promotes the development of the market credit system through finance. This, to some extent, is the inheritance of coordination and overall planning, which forms the two core elements of traditional Chinese culture.

(4) *The spirit of striving for progress evidenced by the saying that "As heaven's movement is ever vigorous, so must a gentleman ceaselessly strive along"*. Chinese ancients had the enterprising spirit of enduring hardships, fighting hard, being thrift, and persisting in creating welfare for the offspring. Development-oriented finance is based on the experience of CDB, reflects the state's will, and aims at future development. It associates the work of CDB and its staff with China's economic development, and the interests of the nation and the people. In that way, CDB shoulders the long-term strategic task with great aspiration, the sense of mission, and responsibility and commitment to innovation, reflecting the traditional spirit of striving continuously to make new progress.

(5) *The stress on the role of the state.* The thought of state economy started early in the long history of China. Its core idea is that when productivity is relatively low, the state can step in to manage some critical sectors. Discourses on Salt and Iron (《盐铁论》), an economic masterpiece written in the Han Dynasty, makes a thorough interpretation of this point. Development-oriented finance has a sharp insight into the actual conditions in China and underlines the role of the state in economic life, particularly in some important projects and events. The idea of drawing upon the organizational strength of the government in carrying out relevant work is just a representation of old wisdom.

(6) *The monetary theory combining metalism and nominalism.* Metal coins appeared as early as in the Shang Dynasty and the Zhou Dynasty in the 11th century before Christ (BC) in China. In particular, the ideology of money credit achieved great development since the 6th century BC. According to the *Discourses of States Discourses of Zhou* (《国语·周语》), at the end of the 6th century BC, Shan Qi objected to the opinion of King Jing of the Zhou Dynasty on making heavy coins and abolishing light coins, and stressed that the weight of the coin should adapt to the level of commodity exchange and actual needs. *Guan Zi Savings of the State* (《管子·国蓄》), a book created in the Pre-Qin Period, not only mentioned that the quantity of commodities determines their value but also recorded the influence of money supply on the purchasing power of money. Paper currency appeared in the Song Dynasty, making China the earliest country to use it in the world. The paper currency in the Song and Yuan Dynasties was merely a congenitally deficient premature compared to that in contemporary capitalist economic conditions. But it played an important role in the mutual promotion and development of nominalism and metalism of the monetary theory. At the end of the 18th century, China's modern financial industry also witnessed certain development with the advent of capitalist sprout and growth of economy. At that time, Shanghai had more than 100 money houses and it established the money trade

association. The credit form through the money club, a kind of self-help organization, appeared in the northern part of Zhejiang, and the credit based on blood relations and family relations of farmers was converted into the credit used in financial lending. In the second half of the 19th century, the money shops in Shanxi allied with some stores with excellent reputation to form a universal financial system that focused on currency exchange and also engaged in taking deposit and lending, which won the honor of "currency exchange for all". Development-oriented finance is developed based on the traditional credit theory and credit building method.

In brief, in the long history, Chinese ancients profoundly understood the people-oriented economic ideology of "respecting virtue and protecting the people". They adhered to the value of naturalism: oneness of man and nature and the dialectic thinking about universe and life on the whole, and embodied the idea of a balanced development. They were born with the endowment of development, and displayed the pioneering spirit of enduring hardship, fighting hard, being economical, and ensuring the well-being of their offspring. They conceived the ethnic sentiment of inclusion, credit as life, and harmony as root and etiquette and had the excellent tradition of helping each other in family, neighborhoods, communities, and in society as a whole. This is what the outstanding traditional Chinese culture is about. Such traditional credit ideology and excellent culture have promoted the development of the human society, exerted an important influence on the reform and development of China today, and enlightened in depth our theory and practice of development-oriented finance. Reviewing history can strengthen our self-confidence and help us find our shortcomings as well.

Ancient Chinese philosophers, like the western sophists, have created a galaxy of immortal works in economic ethics, which took the leading position in the world for a long time. However, modern economy and finance were not first seen in China, and have not achieved great development here, which can be attributed to multiple factors. Historically, the leading position of Chinese economic thoughts in the world prior to the 15th and 16th century was the result of the leadership of China's commodity economy in the world. In the Ming and Qing Dynasties, the government resumed the "silver standard", and used silver as the currency, which ended the use of the paper currency for more than five centuries since the North Song Dynasty, which was against the development trend of the commodity–money relation and formed a stark contrast against the rapidly developing commodity money economy in the Western world. The economic ethics in the Chinese feudal society admired thearchy and imperial power, and dominated the development of the Chinese society, which hindered the development of science and technology, economy and finance in modern China. In particular, since the Ming and Qing Dynasties, China's economic ideology has lagged behind the world's economic development pace. Thus, in essence, China has fallen behind in the contemporary times, and China's financial industry has far lagged behind the industrialized countries, mainly because China lacked the modern credit concept, the thought of advancing with the times, the advanced supporting technology, and the management capacity — factors necessitated for the development of modern finance.

Inheriting and developing the excellent traditional culture is an important condition for our rise after long-term accumulation. At the same time, we should also see that the traditional genes give us some different mindsets and behavioral modes on the way to modernization. Development-oriented finance takes root in the fertile soil of the Chinese civilization and highlights the characteristics of our time while inheriting our tradition.

3.3 Development-oriented finance pays high attention to modern credit responsibility

With the development of the modern economy, the value and characteristics of commodities tend to become differential, diverse, and complex, a trend that increases disguise of fake commodities and deceit of trading process and intensifies the credit issue in the modern economic society. This is an inevitable issue in the transition from a traditional economy to a modern one. It seems more important than ever to build the market credit system, form the code of market conducts with morality as the support, credit as the base and law as the security, so as to make the market credit outcome a conscious conduct. In this sense, traditional ethics and credit need a modernized transformation and interpretation.

In this process, we think "credit" is international as one of the principles that are generally accepted by all nations and in all times. "Truth and loyalty" are universal standards throughout history. However, the key elements of credit stressed by China and the West still differ: The former stresses personal character, and focuses on the internal temperament and personal perfection when establishing requirements for people, while the latter pays much attention to conduct and processes, and belongs to a contractual conduct. The credit mechanism in western industrialized societies is relatively sound while China's credit mechanism remains at the level of "remote control" and emphasizes moral constraint and personal consciousness. Therefore, the connotation of the Chinese concept of credit should be reviewed and enriched from an international perspective. In the contemporary society, credit is a basic condition and essential virtue for the development of market economy. Credit is both equivalent to honesty, reliability, fair trade, and other characteristics, and it also means responsibility and self-control in the general sense. China should not only stress moral constraint but also accelerate the development of the credit management mechanism.

In recent years, China's socialist market economy has developed by leaps and bounds, but the issue of credit disorder in economic life has also come to the fore. It can be seen in every aspect of economic activities and even rampant in some regions and sectors. This is mainly reflected in the following aspects.

(1) The disorder of personal credit, namely, an individual breaking his promise on purpose in business activities and market trade. The conduct of violating contracts or evading debts often happens between individuals or between individuals and economic organizations.
(2) Credit disorder of economic organizations, namely the loss of credit on the part of economic organizations including financial

and accounting institutions, businesses, and intermediary agencies. Examples include chain debts among enterprises, elaborate debt evasion by enterprises from banks, false product advertisements of enterprises, excess package and provision of false information by listed companies, and the partial opinion and private interests of accounting firms, audit firms, asset evaluation firms, and other intermediary agencies. Each year, about four billion contracts are signed in China, but only about 50% of them are carried out. Moreover, contracts only account for 30% of the entire trade volume in economic activities, while the rest is done upon spontaneous agreement. The direct losses caused by contract frauds reach about RMB5.5 billion every year.

(3) Some government institutions do not have credit in economic activities. This is mainly reflected by the facts that some government departments often exaggerate the preferential conditions but fail to offer them in investment solicitation, provide encouraging, not necessarily true, data about economic activities to highlight the government's performance, participate in microeconomic activities for their own interests but refuse to abide by contracts, and resort to deception and black-box operations in tender invitation and government procurement. These three kinds of credit disorder often entangle one another, seriously affect the normal order of economic life, cause a significant confidence crisis in the entire society, increase economic activity cost, reduce economic operation efficiency, curb spending and investment, and influence the healthy development of the society.

Then, why has China's modern credit system not seen due development? Why do Chinese people not have the modern credit concept, the thought of advancing with the times and the advanced managerial skills required for the development of modern finance? We believe that the root causes are as follows:

(1) The traditional social structure and administration system have resulted in a weak foundation for the development of modern

financial credit. In China's traditional social strata, the government is at the top representing the state authority and at the bottom is the collection of scattered individuals under the farming civilization. The information flow between the two ends is vertical, from top to bottom. Scattered individuals do not have stable property rights or the qualification or capacity to negotiate with the top authority. Credit transaction is completely controlled by the top authority, which is an imbalanced structure. In such a dual structure, social resources are mainly concentrated in the superstructure of the society (namely, the government level). Such a distribution pattern determines an individual's behavioral selection and the flow of social resources. To be specific, individuals will have the opportunity to benefit as long as they have the channels to reach the superstructure. When the distribution of interests is badly out of balance, scattered individuals get together as one and use violence to resist the other end (because they have nothing to lose). The result is that they are either cracked down or conferred more economic freedom. However, since there is no corresponding property rights protection mechanism or social adjustment mechanism, the huge economic vitality embodied by such relatively scattered economic freedom and property right owners cannot be injected to the economic growth process. The planned economy inherited and developed such vertical mode of transaction. The economic resources of the entire society are allocated to various organizations by administrative orders from top to bottom; credit is nothing but a negligible auxiliary means, controlled by the superstructure. It is such a vertical credit structure that has destroyed the social foundation for the formation of the middle class. Unlike in Western countries, economic entities such as entrepreneurs and bankers in China are not developed into an important contributor to economic growth and the middle class to cement the stability of social structure. Therefore, the development of credit at the individual level has failed to bring about extensive production or frequent trading in the market. Information relevant to credit is not processed into credit products and sold to entrepreneurs, bankers, and the middle class that need them so that positive information could accumulate to become the drive of credit transactions and accordingly form an important part of the economic operation mechanism. With the acceleration of the market-oriented reform, enterprises started to face market risks independently. However, over the years, enterprises (particularly state-owned enterprises) have been growing in a planned economy, and people's economic activities have been based on the execution and fulfillment of plans, rather than the principle of credit. Therefore, most citizens do not have the right understanding of credit, and thus little awareness about credit. On the road to modernization and market economy, the traditional credit notion has failed to adapt to the needs of a market economy to change for the establishment of a modern commercial credit system and to satisfy the demand of various social classes for the credit system and credit resources.

(2) Lack of a sound legal framework has led to the high cost of keeping credit and the low cost of losing credit, causing the absence of internal drive to build a modern credit system. Credit in China is usually supported by ethical rules and relies on the constraint of social ethics, as is indicated in the saying that "justice lies in the heart of people". The credit system in China's traditional society was also built on the personalized trade relations between acquaintances. In modern society, credit, as an inherent principle for the market economy, needs to be guaranteed by the external force of the law. The law is the compulsory force of the state and the code of conduct that everybody should observe. The law can clearly define the rights and obligations of the value movement and record them in black and white. For example, the property rights regime specifies the rules of how people benefit from economic activities, suffer losses and compensate others, and constitutes the guarantee for various transactions. The regime also defines the relation between behavior and outcome and provides the standard and concrete requirements for credit-based behaviors. In economic activities, if property rights are not defined or protected, it will be very hard for the foundation of credit to take shape. Without property rights, people are not held liable for their behaviors, and thus are unable to predict whether keeping credit could bring them true benefits. The game theory holds that clearly-defined property rights can turn one game between both

parties to a deal into repeated games, and the repeated credit observance by both parties can improve the credit environment. For example, the trade contract system elaborates the performance method and responsibilities of both parties, which is the necessary condition for the normal performance of economic activities. The Marxist economics theory points out that the trade activity is a contract activity, and the subject of the modern market economy is "economic man" or "rational man", all of whose behaviors in the market observe the principle of benefit maximization. Therefore, if keeping credit can bring benefits and losing credit will incur a loss, they will choose to keep credit without hesitation. It is also true vice versa. At present, the development level of the legal system remains low, laws and regulations are unsound, enforcement is limited, the concept of property rights and contract is weak, social rules are immature, and institutional arrangements are irrational. For one thing, the penalty for credit violation is not severe, and for another, the benefit from keeping credit is not inviting. The transaction cost of keeping credit is too high and credit violation involves low cost and generates high income. As a result, the Gresham's Law works. Bad money drives out the good and credit-keeping market entities are forced to exit the market or give up their credit principle. People losing credit do not have to pay a big price, and when others see the benefit of losing credit, they will naturally stop keeping credit for more benefits. Therefore, to develop the economy, strengthening the legal framework to ensure the effectiveness of credit is required. Relevant rules and regulations should be formulated and observed so as to increase the quantity and quality of transactions and optimize the credit environment.

(3) China's fine cultural tradition, including religions and customs, has not been well carried forward, and as a result, there is lack of necessary lubricants for establishing a modern credit system. Credit grows with culture over time. People are the subject of credit. People's behaviors are influenced by their religion, ethics, values, living habits, and other factors which are representations of culture. For example, the credit environment in a region is influenced not

only by the specific religious culture but also by the degree of religious freedom. The world's three major religions, i.e., Christianity, Islam, and Buddhism, have their different believers all over the world, and these believers all regard the religious doctrines as the principles to behave, so the credit-based behaviors in different regions take on particular religious characteristics. Early Christianity advocated "lending in cash, kind, or other forms without any interest". However, with the advent of mass production, the demand for capital grew and the ban on obtaining interest from lending was gradually eased and finally lifted. Islam holds that working is virtue, and lending is allowed, but usury is severely reprimanded. Buddhism advocates charity and salvation, equity, etc., which allow monks to get interest from lending for helping the common people, and emphasizes honesty particularly. In the process of economic transformation, the due role of China's fine cultural tradition has not been brought into full play, and traditional culture and social ethics have not been well utilized to nurture the people and make their behaviors credit-based. Some bad personal ethics and the drive for profits have exerted negative influence on the credit environment.

(4) There is no effective mechanism to bridge China's traditional culture and the modern financial system, which hampers the development of a modern credit system. The modern financial system calls for fairness, equality, and information symmetry, but China's traditional culture is highly organized vertically, and do not foster team spirit horizontally, which tends to cause information asymmetry, i.e., inconsistent information on the same thing obtained by transaction parties. Under the current market economy system in China, information acquired by entities is usually incomplete and asymmetric. For example, the credit reference system is underdeveloped, and financial institutions such as banks are usually passive in the process of gaining customer information. This appears not only in obtaining the information used to decide whether to extend loans but also in supervising the borrower's behavior after he gets the loan. In order to get the loan, the borrower may conceal true information and even provide false information. The incomplete and asymmetric

information distorts the nature of credit to some degree, which will create an impact on the overall status and efficiency of financial credit. With the diversification of financial investment channels and the continuous innovation of investment instruments, the assets of enterprises and individuals are also utilized in multiple ways. However, due to the current segregated management and operation in the financial system, the handling of different investment services is limited greatly, which leads to the asymmetry of financial information. Developing the financial system and running banks in a credit-lacking environment will inevitably lead to a collision with the traditional system, involving economic, political, conceptual, and even interpersonal conflicts. Obviously, there is a higher price to pay. As the financial reform develops further, it will be necessary to seek an appropriate juncture between the traditional culture and the modern financial system, and to change the remote control of ethics into an institutional support for the credit mechanism, so as to combine the development of financial ethics with that of financial legal and advance the financial system reform and credit culture development simultaneously, finally fostering the due value orientation of the socialist financial system. The chain of high leverage ratio, high risks, and high returns in the financial market should be subjected to the regulation by laws and the constraint by the ethics. In the course of perfecting financial regulation, the legal system, moral constraint, industry culture, and work safety shall be put in a more important position to establish a sound credit supervision system, work out the guidelines for different sectors to follow in building credit, strength examination and evaluation, and finally bring forward the development of a modern credit system step by step. Just based on the above understanding and social development, the development-oriented finance is introduced to explore the possibility of stepping up the development of a market credit system in China.

3.4 Development-oriented finance actively pushes the development of a modern credit culture

Development-oriented finance draws on China's fine cultural tradition and the state's organizational strength and propels the development of a modern credit culture by actively integrating and utilizing credit at state, government, institutional, and individual levels.

(1) Formulate working principles reflecting the distinctive features of traditional Chinese culture. Development-oriented finance adheres to three basic working principles in promoting the excellent traditional culture and bringing into play the state's organizational strength. First is the principle of socialization. CDB has put forward the objective to build an inclusive financial system that enables everybody to enjoy equal rights and opportunities to raise money. This is a lofty development objective. In modern society, only when everybody enjoys these opportunities and has the right to access financial services, can they participate in economic development, share the fruits of economic development, and get rich together. Thus, CDB pays particular attention to developing effective modes and creating certain conditions to build a multi-tier credit system that satisfies the diversified needs and provides financing opportunities for vulnerable groups (or groups with immature credit), thereby reflecting the due social responsibility of financial institutions. At the same time, the private sector will also be mobilized to build a socialized risk control mechanism. Second is the principle of guiding by example. The "seed" fund of development-oriented finance is used to attract funds from different sources to "establish a pool of funds" so as to satisfy the largest extent the financing demand of customers at all levels and build a credit system. At the same time, market-based operation is adopted to minimize risks, ensure the effective use of funds, and keep enhancing credit. Third is the principle of being organized. Governments at all levels are mobilized to organize and coordinate relevant work in the interest of providing due institutional support to the establishment of a professional portfolio financing platform. Efforts are also made to develop the standards, products, and procedures for the portfolio financing platform and integrate government, institution, market, and individual credit through intensive, standardized organization so as to accelerate economic and social development.

(2) Make the best of various resources to impel the development of a modern credit culture. First, the organizational strength of the Party is given full play to boost credit building. The Communist Party of China and the Chinese government have developed their organizational capacity and rigid organizational system in past revolutions and economic development. Such capacity and system can help to concentrate efforts on a major task, give play to role of synergy, and introduce the private sector in the development of a social credit system. CDB focuses on bringing into full play the Party's organizational strength, exploring the way to "run the bank well" under the guidance of the Party, making the utmost efforts to create "a learning bank of experts, cadres, and talents", and establishing and improving the management system by integrating business risk control with cadre supervision. By doing that, CDB has just figured out how to facilitate the development of a market credit system and a credit culture through the growth of the Party and the bank. Second, state credit is developed and used to its potential. State credit epitomizes the criteria of honesty and faithfulness, and is also the foundation for major national strategic projects as well as long- and medium-term infrastructural construction. A country with the ability of sustainable development is surely a nation of sound state credit. CDB uses state credit to develop bond financing for long- and medium-term construction projects. Third, the guiding role of government credit is brought into full play. Government credit is the force that leads the development of a credit system. There is no doubt that it is impossible to develop a credit system featuring sound credit and flourishing credit culture without the guidance of the government. CDB brings the role of government credit into full play, promotes the development of credit system, and helps the government establish interactive relations with the market. Fourth, the enthusiasm of institutional credit is given full play. The credit of most financial institutions in China derives from the government credit system. With the constant development of market economy, these institutions have gradually gained more autonomy in the market and have grown into a major social force. However, it is necessary to find a flexible joint between institutional credit and the government and

market credit. Able to realize government goals through market-based operation, development-oriented finance is a natural bridge linking the government and the market, institutions and the market, and helps connect various market entities. CDB is committed to running the bank in an open manner, developing the credit structure, translating the organizational strength of local governments and competent departments into credit advantage, improving the credit concept and financial awareness of local governments and enterprises while offering loans to them. Fifth, the role of individual credit is brought into full play. Individual credit in China is very much influenced by traditional Chinese culture elements on the one hand and lacks the basic consciousness required by the modern credit system on the other hand, namely the consciousness of honoring agreements. CDB supports governments, institutions, and associations in their efforts to do publicity, protect and develop individual credit, and integrate it with the sustainable development of communities and individuals to create a massive and standardized credit system. Through the financing drive, CDB integrates credit enhancement through government coordination and public participation, public morality, and peer pressure effectively to promote the formation of a market-based credit management system, bring together all resources to achieve synergy, and explore the possibility of resolving the retail issue with a wholesale solution and address people's common problems with a standard approach.

(3) Foster a corporate culture featuring development-oriented finance. Leading banks have their particular corporate cultures. Bank culture is the foundation for and driving force behind its sustainable development. While drawing upon China's tradition on credit and the government's organizational strength, CDB works hard to foster a corporate culture featuring development-oriented finance to provide the fertile soil for China's restructuring. The corporate culture of development-oriented finance is a culture of responsibility, innovation, and harmony. It places the emphasis on serving national strategies, performing global responsibility and delivering inclusive finance, introducing innovation in thinking, institution, and business, and putting the interests of the people, the general public,

and the employees first. Building a corporate culture featuring development-oriented finance is about fostering an advanced culture that is characterized by features of the times, the first-class ideology, diligence, pragmatism, quality service, development spirit, and team priority and are based on the core values of teamwork, innovation, devotion, expertise, credibility, honesty, people-centered mindset, and value creation. Employees are encouraged to share what they think with others, pursue progress rather than perfection, take on responsibility instead of vying to take the credit and grasp every opportunity to show their talent. The ultimate goal is to provide customers with the best satisfaction, and employees with the best opportunities for career development.

3.5 Summary

This chapter has set forth the cultural foundation of the development of financial theory and practice. Development-oriented finance is a fruit born by carrying forward the fine traditional culture and by making use of political and organizational advantages (Figure 3.1). Many positive elements in Chinese culture, such as the tradition of mutual aid, the development ideas of moderation and balance, the harmony-centered moral feelings, and the entrepreneurship of diligence and thrift, have great potential strength and function as the historical basis for doing a good job. China enjoys a strong advantage in political organization, which is especially conducive to concentrating its forces on fighting the collective battle and promoting the social credit system construction, and is a crucial condition for the country to boom with long-term accumulation.

The formation and growth of development-oriented finance is essentially a course of carrying forward China's fine tradition of integrity and taking advantage of the political and organizational edges. An important idea of development-oriented finance is to combine the organizational and coordinative strength of the government with the financing advantage of development of financial institutions, attach importance to planning, focus on market construction, collaborate with social forces, and grant financing support for the

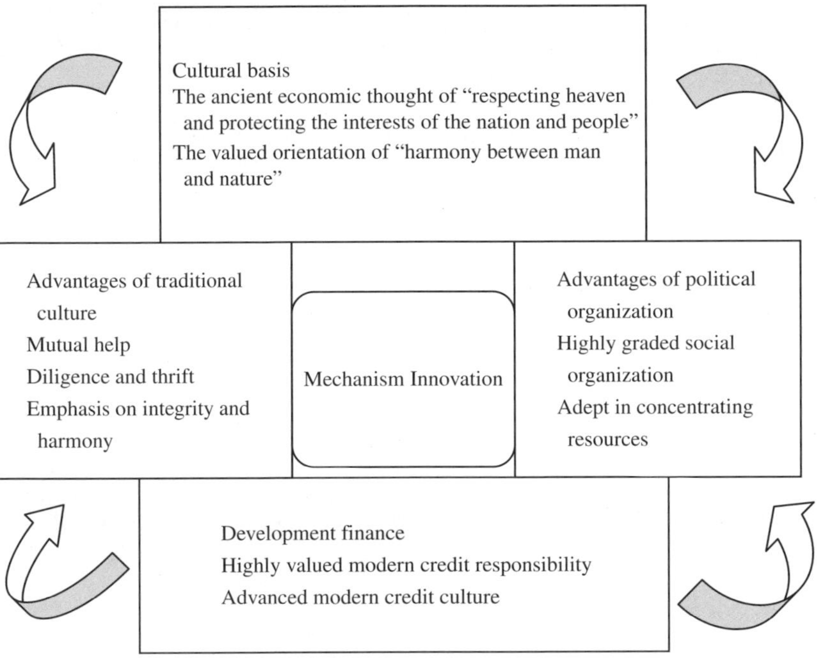

Figure 3.1: Carrying forward the fine traditional culture.

need, so that we can transform the constrained fields in economic and social development into mature areas with market-oriented and commercialized operations, and achieve outstanding market performance while serving national development strategies.

Carrying forward the fine traditional culture and employing the political and organizational advantages mean that development of financial institutions should take full advantage of these valuable resources to speed up the construction of the new system on the one hand and on the other hand, constantly enrich the traditional Chinese culture with modern credit ideas and financial knowledge. Such exploration is helpful and positive. We will continue to deepen our exploration and our research in this regard.

Chapter 4

Philosophical Outlook on Development-Oriented Finance

4.1 Introduction

Development-oriented finance is the outcome of a reform process. It is a finance concept and a mechanism for dealing with bottlenecks. It is policy based, but is not a simple extension of financial policies; it has market functions, but is not aimed at profit-making; it has the nature of a financial enterprise, but more often, it embodies the government's intention.

The research toward theory and practice of development-oriented finance covers aspects such as ideological basis, theoretical essence, operational mechanism, important practices, and international financial-oriented strategies. The ideological basis for theory and practice of finance-oriented development originated from dialectical materialism and historical materialism. They are embodied in the following five aspects:

(1) Singling out and tackling the principal contradictions, especially principal contradictions in mid- and long-term economic-social development.
(2) Exploring realistic ways of solving problems and taking initiatives in solving the contradictions between the enormous demand on finance in socioeconomic development and the backwardness of the finance market.
(3) By applying the Marxist dialectical theory on credit, figuring out conditions for internal qualitative change that leads to the transformation from non-creditability to structure, and promoting the building-up of market creditability through financing.

(4) Inheriting and carrying forward outstanding traditional culture and superiority of political organizations, and speeding up the building of a market credit system to consolidate the foundation for mid- and long-term development.
(5) Making scientific evaluation of the basic direction of sustainable development and driving forced-consumption finance and urbanization, under the conditions of international competition.

This chapter deals with the important contents of ideological basis for development-oriented finance and elaborates how development-oriented finance should persist in dialectics, and apply the Marxist credit theory to explore new approaches of how development-oriented finance with Chinese characteristics can promote economic-social development. Guided by the government's "hot spots", development-oriented finance variably keeps a watchful eye on principal contradictions and puts forward its working policy comprising "sending charcoal in snowy weather to the government's 'hot spots'; planning comes first, building up creditability; stimulating development by financing". So far as the working policy is concerned, credit build-up is an internal factor. Relative backwardness of the development of China's credit system is the fundamental impediment that restricts long-term sustainable development; to promote development by financing is an external factor; the external factor works only through the internal factor. Creditability can be built up and the building up of creditability can be stimulated. The practice of development-oriented finance can accelerate the building of the credit system. In order to speed up the qualitative change of the internal factor, conditions for transformation should be found between passiveness and activeness, incredibility and credibility, and immature market and mature market. That is to say, in order to accelerate the building up of the credit system, it is necessary to have a profound understanding of the essence, functions, and characteristics of credit, disclose and have a command of the basic law of credit activities, and guided by the scientific outlook on development actively explore the new concept of promotion of economic-social development in China by development-oriented finance.

4.2 Have an in-depth understanding of the essence, functions, and characteristics of credit activities

In life, credit has a bearing on almost every one. But what on earth is credit? It is a relatively complicated issue indeed. Many economists and philosophers, like the classical economist Adam Smith, David Ricardo (his Chinese name is Li Jiatu), founder of macroeconomics John Maynard Keynes, and well-known social philosopher Georg Simmel,[1] all performed in-depth study of credit. Therefore, once we have a comprehension of what credit is and are able to achieve a good command of its essence and understanding of its functions and characteristics in economic growth and social development, we are able to somewhat understand the basic problems in our economic development and somewhat comprehend the basic problems in development-oriented finance theory and practice.

4.2.1 *The essence of credit*

Marxist credit theory regards credit activities as the reflection of value form of social practice activities and an important link in the circle of total social capital activities[2] (Figure 4.1). It holds, "Credit, in its simplest expression, is a proper or improper trust. It makes one entrust a certain amount of his capital in the form of currency or in the form of a commodity as an estimated value to another person. The capital must be returned when it is due."[3] This definition expounds the fact that credit, as an economic domain, reflects the interests of different sectors based on credit among people. The essence of this kind of relationship is a social relationship formed by the need to realize one's will to obtain economic interests. In the final analysis, credit is a social relationship that reflects form of value. If expressed in common people's remarks, it is a relationship where "money breeds more money"and "if a tree is improperly removed, it will perish; if a person moves away from where he/she

[1] Georg Simmel, *The Philosophy of Money*, Huaxia Press, 2002.
[2] Karl Marx, *Capital*, People Press, 1975, pp. 116–117.
[3] Karl Marx, *Capital*, People Press, 1975, pp. 410–442.

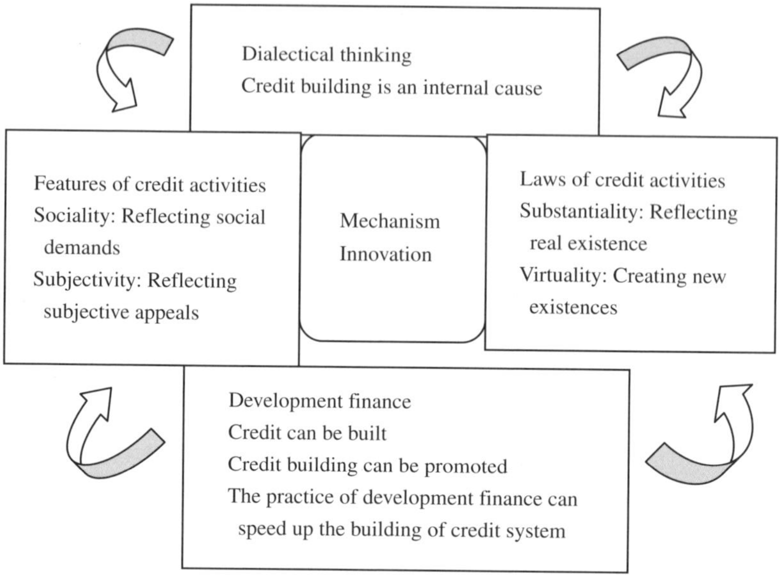

Figure 4.1: Developing the Marxist credit theory.

stays, he/she will become more vigorous; if money is properly operated for investment, it will bring about more money". In a word, money in the process of financing activities is able to create credit. Credit activities are the same as production activities and they can create value. We may have a new understanding in two aspects of the essence of credit-activities related development-oriented finance.

(1) Credit represents the "consciousness cohesion" and way of behavior of the human race, which is central to all transactions. From an enlightened state to maturity, its essence is a process of the sublimation and accumulation of credit consciousness. Unawareness of credit does not mean that there is no credit at all. Once one goes out of the state of unawareness and becomes aware of his/her needs and ability for credit, there will be changes in human behavior. This change is reflected in the success of credit building, which in turn will certainly promote all-round social development.
(2) Credit is spiritual wealth and value resource of an enterprise, a locality, and even a country. It is a unique asset. It is used in

compliance with general use value and the law of value. It is wealth created by laborers, enterprises, and government. One part of the wealth through preliminary distribution goes to workers, staffers, and entrepreneurs in the form of wages, salaries, interests, and rent, which become family income; one part of it is kept by enterprises as retained earnings, which becomes enterprise revenues; another part of it through redistribution in the form of taxes becomes revenues of governments at various levels. Part of the wealth is consumed for maintenance and re-production, and the remaining part becomes credit accumulation in the form of savings. Families, enterprises, and governments are all consumers and savers of financial assets. Inevitably, exchange relationships are formed as well as a market between consumption and saving, or between users of financial assets and providers of financial assets. In this market, the intermediate financial institutions play a key role in the normal operation of credit movements. If the intermediate financial institutions observe credit standards and conduct activities in compliance with regulations, through their remarkable service, they are able to optimize the deployment of credit as a kind of financial asset and provide socioeconomic development with basic guarantee. On the contrary, if intermediate financial institutions violate regulations, there might be chaos of financial order. In 2008, some financial institutions in Wall Street performed their operations in violation of regulations, excessively loosening their control over credit of consumable housing, thus bringing about chaos in social credit order and triggering the global financial tsunami, from which we must draw a good lesson.

4.2.2 *Functions of credit*

Credit is a powerful leverage for promotion of socioeconomic development. To individuals, state, enterprises, and society, credit is an extraordinarily valuable resource and a powerful leverage for solving problems. If one has no credibility, he will achieve nothing; if an enterprise has no creditability, it will not last long. Modern economy is a credit economy. Various transactions in modern society are carried out with credit as the link. In a modern economy, there is socialized credit relationship in the form of a creditor's rights and liabilities, or social credit, which means that the entire society has a relatively strong concept of credit and relatively advanced credit tools; there is organic relations between economic entities through advanced credit tools. A credit relationship is formed through the process of a series of activities such as borrowing, redemption, payments, thus turning scattered resources into a gigantic flowing social resource and effectively meeting the demands of socioeconomic development on resources. If a socialized credit relationship is absent, social resources cannot flow and be exploited in a rational way. Creditability of individuals and enterprises is the foundation of social credit; commercial credit and national credit are the guarantees for social credit. Modern finance is composed of individual credit, enterprise credit, commercial credit, and national credit. The fundamental aim of credit movement is to combine various credits into an organic one to form a credit world and distribute limited resources in a rational way so as to provide credit guarantee to socioeconomic development.

4.2.3 *Characteristics of credit*

In speaking about the feature of credit, we have discovered that credit movement is closely associated with project construction and other social activities, but it has its own unique attributes: sociality, morality, and subjectivity.

(1) *Sociality* reflects the common needs of the society for credit and the broad impact of credit on social development. Credit has close bearing on the interest of common people and involves all aspects of the society. Credit is embodied by the participation of common people; it is expressed in credit exchange; and it is demonstrated in balanced ratios.

Participation in credit-related activities of the common people is more often than not a conscious behavior or an unconscious behavior; sometimes, it is an active behavior or a passive behavior. A credit movement born out of initiative is an active and conscious credit movement — the least that one can do for building social credit. We shall encourage and publicize conscious and active credit movements and accelerate the building of a social credit system. An unconscious credit movement is something natural in social credit. If it exists under an active and effective management set-up, it is as a rule favorable. It may often exert negative impact on an imperfect market system. Passive credit movement is a movement of "being credited", or a phenomenon of being kidnapped by some abnormal credit movements. Therefore, we must be sober-minded that as far as sociality credit movement is concerned, participation of common people shall be correctly guided and their involvement shall be standardized, normalized, and systematized so as to form a credit support network with the participation of the entire society. Efforts shall be focused on solving the two aforementioned problems to speed up the building of a financial system for people's livelihood and provide the entire society with credit service, manifest the equality to finance for all people, while safeguarding financial security by relying on social forces.

Credit exchange movement is the inevitable demand and outcome when society has developed to a certain degree. Along with social progress and development, modes, tiers, and scope of credit exchange movement are constantly progressing and developing. In modern economic activities, credit as an important component of social resources has become an instrumentality element for finance and transactions. This instrumentality element is characteristic of liquidity, or it can be used as a unique exchange tool between different resources and in different exchange processes that reflect different liquidity. For instance, in international revenue and expenditure, liquidity reflects a nation's ability to make up for deficit in balance of external revenue and expenditure and it also reflects its necessary foreign exchange reserve. In the banking system, liquidity reflects banks' ability to satisfy their clients' encashment and also reflects how much cash and short-term assets they have. It can be said that liquidity obtained from various exchanges is another basic feature of credit movement of sociality. We are expected to recognize this feature just to underline the efficiency of credit to guide the building of a healthy credit system and construct social eco-environment that is instrumental to the healthy balance of highly efficient credit movements.

Balance ratio of credit movements is another feature of credit movements of sociality, which reflects the basic characteristics of relationship among departments. There shall be an appropriate ratio between consumption and saving, commodity credit and currency credit, and investment and production; otherwise, there will be an imbalance. When it happens, it will be difficult for credit movements to continue. There is a brilliant exposition in the works of Ye Ziqi of late Ming Dynasty and early Qing Dynasty: "Take the water in a pond for example. The incoming ditch for the water shall be the same size as the outgoing ditch. Then there is smooth liquidity of water in the pond like smooth blood circulation". This vividly illustrates that the balance ratio of credit movements is a kind of dynamic balance and from the perspective of time and space change, an overall and comprehensive consideration needs to be given to it. Analysis of balance ratio of credit movements helps us to correctly plan for credit construction, exploit various resources in a rational way, and conduct various financial or economic activities in proportion and in proper steps.

(2) *Morality*. Credit is the application and solidification of morality in the commodity exchange process. Morality originated from various people's relationships in social development. Along with different stages of social development, morality has increasingly become sociality. Morality in the broad sense is the product of social development and is also its foundation. After the Industrial Revolution, morality was applied extensively to large-scale commodity exchanges. It got expanded, strengthened, and varied; it became a necessary condition and foundation for social development and social framework; and it is a guarantee for commodity exchanges. Honest credit is the soul of a market economy. Commodity exchange among the human race began from bartering to monetary transaction and finally to credit transaction. Credit transaction is based on credit morality, which requires that the transaction behavior and means of

the credit mainstay comply with specific moral principles and social expectation (including honesty, justice, conscience, and compliance). These are the core and basis for financial laws, systems and regulations, and other laws. The universally recognized fact is that credibility has virtue, whereas incredibility lacks virtue. Whoever ignores or loses the bottom line basic morality will ultimately destroy one's market reputation which would be irreparable. The basic moral qualities, such as integrity, moral credibility, fairness, impartiality, scrupulous abidance by privacy, of a credit intermediate organization as a transaction executioner are basic conditions to ensure smooth credit activities. In his speech delivered at the British Cambridge University on March 2, 2009, Premier Wen Jiabao pointed out: "to effectively cope with this crisis, great attention should be paid to the role of morality. Morality is the greatest thing in the world. Its rays of light are even more brilliant than sunshine. Authentic economic theory never clashes with the highest moral code". Economic theory should represent fairness and credibility and equally promote support to all people including the most vulnerable people; lack of virtue is the deep-rooted cause that led to the current financial crisis.

Morality of credit is the most important feature of financial activities. Morality of credit clearly lies in economic qualities and inherent value of financial enterprises, which has direct bearing on the healthy growth and lasting competitiveness of financial enterprises. Meanwhile, credit is also the most important requirement of other social activities, the moral outlook that is absolutely necessary for market economy, the foundation for harmonious social development, and an embodiment of human civilization. It is through building up of credit relationship that human society has established a civilized world, which is different from other societies. Along with unremitting and ever-deepening development of credit relationship, human society is continuously progressing and becoming increasingly civilized.

(3) *Subjectivity*. The mainstay of credit is an important indicator of realization of pursuit of interests, transactions, and dialogues between transacting parties. In essence, all social and commodity transactions are translated into the same language, forming basic

elements for market-orientation of the entire society and turning all economic activities into the mainstay of interests through credit variance. These main bodies are of the same quality and they can conduct transactions. As we know, credit movement is a reflection of the claim of an individual, a unit, and sovereignty interest of a nation, which forms the outstanding characteristics of "subjectivity". This feature also has a structural demand as reflected in the saying "numberless grains of sand can pile up into a pagoda". Individual credits of all tiers jointly form a solid credit combination to provide inexhaustible credit resources to socialized credit movements. Hence, there is "subjectivity" in credit movements. Moreover, there is "symbiosis" between one credit subjectivity and other ones. Under market economy conditions, interests of economic activities are credit-oriented and the credit relationship has infiltrated into each and every aspect of economic development. In credit movements, in order to pursue maximum value, the possible interest credit subjectivity may resort to various means. Then they are liable to lose its credibility. Consequently, credit relationship becomes fragile, credit order becomes chaotic, and transaction risks become very big, thus bringing unfavorable influence to both transacting parties. Therefore, credit economy often needs some professional credit management institutions (like credit checking management corporations and guarantee corporations) to provide the transacting main bodies with relevant services, to guard against risks, and to ensure the healthy and orderly market operation with relatively low transaction cost.

4.3 Reveal with depth the basic law of credit movements

As long as we have a correct understanding of the essence, functions, and characteristics of credit, we will easily find that credit movements follow the three basic laws.

(1) *As social basic activity, credit movements not only reflect actual reality but also create future reality.* Actual reality is the basis for credit movements. However, credit movements are not only a simple reflection of actual activities, but may well also be the

sublimation and extension of actual activities. Let us explain this with a real economy and a virtual economy in economic activities. Real economy is reality that is visible and touchable, whereas virtual economy is a new reality corresponding to real economy. We can easily notice that virtual economy in economic activities is a creation of relatively independent credit movements. Virtual economy is a state relative to real economy and a product of a highly developed market economy. It comes from real economy, but it operates relatively independent from the real economy. That is the reason why quite a number of financial products are getting farther and farther from reality. However, fundamentally speaking, the relationship between real economy and virtual economy is like that between the two sides of a coin. Real economy is the basis, while virtual economy is a reflection of real economy in a unique credit state. If this kind of unique credit form is over-exaggerated, real economy may become a distorting mirror. The process is one of economic bubbles. We shall object to economic bubbles and bring it under control without restricting the requirements of regular laws for credit movements to create a new reality. Otherwise, a catalyst or a vital force may be missing in the economy, because when real economy develops to a certain stage, it needs the expansive function of virtual economy to realize "leapfrog" development. But virtual economy expands to a certain stage and it requires structural adjustment of real economy to achieve sustainable development. The essence of virtual economy is relatively independent movements of capital value form.

According to the degree of virtualization of financial assets, a virtual economy can approximately be divided into the following four tiers: (i) the first tier is creditization of currency. Once currency disengages itself from the gold standard and becomes paper currency, it will create conditions for emergence and development of virtual economy. Modern banks have the function of creating credit, derivative currency. Credit currency is a relatively independent movement from banks. (ii) The second tier is propitiation, instrumentalization, and securitization of real economy that to some extent is virtually associated with real economy, emerging in transactions, such as stocks, securities, and funds. (iii) The third tier is monetization of visible assets and securitization of financial assets. By repackaging housing mortgage loans, automobile mortgage loans, and credit card loans, banks have them securitized or some securities of higher rating are added and used as mortgage to issue new securities, thus improving the liquidity of assets. In doing so, the already virtualized capital now becomes more virtualized. (iv) The fourth tier is a virtual state which has completely separated from real economy and is independent. This is achieved by emergence and application of several financial derivative instruments which form highly virtual capital, such as financial options, financial futures, forward agreements, and financial exchange. Neither the selling nor the purchasing parties directly holds the securities or currency under the contract and they do not have to buy or sell those securities or currency when transaction is finally settled. Especially for transactions of indexed futures and options, in fact, it is a kind of gambling on the rise and fall of indexes without anything in kind. This is out-and-out virtual capital. Historically, the development stages of virtual economy — capitalization of idle money, socialization of interest-bearing capital, marketization of negotiable securities, internationalization of financial market, and integration of international finance — have reflected the development of real economy.

(2) *In the process of creating a new reality, credit movements can play either a positive or a negative role.* Let us also take the existence of virtual economy in economic activities, for example. Independent movements of virtual capital value constitute another economic form that corresponds to a real economy or a virtual economy. The emergence and development of a virtual economy provide the human race with approaches to scattering risks and instruments to circumvent risks in risks-permeated economic cooperation, standardize practice of transaction and investment, and promote professional division of work. All these help in lowering transaction costs and in enhancing scale benefits. That is to say, virtual economy plays an important and irreplaceable role in optimizing resource allocation and accelerating assets regrouping. However, today, virtual economy that has undergone development over the years is like a hard-to-control runaway

horse. A lot of actual and expected financial wealth that has separated from real object is moving and rapidly swelling in virtual state, bringing enormous uncertainty and instability to economic society, which we must be vigilant against. Judging from the perspective of the development track of a virtual economy, creditization of money, capitalization of credit, securitization of assets, and pricing of invisible assets act as the bridge or link leading the real economy to the virtual economy. Expectation of future revenue is the soul of virtual economy.

Electronization, networkization, and digitization are boost motors that accelerate development. By "playing the fool" and "currying favor with the majority", one may be eager to pass his "relay baton" to the next person, expecting to obtain a large amount of risk income brought about from speculation. These inherent driving forces result in rapid development of a contemporary virtual economy. Only by recognizing the existence of virtual economy and being aware of the connotation can we bring the role of virtual economy into play. If we overlook the adverse impact virtual economy is liable to have and if we cannot exercise macro-control over it, we would be planting the root of trouble for the occurrence of a bubble economy and the outbreak of an economic crisis.

Virtual economy may bring us tremendous revenue, but is often coupled with risks. The major risk is economic bubbles, which is coexistence. When the market value of virtual capital is bigger than the counterpart of actual capital, there must be economic bubbles. Economic bubbles are mainly caused by speculations. In the capital market, as long as investors have the same anticipation and before the reverse anticipation becomes the mainstream, the market relay baton may not have to worry about the next runner. Thus, the market will become increasingly prosperous. What investors are most concerned about are the price-difference earnings when they are engaged in buying and selling. They do not know much and have little interest in the operation of real economy to which the virtual economy is attached. Hence, capital prices depart from their value and bubbles emerge. Of course, though real economy exists in the form of "objects", it does not necessarily mean that it will not produce bubbles. For instance, repeated low-level construction results in surplus capacity and surplus products; if capital of enterprises' bank loans or stocks or securities exceeds actual capital that the enterprises in question can endure, there are surely economic bubbles. Economic bubbles include bubbles resulting from speculations on capital market and shrinkage of actual capital. The main reasons are: (i) the basic structure of economy must have gone wrong and (ii) there must be excessive speculations on the capital market. In the past two decades, the Japanese bubble economy has broken up, financial crises have taken place in Mexico and Brazil, financial storm has hit Southeast Asia, and in 2008, the whole world began to suffer from the global financial crisis. They differed in a thousand and one ways, from the formation of economic bubbles to the outbreak of an economic crisis, however, the basic mechanism remained the same without deviating from the aforementioned two causes.

(3) *Credit can be built up and credit construction can be promoted.* In the historical process of a market economy growing and maturing, there were always struggles between observance of credit and violation of credit. While the overwhelming majority of important transactions observed standards, there were nevertheless a few obsessed with the desire for gain. In the market, they are engaged in all sorts of fraudulent activities for ill-gotten gains. Only after more than 100 years did market order in European and American countries gradually become full-fledged. China's system is under transition from a planned economy to a market economy, in which counterfeiting and selling children, tax evasion and false declaration, economic fraud and vicious debt evasion, and debt cancellation that undermine credit are common occurrence. However, credit will certainly gradually be strengthened and overcome the wrecking disturbances, open up the way to normal operation, and in the end establish its dominant position in market economy. An in-depth analysis shows that the synergy formed by the law of value, law of supply and demand, and law of competition in the development of market economy brings about a market mechanism for check and balance allowing the fittest to survive and the inferior to perish. Of course, it is inadequate to depend on the "invisible hand only". The superstructure is required to adopt

necessary measures and an effective mechanism can be established to accelerate the process. Credit movements can be developed and built up like productive forces. If external elements (like coordination conducted by the government for optimization) are combined with foundational functions of the market, building of market credit system can undoubtedly be sped up. Developed market economy systems in Western countries are influenced by their own culture, ideology, and politics and they seem to have experienced a natural evolution process, in reality, their governments have played a *sine qua non* role — an indispensable role. China and a large number of other developing countries, the new emerging countries, do not have the time and space for free evolution and re-growth and neither have the financial capacity to bear the gigantic cost of free evolution. What they can do is only to take the initiative to develop and build up credit to catch up with the wheels of the times.

4.4 Actively explore the growth concept of development-oriented finance

In view of the above-mentioned essence, function, characteristics, and regular law of financial activities, China Development Bank focuses on financing bottlenecks in socioeconomic development. It vigorously promotes the building-up of market credit system in the basic fields of social-economic development and relatively weak fields. In order to actively develop and build up market credit system, China Development Bank understands the importance of advanced concept better and that advanced concept guides actions and is imperative in guiding development-oriented finance. Therefore, in practice, China Development Bank persists in the combination of concept and practice, focusing on key problems in development and raising capital in identifying solutions to problems, but it does not want to be led by the nose. It wants to become a force of active development, by launching offensive attacks, fighting battles with multiple forces joining in, so as to turn passiveness into activeness, change incredibility to creditability, and turn an immature market into a mature market. The Bank's important concepts of development include "planning first", "strategy options", "combined capital raising", "socialization of finance", "organization of credit increase", "benefits after obligations and cooperative development" in international financial operation, "doing a good job in Party construction, running the Bank and supporting development", and the concept of creation. These concepts guide China Development Bank's practices and its proper promotion in the building of a market credit system.

4.4.1 *Development-oriented concept*

Secretary-General Hu Jintao gave a speech on development-oriented poverty alleviation in Guizhou, which embodied the development-oriented concept. When we learn about the essence of Mr Hu Jintao's speech, we can easily understand that opening up is none other than development. An exploitation process is a development process, or a process to improve one's ability of self-accumulation and of self-development. Principal contractions in the development process must be grasped and solved. China is still in the preliminary stage of socialism. It is the characteristic of operation of macroeconomy, and the backward credit system cannot meet the needs of rapid economic-social development. This is the principal contradiction of this stage. Obviously, China is short of resources, its utilization rate of resources is low, there is much room for improvement in credit system and credit mechanism, and there are some uncertainties in economic construction. Rational arrangement of economic resources, provision of stable and long-term construction funds, and realization of basic balance between current consumption and long-term investment returns are prerequisites for assuring sustainable development. Difficulty in financing is a major bottleneck in free economic–social development, especially in "hot" social fields such as housing, medical care, and education. Breakthrough in the bottleneck and straightening out the links that enable economic–social development will experience a plain sailing and the result of "one thing is sorted out, the rest is sorted out too", thus achieving the purpose of half the work with twice the result. We consider problems from the angle of development, firmly grasp the key to credit bottleneck, and promote building-up of a credit system with development principles to realize rational arrangement of capital. We firmly maintain that credit can be built. To solve the issue of credit, it is necessary to put people first and take the institution as the mainstay. If the mainstay for fund-raising proceeds without subjective initiative and good credit structure, all financial activities would be likened to a tree without roots or water without a source. Therefore, we attach great importance to the strengthening of a market's legal systems, displaying people's subjective initiative, and developing the inherent potential of the credit mainstay and governmental departments' dominant position in organization and resources in all fields, thus retaining the everlasting vitality of the credit mainstay. We not only have to inject blood into the organs that lack blood but also to teach them how to enhance the "blood making" capacity. In this way, we are able to turn immature credit mainstay into mature one and bottlenecks into highlights. This is exactly the result of concept guiding its action.

4.4.2 *Concept of planning first*

Planning is an idea of development and is a strategic deployment or actual arrangement for future development. No matter whether the level of planning is high or not, it reflects the realm of ideological level. Scientific planning on development is the combination of the theory of knowledge and that of practice. "Being scientific" refers to the theory of knowledge, mainly embodying cognition of the relationship between men and nature, the cognition of basic systems of the economic society, the cognition of national conditions, the cognition that backward countries have to achieve "leapfrog" development, and stick to their own development roads. "Development" refers to putting theory into practice, not only in the field of science and technology, but also in the society and market. Scientific development is a continuous process of combining cognition and practice resulting in development that is all-round and three-dimensional, both in time as well as in space. Only by being deepened by historical experience of economy and social changes at home and abroad and through constant practice can comprehensive contents and broad range of scientific development be enriched and tested. Scientific planning of development is an important aspect and prerequisite for scientific development, by which developing countries may turn passiveness into activeness, avoid twists and turns, and speed up their development. Development process in developing countries is vastly different from that of developed countries. The former must depend on ways suitable for them and bring into play their characteristics of advantages and accelerate the development process. Hence, they are required to encourage continuous cognition based on their own successful experiences and failures and those of their rivals as well. The planning process is a process of gradual cognition. Planning helps us achieve success and to detach ourselves from routinism, to integrate theory and practice, and to reflect the features of the objective matters in a more profound, more correct, and more complete manner. In taking stock of the objective matters as a whole, a great and farsighted goal will be worked out, a further clear-cut policy will be advanced, and effective strategic measures will be drawn up. This is a scientific undertaking, allowing not in the least falsehood or exaggeration, on the contrary, a pragmatic and prudent approach is required. Development-oriented finance is required to abide by the principle of Planning First and committed to turn planning into a core competitive edge, bringing into play its role in guiding the overall situation in an effective way.

4.4.3 *Concept of strategic options*

Strategic options are also a combination of the theory of knowledge and the theory of practice. Strategies are related to the theory of knowledge, planning, and cognition for the future; options are related to the theory of practice and are an application of financial technologies. Strategic options are an important source of ideological technology to plan proper scientific development. In formulating planning for investment and financing for a region or a department, full consideration shall be given to the ground realities, potential advantages, and development levels of the region or department in question. Their development performance in the days to come shall be rationally employed to decide credit support to the needs of current large-scale construction. In the development process of a region or department, its superiority stands out and its development performance in the days to come becomes obvious. It can solve its problem of insufficient construction capital through local capital-raising channels in a proper way. When development-oriented finance supports localities and important industries, a long-term risk related to large capital may be concentrated. This risk in reality relates to insufficient capacity for generating profits leading to insufficient cash flow, and therefore, options are needed to cover. As China is a developing country, it is necessary for development-oriented finance to deal with projects for which there are no sufficient gains in the prior period; correspondingly, it is necessary to develop options that can be liquidated after the development prospect is realized, options that can guarantee gains, and achieve break-even balance in general. Development-oriented finance persists in developing the space of strategic credit, analyzing the prediction of development prospect, making full use of development-oriented financial capital with government credit or its background to realize guidance, and collection of socialized capital and its coordinated operation. Development-oriented finance deploys a small amount of development-oriented capital as seed capital to synergize the growing social capital in order to provide joint support for construction of projects in economic development. Development-oriented finance, with credit build-up as the main thread and through system building, makes full use of the finance leverage effect and principles of option investment to design a rational credit structure that can cover the credit of current construction projects to ensure realization of profit–loss balance. Meanwhile, with sustainable capital, development-oriented finance endures to solve problems and gain feasibility of long-term investments by providing financial services.

4.4.4 Concept on combined financing

Combined financing is a capital-raising mechanism and an idea of integrating resources "shoveling the peak, filling up the valley", hedging risks, and coordinating development. We maintain that a comprehensive consideration shall be given to capital exploitation and risk control in development, fight a battle by pooling all resources together instead of a guerilla warfare. All are to be mobilized to promote the building-up of one field and all efforts are put together to support the coordinated development of one region. Various resources from the government, banks, enterprises, and other credit measures shall be exploited in a comprehensive manner. Plans for financing in an all-round way with an appropriate credit structure and cash flow, in general as reference, are to be worked out along with dynamic monitoring and adjustments to avoid concentration of risk in combined capital raising including within/off-the-statement operation risks and implementation of risk quotas and anticipated loss of combined financing, which not only provides great support for economic–social development but also manages risks in an effective way. Through the design of combined financing, development-oriented finance by maximizing finance to medium- and large-size construction projects "encases" together in a certain field and arranges capital resources and capital application in a unified and coordinated way to provide local governments with packaged services. This not only satisfies the need of capital for current construction projects but also makes an overall arrangement for medium- and long-term capital needs; it not only improves the current market but also helps localities gain opportunities to seek sustainable and profitable growth. This is undoubtedly instrumental to overall development of the region or the field in question. For instance, by way of securitization of social capital, development-oriented finance raises a large amount of capital, turning non-productive, short-term, scattered, and idle social capital into productive, mid- and long-term, orderly capital of scale, thus achieving rational arrangement of resources for long-term construction projects, creating high-speed capital accumulation with distinctive Chinese characteristics, forming effects of scale and realizing unconventional development of a developing country. In the combination process, development-oriented finance further enhances its market competitive edge.

4.4.5 *Concept of socialization of finance*

When in pursuit of wealth, self-disciplined enterprises that undertake social responsibilities along with professional ethics can reach the highest realm of a modern enterprise with synchronous development. It is this consciousness of responsibility that puts forward the guiding line of "socialization of finance and "financialization of society", which means enterprises shall give back as much as possible to the society, serve the society, and devote themselves to the joint development of real finance and economic society; enterprises shall keep a close eye on the needs of social development, be concerned about the need for livelihood-related projects, and the need for capital for creation of undertakings and re-employment of the disadvantageous social groups; they are expected to build up socialized, instituted, and standardized credit system and conduct socialized distribution of gains and risks through socialized organization and management of credit resources to manifest "fairness, justice, and transparency" and realize the goal that everyone enjoys the right to raise capital. Realization of socialization of finance not only relies on the government but also on the market and the society; it needs to display the government's organizational advantage and activeness from all walks of life; the realization can be achieved by accelerated building of the market and relevant systems. Market building depends on the publicity of the development concept of marketization, guarantee of returns from investment and efficiency, while system building is to ensure that risks can be controlled, compensated and balanced. Factors such as awareness of credit systems, moral behavior code, mutual help between ethnic groups wherein the system holds each responsible for the action of others, conducting operations in compliance with regulations, government's guarantee and international trans-period profit loss coverage constitute the foundation for smooth operation of socialization of finance and financialization of society. Development-oriented finance is required to actively display its advantages of market build-up, system build-up, and raising capital to push forward socialization of finance. We persist in "socialization of finance and financialization of society". While continuing to raise finance to support "two foundations, one pillar", we should actively develop livelihood finance, further strengthening the development of projects devoted to people's livelihood, supporting credit policies in employment, providing grant-in-aid for students and for post-disaster reconstruction, sharing of resources and raising capital to solve "bottleneck" problems so as to satisfy the direct needs of the masses in socioeconomic development and build a harmonious society.

4.4.6 *Concept of increasing creditability through organizational efforts*

In order to solve the contradiction between a backward credit system and the rapid growth of economy, it is essential to combine both the government role and the market role. The key to accelerate mid- and long-term financial markets is to establish a full-fledged and developed basic set-up and micro-system for finance. In a big developing country like China, we cannot wait for the natural formation of a credit market. To speed up development, we must integrate components of resources such as government, market, finance, and enterprises. It is necessary for developed countries to increase creditability through social efforts, but it is not a means to solve problems once and for all. By relying on the government's advantages of organizational ability, we can build market credit and a market system that are active, highly efficient, and systematic thus resulting in enormous system efficiency and market efficiency. We shall make full use of the foundational role that government credit can play to enhance the interactive efficiency of credit loans and raising of financial capital and actively create conditions for capital raising to enter a capital market, which is instrumental to promote a coordinated development of healthy enterprises, finance, and economy. Development-oriented finance is aimed at combining its own capital-raising advantage and the government's advantage of organizational ability, that is, development-oriented capital is expected to integrate, in essence, quasi-bonds and management of financial assets, improve development capital-raising mechanism, push forward the building of credit as the mainstay of economy and platform for investment and capital raising, a platform which combines the government, enterprises, and market mechanism, so as to transfer national credit, bank credit, and credit of local governments to enterprise credit. In doing so, on the one hand, safety of assets is ensured; on the other hand, support to all-round, coordinated, and sustainable economic development is guaranteed.

4.4.7 *Concept on international development*

This is "obligation first and profit second, followed by cooperative development". China Development Bank is active in formulating strategies to support enterprises in implementing their energy resources to "go global". Gradually, the way of thinking about "sending charcoal in snowy weather; making careful planning; and having the future in mind" is formed. The Bank emphasizes on joint development with developing countries, upgrading friendships in politics, among people and cultures to strengthen strategic partnerships, which would lead to mutually beneficial economies and win–win cooperation. Realization of effective connection with Chinese modes has been achieved through helping a great number of less developed countries in building their own development capability and markets. This is an important basis for our new pattern, new order, and new policy, with which we can participate and exert influence on the growth of global economy and finance.

4.4.8 *Concept on doing a proficient job in Party construction and in the running of the bank; supporting development*

We regard Party construction and running the Bank well as an inseparable entity which shall remain unified in the advanced nature of the Party. Ideology shall remain unified, strength shall be cohered, and planning strategy shall be developed under Party construction so as to speed up development. In addition, mechanism and risk prevention shall be improved and building of market, credit, and systems shall be promoted under Party construction. We shall earnestly transfer the Party's political and organizational advantages to the competitive advantage of the China Development Bank; we ought to establish and improve an inspection system for Party construction. All this is an important measure for creating the culture of development-oriented finance.

4.4.9 *Concept of renovation*

This includes renovations in ideology, system, and technology. All these renovations are aimed at overcoming difficulties in development and in reducing the transaction costs. Renovations in ideology refers to interaction among people, which is a evolution of how the human race shall restrict itself; renovations in the system is interaction between people, which suggests the development of an ideal system; renovations in technology refer to interactions between the human race and nature comprising the act of men in transforming nature and in protecting the environment. Renovations in ideology are instrumental to reducing the cost of system building; renovations in systems are instrumental to reducing the cost of revolution of technology; and renovations in technology are instrumental to reducing production cost. The process of economic development is one of constant renovation and also one of cost comparison. Every one or every department has his/her or its comparative advantage and realizes his/her or its comparative cost through transactions. Comparative advantage leads to professional specialization and professional specialization leads to labor efficiency. Professional specialization is followed by commercialization and then monetization. Monetization is a typical embodiment of reduction of transaction cost. Financial activities related to reduction transaction cost emerged after monetization. We persist in financial renovation by aiming to integrate some resources and conditions into financial activities that we have not so far applied and providing better financial services in fostering economic–social development by reducing uncertainties and lowering financial transaction costs and risks, while ensuring sustainable and better gains for development-oriented finance. Development-oriented finance is expected to establish its theory with distinctive Chinese characteristics through renovations in theories, systems, policies, and products, thus building a modern credit set-up on the basis of optimized operation of the microeconomic mainstay to stimulate the formation of a modern credit system, establish regulations of economic acts or rules of the game that conform to reality in China, improve bank performance, raise economic efficiency, and enhance market confidence. As for problems and contradictions in development, development-oriented finance is to solve those problems that cannot be solved in the current financial system and turn some uncertain tentative ideas into operable plans. For instance, through renovated government–bank–enterprise–market credit system, that is, "four in one" credit system, development-oriented finance brings all efforts into full play, thus turning the unfeasible into the feasible and social resources into reliable credit. In the end, numerous projects, ranging from large projects such as infrastructure facilities to small and intermediate enterprises, including providing support to school going children, are supported by the credit system. In fact, a development-oriented market is constructed with approaches of development-oriented finance to explore fields where development-oriented economy is vigorous. Successful practice of development-oriented finance indicates that our renovation has reached a high level. Nowadays, having enough to eat is no longer a problem, as we are aware of the overall situation, we have sought far and wide for "what lies close at hand" to establish an advanced credit system, and pursue higher and farther goals. It is through our planning that we are turning the unfeasible into the feasible. Commercial banks must be surprised and think that it is inconceivable, but this is where the success of development-oriented finance lies. By expanding our thought process about development-oriented finance and exploring new approaches, development-oriented finance has its share in economic growth.

These concepts are interrelated and are mutually complementary. They have jointly formed the concept of overall development of development-oriented finance and are constantly being enriched and improved in practice and in discussions.

4.5 Summary

In this chapter, we have discussed the philosophical basis for the theory and practice of development-oriented finance, which results from adhering to the dialectical thinking and giving full play to the initiative. Analyzing the nature, characteristics, and law of credit activities from the perspective of epistemology and practice, we can draw the following crucial conclusions: (i) credit can be built, (ii) credit building can be promoted, and (iii) the practice of development-oriented finance can speed up the building of the credit system.

The modern economy is in essence a credit economy. Credit, which is a representation of the human's cohesion of sense and way of behavior, is central to all transactions. For individuals, businesses, state, and society, credit is a precious resource and is a powerful lever to solve problems. Credit is a kind of social relation reflecting the form of value. Credit activities, as the basic activity of a society, reflect both the existence in reality and create new existence, and may have a positive effect or negative effect on the creation process. Credit activities are closely related to social activities like project construction and meanwhile have relatively independent activity patterns. In compliance with the law of financial activities, development-oriented finance persists in combining epistemology and practice, concentrates on the key issues, gives full play to the initiative, and innovatively develops ideas and measures to properly handle the relationship between long-term and short-term development, between internal and external causes, and between maturity and immaturity while vigorously promoting the building of market credit system, and provide financial services for the modernization drive.

Chapter 5

Rational Judgment of Development Trend and Dynamics in the 21st Century

Development-oriented finance upholds international strategic thinking and scientifically explores the basic direction and dynamics of sustainable development against the backdrop of economic globalization.

Today, there are the following two types of globalization in the world:

(1) Globalization that is driven by American consumption constitutes the consumption engine for global economic development.
(2) Globalization that is driven by China's urbanization constitutes the urbanization engine for the rapid development of developing countries.

After an examination of the unique features, trends, and interactive relations between the two engines, we can come up with the following important conclusion: China needs development-oriented finance in the 21st century, and development-oriented finance is important in accelerating the development of China's urbanization and consumer economy.

5.1 Correctly understand consumption-driven globalization

5.1.1 *Meaning of consumption*

Consumption is the purpose of production. It is also a way people convert all sorts of products according to their aims. Without consumption, there will be no production. All production activities are designed to meet the demand of consumption. Consumption is a basic demand of people, and also the lifeline of society. A consumer society is surrounded by commodities and features the mass consumption of commodities. This mass consumption of commodities not only changes the daily requirements of people but also changes the social relations and lifestyle of people. With advancements in production technologies, consumption continues to enrich and enhance its contents and levels and the consumer society continues to advance to new stages.

In the early 20th century, a consumer credit revolution occurred in the United States, in which installment shopping became a universal lifestyle in society. As a result of the drastically higher productivity and the increase in material products arising from the Industrial Revolution, consumer demand gradually replaced production capacity and become a major bottleneck to the growth of the American economy. In order to meet the demand of mass consumption, Americans developed consumer loans for installment shopping. This consumer loan gave an immense boost to the building of a modern credit system, helped vast numbers of consumers to realize their consumer demand, brought a fundamental change to the wealth management model of American families, and enabled American citizens to buy expensive consumer durables. In short, it made the American dream come true. Accordingly, consumer loan became a powerful wave once it was recognized by society, and appeared before people as America's most authoritative culture. Its impact and influence overwhelmed the social custom that churches, families, and the state tried to control market worship for material desires. Consumer loan created mass consumers who were happy and confident to borrow money that they looked upon as a "beautiful loan". Meanwhile, as loan repayment required work and restraint, consumer loan itself became a sort of control mechanism, which made borrowers respect strict repayment schedules as loan repayment was not so light-hearted. The reason why consumer loan could develop in a sustained and rapid way was precisely because this consumer culture not only contained a fashionable concept of consumption but also preserved the traditional concepts of prudence, thrift, and hard work. In such a situation, this consumer culture was a specific lifestyle and also an attempt to realize the meaning of life from daily life, namely from the process of marketing, shopping, consumption, and disposing of commodities. In this consumer culture, consumers believed that they could discover the meaning of life in the course of consumption. It was in the course of consumption, rather than production, that people felt they were most dynamic and humane. Accordingly, consumer culture became an important content of modern American culture. Consumer loan created consumer society. History indicates that this consumer culture formed in capitalist countries became an engine for modern economy, which provided astonishing power for modern economy. The personalized pursuit and overall development of mass consumption promoted the change of the mode of industrial production and the transition of American economic growth from being production driven to consumption driven.

5.1.2 *Change and development of "consumption engine"*

From the early 20th century to the early 21st century, the American economic growth driven by consumption lasted for about one century. This was a century in which the seller's market was replaced by the buyer's market, a century in which the consumer society developed from Fordism to post-Fordism, a century in which the "production"-centered society was replaced by a "consumption"-centered society, and a century in which the overall rise of mass consumption was replaced by individualized development. An analysis of the development and change of the century-long consumption-driven economy can help us further understand the unique features of the "consumption engine".

In the initial stages of the "consumption engine" that was developed in the early 20th century, the mass consumption society had a close relationship with the mode of mass industrial production established by Henry Ford. Mass production dominated the economic life, consumer market was rather elementary and simple, consumption was rather mass oriented, and market on the whole was a seller's one. As enterprises introduced centralized management, workers were clearly divided into classes and commodities were produced according to uniform designs, and most commodities were not distinctively targeted on specific markets. Individualization was weak, but new commodities always continued to appear. As a result, consumption was essentially mass oriented, uniform, and standard. Consumers had small room to choose, and market commodities generally reflected the interests of producers, instead of the demands of consumers. In general, corporate production guided consumption. Consumption did not have a visible level of contribution to economy and society.

Thanks to the continuous innovation of technologies, products, and markets, the nature of production and consumption underwent many changes. In the early 21st century, in particular, corporate production was growingly organized according to "flexible specialization". In other words, production was organized in flexible forms, in which producers emphasized innovation and pursued individualized commodities so as to boost the life force of products and the capacity of enterprises. Enterprises, which defined themselves as the engine of their times, not only defined the commercial models and concepts for production marketing, and the whole industry but also widely used the network technology and advanced communications technology to arrange their production worldwide. Product exhibition, packing, promotion, and after-sale service played growing roles, gavc a strong boost to the development of the service industry, and turned the consumer market into a typical buyer's market. In a buyer's market, the consumer was god and the consumption pattern presented many new features such as the following:

(1) Market commodities were diversified. The change of fashionable models and individual styles made commodities even more differentiated and consumption even more specialized, giving birth to the model of individualized consumption.
(2) Market segmentation appeared in light of different product preferences, turning consumer activities into an important way for social status identification.

(3) Consumers became changeable, with their preferences changing more frequently and their consumer demands becoming growingly difficult to forecast. This shortened the life span of every product.
(4) Consumer shopping became a form of modern activities and assumed growingly diversified forms, from store shopping to mail shopping and further to online shopping. They gave birth to new logistics industries.
(5) Consumption was not only a basic demand but also an entertainment demand. Consumer culture became an important component of social life, and sports and leisure consumption were on the steady rise.
(6) Shopping and consumption venues were integrated. While superstores became a symbol of urban development, consumption environment emphasized individualism, comfort, and function.
(7) Brands became a totem, a worshipping symbol, and a trust to the general public.
(8) Consumption became a vogue, giving birth to consumption school and consumption liquidity.
(9) Group and government procurement became an important force in consumption.
(10) Both the level of consumer crimes and anti-crime technologies continued to grow. For example, credit card fraud, mobile phone fraud, and online fraud were on the rise, and remote-controlled surveillance cameras and other anti-theft technologies were also growingly updated.

These were all the unique features of the so-called "post-Fordism", which emphasize flexibility and elasticity and provided new impetus to the development of consumer society. Under the guidance of "post-Fordism", consumption created new production demands and consumer demands stimulated innovation and production desires. Consumption became a major force to drive social development and made a growing contribution to economic growth and social development. The consumer market in the age of "post-Fordism" made human exchanges to increasingly wider directions. As a result, the opportunity economy replaced the scale economy, with both production process and marketing method becoming increasingly flexible.

However, the role of consumption in driving economic and social development cannot be infinitely amplified and the contribution of consumption to economic growth cannot entirely replace production and investment. While consumption produces positive impacts on economy and society, it also has some negative impacts on them. China should correctly understand and treat consumer economy and consumer society for several reasons such as the following:

(1) The change in the nature of production and consumption does not change the inherent links between them. Although the activities of consumption have shown a growing relative independence from the activities of production, there exists no consumption that is divorced from production. Consumer culture is based on material culture, and material culture must be based on the productive relations of enterprises. Consumption as a whole cannot be separated from material reality. In the world amassed in commodities, most commodities are available from industrial production.
(2) The specialization of consumption is closely related to the application of expertise and technical know-how in the course of production. Many elaborate science and technology and complex technologies ensure the health and taste of consumption and support the development of consumer culture.
(3) Consumption is closely linked with the environment of human life. While consumption can increase the vitality of the environment, the environment can also affect consumption. The level of consumption of a beautiful city must be higher than that of a backward city.
(4) The consumption advertisements generally cannot reflect the real nature of commodities and are generally exaggerating the nature of the commodities. Meanwhile, the consumer market is generally a world without ideological depth and consumers tend to be misled.

(5) More and more consumer goods are regarded as the symbol of status, which tend to produce demand surplus that cannot be met and which tend to lead to economic instability and improper or excess consumption. Excessively competitive mass consumption generally can disturb modern economic order and have harmful impact on society. Therefore, consumption as the impetus to social development must be compatible with the level of production and the natural resources. The use of the consumption engine must be proper.

5.1.3 *New commodity fetishism*

What we need to mention here is that with the rapid development of the marketized environment, an excessive part of human life has been commercialized, giving birth to the new commodity fetishism. Commodity fetishism worships not only commodities but also capital, brands, and reputation, and invests underserved powers in these things. In essence, this is a result of the abuse of consumer credit, and China must pay high attention to its harmful effects. Karl Marx made a profound exposition of commodity fetishism in his work "Das Capital". He noted that commodity fetishism means people regard the value of products as being inherent in these products. In fact, value is created by people. When commodities are materialized, the value of commodities seems to have become the natural attribute of commodities themselves (Marx, 1976, p. 165). Today, the capital is also materialized and so is the brand. The phenomenon of materialization appears not only in the sphere of commodities but also in many other spheres. What consequences will this phenomenon of wider and deeper materialization bring to society and the economy? We cannot deny that the leadership of market mechanisms finds a full expression here. But we must also see that with the high development of market economy, market operation further conceals the nature of value exchange. Value seems to have become a natural attribute of commodities, capital, and brands, which further highlights the material relations between man and man, and dilutes the social relations and the sense of responsibility between man and man. In a market environment where both demands and commodities have become more and more complex and feign, the tools attempting to be used to meet demand have become more and more ambiguous. As individuals cannot acquire the "technical know-how" for all commodities and cannot possess complete or full information about the quality of goods, personal pursuits are generally difficult to be truly realized. Accordingly, consumers are perplexed about the nature of their demands. Commodity fetishism has brought major changes to the meaning of the concept of credit, doubting installment payment in the early 20th century to desiring installment payment, to owning credit cards, and to materializing credit card and regarding it as a symbol of status and an irresistible force. To some extent, it has fostered hedonism and caused excess consumption and forward consumption. Excess consumption is undeniably an important factor that triggered the 2008 subprime loan crisis in the United States and thus the global economic crisis.

In the 21st century, green consumption has become fashionable. Green consumption refers to a type of consumption that arises from reflections and is thrifty and environmentally responsible. In the course of reflections, all players in the sphere of green consumption, including social groups, retailers, producers, market researchers, all consumer groups, and government departments that emphasize environmental protection, gather together, with each group using different ways to express its awareness and responsibility of green consumption. Green consumption is increasingly linked with reality and responsibility. In a sense, green consumption is a correction to the new commodity fetishism.

5.2 Expedite globalization driven by urbanization

5.2.1 *China's urbanization is the world's largest modernization drive*

The urbanization engine is in fact the economic and social development driven by China's urban infrastructure construction and industrialization. Compared with the Industrial Revolution in Britain and the Meiji Reform in Japan, China's urbanization is far more difficult. It is a great social revolution and also has greater potential and prospect. Accelerating urbanization in a big country with 1.3 billion people requires enormous resources and market. This will be the basic force to drive China's economic development in the next 50–100 years, and also to drive the future growth of the world economy.

Currently, the level of China's urbanization is still fairly low, at about 47%. If China is to reach the level of urbanization in developed countries, it still has to transfer over 700 million peasants to urban areas. As it is impossible to transfer all these people to large cities, China needs to actively develop small and medium-sized cities and especially small towns so as to promote urban–rural integration. A small town is the preliminary form of a city, and residing in small towns does not mean "urbanization" in the full sense. But in light of China's unique national condition that rural people account for half of the total population, the development of towns and cities remains an inevitable choice for the realization of China's urbanization. Urbanization is a concept in development. In essence, urbanization means a continuous transfer of rural people and the secondary and tertiary industries to urban areas, and thus increases the number of towns and cities and the number of urban residents. Before moving to urban areas, Chinese peasants are mostly self-sufficient. When they become urban residents, self-sufficiency is replaced by commoditization, thus releasing a great amount of social demand and expediting the social division of labor and the development of various industries. Therefore, urbanization can drive forward industrialization and the development of housing, transport, medical care, education, and other social undertakings, and can integrate all factors required for development. An accelerated urbanization can allow more peasants to have opportunities to work and live in urban areas, integrate them with mainstream society, and share the fruits of development. When social tolerance becomes higher, contradictions will lessen and society will become more harmonious and stable. Therefore, urbanization is a fundamental way for China to spur domestic demand. Urbanization and urban infrastructure construction are an important development strategy for China in the 21st century. In particular, small towns constitute a key link that can receive industrial extension and information spread from central cities and can serve vast rural areas. They play important roles in forming a rational system of towns and cities, absorbing rural surplus labor, and effectively driving the development of county economies. In the next 50 years, the construction of county cities and towns will become a new development priority and it will form a new large market.

5.2.2 *Long- and medium-term financing mechanisms constitute the most important force of urbanization engine*

The expedition of urbanization must be backed by long- and medium-termed financing mechanisms for infrastructure construction. Thanks to three decades of reform and opening up, China has accumulated certain social wealth. As long as it has rational mechanisms to mobilize all resources, it can effectively advance the process of urbanization. The responsibility of China's urban construction rests with regional governments, but the fiscal resources available to these governments cannot meet the huge funding demand. In the meantime, China's existing legal environment and fiscal system do not allow regional governments to directly float large amounts of debts. This is where the institutional contradiction lies between urban development and urban construction financing demand. In the course of supporting the development of infrastructures, basic industries, and pillar industries, development-oriented finance has developed a financing mechanism for urban infrastructure construction, which has effectively brought China's urbanization to a new high and expedited the process of urbanization. In August 1998, CDB signed an agreement on development financing cooperation with the People's Government of Anhui Province, which creatively used government's organizational strength to build a new financing mechanism for urban infrastructure construction. In this new financing mechanism, the government is responsible for establishing an urban construction and investment company which can perform the urban construction financing function on behalf of the government and under the guidance and coordination of the government. At the same time, the government is committed to the gradual improvement of the company's corporate governance, structure, and systems. This creation has successfully incorporated the government's credit resources in urban construction and integrated government credit and the credit of development-oriented finance with corporate credit. When government credit is used as the guarantee of corporate credit or is converted into corporate credit, it can enhance the financing capacity of enterprises. This new and effective government credit building mechanism can better solve the problems such as fund shortage, time shortage, and the irrational structure of fiscal construction funds. This mechanism also combines planning with financing credit space for long-term survival, development, and self-renewal. It is a snowballing development model.

In the course of economic globalization, world resources in a sense are also globalized. With advanced mechanisms, China can also mobilize international resources to speed up its urbanization construction and at the same time provide market space for the international community. China's huge population, huge scales of urbanization and industrialization, and green construction project to renovate over four billion square meters of shabby urban houses across the country must be backed by huge industrial chains and supply chains. Domestic resources alone cannot meet the demand. It must take advantage of global energies, minerals, technologies, raw materials, farm products, and other resources. Development-oriented finance should not be content with incubating itself in the course of America-centered globalization and with the achievements it has made in China. Instead, it should seize opportunities to carry out international cooperation, widen development space, and build China-led global industrial and supply chains to meet the demands of China's long-term construction and development.

Urbanization is a historical process. As a social and historical phenomenon, urbanization is both a manifestation of the advance of material civilization and a driving force for the advance of spiritual civilization. Currently, China's regional distribution of towns and cities is irrational, its urban–rural relations are uncoordinated, the functions of towns and cities are unsound, and the overall carrying capacity of towns and cities are weak. Therefore, China is unlikely to complete urbanization overnight. In this process, China needs to correctly handle the relations between the promotion of urbanization and farmland protection, efficient utilization, the relations between the building of modern towns and cities, and the preservation of historical towns and cities. While China gradually raises the rate of urbanization, it should pay more attention to the improvement of the living conditions of urban and rural residents, the availability of public service facilities, the enhancement of industrial quality, and the coordinated development of urban and rural relations. China has to accelerate the rate of urbanization and at the same time improve the quality of urbanization. It should refrain from the blind construction of towns and cities and must emphasize the following four plans: (i) the strategic plan, (ii) the overall plan, (iii) the land-use plan, and (iv) the industrial development plan. In short, urbanization must emphasize both speed and quality.

5.3 Analysis of two engines

In the course of fighting against global economic recession and building new international economic order, we can easily discover the following problem when we compare the two engines: the world economy driven by commodity consumption is in fact fraught with some excess consumption and waste and has exerted great pressure on resources and the environment. We cannot deny the positive roles of the consumption engine. But the international community must conduct effective regulation and restraint over the consumption engine. On the other hand, the world economy driven by urbanization has an enormous space for development. As a major developing country, China still has a fairly low level of urbanization. This means that China still has a long and arduous task to build the country. It also means that China has huge potential. If this potential is tapped, China will be able to maintain steady and fast economic development for a long time and make contributions to the world economy. From the global and long-term perspective, the consumption engine must properly reduce its speed and the urbanization engine must properly increase its speed. This is a trend of balanced international economic development in the 21st century. The outburst of the international financial crisis has weakened the America-centered driving force for globalization, and the globalization featuring the development of multi-polarization has the opportunity to develop.

5.3.1 *Development trend of two engines*

Figure 5.1 compares the changes in the world GDP ratios of economic growth of two typical countries (United States and China) using the two engines. From this comparison, we can infer the following:

(1) The great achievements made by China in economic construction over the past 30 years since the beginning of reform and opening up have elevated China's global status. China's contribution to the world economy has become visibly higher and its influence has become greatly stronger. Over the past 30 years, China's share of the world GDP has risen sharply. In the past decade or so, in particular, the growth rate has been most conspicuous, rising from 3.4% in 1998 to 8.9% in 2011. Since 1998, China has enforced a proactive fiscal policy to implement the urbanization development strategy, intensify infrastructure construction, spur the domestic demand with construction investment, stimulate economic growth, and bring urbanization into a period of accelerated development. China's rate of urbanization rose from 34% in 1998 to 47% in 2011, an average annual growth rate of 1.11 percentage points. This has greatly driven the growth of GDP. At the current conventional and rational development speed, China's GDP is likely to surpass that of the United States in the middle of this century. But China's overall strength will remain far weaker than that of the United States, and the 21st century will remain an American century.

(2) What is in sharp contrast is that the world GDP ratio of the consumption-driven American economy has been declining.

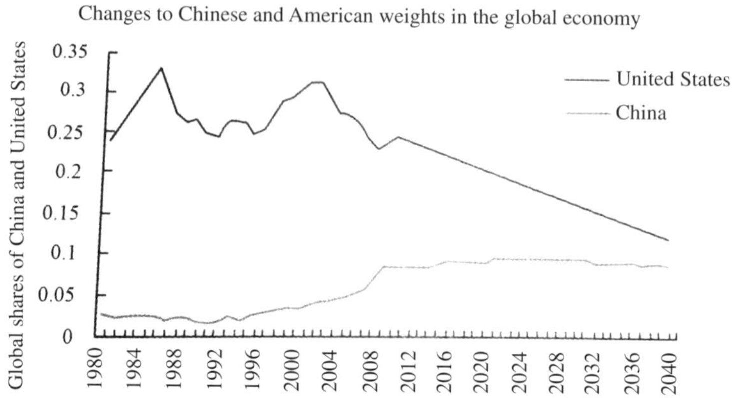

Figure 5.1: Changes in world ratios of economic growth of United States and China.

Note: The basic data originated from the annual data published by the World Bank website www.worldbank.org.cn; on the basis of an integrated analysis of these basic data and the normal speeds of economic development of the two countries, the author worked out the world GDP ratios of China and the United States; the 1980–2009 data are the true data published by the World Bank, and the 2010–2050 data are projections (relevant regression analysis).

Over the past 30 years, the contribution of the United States to the world GDP dropped about two percentage points every 10 years. In the 1998–2009 period, in particular, this contribution dropped to 23.6% from 29.3%. But the United States remains the leader of the world economy.

(3) Consumption remains the main force to drive the development of the American economy. While the United States has seen its share of the world GDP continuing to decline, the contribution of consumption to the American GDP has continued to rise, at as high as 80%. This is an indication that the consumption engine remains the most important force to drive the American growth. The global economic crisis is the most serious event since the Great Depression in the 20th century and has had certain impact on this consumption engine. But the American growth model featuring consumption with borrowed money is unlikely to change. Its financial imperialist model is unlikely to end either. It will not

change in essence, only shrinking in degree. An examination of the crisis indicates that the systematic risks accumulated by unsound consumer credit pose a major hidden danger and even a serious damage to steady economic performance. For this reason, establishing sound consumer credit mechanism and boosting the risk-resisting capacity of the consumer economy will be the necessary steps to ensure consumption-driven globalization.

5.3.2 *Development-oriented finance is an accelerator to urbanization development*

The world order is undergoing great changes and adjustments. The international financial crisis will have a long-term impact. The negative impact of the global financial crisis on economic growth may last for a long time. When summarizing and studying the driving force and direction of global development, many countries take urban infrastructure construction as an important measure to resume economic growth, increase job opportunities, and elevate development level. According to the 2011 Global Infrastructure Summit Forum, the funding demand for the construction of strategic infrastructures around the world in the next 30 years will reach 35 trillion dollars. Likewise, China will also take urban infrastructure construction as a key step to spur domestic demand, adjust industrial structure, and promote economic growth for a long time to come. This will determine, to a very large extent, the trend and the following unique features of China's economic situation:

(1) The driving role of infrastructure construction has become more tangible. As a developing country, China has long been in a stage of construction. While urbanization is a lasting force to drive economic growth, infrastructure construction plays fundamental, long-term, and overall roles in accelerating urbanization. In the course of spurring domestic demand, railways, highways, airports, other transport networks, and the construction of urban infrastructures have become priorities. As a result, many second-line cities and even county cities have also expedited their development.

(2) The task of industrial restructuring has become more difficult. An important content of spurring domestic demand is to optimize industrial structure, featuring the enhancement of indigenous innovation and the closer coordination between the primary, secondary, and tertiary industries. The financial crisis has drastically reduced China's external demand and exerted a tremendous pressure on China to expedite its own industrial development. If China can seize this opportunity and intensify support for the development of priority industries, promote the construction of an industrial system which is fully fledged, independent, and technologically competitive, and enhance its international competitiveness, China will be able to turn this crisis into an opportunity and continue to hold the initiative in its own hand in the new round of economic growth.
(3) The development of small and medium-sized enterprises has become more and more important. Small and medium-sized enterprises are an important force to drive economic growth and offer employment. Their ratio in the whole economy will gradually become higher, laying a foundation for the accelerated development of the circulation industry, service industry, processing and manufacturing industry, and other sectors.
(4) The call for easing resource constraint through international cooperation has become ever stronger. Currently, China faces serious resource constraint, with over half of major energy and mineral resources having to be imported. Most of these major resources are monopolized by multinational companies in the West, which has placed China in a very passive position. The government requests Chinese enterprises to seize new opportunities for overseas investment, expand their overseas operations more actively and prudently, and strengthen cooperation with foreign partners in the fields of badly needed rare resources and key technologies.

Apparently, all the above major unique features are closely related with development-oriented finance. On the one hand, development-oriented finance must play the roles of an accelerator and regulator. On the other hand, development-oriented finance will have an important opportunity for accelerated development. Development-oriented finance has the duty and ability to remove bottlenecks and mobilize both domestic and foreign resources so as to promote the building of industrial chains and supply chains for urban infrastructure construction and to meet the demand of China's long- and medium-term construction and development.

5.4 Summary

In this chapter, we have discussed the international background in which China's development-oriented finance took root and moved forward (Figure 5.2). Development-oriented finance is based on the globalized strategic thinking and is generated from correctly analyzing and following the basic direction and momentum of sustainable development in the international competition. In economic globalization, the huge demand brought about by China's urbanization has provided new opportunities and incentives to improve the

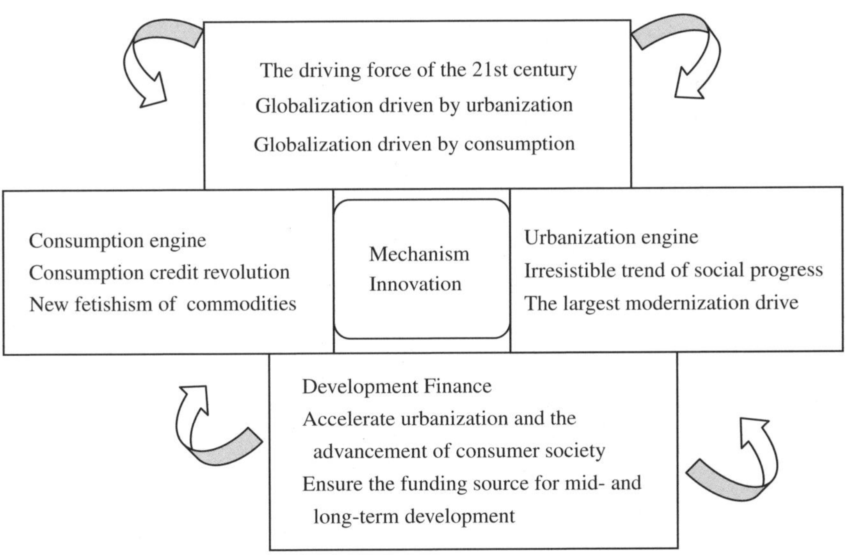

Figure 5.2: The driving force of the 21st century.

modern credit system. Speeding up urbanization in a country with a 1.3 billion population will definitely create a huge demand market which calls for supply on a global scale. Just as the credit consumption revolution in the United States in the early 20th century provided sufficient funds for consumption, development-oriented finance can provide sufficient credit support for urbanization and boost the engine power for urbanization. When it comes to sticking to the globalized strategic thinking, it follows that: (i) the positioning of development-oriented finance is an important component of China's long-term development strategy; (ii) the theory and practice of development-oriented finance are important parts of the socialist market economy; (iii) to establish the long-term, effective mechanism for preventing financial crises and ensure the sustainable, steady, and rapid development of China. It is imperative for development-oriented finance to fulfill its key role in the economic development and institutional building. From an international perspective, urbanization is a long-term and arduous task worldwide and developed countries are also in face of urban renewal and reconstruction, so the theory and practice of development-oriented finance will also be useful for the international community.

Part II

The Theoretical Contents of Development-Oriented Finance

The theory of development-oriented finance is built to support development and avoid risks stemming from under-developed credit system. It meets the capital demand of mid- and long-term infrastructure building, vital fields, and relatively weak areas. Development-oriented finance as practiced by CDB offers a good solution to answer how to raise enough money through market under the background of disadvantages in total amount of money, time, and structure. It also offers a solution to less developed countries to make great development and to China for enduring with a sustainable development. Its core contents are the following: planning should be put in the first place, finding all potential to ensure economic development, making full play of the government's organizational advantages, developing portfolio financing, promoting socialization of finance, carrying forward the fine traditional culture, resolving conflicts of credit, breaking the financing bottleneck, and promote a stable and rapid economic development in a sustainable way. In this part, we systematically analyze the theory of development-oriented finance, trying to answer the question of "What is it?". Table P2.1 includes the basic elements and contents of development-oriented finance.

We should emphasize that development-oriented finance is a theory derived from practices and creativity, which is China's local theory. Development-oriented finance is always improving itself, which calls for support from other fields. We sincerely hope that people in other fields could lend us help and give some suggestions to make the theory more complete. Development-oriented finance assists in China's mid- and long-term development, which is also valuable for the world.

Table P2.1: The basic elements and contents of development-oriented finance.

Elements	Basic contents
Definition	The theory of development-oriented finance offers a solution to less developed countries to make great sustainable development.
Contents	Reveal the relationship between planning and long-term development.
	Reveal the relationship between credit system building and long-term development.
	Reveal the relationship between the advantage of the government organizations and medium- and long-term development.
	Reveal the relationship between the portfolio financing and medium- and long-term development.
	Reveal the relationship between the socialization of finance and medium- and long-term development.
	Reveal the relationship between the culture of development-oriented finance and medium- and long-term development.
	These six relationships offer a solution to the contradiction between the immature financial system and the rapid economic development under the background of tight macroeconomic operation so as to avoid the risks and keep the economy from developing quickly.
Conclusions	Planning is the core competence.
	The construction of credit system is the fourth driving force of economic development.
	The government forces and the market forces could be transferred to each other so as to quicken the development of economy.
	Portfolio financing and integrated operation can support economic development and avoid risks.
	The socialization of finance is a vital force of the 21st century.
	The theory and practices of development-oriented finance diversify the scientific concept of development, which is an important part of the socialism market economy with Chinese characteristics demonstrating the ability of CPC.

(*Continued*)

Table P2.1: (*Continued*)

Elements	Basic contents
Process	Coming from practices, we should go to practices again; from China's situation, we should absorb advanced theories to make innovations.
Model	There are several kinds of model, such as infrastructure model, city building model, strategic industry financing model, people's livelihood and financial model, the new mode of rural development. These models embodied the method of using the market to achieve government targets.

Chapter 6

Planning is a Core Competitive Edge

6.1 Introduction

The major objectives of development-oriented finance are to (i)reveal the relationship between planning and long- and mid-term development, (ii) illuminate that planning is a core competitive edge, and (iii) bring into full play the role of planning in order to realize a sound and rapid development. Development-oriented finance has the following characteristics: (i) persists in placing planning first and seizing the initiative of development, (ii) insists on planning from a high starting point and implementing plans without deviation, (iii) publicizes actively the concept of scientific development, and integrates government, financial, and market forces, (iv) discovers major projects, (v) identifies resource potential, (v) brings into play the initiative of all parties, (vi) predicts scientifically strategic credit space, (vii) utilizes existing resources and future resources rationally, (viii) arranges funds in a unified and coordinated manner for mid- and long-term infrastructure construction, development of priority sectors and weak links, (ix) takes cash flow balance and profit-and-loss balance into overall consideration, and (x) promotes jointly the building-up of credit, systems, and markets with relevant parties. It can support development and avoid risks, thus promoting a healthy, rapid, and sustainable economic development.

Planning as a core competitive edge is embodied in five aspects:

(1) It conducts vertical and horizontal comparisons, makes scientific evaluation, commands the trends of economic-social development to find out the key projects of mid- and long-term significance, solves the bottleneck issues that affect mid- and long-term development to greatly enhance the competitive edge, thus

embodying the strategic requirement in economic-social development.

(2) It gives comprehensive consideration to mid- and long-term development stretching to hundred years, of population, resources, industries, society, and markets in a nation or region; it incorporates various uncertainties into the entire environment, deploys elements of productive forces in a scientific way, and taps deployment potential of production elements; it puts forward a package of design and construction, offering a one-off demonstration of construction scale and development framework for a period of time to come, and carries out project construction in a coordinated way to avoid "roads with zippers" and "whiskers projects" and ensures development quality and speed, thus embodying the requirement of comprehensiveness in socioeconomic development.

(3) It integrates various resources (including potential elements) and deploys them in proportion so as to keep a certain degree of balance, which is instrumental to hedging mid- and long-term construction risks, enhancing the efficiency of resource utilization, strengthening the momentum of sustainable development, expanding the effectiveness of productive forces, thus embodying the requirement for balance in socioeconomic development.

(4) It scientifically sets "pillar industries" and strategic options through optimization of the economic structure, thus bringing into play the extended function of credit, expanding the space for strategic credit, discovering growth potential, expanding the production range, and creating new markets. Planning embodies the requirement of innovation in socioeconomic development.

(5) "He who doesn't plan for the future will find trouble at his doorsteps"; from the perspective of the historical development of mankind, conducting research of the development trend of productive forces, contributing to the cognition and application of the laws of economic development, which will play an important guiding role for a long time to come, thus embodying the historical requirement in socioeconomic development.

6.2 The strategic value of planning

6.2.1 *Planning is both a strategic tool and a strategic idea*

Planning is a necessary tool and means for mankind to learn about nature and change the world. The terms planning and plan are different yet related. Planning represents an instructive and directional goal in terms of overall characteristics; it refers to a relatively long-term development plan and it suggests space. Technically, planning often chooses fewer object variables and relies on relatively mature technologies. The time and space involved are relatively large in magnitude. Take infrastructure, deployment of state-owned land, and exploitation of water resources, for example. These objects have relatively few variables, cannot be duplicated, and are more often than not irreplaceable, but their timelines are exceptionally long and last for several decades, even a century. Therefore, the contents of planning must be far-sighted and strategic. A plan is the product of the planned economy period, focusing on the short-term; plans are the specific links in planning or arrangement of specific projects that evolved in the operation of planning. For example, in the electronics industry, there is planning for cell phones from the second, third to fourth generation. It is not so much a kind of planning; it is rather a plan or a scheme for a product and technology, or, as the Japanese and Koreans call it, it is rather a plot. Its characteristics are the following: technically complicated, chooses relatively large number of variables, depends on advanced technology, and variables of time and space are small in magnitude. In economic development, the final result of planning or a plan is the formation of projects and specific construction plans. In the process of economic and social development, mankind not only needs short-term plans to deal with multiple variables and scenarios but also plans dealing with fewer variables and longer timelines. This is where planning steps in. Long-term planning is the foundation for short-term plans. It reflects mankind's overall initiative for dealing with nature, originates from objective cognition, and is a kind of reform of the objective by the subjective.

"Without a long-term strategy, short-term achievement is unattainable; without consideration of the overall situation, local governance is impossible." As a strategic idea, planning puts forward scientific development recommendations and schemes to satisfy people's demands for development. China's development strategy for the 21st century (including a three step strategy) is to gradually complete the construction of the preliminary stage of socialism by 2050 or within 100 years. There is a demand for development space in each respective stage. It is necessary to consider them from a macro-strategy viewpoint and in a unified and coordinated manner. The strategic height of planning lies in its comprehensive consideration of national interest, regional well-being, prospect of industries and enterprise development, to guarantee positive externalities of the overall effectiveness of capital invested in major projects, and lay a good long-term internal foundation for economic development, so that effective deployment of capital, resources, manpower, and technology is achieved. Planning is a study with clear-cut targets and is also a piece of organization work with comprehensive coordination. Planning is a process of unifying cognition, and an important step for strengthening the study of strategic decision making. Planning should be concerned not only about science and technology, material production, and development of industries, but it should also be concerned about development of organizational structures, financing systems and market systems, and striving through market building to make possible the promotion of fields that could not be done by capital financing in the past.

6.2.2 *Planning is rational strength based on man's continual cognition of nature and society, manifesting scientific, technological, and social progress and the evolution of systems*

In the course of learning about the laws of nature and society, people gradually began to attach importance to ecological environment protection, resources conservation, independent innovation, development of advanced technologies, energy conservation and consumption reduction, and the development of a cyclic economy, transforming labor-intensive processing industries into high value-added industries focusing on intellectual innovation. This is the general trend of human progress. It is because of human cognition of this trend and also for better adaptation to this trend that various forms of planning appeared. In retrospect, although the manuscripts of design principles for airplanes, submarines, and tanks put forward by Leonardo da Vinci 500 years ago were scientific fantasies then, it can be said that they contained elements of primitive planning for science and technology. In a broad sense, in *Das Kapital*, Marx and Engels' criticism of capitalism and the visualization that the proletarian class can seize political power is a piece of early planning for political and social development. The Paris Commune did not achieve this planning, but Lenin did and then planning for industrialization was worked out, thus finding the path for backward countries to realize rapid development. It was quite successful for a short time and the world was greatly shocked.

Economic planning originated in France; it was developed in the Soviet Union and the best implementation took place in the United States. Since the Industrial Revolution, France began to lag behind Britain. France was eager to find an approach to speed up its economic development. The approach was none other than the formulation of economic planning. France combined economic planning with advanced industrial technologies, thus accelerating economic development. After the October Revolution, the Soviet Union drew on the approach and expanded it, which evolved into planned economy and played an important role in promoting the development of new industries. When the first Five-Year Plan was completed, the Soviet Union had turned itself into an industrial country from an agricultural one. When the second Five-Year Plan was completed, its gross industrial production was ranked first in Europe and second in the world. However, the Soviet Union regarded the state as an enterprise and exercised direct control over material products and projects. Now things went wrong, as a plan is not equivalent to planning. Some major capital construction projects often have bearing on the long-term economic and social development. Not only are methods of operations research for enterprise operation needed, but planning is also needed. The success of the American model was attributed in a large degree to its combination of science, technology, trade, finance, and European political systems on the basis of the Industrial Revolution. It also drew on experience and lessons of development from other countries. Scientific planning and realistic goals played an important part. During the late Qing Dynasty, China suffered untold invasions and humiliation. Its defeat in the Sino-Japanese War of 1894–1895 awakened the Chinese people. Chinese Communists headed by Mao Zedong combined Marxism with actual practice of China's revolution. This was a piece of gigantic planning. This kind of planning enabled China's revolution to embark on the path of success. During the period of socialist revolution and construction, it was also due to good planning that socialist construction scored achievements that attracted world attention. History is a mirror. The process of planning is the process of looking into the mirror. On the one hand, we look back at history and learn why we were backward; on the other hand, we analyze the reality and find out how great the gap is between ourselves and the developed countries.

6.2.3 *Well drawn-up planning in developing countries is the fundamental prerequisite for achieving a leapfrog development*

In developing countries, apart from the backwardness of material production and markets, another important lag is the lag in planning. To a large extent, many developing countries either do not have proper planning measures or they employ only weak planning measures in many fields. This results in indiscernible construction and unscientific progress within a country. Therefore, if a developing country has to scientifically progress and realize a leapfrog development, it should draw-up proper planning measures and look into the mirror and find out the advantages of other countries and, in comparison with them, where it falls short. Thus, only through proper planning and implementation of specific plans, can a developing country achieve a leapfrog development. To a large extent, planning relies on mature technology, not necessarily sophisticated advanced technology. It is easier for developing countries to do things that require mature technology with not too many variables. For instance, the construction of expressways, railroads, airports, power plants, and urban infrastructure is basically mature technology. Leapfrog development can be achieved by relying on mature technology, well worked out planning, management of the design process and subsequent construction. Actually, planning is an important approach for developing countries to turn passiveness into activeness, make fewer detours, and speed up scientific development.

6.3 Basic requirements of development planning with distinctive Chinese characteristics

China is a big developing country, whose development path is different from that of the developed countries. There must be scientific planning that exploits China's own advantages and characteristics, thus taking its own development path. China has been and will still be in the preliminary stage of socialism for a long time. Mid- and long-term infrastructure construction tasks are quite demanding and for a long time many fields and regions have not received financial support; the task of market building and system building is also arduous. The macroeconomy will be in a "tight" operating state for a long time to come. Relatively speaking, China's current levels in science and technology are lagging. There is also much room for improvement in its market system. It is necessary for China to achieve a leapfrog development through scientific planning to shorten the gap between it and the developed countries, to complete what it took them a century or even several centuries to complete. The important approach for us to reach our strategic goal consists of attaching strategic importance to planning, accelerating the building of a market system, utilizing limited resources and capital in a planned way, and really satisfying the demand of capital of mid- and long-term infrastructure construction. Under the present situation, "planning first" is especially important for the expansion of domestic demand and the promotion of stable and relatively rapid economic development. Scientific development planning is the component with the most scientific value in a traditional planned economy, and should be inherited and carried forward.

(1) *Planning embodies the advantage of political organization.* China's economic development is greatly different from that of the West. Economic development of Western countries started from the Industrial Revolution. Peasants became workers and the proletarian class; landlords became capitalists; urbanization and industrialization were driven by the capital and the market. China's economic development and urbanization process is largely driven by social revolution and social progress. Urbanization is a spatial concept, a physical concept, a developmental concept, and also a societal concept. The case of peasants becoming urban residents is a change in social relationship. In China's history, there were situations when a political organization drove a "great-leap-forward" change in the social relationship, but that is an extreme approach driven by the social revolution; the methods and objectives were problematic. Now, we advocate "planning first" through scientific planning by transforming the mode of socioeconomic development with few variables, long timelines, and driven by mature technology into a development mode that is programmed, organized, and advancing on a gigantic scale. Although there are tinges of being driven on a grand scale, it is neither blind construction nor repeated construction in the various localities. Instead, it is guided by planning and driven by scientific methods and market-oriented approaches. Thus, we have replaced "driven by social revolution" in the past with "driven by scientific organization" after planning. For years, development-oriented finance has been actively exploring effective approaches to scientifically organize and drive economic and social development for the purpose of pushing forward China's market development and the reform of its investment and financing system, promoting scientific development, and social harmony. In the course of financing to support local construction, development-oriented finance advocates "planning first". Through planning for scientific development, the

comprehensive forward looking initiative in work, and the unified and coordinated deployment of important resources are strengthened. This results in risk prevention and elimination of blind investment and repeated construction.

(2) *Planning includes not only material construction, but also market building and society building.* Marketization of economic operation is the basic requirement of a market economy. Marketization involves the driving force for development of millions of households, individuals, and all micro-bodies. For instance, everyone would like to set up a company and earn profits. This way the market starts to work. This gives us some food for thought: planning should include not only material construction but also market building and society building. The understanding of this covers two aspects: balance between ecology and resources refers to adopting a scientific outlook on development and realization of energy conservation and emission reduction; on the other hand, balance between harmony and efficiency refers to prevention of widening of social gaps and ensuring a harmonious society — harmony and efficiency should be dealt with at the same time. There is one-sidedness in the saying "efficiency first, while at the same time giving consideration to fairness". Because if we one-sidedly allow a minority to get rich and then transfer wealth to the masses through the financial transfer payment, this kind of social adjustment process will not be applicable to China. China should provide everyone with equal opportunity in its primary distribution and emphasize prosperity through labor. Migrant workers and urban residents should enjoy equal treatment in securing education for their children, employment, financing, medical care, and housing. Only thus can everyone have the same opportunity to prosper, through individual effort instead of realizing equal wealth in society through secondary distribution by the government. The range of people relying on secondary distribution should be small; this range mainly includes people who have lost their ability to work. Their minimum living standard can be maintained with the help of charity. It is expected that people, generally, should acquire wealth through labor and employment. The government should create job opportunities for them, encourage them to work, develop medium

and small enterprises, and also private enterprises. As for those medium, small, and private enterprises that lack the necessary conditions, these can be created by way of training, education, guidance, and financing to promote their growth. When these enterprises have developed, social responsibility should be demanded of them, to regard the future of their country as their own responsibility and make contributions to society. These are what should be considered in planning. Only if such planning is done well can the economy witness stable, healthy, and coordinated development.

(3) *Planning is an overall systems project that involves the following planning measures:* (i) it starts with regional and urban planning — planning for cities and towns based on population and land; (ii) industrial planning — deployment of industries according to local resources; (iii) social planning — deployment of schools, hospitals, and cultural facilities according to regional and industrial development; (iv) market planning — building up market systems and mechanisms that are full of vigor and efficiency, and suit the needs of development; (v) planning for enriching the people — designing approaches that enable ordinary people to get rich, realizing a path of common prosperity; and (vi) finally, financial planning — mobilization of social capital to ensure the financial needs for development. This is a systems and interdisciplinary project that mobilizes the economy and society in a unified and coordinated manner. Therefore, planning is a branch of science. If planning is ever to be done well, it is essential to break free from the practice of "each administering its affairs regardless of the overall interest" and pool various resources in a unified and coordinated way to come to a consensus and form a synergy. Scientific planning must be forward reaching. Planning for the future is nothing to be worried about and neither are changes midway; what has to be worried about is the absence of planning. We do not have to worry about our current small economic aggregate and low real GDP per capita. Although the latter is only US$1,000 or US$2,000 or less, future income can be treated as a component for planning, this way planning can be done in one shot, covering 30, 50, or even 100 years.

Otherwise, building today and tearing it down tomorrow will result in a lot of blind investment and repeated construction. Our point of departure should be from our national condition of a current population of 1.3 billion and a future population of 1.5 billion. We should do our planning on 9.6 million m^2 of land, conducting surveys, and computation of the bearing capacity of various resources, to obtain the amount of urban space, agricultural output, raw materials for industries, consumer goods, and corresponding infrastructure facilities of electricity, transportation, telecommunication, etc. required in the next 50 years or 100 years when income per capita reaches tens of thousands of USD, when land, water, air and ecology resources could be distributed and exploited in a scientific way — in a word, planning what China should be in 100 years. On 12 June 2010, the State Council examined and passed, in principle, the planning for major national functionality zones. The national land is divided into four types of zones: zones of optimizing development, key development, restrained development, and forbidden development, and the scope, development goals, development direction, and development principles were determined respectively for those zones. This planning is of enormous significance.

(4) *Development-oriented finance planning is an important component of national planning.* Development-oriented finance planning, guided by scientific outlook on development, aims at integrating various resources and enhancing the application efficiency of capital, thus fully embodying the goal of national development in a unified and coordinated way. It focuses on compensating and enhancing the degree of regional, industrial, social, and market development through development-oriented finance, and highlights market and systems building. Development-oriented finance planning and national development planning are common yet carry some different characteristics. They are common, in that the contents of national development planning all are the goals China Development Bank seeks after, most of which are indices for material construction and finally formed projects, while development-oriented finance planning highlights the characteristics of market building, with more

detailed scientific content on regional, industry, social, and market development. Development-oriented finance planning integrates national development goals for the 21st century with major national projects, key projects, fields of innovation, and support plans pertaining to socioeconomic development, and a train of thought for financing, in order to promote scientific development. Development-oriented finance planning is more difficult, more detailed, and more substantive.

Development-oriented finance planning interacts with government planning and institutional planning. Problems of blind investment, repeated construction, and poor asset quality can be solved to a large extent by strengthening the early stages of planning and deepening cooperation with localities and industries, to achieve the goals of macro-control and macro-regulation. By scientifically formulating development planning, development-oriented finance begins at the up-stream and connects the development of China Development Bank with government planning and development planning of various parties to initiate strategic operations that are comprehensive and forward-looking. Development-oriented finance helps local governments and enterprises prepare emergency plans and scenario plans, integrate resources of various parties, enhance the efficiency of capital, and guard against financial risks, so as to earnestly implement the scientific outlook on development. Under the situation of macro-control and macro-regulation, through "planning first", China Development Bank extends its operation to the "upper reaches" and expands in all directions, which is instrumental to maintaining its advantageous position in infrastructure and major industries, and to rapidly occupying an advantageous position in new "blue water" fields.

Development-oriented finance planning lays emphasis on seeking appropriate plans for capital raising on the basis of strategic studies, which is different from conceptual planning, land use planning, and construction planning in the usual sense and neither is it the same as scenario planning, which addresses various possible occurrences in operation and is considered an aspect of internal planning work that deals with market fluctuations and is more characteristic of work to be done in the "lower reaches".[1] Development-oriented finance planning starts from the "upper reaches" and connects with national development planning and various other development planning. It pursues the best development result in client–institution relationship, supply–demand relationship, and in interaction of all aspects. In the past, we thought that the market was static and inflexible. All were vying for a bigger share in the limited market and playing a zero sum game. Now we have benign interaction with local governments through scientific development planning, thus expanding the market. The market is not grabbed; instead, it is offered due to government cooperation. Development-oriented finance planning is different from the simple material production planning that was carried out in the past. Instead, it is devoted to building up a highly efficient market and financing system, manifesting the contents of system building, market building, and finance building. It can raise capital for major national projects and large infrastructure on the one hand and provide service to communal finance and construction of new-type of rural areas on the other hand, so that equal opportunity for raising capital is available to all, enabling every micro-body to achieve healthy growth, and finally realize the coordination of finance and urban and rural development, finance and regional development, and finance and socioeconomic development. It promotes the realization of the "Five Balances" through the development of finance and the market, embodies all the requirements of scientific outlook on development, and serves as an important force in driving socioeconomic growth.

Development-oriented finance persists in planning first, grasping the initiative of development, focusing on development that does more for the country, and applying first-rate performances to support national economic targets, social targets, and targets of national competitive edge. Speaking of finance for finance's sake will always

[1] Gu Chaolin: *Conceptual Planning — Theory, Approaches and Examples*, pp. 3–9. Conceptual planning lays emphasis on the study and analysis of development strategies, puts forward conceptual frameworks for development; land use planning and construction planning lay emphasis on the spatial deployment of resources, implementing strategies of economic development in land use and construction of facilities.

be partial and passive. Only by starting from the overall situation of socioeconomic development, can one occupy the commanding height and seize the initiative. For instance, at the county level, projects are like small fish. You cannot set your eye on each individual fish. What you should do is to weave a net to catch the whole lot in one dragnet. This "fish net" is planning. We must weave good "fish nets" so that risks are managed, projects are covered, and management funds are provided in time. Only then can operations at the counties level develop at an accelerated pace. Development-oriented finance planning focuses on solving problems of construction risks of mid- and long-term projects, to promote market building and harmonious social development. The construction cycles of major projects, represented by infrastructure, are long and their risks are high. These projects need long-term consideration and thorough planning, including analysis of economic cycles, painstaking design, and steady progress, to realize sustainable development. Specifically, development-oriented finance planning must conduct targeted studies and plan the design after fully grasping the development trends and comprehensive consideration of the synergy between the present development level and the development potential of the resource environment. This will help to calculate, using qualitative and quantitative methods, the credit space that can be provided by strategic development targets, make coordinated arrangements for the priority and progress schedules of project construction, formulate plans for deployment and provision of limited resources, consider comprehensively the cash-flow balance and profit-and-loss balance of project construction and social development, reduce systematic risk exposure, and realize scientific deployment of productive forces and sustainable development.

In accordance with the arrangements of the Central Committee of the Chinese Communist Party and the State Council, the overall situation of the market economy and requirements of macroeconomic control, China Development Bank has actively conducted regional planning, industrial planning, social planning, market planning, financing planning, livelihood planning, planning for enriching the people, and planning for international cooperation. This not only fills the gap in planning for localities as in "sending charcoal in snowy weather", but also works out a large number of effective projects, thus forming an endless stream of projects for development-oriented finance, laying down a good foundation for future work, and promoting development of various aspects through 100-year planning.

6.4 Establishing a study model of strategic credit space

6.4.1 *Connotation of strategic credit space*

In mid- to long-term development, it is essential to attach great importance to the study of strategic credit space to balance the cash-flow and profit-and-loss and to ensure the actual effectiveness of planning. China's economic development is in an important period of strategic opportunities. Expectation of rapid economic growth can not only create a lot of opportunities and space, but also highlight basic contradictions between a backward financial system and financing needs arising from rapid economic growth within a tight state of economic operation. If opportunities are grasped and contradictions are solved, possibilities to form a new credit space exist to support development and realize strategic goals. In its planning process, China Development Bank attaches great importance to the study of strategic credit space, gives full consideration to changes in scenarios that may bring opportunities and risks, appropriately utilizes strategic option to avoid risks, all of which are instrumental to expanding the long-term market space with strategic developmental significance, to realizing the cash-flow balance and the profit-and-loss balance for mid- and long-term infrastructure and construction in bottleneck fields. The development of a strategic credit space has a bearing on the scope and direction of the long-term development of development-oriented finance. This is an important hallmark in differentiating development-oriented finance from commercial finance.

Strategic credit space refers to the comprehensive evaluation, deployment, and consideration of the prospects of development of mid- and long-term credit, after a series of scientific assessments of the credit environment, credit ability, credit potential, and credit system of financing bodies, including governments at all levels, enterprises, and individuals, during a certain period of time in the future. The study of a strategic credit space is mainly devoted to the development and assessment of credit space from the four dimensions of region, industry, society, and market, with emphasis on ensuring the security of capital demand and supply for mid- and long-term development. For China to become a moderately developed country in the 21st century, how much capital will it need? How many channels are there to raise the capital? How big is the existing gap? Are there basic conditions for credit? What are the solutions? Answers can be found by conducting a solid and scientific study of the strategic credit space. In-depth study and planning of the demand space of development and its possible boundaries within a given time period, including population growth, material production, change in social systems, and spiritual civilization development, for the region, the nation, localities, industry, society, and the market, and design of a relatively reliable capital supply chain and a plan for building a market system, can form a four-in-one (development of regions, industries, society, and market) credit development space. These strategic credit spaces are based on the market development level, credit structure, and characteristics of the economic environment. These spaces refer to realms with improperly functioning markets and imperfect systems and mechanisms, but with prospects of unbounded development; they are also the "bottleneck" realms that affect China's economic development and the building of a moderately prosperous society. China Development Bank, by applying the theory of development-oriented finance and setting credit building as the main thread, analyzing and predicting development prospects, designing credit structure, bringing into play its excellence in capital raising, making breakthroughs in bottlenecks, and through systems building and mechanisms innovation, turns immature markets into mature markets, thus maximizing the value of development-oriented finance.

6.4.2 *Structure of strategic credit space*

The strategic credit space we have put forward is a credit development space consisting of regions, industries, society, and markets in time and space. Of the four elements, regional development takes the lead, which can give impetus to industrial and social development; market development is fundamental and runs through the whole process, which reflects the depth and width of economic activities; industrial development is the pillar, manifesting national core capabilities; social development is the purpose, embodying people-oriented requirements and results.

(1) *Regional development.* It is devoted to the study of the infrastructure and industries that can be carried within a region and the development space available for construction of new rural areas and small- and medium-sized enterprises. Regional development is guided by regional planning. Regional planning is a comprehensive embodiment of the distribution of social functions, deployment of industries, sustainable utilization of natural resources, population, and protection of the ecological environment. It is the core of all planning. Regional development-oriented finance planning is mainly devoted to urbanization and infrastructure, covering all the provinces, cities, and counties. On the basis of calculating the region's future synergy of population, land, resources, and environment, the regional development-oriented finance back-calculates the construction scale, functional zoning, and industry deployment of cities and towns, and the distribution of infrastructure such as energy, roads, water, etc. The emphasis of regional development is urbanization whose driving effect of can improve the environment, enhance land values, and turn land into government's tax revenue and credit. Development-oriented finance firmly seizes the key link of turning land into assets, which is also a core link in risk prevention, the credit chain and financing chain, to construct a platform for infrastructure and regional development on the basis of land development and utilization to promote industrial and social development. There are two modes of risk prevention for regional development — one is integrating transfer payment and the other is turning land into assets. Integration of

transfer payment is achieved through rational arrangement and utilization of resources to solve the problem of imbalanced development. Two conditions are required for turning land into assets: The first is that there must be urban planning and rural planning; secondly, there must be investment in infrastructure. Once these two conditions are in place, land can become assets and regional development will be achieved. This is the main thread in regional development.

(2) *Industrial development.* Unlike regional development, technological R&D takes the leading role in industrial development. Once changes take place in upstream technology, downstream production and circulation will be affected. Therefore, the emphasis in industrial development is in working out early project planning. According to requirements of scale development, development-oriented finance determines working goals for the development of near-, mid-, and long-term projects, plans and prepares projects at the source, to create space for mid-stream and downstream development. If development-oriented finance does not have a project flow, it will have no fund stream and cash flow. It will be water without a source or a tree without roots, and is doomed to dry up and perish. At present, in China, the huge cash flow formed in the downstream industrial development is not fully supporting R&D of upstream new products and the capital-raising chain and credit chain are broken. Development-oriented finance is concerned about each and every important link and its development prospect, striving to use the fund chain to cover the industry chain. Development-oriented finance's study of the industry chain is not aimed at mastering the know-how to be directly engaged in research, construction, and production in relevant fields, but at studying the capital-raising system and building up a credit chain and credit system. This is a main thread in the industry chain and development of industries, a thread where development-oriented finance is highly concerned about industries of high socialization, because they are the foundation for social security, national security, national interest, and people's livelihood, such as grain, basic energy resources, water, transportation, communication, circulation, which are products and services that are closely related to the livelihood and survival of the masses.

Meanwhile, development-oriented finance actively supports the protection and application of independent intellectual property rights, encourages enterprises to possess sophisticated technologies, uses the fund chain to cover high-end industries including major special projects on science and technology, major special projects on equipment, and major special supporting projects. It is also active in helping medium and small enterprises to conduct innovation in science and technology, which includes stock industries and incremental industries. There is also an interactive relationship between the industry chain and land resources in industrial development. For instance, consider the case of Shenyang, where demolition in the eastern part of the city and construction in the western part took place, and the case of the textile and iron- and-steel industries in Tianjin. All these cases are examples of positive experience of helping industries to develop by using land as the intermediary and turning land into assets. Practice has proved that land is an important vehicle that connects the industrial chain and is an important link between finance and industry. The gigantic capital operation capability formed by upward revaluation of land is instrumental to promoting industrial development. The industrial platform is where land, industrial and regional development converge. Development-oriented finance properly combines land assets and the industrial platform to help the platform expand its assets scale, provides industries with a helping push during its start-up period, enhances their development speed, and ability to sustain debt. This not only promotes healthy development of enterprises but also alleviates financial burdens.

(3) *Social development.* There is much overlap between social development and regional development. They are both related to transfer payment and turning land into assets, but they are not entirely the same. In terms of credit structure and risk prevention mode, social development is more complicated. In particular, mechanisms for social risk supervision and risk sharing have new characteristics. In development-oriented finance, social development planning centers around population numbers and the all-round development of people. It arranges social undertakings like education, medical care,

public health, culture, employment, and environmental protection in a unified and coordinated way.

(4) *Market development.* It is the most difficult issue among the four developments, because all development is to be manifested in market development. Market success depends on platform construction or construction of legal persons. Without a mature platform, there can be no mature market. The stimulating force produced in the course of market building is a marketized stimulating force, which can bring about a gigantic release and development of forces in the economy and society as a whole. This development is multifaceted, all-rounded, and its results are immeasurable. Development-oriented financial market planning, in combination with the local market platform, capital-raising platform, system building, institutional structure building, and credit building, helps to promote diversity in capital raising, strives for investment of social capital, and actively expands the export capital market of projects.

Development-oriented finance develops and assesses strategic credit space from the aforementioned four aspects, giving expression to the requirements of scientific development. Its core is to focus on market development, and through it, drive the development of all other aspects. Being driven by development-oriented finance is different from governmental financing. Funds of development-oriented finance are to be retrieved. Therefore, market systems must be built, extending market building from single projects to a systematic market. Only by filling the gaps and deficiencies of market building, can regional development, industrial development, and social development be realized. Through cooperation with localities and various industries, development-oriented finance absorbs their advantages in technology and materials, and complements the advantages in technology and materials to promote development.

Development-oriented finance develops and assesses strategic credit space, with the main objectives of forming a project flow, a funds flow, and a risk management system to ensure currency flow balance and profit-and-loss balance of mid- and long-term development. Development-oriented finance is different from commercial banks that draw savings deposits. Commercial banks ensure cash flow on the basis of savings. That is to say that regardless of the number of projects handled, there is no reduction in savings; since development-oriented finance has no savings deposits, once project flow decreases, capital flow decreases correspondingly. Therefore, development-oriented finance is concerned about project flow and strives to take the initiative. Development-oriented finance sees the gap between its operation and the requirements of the development of the current situation, tries its utmost to expand the work volume of project development, with emphasis on advance work and with sufficient project flow to satisfy the needs of sustainable, rapid, healthy, and long-term development of development-oriented finance institutions and the needs of national development.

6.5 Strategic credit space assessment techniques

From its practice, development-oriented finance has summarized and formed a set of techniques for the assessment of strategic credit space. The key points being setting development as its core, sustainability of population as its driving force, sustainability of environment as its boundary, establishing analysis indices that cover regions, industries, society, and market in time and space, setting up a development forecast model, calculating basic credit quota, risk quota, total volume boundaries, forecasting the degree of development, and on this basis putting forward a specific and scientific concept and idea of strategic deployment.

Development-oriented finance considers cash flow balance and profit-and-loss balance in the strategic credit space. It is done on the basis of economic analysis and assessment of public projects, not solely on the basis of financial analytical indices. Financial analysis focuses on what the internal rate of return of a project is and studies financial revenue and expenditure of a project with various financial analytical indices to decide whether the project is financially feasible. If a project is financially feasible (for instance, the internal rate of return meets the investor's requirement), it does not necessarily show that it is economically feasible. The fields that development-oriented finance supports are those that consist of "two foundations and one pillar" and bottleneck fields, that is to say, priority is on public engineering projects. The market for these fields or projects is usually immature and more closely associated with social effects, and is difficult for commercial banks to access in the early stages. Therefore, it is necessary to consider their cash flow balance and profit–and–loss balance from the perspective of economic analysis as well as public project assessment. In speaking of economic analysis, it means to estimate the economic profit and economic cost of a project, and decide whether it is feasible from the perspective of the national economy. The starting point of economic analysis is the interest of the nation as a whole, hence the definitions of cost and benefit are often different from those used in financial analyses. These differences mainly result from the two assessment methods using different prices for what is invested and what is produced. Economic analysis uses economic prices, while financial analysis uses market prices. Economic price is usually called "shadow price", reflecting the real degree of scarcity of certain things in the national economy. In a fully competitive market (where market competition is not distorted), the value of a product should be measured by its market price. But in many cases, the market is not fully competitive. Prices are distorted by various factors. In economic analysis of public projects, we need shadow prices to calculate the value of products. The shadow price of a product refers to its marginal economic benefit, that is, the additional economic benefit brought by adding one more unit of the product in question. Besides, although economic analysis and financial analysis use some similar assessing methods, such as net present value, cost-benefit ratio, payback period, internal rate of return, the data on costs, benefits, and discount rate they use are different. For instance, "social discount rate" is usually used in the assessment of public projects. When benefit is looked at from the society, consideration is not only given to the benefit of investment for the current generation but also for the next generation. Therefore, social discount rate or the social opportunity cost is often higher than the investment return rate resulting from financial analysis. Investment in many public projects will bring "external effects" — these projects not only benefit investors but also people who do not participate in investment. When we consider a project, we must bear in mind the interests of the country as a whole in determining its feasibility.

6.6 Input–output analysis model for strategic credit space

One important feature of our study of strategic credit space on the basis of economic analysis is that we set system building, mechanism building, and market building as important input–output factors, as the degree of perfection of a market system is closely associated with the efficiency of utilization of various elements of production, or with economic efficiency. Today, we promote market building through financing, and the market efficiency may change remarkably tomorrow. This is also a kind of input–output. Therefore, to put it briefly, when we analyze the funds flow balance and profit-and-loss balance of mid- and long-term infrastructure construction and construction in social bottleneck fields, input–output can be simply divided into hard input, soft input, hard output, and soft output. Hard input includes all hard resources such as capital, labor, natural resources, production, and transportation tools, etc., whereas soft input refers to soft resources such as credit system building and management, etc. Hard output includes realization of material wealth such as capital gains, increase of earned income, newly developed resources, new production, and transportation tools, etc.; soft output includes degree of credit development and enhancement of management level. Based on qualitative and quantitative analyses on the soft and hard input elements, and incorporating government, enterprises, and social investing bodies into the overall strategic credit space development framework through planning to establish a sound system of project flow, funds flow, and risk control, and on the basis of real-value creation and renovation of systems and mechanisms, it is possible to realize sustainable circular development of input and output (soft and hard elements), that is, realize cash flow balance and profit-and-loss balance of mid- and long-term development, and solve the problem of potential risks in mid- and long-term infrastructure construction and construction of social "hot spots".

Figure 6.1 summarizes the analysis process of cash flow balance and profit-and-loss balance of strategic credit space.

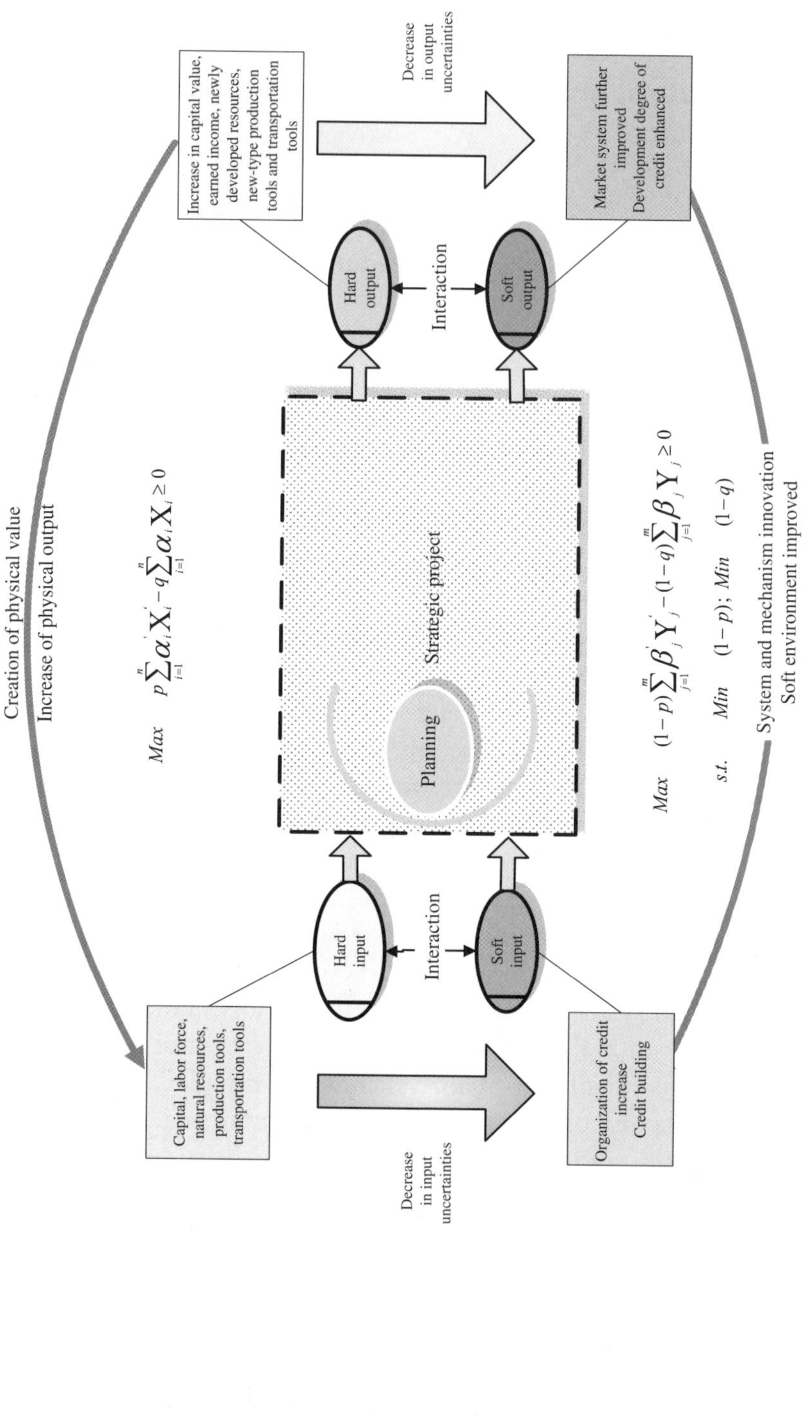

Figure 6.1: Cash flow balance and profit-and-loss balance of input and output under the strategic credit space model.

The below input–output circulation system has the following quantitative relationship:

$$\begin{cases} \text{Max} \quad p\sum_{i=1}^{n}\alpha_i^{'}X_i^{'} - q\sum_{i=1}^{n}\alpha_i^{'}X_i^{'} \geq 0 \\ \text{Max} \quad (1-p)\sum_{j=1}^{m}\beta_j^{'}Y_j^{'} - (1-q)\sum_{j=1}^{m}\beta_j Y_j \geq 0 \end{cases}$$

Restraining condition: Min($X + Y$)
Of which, X-Hard input; Y Soft input;
X'-Hard output; Y' Soft output;
p Ratio of hard output, $1-p$ Ratio of soft output;
q Ratio of hard input, $1-q$ Ratio of soft input;
α_i, β_j Adjustment coefficients of various inputs;
α_i', β_j' Adjustment coefficients of various outputs.

Here, it is assumed that there is a certain total input and a total output. To reach a certain amount of output, increase of soft input can correspondingly reduce hard input, or to reach the goals of a certain output and development, the better the market system, the input of capital, technology, and labor can correspondingly be decreased; otherwise, there must be more inputs.

This quantitative relationship demonstrates that as long as input and output satisfy certain conditions, cash flow balance and profit-and-loss balance can be achieved. In summarizing the practice of China Development Bank we have found that there are three major factors that restrain cash flow balance and profit-and-loss balance for mid- and long-term development: (i) project flow (group of strategic projects), (ii) cash flow (cash sources with sustainable circulation), and (iii) degree of development of credit (risk control mechanism).

(1) *Project flow* refers to groups of strategic projects bearing on national interest and people's livelihood. These strategic projects during a long period of time are of certain significance as

markers for national economic and social development, and are important components of national mid- and long-term core competitive strength. They ensure momentum for sustainable economic-social development. Therefore, we are required to take on the issue upstream and ensure project supply at the source. Planning first is precisely the important means to ensure incubation of strategic projects. Through cooperation with governments at various levels and strategic enterprises in planning and by relying on and organizing active participation of social resources in planning, a sustainable flow of strategic projects for the entire society can surely take shape.

(2) *Cash flow* refers to fund sources that can carry out sustainable circulation. There are three channels of capital for mid- and long-term projects. (i) *The future revenue of the projects themselves*: this is the primary foundation for assurance of cash flow balance and profit-and-loss balance. Usually, the cost and risks of mid- and long-term projects are higher in the early stages and lower in later stages. The opposite is true with their cash flows. Planning is able to conduct benign jointing between imbalance of cash flow and imbalance of risks, and arrange delayed re-payment of short-term cash flow imbalance risks until later stages to avoid financial difficulties in the early stages of development. (ii) The large-sum, stable, long-term, and sustainable quasi-sovereign securities financing of development-oriented financing institutions can, through the securities market, publicly collect and assemble from consumers small-sum, idle, short-term, and uncertain savings capital, realizing separation of national capital accumulation and private saving structure (a part of private savings have long-term precautionary requirements, such as education). This will, for quite a long time to come, help alleviate financial resource restraints and insufficiency arising from the lag in capital market building in China, but the prerequisite is that there needs to be a government-backed development-oriented financial institution that uses national credit as an important support, to realize rolling development of financing through securities. As long as the nation is there, national credit space can be or should

be utilized to the full. For this, the legal system needs to provide enough guarantee, such as enacting specific "Management Regulations for Development-Oriented Finance", or "Management Regulations for Policy Banks". (iii) *The rational introduction of socialized capital*: this requires a rather sound and healthy credit system environment to create conditions necessary for the entry of private capital, commercial finance, and foreign capital into the mid- and long-term construction field.

(3) *Degree of credit development* refers to the development level of the credit system. We can realize effective control of risks in mid- and long-term strategic projects and the "hot spot" fields in society and people's livelihood by planning in advance and controlling the risk at the source, by collecting and assembling all resources to achieve socialization of finance, through establishment of a society-wide credit system and risk sharing mechanism and improvement of the legal protection system. For instance, the bundled loan that China Development Bank is exploring in its practice is an innovative means for enhancing the degree of credit development, accelerating project construction, cash-flow building, and credit building. Through collecting, sorting out, assembling, and systematization of scattered credit resources, the conglomeration and scale-up of credit building is thus achieved on the basis of credit structure and overall cash balance and policy making. Sustainable credit expansion vitality is thus injected into the development of regional economies that have the "shortest plank effect" soft restraint mechanism. Of course, this practice requires constant improvement.

In a word, paying due attention to project flow (group of strategic projects), cash flow (cash sources with sustainable circulation), and degree of credit development (risk control system), strengthening the building of strategic credit space is not only a risk control technique but also a planning idea and development strategy. In the area of mid- and long-term financing, measures such as persistence in placing planning first, strengthening the study of strategic credit space, conducting comprehensive, meticulous, and in-depth feasibility studies on project screening, capital arrangement, market building, and system building, seeking and developing sustainable strategic credit space will help to reduce various uncertainties in the input and output of mid- and long-term development. Such measures will also help to deploy resources as rationally as possible, to seek to maximize various outputs while minimizing uncertainties (or risks), with the prerequisite of there being no negative soft output and hard output (i.e., output is greater than or equal to input), to realize cash flow and profit-and-loss balances for mid- and long-term construction projects which is of importance to guard against systematic risks in major mid- and long-term projects and in ensuring stable, rapid, and sustainable development of the economy.

6.7 Establishment of a study model for strategic option

The strategic option planning model is in reality a deepening of the strategic credit space planning model. It focuses on the study of the option aspect of strategic credit space. Rational development of the strategic option is of utmost importance to reducing uncertainties in economic activities, using minimum cost to avoid potential risks, helping governments at various levels and the development-oriented financial institution itself enhance their capability to deal with changing situations and ensuring the rationality of strategic planning.

6.7.1 *Connotation of strategic option*

The option is a contract, which gives a holder the option of the right to buy or sell a certain asset at a specific time and under specific conditions. Compared with other financial agreements, its uniqueness lies in the right, not in the obligation. An option holder exercises his/her option only when there is profit to be gained. Under other situations, he/she might give up the option. W. Carl Kester was the first to associate the option theory with strategic management, making it an important component of strategic risk management. He holds that managerial personnel should regard investment opportunities as the future growth option of a corporation.[2] To realize the investment opportunity in the future, it is necessary to develop and design strategic option, which may serve as an operable tool for managerial personnel to deal with the uncertainty of the future effects of present policy decisions — through incessant perception that risks are coming and the ability to seize available new opportunities, in order to formulate new strategic plans and strategic options.

We have a better understanding and have creatively applied Wall Street's option theory and formed the concept of strategic option of development-oriented finance in association with the actual conditions in China and its development-oriented finance practice. That is, on the basis of the given strategic intention and under the prerequisite of clear and specific long-term strategic goals, to seek, discover, and create a series of opportunities for making strategic decisions. Through development and design of a series of strategic contracts, and choosing to execute or abandon these established strategic contracts in a certain period of time, we ensure the flexibility and rationality of formulating strategies in an uncertain environment and reduce uncertainties in economic activities, thus enhancing the probability of value discovery, and realizing the flexible strategy transfer. Such processes would help us to avoid potential risks in committing serious mistakes in strategy making. The role of strategic option lies in reducing risks brought by uncertainties, and creating opportunities for choice of strategies in future changing situations, thus providing opportunities for possible growth of a region and an enterprise. The uncertain risks we are talking about here are in reality strategic risks, which mainly come from changes in various elements such as the market, products, technologies, management, external environment, etc., which exert important influences on the formulation and implementation of development strategies. The core value of strategic option comes from its value of resisting risks, its value of obtaining opportunities for growth, and the additional value that governments at various levels may get. The goal of strategic option

[2] W. Carl Kester, *Case Problems in Finance.*

is to guarantee reliability of investment, realize sustainable development of credit, and ensure the momentum for long-term development of a nation, regions, industries, and enterprises. On the basis of strategic option in economic development, development-oriented finance forms a unique framework model for credit evaluation and strategic planning. When a development-oriented financial institution assesses government credit, it actually turns the government's ability to perform coordination and system building into a product with cash recovery and gigantic development potential, or a strategic option. This kind of option is an essential characteristic of development-oriented finance and is a concrete embodiment of its role in offsetting market immaturity and market malfunctions.

6.7.2. *Structure of strategic option*

The strategic option we have proposed is divided into three tiers. As strategic option is continually developed and exploited, strategic credit space will be further expanded and defined, and risk exposure will gradually be reduced, thus realizing coverage of future risks by economic development.

(1) *Strategic option of the first tier.* On the basis of national planning for macroeconomic control and structure adjustment, the strategic option of the first tier brings into full play the professional advantages of a development-oriented financial institution, to help local governments and enterprises identify and tap the realistic potential advantages and turn these realistic potential advantages into material options and clearly identified investment decision opportunities. Once conditions are mature, local governments and enterprises can invest, while development-oriented finance can, at the appropriate time, provide governments and enterprises with financial services such as financing support and financial consulting, etc., and help its clients implement these material options, enabling them to have new opportunities for development and benefits.

(2) *Strategic option of the second tier.* On the basis of the anticipated economic benefit of local governments and enterprises over a relatively long period of time, development-oriented finance makes commitments involving large sums, using market funds, and funds in the

future to help its clients arrange planning for the next 5 and 10 years, strengthens the localities' capability of and confidence in long-term development, and promotes coordinated development of the localities. Facing the picture of great economic-social development everywhere in China, development-oriented finance not only waits for the end, or providing capital only when a project is ready; instead, it gets involved at the very beginning. It takes the initiative to decide policy loans of significant amounts on the basis of government's development planning and overall investment scale and gives a comprehensive consideration to the funds needed for planned projects, thus making planning more rational and accurate and instrumental to implementation. With rational commitments, development-oriented finance drives synchronized growth and synchronized maturity of projects groups and cash flow everywhere in China, promotes the integration of forces of government, finance and market, pushes forward the implementation of regional investment plans and industries investment plans, and manifests its initiative of implementing the requirements of scientific outlook on development.

(3) *Strategic option of the third tier.* On the basis of current value and conditions, choice of future opportunities for investment, probability of improvement in conditions, and changes in the situation, development-oriented finance helps its clients revise and improve their mid- and long-term development planning on a rolling basis.

Scientifically established development approaches and strategic targets, including national strategic targets, targets for eradication of economic-social bottlenecks, targets for system building, at the same time creation of conditions to remove as much as possible various uncertainties, including technology risks, governance structure risks, market risks, and management risks, provides call options to development-oriented finance, clients, cooperation partners to boost society's confidence. Scientific and rational call options manifest not only synchronized development and mutual-matching of project groups and funds flow but also the trend of technological transformation, upgrading of industries, structural adjustment in national development, and the demands of systems-, market- and credit-building. Scientific and rational call options have a certain stability and necessary elasticity. Stability calls for relatively accurate prediction of the

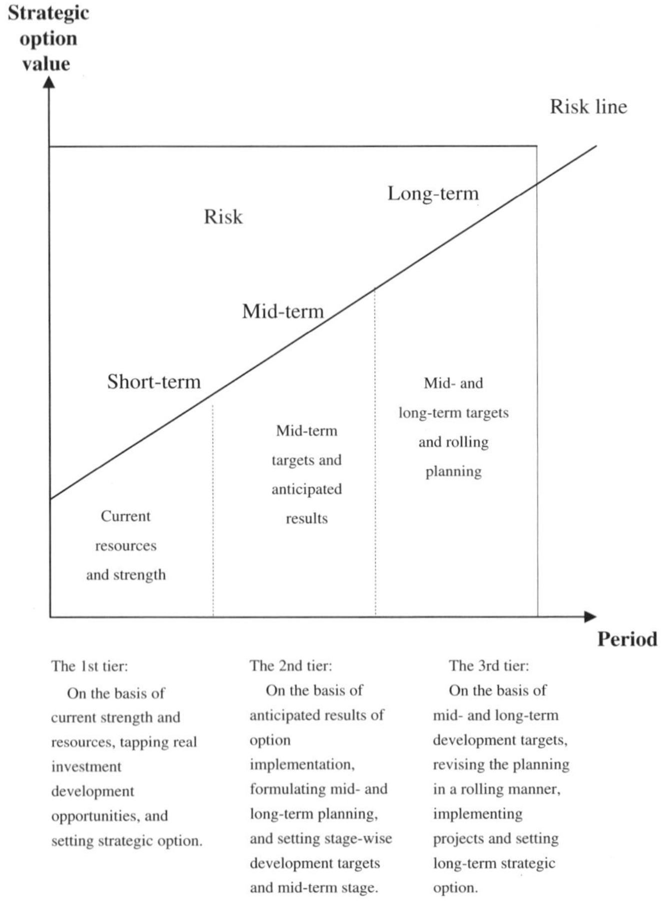

Figure 6.2: Periodic evolution nature of strategic option.

market and prospects and elasticity requires capability of responding and adjusting to changes in the situation. Development-oriented finance not only provides society with call options but also shares call options with commercial banks through assets management and strategic cooperation to jointly advance the process of modernization and enhance China's international competitive strength, manifesting the leading, guiding, and promoting role of development-oriented finance. Figure 6.2 illustrates the stagewise evolution nature of the analysis framework of strategic option of development-oriented finance.

As shown in Figure 6.2, the following conclusions can be drawn from the analysis of the stagewise evolution nature of the strategic option: along with the in-depth progress of the work on planning and its continual rolling revision, mid- and long-term targets become increasingly clear, risk exposure is gradually reduced, the strategic option value continually increases, and the anticipated benefit of current capital expenditure increases. Arrangement of strategic options and application of integrated management tools can reduce the risk exposure ratio, realize effective hedging of strategic risks, and maintain flexibility and elasticity of strategic development. In the long run, this manifests itself as a sustainable credit building process for mid- and long-term projects. In terms of a macro view, if projects scheduled for several years in the future are carried out now on the basis of scientific planning and giving adequate attention to the changing economic development scenario, concentrating resources, starting high, and taking large steps, it is possible to produce a spillover effect of resource scale and increase mid- and long-term cash flows and positive earnings probability. In terms of a micro view, development and application of strategic options can help credit bodies which hold option agreements guard against breaking of a capital chain that may be brought about due to market changes, and losses that may be caused by price fluctuation. This is why strategic options can guard against risks. The development and application of strategic options is like fuzzy mathematics; it does not require, nor achieve precision, but it reveals the regular patterns and characteristics of the support of development-oriented finance for mid- and long-term infrastructure construction: first, it possesses the comprehensiveness, long-term nature, integrity, and competitiveness of strategy; second, it manifests systematic and structured strategic financing polices; and third, it reflects the flexible overall strategy of dynamic planning and dynamic implementation.

6.7.3. *Application of strategic option*

There are many successful cases of strategic option as an important idea of development-oriented finance. Take Suzhou Industrial Park for example. During the early period in which development-oriented finance was involved, excavation of the "Golden Cock Lake" was the first project chosen, followed by construction of other infrastructure. This is a kind of development and design of strategic option, listing the environment issue as something for long-term consideration and incorporating supporting projects into the general planning, thus creating invaluable returns for the all-round development of the Park in years to come and ensuring sustainable credit conditions. Another example is combining Russian R&D and its technology with the broad Chinese market through strengthening cooperation with Russia in the aviation industry. It is possible for China and Russia to become a third important force besides Boeing and Airbus in the worldwide aviation industry which could play a gigantic stimulating role for the Chinese as well as Russian economy. When considering long-term projects, we should have a long-term strategic vision. Many projects will take decades or even longer to complete, however, we can start to give certain preliminary considerations, which include promoting academic exchange between economic departments of various countries to facilitate the forming of a consensus among the financial community, enterprise community, and academic community. With a consensus and long-term targets, we can move a step further and start with planning, with early deliberation, formulating plans, and implementing the targets step by step. It is through scientific and in-depth analysis in the planning stage that development-oriented strategic option develops and exploits a series of strategic credit spaces — taking projects that are not very clearly defined and moving them from long-term plans and implementing them in the near-term, and similarly, postponing implementation of near-term project plans to a later period, and through establishing options, achieve flexibility and balance in policy making. This kind of time-space transformation can effectively change the marginal benefit and risk boundaries of investment, reduce systematic risk exposure, increase risk limits and credit space of capital-raising bodies or regions, and realize cash flow balance and profit-and-loss balance of project investment.

The reason that development-oriented finance regards planning as a core competitive strength is because planning can play the magic role likened to "a force of 4 ounces can deflect a force of 500 kilograms". This unique ability is attributed to development and exploitation of strategic option. Planning itself is "designing the whole and laying out the structure", or incorporating all possibilities into the range of consideration, including development and design of strategic option. The key in strategic option development is to "know the enemy and know yourself, and you can fight a hundred battles with no danger of defeat", which mainly depends on the channels and degree of difficulty of information access. Through planning, information can be fully collected, problems can be analyzed, breakthrough points can be found, and various organizational forces can be brought into play in order to create possible opportunities for development of the strategic option and ensure flexibility of the strategy change. Strategic option design is a forward-looking technical effort, including considerations regarding the macro-environment, bottlenecks in development, credit risks, cash flow balance, system building, and operation strategies. Furthermore, strategic option design is also an important tool to incorporate a given strategic credit space into an operable planning system to ensure that system building develops in a clear and set direction to realize "keeping pace with the times".

6.8 Summary

In this chapter, we have carried out an in depth analysis of the strategic significance and characteristics of planning, and established an analysis framework for the strategic credit space and the strategic option, and answered the question of how to guard against risks in mid- and long-term infrastructure construction and social "hot-spot" construction in a targeted manner — a question which the society is most concerned about (Figure 6.3). China's development strategy for the 21st century (including a three-step strategy) is to gradually reach the level of a moderately developed country within 100 years. Each stage has a relative development demand space. These need to be considered in a unified and coordinated way from a macro strategic perspective. Planning first is based on the development concept of

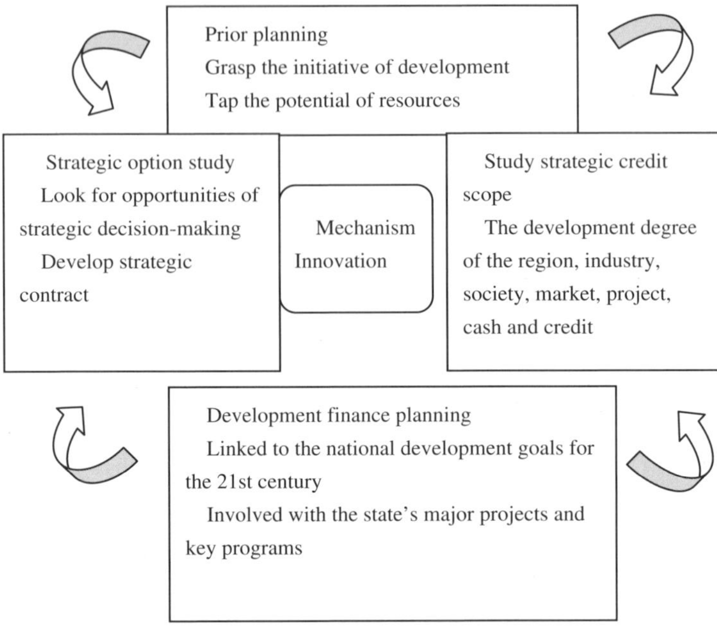

Figure 6.3: Planning is a core competitive edge.

making planning the antecedent of all economic activities in order to achieve sustainable economic-social development through highly efficient, all-round, accurate, and systematic plan design and structure deployment. Development of this kind is usually unconventional and has latecomer advantages. If development oriented finance starts from planning, discovers projects of great significance, taps resource potential, brings into play the enthusiasm of various parties, and seizes the development initiative, it is able to support development and avoid risks. Of course, its basic condition lies in the situation of credit system building. Because, whether it is the development and exploitation of the strategic option or the study of the strategic credit space, they are all closely associated with the maturity of the credit system. In other words, formulation of scientific planning and results of its implementation depend upon the maturity of the credit system. The essence of finance is social credit; the foundation of a developed financial system is a sound credit system; the foundation of scientific planning is also a sound credit system. Therefore, if planning is expected to enhance efficiency, the key lies in establishing, creating, and maintaining a consistently improving credit system environment, and through credit system building, minimize various uncertainties, thus realizing the rationality, long-term nature, comprehensiveness, and operability of planning, which is the most important condition to ensure planning efficiency. We will be dealing with it specifically in the section "credit system building is the fourth propelling force of economic development" in Chapter 7.

Chapter 7

Building the Credit Market Constitutes the Fourth Driver for Economic Development

An advanced credit market system is a driver for economic development. It can organically integrate all social forces and especially credit-related market factors such as plans, political strengths, and traditional cultural considerations. By releasing the demand and energy of market players, an efficient system can promote the improvement and development of credit markets and ensure the normal operation of social order and the market economy. This is a long-standing endogenous mechanism that has been employed to ensure China's medium- and long-term sustainable development.

Development-oriented finance has played a major role in building the credit market systems in China. By way of summarizing our bank's practice of development-oriented finance, I would note that we have formed our own theory of development-oriented finance. This theory, which is based on national conditions and draws on extensive experience at a high level, is designed to promote sustainable economic and social development. It is a theory that results from practice and returns to practice and has stood the test of China's economic development. It is also a theory that can expand from the reform and development of the financial industry to the reform and development of other industries and from China's development to the development of other countries. In short, it is a financial theory of China's own that has been proven over time under a wide range of conditions.

An important content of the Chinese theory of development-oriented finance is to reveal the relation between a nation's credit market system and national medium- and long-term development, where we define credit market system building as the fourth driving force for economic development, and introduce an analytical model in pursuit of its validation. This theoretical model introduces the factor of credit market systems into the traditional model of economic growth, and can objectively reflect the real conditions of economic development in developing countries. The model helps to guide us in our efforts in building a credit market system, where we might lock in upside risk and mitigate development risks in practical work. By establishing an evaluation system for the development of the credit market, credit building can develop from scattered, isolated, and qualitative risk prevention measures to a systematic, targeted, and quantitatively measurable operating mechanism, and can allocate and use social resources more rationally and promote sustainable economic and social development.

7.1. Origin of the issue

Robert M. Solow and other Western economists have made an in-depth analysis of the key factors impacting economic growth. They note that capital, labor, and technology are the key factors that determine a country's production of materials and labor service.[1] In other words, capital, labor, and technology are the sources of the three acknowledged drivers for economic growth, but this theory has failed to consider the market base on which these factors spur economic growth. This is because they are postulated on the assumption that markets are already mature; under such conditions, once economic growth begins, the market system can automatically stabilize and sustain the growth. However, a host of empirical data contradicts this theory. In fact, market systems are always in need of improvement and development. In developing countries, in particular, market systems are mostly unsound and underdeveloped. The three-driver theory cannot explain why different countries have

[1]Robert M. Solow: A Contribution to the Theory of Economic Growth [J], *Quarterly Journal of Economics*, 1956, 70(1): 66–94.

very different economic growth patterns. In the course of economic globalization, the free flow of capital, technology, labor, and information has constantly improved. This begs the question: Why has the difference between the developed and developing countries tend to widen rather than narrow? Of course, a considerable portion of the wealth gap between different countries can be attributed to their resource endowments. But there also exists a wide development difference between countries with roughly the same resource endowments. This makes it necessary to look at economic growth through the lens of market systems. Economists have attached growing importance to the roles of market systems in sustainable economic and social development, and there have been many significant research studies yielding important results on this subject.[2] What we want to further emphasize here is that the difference between the developing and developed countries does not exist merely in capital, technology, and labor; the most fundamental difference exists in their market systems. In a major developing country like China, market systems building has in fact become a basic factor impacting the efficiency of the three major drivers. Defective and outdated market systems are a fundamental constraint on economic and social development. On the one hand, it is unable to effectively regulate the difference in income distribution between different regions and between different members of society and to provide public products and public services. These include the problems regarding countryside, agriculture, and peasants; the problem of social security; the problem of employment; and the protection of the eco-environment. On the other hand, economic transition breeds enormous systemic risks caused by outdated systems. In the financial sector in particular, the main expressions are the absence of social credit, ineffective regulation, and outdated investment and financing systems, both at the micro-system level and at the basic

---

[2] St. Fishcer and A. Gelb: The Process of Socialist Economic Transformation, *The Journal of Economic Perspectives*, 1991, 5(4): 91–105.

O. E.Williamson: Comparative Economic Organization: The Analysis of Discrete Structural Alternatives, *Administrative Science Quarterly*, 1991, 36(2), 274.

financial system level. As a result, policies cannot be effectively transmitted, macro-regulations cannot be effectively followed, market efficiency is low, the costs of investment, consumption, and export are relatively high, and the whole economy operates on a capital-inefficient basis. Credit market systems are the most important core contents of the market economy in developing countries, and all market problems are fundamentally related to the credit market system. For this reason, we have focused our research on credit market systems, which will help us to reach the heart of the issue and find practical solutions. In order to be brief, the systems or market systems we shall mention in the following part of this chapter mainly refer to the credit market systems. Our basic view is that accelerating credit market system building is necessary for developing countries to achieve deliberate, active, sustained, steady, and healthy development.

7.2. Exploration of new development concepts and procedures

In order to accelerate development and keep pace with the times, the developing countries must conduct an integrated study of the contributions of systems, capital, labor, and technology to economic growth, recognize both the economic and social components of economic development, study the input and output from a broader perspective, and incorporate more factors to form a new way of thinking. This new way of thinking occupies a four-dimensional space that takes systems, capital, labor, and technology as the independent variables and takes economic growth as the constrained variable and can briefly, clearly, and comprehensively demonstrate the issues that occur. Although system, compared with the hard factors of capital, labor and technology, is invisible, intangible, and less independent, its role can be entirely regarded as a dimension. With constant improvements, financial systems have had growing impacts on economic development. In the edifice of modernization, system is a wall. Only when a sound system is established and improved can the edifice of China's modernization truly stand up. Of course, analysis of this nature involves unprecedented span and difficulty and has unprecedented implications.

Through an integrated study of system, capital, labor, and technology, we attempt to solve the following three specific issues:

(1) To provide a more generalized growth interpretation model for developing economies on the basis of China's experience.
(2) To explore the real relations between system, capital, labor, and technology on the one hand and economic growth on the other.
(3) To enrich and deepen the field of development economics to quantitatively reflect China's economic and social development that is consistent with China's actual experience, and thereby make it as an important content of the principles of Chinese-style development finance.

Consistent with such an understanding, we recognize that economics is "merely" a part of sociology and economic issues are inextricably social issues. Crudely put, economics is a facet in people's lives and people's lives are significantly affected by their nation's economic development as well as by their own personal economic progress. A market system with credit market system building as its core content is more of a social issue than an economic one. It is only natural that our study combines economic laws with social ones. The greatest difficulty of our study is to find the specific relations between system, capital, labor, and technology on the one hand and economic growth on the other hand. If this issue is solved, the first and third issues will be readily solved. In the relation between the four-driver system and economic growth, system building is the fourth driver for economic development. This is not merely our empirical understanding; the system contains objective inherent relations. Just like the close relation between technology advance and labor productivity enhancement, system building also has close relations with the efficiency of capital use. Just as technology advances are an endogenous force for economic growth, system building is also an endogenous one for economic growth. Developing countries do not have inherent high-efficiency systems.

Their systems are systems in development, and their markets are markets in development. We must consider the impact of system building on economic growth. Robert M. Solow won the 1987 Nobel Prize for economics for his exposition that technological advance based on high-efficiency systems was an endogenous force for economic growth. Our analysis of the relations between system building and economic growth is not intended to win a prize. Instead, it is intended to solve the issue of credit system building in the course of China's economic development so that the economy can develop in a better, faster, and sustainable way. Our analysis is of a preliminary nature, with a preliminary framework being established. Great efforts are required to replenish and improve this analysis.

Robert M. Solow explored the relation between technology and labor at depth. He introduced the new variable of technological labor and took technology as an endogenous force impacting economic growth. Therefore, the model of economic growth he developed looks brief and effective. By drawing on his method of research, we do not intend to elaborate on discussions on the two factors of labor and technology, for the impacts of these on economic growth have already been fully discussed in other papers. Here, we shall focus our discussions on the relations between (credit) market systems and capital, and introduce a new variable of credit capital. Credit capital refers to the credit resources when credit market systems reach a certain degree of development. The efficiency of credit capital use is closely related to the decree of credit market system development. Therefore, we can use credit capital to reflect this relation, to explain the relation between market system and economic growth, and to explore whether market system is an endogenous force for economic growth. The impact of market system on economic growth is evident. In a sense, market system can make production more efficient and can increase output with less input, as technology advance does. Market system can also stimulate economic players, which technology advance cannot. Below, we attempt to introduce the model of economic growth added with the variable of the credit market system.

7.3. Preliminary framework of theory of four-driver economic development

We believe that in the initial stages of the Chinese-style socialist market economy and those economies of other developing countries where market systems are relatively backward, economic growth has close relations with the four independent variables of system (M), capital (K), labor (L), and technology (E). This relation can be briefly expressed in Figure 7.1.

Sustainable economic development here is an integrated, comprehensive, and long-term development. To facilitate our research, we use the commonly known GDP to represent sustainable economic development. Although GDP cannot fully reflect the state of sustainable economic development, it can roughly reflect the meaning of such a development. This simplified method can help us to theoretically explore the relation between sustainable economic development on the one hand and (credit market) systems, capital, labor, and technology on the other hand.

We all know that a utility relation exists between labor and technology. This relation has been fully explained by Solow in his theoretical model of economic growth and can be represented by $V(L(E))$, a utility function of technological labor. Likewise, a utility relation also exists between system and capital. In other words, credit system

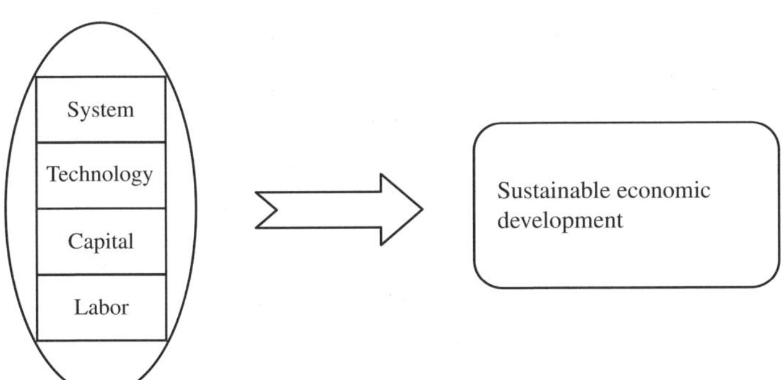

Figure 7.1: Four major drivers and sustainable economic development.

development is closely related to capital use efficiency. Therefore, we can use $U(K(M))$ to represent the utility function of credit capital.

Let us draw on Solow's research results. In the Solow model of economic growth, the impact of technology advance on economic growth is mainly expressed in the impact on labor. In other words, technology advance is expressed in Herald's neutrality.[3] When the technology variable is effectively combined with the labor variable, labor is called technological labor. Our theory of development-oriented finance believes that the impact of credit market systems on economic growth is mainly expressed in enhancing the efficiency of capital use through elevating credit market development. When the variable of the credit market system is effectively combined with the capital variable, it is called credit capital. Accordingly, the market system can also be roughly expressed in the neutrality of development finance.[4] This can easily be proved by practical experience. If a credit market system is relatively sound, the capital liquidity of this market will be greatly higher and the efficiency of capital investment will also increase in a positive direction. Therefore, we can use the credit market system as a factor in the model of economic growth we shall introduce. In this way, we can develop a new model of economic growth that contains the utility function of credit capital:

$$Y = F(U(K(M)), V(L(E))).$$

This function reflects the impact of market system on economic growth introduced by development finance. Specifically, Y stands for the end-product output under the conditions of certain capital utility and technological labor utility; $K(M)$ stands for the credit capital, $L(E)$ stands for the technological labor, and $U(K(M))$ and $V(L(E))$ stand for the utility function of credit capital and the utility function of technological labor respectively.

[3] Herald's neutrality in technology advance means that technology advance increases output by way of increasing labor stock, which is also called labor-intensive or labor-extensive technology advance.

[4] The market system with the neutrality of development finance refers to enhancing output through building the credit market system and enhancing the quantity and value of credit capital stock. It is also called the intensive capital.

If we use X to replace $U(K(M))$ to represent the total utility of credit capital and use Z to replace $V(L(E))$ to represent the total cost of technological labor, the above model can be expressed:

$$Y = F(U(K(M)), V(L(E))) = F(X, Z) = X^{\alpha}Z^{1-\alpha}.$$

In the model, $0 < \alpha < 1$. Here, we can have a classic expression of production function, which is similar to the Cobb–Douglas growth model. This function can meet the basic hypothesis of the neo-classical production function. It has three properties:

(1) The marginal outputs of all factors are bigger than 0 and their growth rates decrease progressively, namely $F_1 > 0$, $F_{11} < 0$, $F_2 > 0$, $F_{22} < 0$. Specifically, F_i and F_{ii} ($i = 1, 2$) stand for the first and second partial derivatives of the function F respectively. The first partial derivative reflects the slope ratio of the function and indicates the direction of the change of the production function of social end-products. The second partial derivative reflects the curvature of the function and indicates the speed of change of the function of the social end-products.
(2) If the scale of production remains unchanged, the production function has a linear homogeneity, namely $F(\lambda X, \lambda Z) = \lambda F(X, Z)$. It is tenable to any λ. In other words, the inputs of various factors have a proportional relation to the production function. Therefore, it can be used as a constant (λ) and placed outside the function.
(3) The Inada conditions. When X and Z tend to 0, the marginal distribution of the function F (F_x and F_z) tends to infinity. When X and Z tend to infinity, the marginal distribution of the function F (F_x and F_z) tends to 0.

If the two sides of the model expression are divided by Z, we derive the following singleness of function homogeneity:

$$Y/Z = F(X/Z, 1).$$

If $k = X/Z$ and stands for the credit capital utility possessed by each technological labor unit and if $y = Y/Z$ and stands for the economic growth rate at the cost of unit technological labor, we can work out the functional relation between economic growth and the credit capital utility possessed by each technological labor unit:

$$y = F(k,1) = k^{\alpha}, \text{ namely } y = f(k).$$

Here, k stands for the credit resource possessed by a unit of technological labor under the condition of a certain degree of credit market system development. The bigger the value, the sounder the system and the greater the stimulus to economic growth by other factors operating under a high-efficiency system. Apparently, the above functional relation reflects that the degree of the credit market system development (credit) is an endogenous force for economic growth. This is because credit capital is closely related to the degree of the credit market system development. In other words, the degree of credit market system development impacts the efficiency of capital use and in turn the economic growth. In this way, we can come up with a regularity understanding: the acceleration of credit market system building by tapping the strength of government organizations and the role of development finance can increase the utility of credit capital, can raise the **total factor productivity** and in turn the total wealth of society, and can promote sustained economic growth. In short, the strengthening of the credit market system building can promote sustainable economic and social development.

There is an interesting corollary to this theory that is a result of its application as a measurement tool in a time-differential perspective of national productivity. If L is the measurement of a nation's entire labor pool, and the other variables (E, M, and K) likewise represent national characteristics as quantified elements at a given time $t_{x'}$, then

if $Y = F(U(K(M)),V(L(E))) = F(X, Z) = X^{\alpha}Z^{1-\alpha}$,

$Y_{t'} = F(U_{t'}(K(M)), V_{t'}(L(E))) = F_{t'}(X, Z) = X_{t'}^{\alpha}Z_{t'}^{-\alpha}$. Hence $Y\Delta t = Y_{t1} - Y_{t0}$

$= F(U_{t1}(K(M)),V_{t1}(L(E))) - F(U_{t0}(K(M)),V_{t0}(L(E))) = F_{t1}(X, Z) - F_{t0}(X, Z)$

$= X^{\alpha}_{t1} Z_{t1}^{1-\alpha} - X^{\alpha}_{t0} Z_{t0}^{1-\alpha}$.

If we assume that technological labor and credit capital advance over the course of a given period, say one year, in a positive manner that can be approximated as linear relations (an acceptable postulate for today's China), then,

$X^{\alpha}_{t1} = X^{\alpha}_{t0}$, ${Z_{t1}}^{1-\alpha} = {Z_{t0}}^{(1-\alpha)}$ so that $X^{\alpha}_{t1}\, {Z_{t1}}^{1-\alpha} - X^{\alpha}_{t0}\, {Z_{t0}}^{1-\alpha}$

$= mX^{\alpha}_{t0}\, n{Z_{t0}}^{(1-\alpha)} - X^{\alpha}_{t0}\, {Z_{t0}}^{1-\alpha}$, where $m, n > 1$.

Consequently, we can say that technology advance coupled with credit market system building (technological labor multiplied by credit capital) interact to increase China's production advance in a manner we associate with compound interest. Of course, this is exactly the phenomenon we associate with developed countries, "The rich gets richer and the poor gets poorer", because the confluence of both attributes, with them both consistently being positive and greater than one, is normally associated only with developed economies.

Note that if we neglect that portion of national income associated with national resource liquidation, FDI and capital outflow, the above result, $X^{m\alpha}_{t0} {Z_{t0}}^{n(1-\alpha)} - X^{\alpha}_{t0}\, {Z_{t0}}^{1-\alpha}$, when the variables are quantified with appropriate measurement units, accurately state the change over time in a nation's GDP. Since all can be redefined to operate as virtual labor leveraging factors, then the consequence is to quantify and explain mathematically what China's political leaders have intuitively long understood in a resource-strapped country like ours (considering its population), "The greatest factor in our national income is our people." So long as population constraints inhibit tendencies to runaway population growth and we are able to continually improve our technology and our credit market systems, China should markedly increase its GDP. Our latecomer status to technology advance and credit market system building means we have latecomer opportunities in terms of labor and capital leveraging.

To a great extent, the system of national opening up and economic reform was responsible for China's economic growth from the late 1970s through the mid-1980s, but this developed as a philosophical notion rather than in a calculated economic framework. Since that time, the nation's political and economic leaders have deliberately utilized the bulk of our nation's disposable income for capital projects intended to further technology based on application of an increasingly well-understood four-driver platform for economic development. This is possible due to relatively unique Chinese political, economic, social, and cultural considerations and perhaps adaptable only to certain developing nations. We at China Development Bank (CDB) and other policy banks have cooperated with the aims and objectives of our national leaders by furthering efforts toward financial system reform and consequent increasing of China's GDP growth through credit market systems building.

We once stated earlier that developing countries are noteworthy for inefficient markets and outdated financial and credit systems. China is, or was, no exception to this generalization. When I was appointed governor (CEO) of CDB in 1998, it was saddled with over 41% non-performing loan (NPL), a polite way of stating that 41% of all money it lent was not being repaid according to the terms of its loans. Through the institution of policies consistent with the four-driver theory, we modernized the bank and its policies, and drove home the theory of credit market system building to all our borrowers, their communities, the facilitating and cooperating banking, and other financial institutions and all other stakeholders in the development banking arena in which we operate. The result has been dramatic: the bank's NPL ratio has dropped precipitously, reaching NPL levels below 1%. For the last five years, for every calendar quarter, CDB's NPL ratio has been under 1%. Meanwhile, the bank's loan portfolio has exponentially grown at a compound annual growth rate (CAGR) of approximately 23%, and our outstanding loan balance now equals an amount roughly equal to 12% of current national GDP. It is theory, practice, and hard work, but it has changed China and consequently the world economy.

This conclusion can be further elaborated as follows:

(1) An efficient system is a guarantee for other factors of production to fully play their roles. The factors impacting a country's economic growth are interlinked, and the factors of capital, technology, and labor are combined with each other and operate under

specific systems. System is an important variable in the course of economic growth, and also an important factor for realizing steady economic growth. An appropriate system is a prerequisite to ensuring other factors efficiently play their roles. A good system has direct economic implications and can better regulate human relations and reduce information cost, uncertainty, and transaction cost. Based on the impact of the known factors of production on economic growth, we can have a new and deeper understanding of the factors impacting economic growth. Or in other words, we have further identified the impact of system building, as a factor of production, on economic growth: the input of the factors of production determines the intercept of the trend line of economic growth and translates the intercept upwards, while the efficiency of system determines the slope ratio of this curve and the sounder the system, the greater the slope ratio of the trend line of long-term growth (see Figure 7.2).

Note that Figure 7.2 contains four expressions besides that of the nominal $y = f(k)$, or $y = f(M, t)$ in which M represents market system driver force, and t is time. The middle line represents the theoretical economic development level (not the growth rate) for a given M for a given general time frame. The first and third lines represent the economic system growth given maximum/minimum M, it being assumed that advances in credit market systems building are negligible in this interval; note that the driver M constrains within

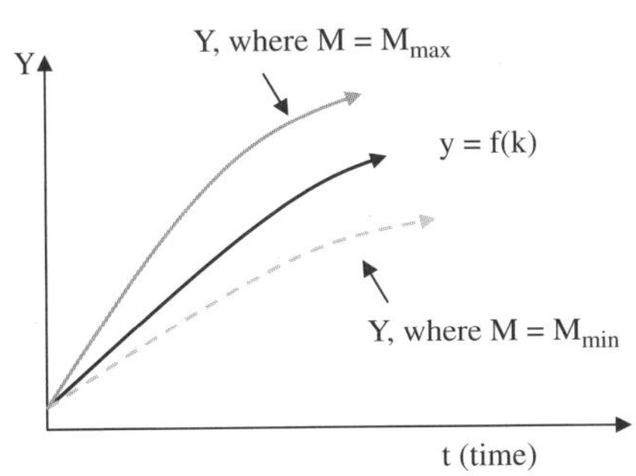

Figure 7.2: Effect of credit market system building on economic growth patterns.

the $M_{max} - M_{min}$ growth envelope even as *M* and a larger *Y* increasingly leverage the effect of capital (*K*) as t increases. *Y*-axis does not represent GDP; rather it is best designated as "gross economic development level", which we have earlier equated to *Y*. *X*-axis is *t* (time), but note that *E*, *L*, and *K* are fixed in this view; in reality *E*, *L*, *K*, and M are independent variables. Figure 7.2 shows the effect of credit market system building on economic growth. This further explains that an advanced credit market system is an important factor for long-term economic growth.

(2) Credit market system building is the basis for all financial system innovations. An effective credit market system can rationally mobilize and regulate the flow of social funds and move the surplus funds of some sectors to those where funds are needed. It is a regulator in the circulation of social funds. By creating financial assets, an effective credit market system can effectively integrate scattered credit behaviors, such as savings behaviors and investment behaviors. This can both elevate the overall levels of social savings and investments and effectively distribute savings among various investment opportunities so as to promote the development of the whole social production and form an effect of induced economic growth. In this sense, the credit market system is the basis for all economic systems. If system innovation can push forward sustained economic growth, credit market system building is the source of the primary drivers for economic growth. The higher the level of credit development is, the stronger the impetus for economic growth will bc. Effcctive credit market system building can promote economic growth, and sustained credit market system building is the basis for all system innovations.

(3) An advanced credit market system is a guarantee for sustained, healthy, and rapid economic and social development. We should affirm the roles of capital, labor, and technology as they advance economic growth, but from the perspective of capital, labor, and technology alone, they cannot eliminate all obstacles to economic growth or automatically provide an appropriate environment for them to fully play their roles. Only system changes can eliminate some non-technical obstacles to economic growth and can fully

release the energy of capital, labor, and technology, because systems are the concrete forms of the relations of production. As a superstructure, the relations of production restrain the basic factors of the economic base. An advanced credit market system represents an advanced relation of production and therefore is an important driver in economic and social development.

The model of economic growth developed by us is a model established by incorporating the credit market system as a factor of economic growth into economic analysis. Compared with the neo-classical model, this model has the following unique features: (1) It retains the exposition of the neo-classical model that three factors determine economic growth. (2) It explains the stimulus role of system changes to economic growth. (3) It explains that system development is both a result of credit capital, human capital, technology advance, and economic growth, and also an inherent need and driver of economic growth. (4) A country can better ensure its rapid economic growth as long as it establishes a fairly developed credit market system in keeping with its national conditions. Incorporating a credit market system as a factor for economic growth into economic analysis and establishing a related model can reveal the relations between credit system development and long-term economic growth and can reveal the roles of market systems neglected by traditional economists. This model indicates that "efficiency" is the key factor that determines the level and speed of economic growth. Among the diverse "efficiency"-impacting factors, the "efficiency of the credit market system" is the central one. The practical experience of reform and opening up indicates that system development is a fundamental development and effective systems can promote economic growth and development. Conversely, ineffective systems can contain and even impede economic growth. This conclusion is tenable, inherently logical, highly compatible with practical conditions, quantifiable, and real.

Development-oriented finance has a profound practical understanding of the above basic conclusions. Financing promotes credit market system building and plays an important role in ensuring that other factors of production efficiently play their full roles in improving the Chinese-style socialist system and in promoting sustainable, healthy, and rapid economic and social development. In this respect, we have many case studies[5] but we do not elaborate on them here for the sake of tightening our theoretical thinking. What we must emphasize here is that the model of economic growth introduced by development finance comes from practice, is used in practice, focuses on solving practical issues, and therefore has a solid practical foundation.

7.4. Theoretical analysis and discussions

The fact that system is the fourth driver does not mean its importance ranks fourth. As there has been sufficient research conducted on the impacts of the three factors of capital, labor, and technology on economic development, we now introduce system as a new factor for economic development and focus our research on it. In our model of this fourth driver to growth, we place system on top of all other three factors for special considerations. As a developing country, we need capital, labor, and advanced technology but, more importantly, we need a sound and developed credit market system. The state of the credit market system reflects the development level, the development environment, and the development conditions of a country or a region. Nearly, all developed economies are in countries that have fairly sound credit market systems. China is now in the preliminary stage of a socialist market economy, and is badly in need of the support of a sound, uniform credit market system. It is unimaginable that a country with an outdated credit market system would experience a very smooth economic transition in the course of its economic development. In a credit-based modern economy, credit activity reflects social activity in a value-based form. It is also the most important feature of financial activities and, by deduction, the foundation for social harmony and development. Therefore, we regard the credit market system as the central part of the Chinese market

[5] China Development Bank/China Renmin University joint research group: Typical Cases of Development Finance [M], China Renmin University Press, 2007.

system, and the issue of system naturally becomes the primary one for a four-dimensional analysis. The traditional (or Western) development economics and its development policies are based on the premise of the current and effective (not necessarily highly effective) market system of one country. This premise does not exist in most countries. Chinese experience lies in how to establish and cultivate this system during the course of continuing economic and social development. The core of this system is the credit market system, especially the one across geographical and kindred networks. Our practice of development finance has formed successful examples in financing and promoting credit market system.

For example, the concept of "degree of credit development" (or credit in short) was introduced and used by CDB fairly early in its practice of development finance and has been expanded to become a complete set of methods and indicators for evaluating credit market development. Credit means the degree of credit market development in a region. The method is to evaluate the state of the customer's credit development and grade its credit development on the basis of investigation, research, and integrated analysis and by combining qualitative analysis with quantitative analysis in five aspects: (1) the credit concept and legal awareness of the customer, (2) the structure of its corporate governance, (3) the quality of its credit structure, (4) the prospect of its credit development, and (5) the diversification of its financing. In practice, credit can be divided into many grades and each grade has a linear functional relation with the efficiency of capital investment and use. Here, according to the state of credit development on the market, we preliminarily divide credit development into five types, namely (i) enlightenment, (ii) take-off, (iii) building, (iv) shaping, and (v) maturity, and further divide them into 12 grades, namely enlightenment into the grades of C and BB; take-off into the grades of BBB–, BBB, and BBB+; building into the grades of A–, A, and A+; shaping into AA–, AA, and AA+; and maturity into the grade of AAA. Their general features are described in Table 7.1.

The preliminary grading of credit development indicates that credit building proceeds in stages, is a process of dynamic development, and can show a leapfrog growth. In different stages of the

Table7.1: Credit development grading.

Grading		Basic contents
Enlightenment	C BB	Being influenced by concept of fiscal financing and being in a state of spontaneous creation of credit building; being unaware credit is wealth, and possessing no such credit.
Take-off	BBB– BBB BBB+	Beginning to have preliminary (passive) understanding of credit building due to external restraint and pressure or due to influence of publicity and promotion of development finance; having no firm direction and being likely to breach contract whenever there is opportunity; believing credit is only a very small wealth component and its value is not worth the effort necessary to increase it.
Building	A– A A+	Having deeper understanding of credit building; knowing credit can become wealth; being actively involved in creating value through credit; having active demand for credit building; making substantial progress in building credit structure and in accepting market supervision, information disclosure, and external audit; having very clear direction; still lacking a sound credit structure.
Shaping	AA– AA AA+	Having credit structure basically in shape; knowing value of its own credit; beginning to protect its value and utilize this asset; recognizing and introducing diverse external forces for credit protection and supervision.
Maturity	AAA	Having credit structure in conformity with new requirements of investment and financing systems; being fully aware of its own credit value; doing all it can to protect and utilize this asset; pursuing financing diversification; gradually turning to commercial banks for short-term loans and to capital market for financing; gradually reducing demand for loans from development finance.

maturing of financial markets, credit market systems building shows the greatest diversity of any sector. Credit market building is not a spontaneous process that cannot be pushed forward. Instead, it is a development process in which we can pursue growth and even leapfrog growth with our social efforts and which does not require several hundred years to repeat the tortuous road of credit building under the capitalist system. Through organized and active pushing, we can move from unconsciousness to consciousness and from unease to ease and develop credit from scratch and lay a foundation for the market economy, monetary economy, and virtual economy. We can build and utilize the indicators of credit market development evaluation as an important tool and measure to push forward credit building. The evaluating indicators should emphasize the forecast for upgrading the degree of customer credit development and the establishment of upgrading marks and completion timetables so as to promote credit market system building. The objects of evaluation are the regional governments, industrial authorities or associations, and enterprises. All customers wishing to enter the new investment and financing system and to enhance their credit awareness can become the objects of credit market development evaluation. The time-points of evaluation include the processes of project development, evaluation, loan release, and principal and interest recovery. In other words, credit market development evaluation should run through the whole banking process, which in turn is also a process of credit market building. Therefore, the evaluating indicators not only reflect the credit development process of an object of evaluation but also examine the results of development finance's push toward credit market system building. While we evaluate the current credit development of a customer, we may also make semiannual, annual, biannual, and five-year upgrading forecasts for the customer, specify the timetable for completing the marker events of future upgrading, and make judgments on the long- and medium-term trends of its credit development.

The above analysis indicates that the model of the fourth driver for economic development introduced by development-oriented finance and the related theory of credit market development can produce the following conclusions: the degree of a region's credit market development is closely related to the level of its economic development; a region with higher credit also has a higher development level of its market economy; elevating the degree of credit development can promote the steady and fairly fast development of a market economy; and credit market development runs through the whole process of economic operation. At present, China's integrated economic and social development fails to receive the required financing support. It is especially so with the countryside, agriculture, and peasants, the small and medium-sized enterprises, the development of the western regions, the rejuvenation of the northeast and other old industrial bases, and the county-level economies. This state of affairs can be attributed to the degree of credit market development and to the separation of the demand for economic and social development from the development of finance.

7.5. Practical factors of the fourth driver theory

The practical factors of the fourth driver theory are the factors that restrain the development of the credit market system. In other parts of the theory of development finance, we analyzed the root causes of the slow development of China's credit system from the following four perspectives of society, law, culture, and mechanism:

(1) The traditional social structure and management system have weakened the country's foundation for acceptance and appreciation of modern financial credit.
(2) The unsound laws and regulations have caused a high cost of good faith, a low cost of bad faith, and an insufficient inherent impetus for China's modern credit system building.
(3) China's failure to develop its outstanding traditional culture, including religious practices, has caused the lack of an indispensable lubricant for China's modern credit system building.
(4) The lack of effective linking mechanisms between China's traditional culture and modern financial systems has caused the lack of effective regulation over China's modern credit system building. Instead of elaborating on the above factors, we want to further analyze the economic factors impacting the credit market system.

These following factors include the level of a region's economic development, the degree of its marketization, the level of its urbanization, the level of its informatization, and the level of its corporate development.

(1) A region with a more developed economy will have more credit activities and will find it easier to obtain credit. Therefore, the level of a region's economic development is generally a typical indicator of the region's credit environment. Likewise, the level of a region's credit development is highly correlated to the level of its economic development. The Maslow Hierarchy of Needs holds that after their physiological needs are met, human beings will pursue the needs of respect and self-actualization and place more emphasis on reputation and other social attributes and, as a result, the regional economic environment also becomes more creditworthy. At the same time, a fine credit environment can promote economic development as it leverages capital. The two supplement and promote each other. Research indicates that when the per capita GDP ranges between 300 and 500 dollars (US dollars, real, per annum), credit is regarded as non-essential; when the per capita GDP ranges between 500 and 1,000 dollars, credit in general is recklessly damaged; when the per capita GDP ranges between 1,000 and 3,000 dollars, the credit market receives growing attention and develops; when the per capita GDP ranges between 3,000 and 5,000 dollars, credit is in stage of reorganization; and when the per capita GDP exceeds 5,000 dollars, credit enters a stage where its virtue is generally appreciated. China's per capita GDP has long exceeded 1,000 dollars and is now close to 3,000 dollars, and this is precisely a crucial period for credit market system building. Improving the credit market system in a major way is vitally important to China's sustained and sustainable development in the 21st century. Under the guidance of the fourth driver theory, we can build a complete set of credit market evaluation indicators and use this system to evaluate, promote, and guide market system building in various regions.

(2) The higher the level of economic development in an area operating under a market economy, the higher the degree of

marketization will be and the more developed the transactions will become. According to repeated game theory, when transactions occur frequently, transaction participants will rationally choose credit in pursuit of long-term interests. Adam Smith discovered that the Dutchmen in the 16th century were more creditworthy than Englishmen, which could be attributed to the relatively more developed commercial economy in the Netherlands at that time. Our studies indicate that in a region where the degree of credit market development is relatively low (at 10%), a 1% growth in the degree of marketization will increase the region's credit by 5% and further improve the region's investment efficiency. Compared with China's east region, the market system in the west region is relatively backward. While the west region's efficiency coefficient of investment in fixed assets is 0.301, the east region's is 0.365, with the former being 17.8% lower than the latter. Therefore, the acceleration of credit market system building is very important to improving the driving effect of investment.

(3) The level of urbanization impacts the regional economy and in turn the credit environment through economic operation. The higher a region's level of urbanization is, the better the expected credit environment will be. Famous urban planning scientists Lewis Mumford and Ebenezer Howard use the theory of magnetism to analogize the convergence and radiation functions of cities. Like a huge magnetic field, a city can attract various factors from the surrounding areas, converge large amounts of resources and credit, produce productive forces through economic activities, radiate to the surrounding areas, and spur the economic development in the radiated areas. The next three decades will see China's second wave of urban development and urbanization, and also a tide of credit market system building. Combining the two together and planning them in a unified way can help China achieve a leapfrog development.

(4) A higher level of informatization can increase the frequency of information exchange, make information more open and comprehensive, and increase the rate of success of credit activities. This will help promote the development of a market economy. A

fine information environment can undoubtedly give a great boost to the whole credit environment. One of the basic hypotheses of today's Western economics is that information is generally full and complete and its acquisition cost is zero, but this friction-free state is basically untenable in reality. Information incompleteness and asymmetry exist in various economic activities. Information asymmetry can trigger opposite selections and moral risks and cause a gross absence of credit. In commodity transactions, sellers hide quality, price, and other information in order to reap extra earnings, and the imitation of such behavior by other sellers will trigger a phenomenon of "inferior goods driving out superior goods". In order to offset the risks arising from information asymmetry in credit markets, banks can likewise drive out "superior" borrowers by unwisely choosing to increase their interest rates. Therefore, drastically raising the level of informatization can effectively promote credit market system building and accelerate economic development.

(5) The level of corporate development is related to corporate credit systems. In a credit-based modern market economy, an enterprise's credit-based activities are increasingly frequent, subject to change, and with ever-increasing transaction size. Corporate credit systems are an important component of modern credit systems. Enterprise credit behaviors are mainly manifested in their external credit relations with their customers, other enterprises, banks, and other lending institutions, in their internal credit relations with their employees, and in their credit relations with government and other public institutions. Governments, banks, and enterprises are all key players in regional economic development, and the credit behaviors between them also constitute an important component of the regional credit environment. If an enterprise is larger in scale and stronger in competitiveness, it is more trustworthy. State-owned enterprises often represent government credit, and the degree of development of private enterprises truly reflects the degree of development of social credit. The entry of foreign-invested enterprises represents the affirmation of the credit environment by international organizations pursuing profit

maximization. We should continue to tap into the strengths of state-owned enterprises, actively promote private enterprise development, and encourage foreign-invested enterprises to enter China. These are all positive steps to credit system building.

Economic analyses clearly indicate the following two points:

(1) The credit market system is the foundation for the development of a nation's market economy and is of continuing overall and fundamental significance to the system of a market economy. Credit building represents the highest grade of system building, and is a key factor to the development of the market economy. Actively building and improving a more transparent credit market system constitutes an important driver for long-term economic development. The fact that developed countries are advanced is, to a very large extent, due to their advanced systems. The success of the United States is, to a very large extent, due to the success of its market building. As China is a developing economy, a developing market and a developing systems builder, its task in system building is quite tedious. Accelerating system building is the only option for a developing country like China to pursue better, faster, and sustainable development. In the wave of economic globalization, failing to accelerate system building can seriously impede the internal building of a well-off society in a comprehensive way and expose China's overall competitiveness, national competitiveness, state security, economic security, and financial security to further external threats.

(2) The market system building cannot rely entirely on spontaneous market evolution. The formation of developed market systems in the West has undergone a very long process mostly through spontaneous evolution and sometimes through governmental intervention. China cannot imitate the old track of mainly depending on spontaneous evolution of Western countries, because fierce international competition allows no time for a "free" evolution and rejuvenation of China's market mechanism and because China lacks the financial resources to bear the huge

cost of natural evolution. China should fully tap its latecomer advantage and rely on the joint efforts of the party and youth league organizations, governments, financial institutions, enterprises, and the general public to accelerate market system building through conscious and active market cultivation. Governments are of a social and public nature, their behaviors are governed by public interests, and their impacts are far-reaching and complex. The credit behaviors of governments can be classified into two categories, leader and participator. As systems leaders, governments can play a leading role in building social credit management system. As the participator, governments can practice the credit system. When governments have credit, society will have credit too. However, a government-led credit market system is different from the credit market system built according to the inherent law of market development, and can harbor and accumulate overall risks. This is mainly because overall risks are often closely linked with the government-involved social, political, and economic policy factors. For this reason, governments should avoid excessive direct participation and intervention in credit markets. In this instance, development-oriented finance can play a very important role. Development-oriented finance, based on national credit and backed by market performance, combines government strength in organization and coordination with its own financing strength. Through financing, it can mobilize various social forces for joint credit building, system building, and market building, and can achieve the development goals of governments by way of market building. Through market building, development-oriented finance can penetrate capital, advanced concepts, and management expertise into each and every capillary of the society and economy, and promote the building of the financing system, the risk control system, the healthy operating system, and the coordination and cooperation system that cover the whole society. Accordingly, it can dramatically amplify economic efficiency and growth and play a unique role in pursuing economic and social development and financial stability.

7.6 Summary

This chapter analyzes the important role and the characteristics of market credit system building, and establishes the analytical model of how the market credit system building promotes economic growth (Figure 7.3).

In addition to the three major driving forces of capital, labor, and technology proposed by Western Economics, developing countries have the fourth driving force for economic growth — market credit system building, which can improve the **total factor productivity**, and form a latecomer advantage. The process of developing market credit system is in fact a process of nurturing the market entities and deepening human capitals, so there is every reason to take market credit system building as the endogenous growth force for economic development. To accelerate the building of market credit system, it is essential for the government to employ its organizational advantage and for development-oriented finance to play an

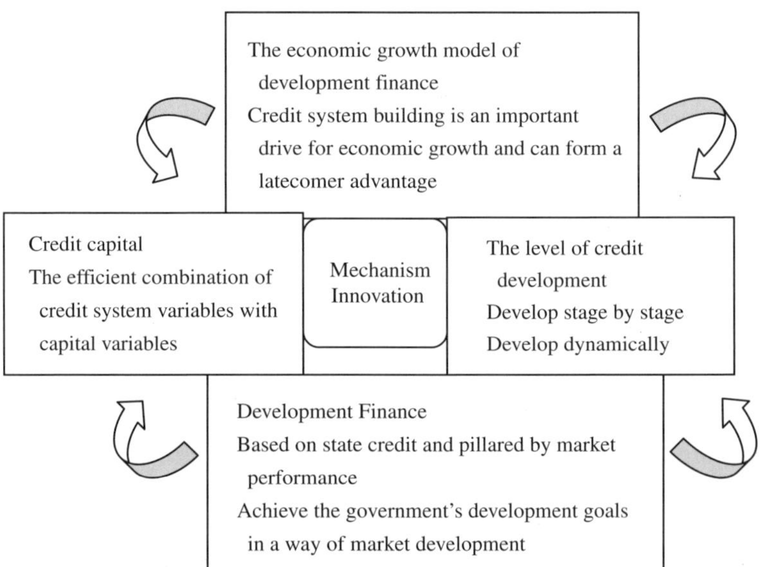

Figure 7.3: Market credit system building is an important drive for economic growth.

active role. This is because the government has a great number of resources in modern society and has an enormous influence. Development-oriented finance is a special force of the government based on macroeconomic objectives and is aimed to address the practical problems of backward institutions and market failures, promote market credit system building, safeguard national financial security, and enhance economic competitiveness. As the study on development-oriented finance is still in its infancy, only after several rounds of test, modification, and supplement and through collective efforts can it improve and provide reference for the sustainable economic and social development.

Chapter 8

Organizational Credit Enhancement Accelerates the Construction of Market Credit System

The development-oriented finance theories aim to reveal the relationship between functioning of the government's organizational advantages and the medium- to long-term development, expound the rules of interconversion between the government forces and the market forces, and accelerate market construction and economic development. Herein, organizational credit enhancement refers to the mechanism where financial institutions capitalize on the state credit and utilize the organizational advantages and the political advantages of the country and of the governments at all levels to make up the market defects through construction of system, mechanism, and rules, in order to guide and regulate the market behaviors and enhance the credit awareness and the credit competence of market entities. The essential of organizational credit enhancement is to construct and upgrade the imperfect financial market. In an imperfect financial market, the irrationality of market players and the asymmetry of market information will generally lead to the failure of financial market and thus increase the risks. Development-oriented finance brings the government's organizational advantages into play in an imperfect financial market, creatively constructs a financing mechanism that is in line with the practical situation of China, and functions under coordination of the governments, boosts the credit system construction, successfully meets the financing demands of urban infrastructure construction, major projects, and hot issues, and accelerates construction of the "infrastructure, fundamental industries, and pillar industries" and the development of livelihood finance.

8.1 Relationship between the market and the government

Since the formation of theories of classical economics in mid-1700s, numerous economists have been devoted to studying the inherent relationships and operational rules of modern economic development, of which the most important theme is the relationship between the market and the government. Is it necessary to bring the government's role into play in the modern market economy? Is the market omnipotent? The theorists and the academics have always been haggling on these questions. Adam Smith emphasized that the market is an "invisible hand" and wished to promote the economic development through free competition and free trade. The successors represented by Alfred Marshall further improved the economic liberalism theory of Adam Smith and came up with the neoclassical economics, believing that the liberal market economy is an engine that can automatically adjust itself to resolve all kinds of conflicts. The economic crisis in the 1930s not only heavily hit the capitalist economies but also proved that the economy could not spontaneously strike the balance. The government intervention theory of Keynes emerged in such a background and has guided the governments to step up their macroeconomic management to a certain extent. The technical analysis means of it, for instance, the analysis of marginal return on capital, were proven very useful. However, Keynes failed to put forward the concrete transmission route and mechanism. Between the 1950s and 1960s, the Keynesian economics was split into two parts: (i) the leftists, represented by Robinson, isolated the neoclassical economies completely from the Keynesian economics and established the Cambridge school, trying to solve the problem through distribution and (ii) the rightists, represented by Samuelson, combined the government's interventions with the market and the macroeconomy with microeconomy and established the neoclassical synthesis. The latter is of greater reference significance to our studies. The theory of structure of the development economics developed by Lewis became the theoretical foundation for the planned economy in the 1960s, which boosted the development of some national industries but ignored the agriculture, the disadvantaged groups, and the market function.

In the 1970s, Mckinnon put forth the issues of financial repression and financial deepening and profoundly explained the role of finance, foreign trade, and fiscal policies. But Mckinnon did not answer how to design the financial development mechanism of developing countries. In developing countries, the functioning of the government should rely on a relatively sound intermediary transmission mechanism and should have the credit system construction and development placed on a very important position. Transition economics takes system as an endogenous variable of the economy and provides certain theoretical support for our reiteration of stepping up the credit system construction. The social cost theory of Coase lends some technical support for our innovation of the mixed financing model. By reviewing the economic theories, we find that there is certain theoretical foundation for the government to act and play functions in the market. To this end, we will analyze the characteristics of interconversion between the government forces and market forces in line with the situations of developing countries, especially the practical situation of China and development-oriented finance practices, in a bid to provide theoretical basis for the correct exercise of the government's and the market's roles.

8.2 Transformation of the government's functions

The government's role in a market correlates closely with the economic development levels and the transformation of the government's functions. To play its role, the government must determine its functions that are adjusted with the changes in development environment. In the early period of capitalism, the rapid growth of the economy was mainly driven by market forces. However, market forces could not help maintain the national security and stability, which created opportunities for the government to extend its functions in certain special periods and under special conditions. From experiences during the two world wars, people gradually became aware of the government's high efficiency in collecting social resources to respond to emergent events. In wartime, the supply of military materials and the conscription of defense forces could not be carried out in accordance with the market rules in general. Under such circumstances, the government was generally more efficient than the market, and especially, people became to accept that the government outstripped its function limits in the emergent conditions. This paved a foundation at the level of social psychology and political culture for the re-extension of the government's functions. When the economic crisis broke out in the 1930s, the Roosevelt administration's intervention into the market did not encounter excessive objections and contravene. After the crisis was successfully overcame, correction of the market failure became a major reason to extend the government's functions in the peacetime. Wars and economic crisis changed the relationship between the government and the market, as well as the people's views on government intervention, thus creating opportunities for the further expansion of the government's functions. After World War II, the governments of western countries not only helped maintain the market order in the economic activities in the capacity of market monitor but also adopted active behaviors to redress the market defects and change the market conditions. This indicates that western governments have developed from a "night-watch government" to an "active government". The governments of developing countries and socialist countries generally pursued the strategies of catching up with and surpassing developed countries and were accustomed to use the centralized planning method to strengthen the foundation of national economy. In the course of economic development, the governments not only served as the "navigator" but also directly organized and participated in the national economic activities. In this way, governments of the developing countries and socialist countries became a "proactive government", thus exerting functions on almost all of the economic and living aspects. The excessive intervention and the excessive arrangement by the "active government" had led the government's role to the opposite side. After 1970s and 1980s, with the transition of planned economy toward market economy, the government's functions were largely slashed and the construction of an effective government became an important orientation for the government reform.

It is the international convention practice to bring into play the government's important role in market and system construction and implement organizational credit enhancement. Even in the developed countries, the government will directly invest and incorporate development-oriented financial institute to realize the connection between bank loans and the capital market and redress the structural deficiencies in the market and system building as well as the market failure and system defects in certain fields. In 1930s, in response to the credit crisis in the US mortgage loan market, the credit imbalance, and different interest rates between regions and the unstable market and in order to eliminate the market defects and realize the social development objective of "house for everybody", the US government started with the market construction and established a number of policy financial institutions such as Fannie Mae (Federal National Mortgage Association) and the subsequent Freddie Mac (Federal Home Loan Mortgage Corp). As intermediaries between the government and the market, these institutions were responsible for creating the secondary market for housing mortgage loans. In order to quicken the market construction, the government capitalized on organizational credit enhancement and granted these organizations with many preferential policies such as the invisible debt guarantee, tax relief, credit limit provided by the US Department of The Treasury, classification of securities into low-risk asset class and other business privileges in order to support these institutions that were operating on the market terms. Fannie Mae and Freddie Mac achieved remarkable results in the construction of the secondary mortgage loan market, continuously eliminated the market defects, evidently raised the housing ownership rate, and successfully attained the government's objectives. The market forces were transformed into the government forces and the government was able to play a more active part in the macro-control. In 1990s, the return on equity (ROE) of these two institutions reached more than 20%, far above the returns of insurance companies, commercial banks, and savings institutions. Development paths of the Federal National Mortgage Association and Federal Home Loan Mortgage Corp reflect the philosophy and methods that the government builds market through institutions and the market development boosts the improvement of institutions. Airbus is another typical example of the organizational credit enhancement. In order to cope with the monopolization of US Boeing and to redress the market failure, Airbus was established as a united non-enterprise legal person entity by the then Aerospatiale of France, Deutsche Aerospace, British Aerospace Corporation, and the Chinese Association of Shipping Agencies with supports of the French, German, British, and Spanish governments. Airbus integrated the government's financial strength, scientific research, development, and production of all its member countries into the same institution, replaced the management of assets and liabilities for government coordination and government commitments through cross-national organizational credit enhancement, and realized the conversion between the government entry and the market exit. It was developed into an independent enterprise in 2001 and was listed on the stock market later on. This is a process where multiple countries brought the government's organizational advantages into play in cooperation and promoted the project gradually to the market. It is also a process that the government actively built the market, system, and credit to make up the system deficiencies and accomplished dual success in the project construction and system building. The government made use of the organizational credit enhancement to promote leapfrog development of the market and exercised the government's functions in the new stage of social and economic development. In this process, the government's functions are reflected as coordination, promotion, and service, and the government gradually changed into a service government (Table 8.1).

Along with the development of society and economy, the government's functions gradually develop from a "night-watch government" to an "active government", and then to a "proactive government" and a "service government". The government's functions evolve from emphasis primarily on external guarantee to the internal coordination and social services, and there appears a trend that the government's functions gradually change from small to medium and then to a proactive government. The small functions emphasize on the provision of pure public goods: national defense, laws, property rights macroeconomic management, and basic medical care; the medium functions

Table 8.1: Types of the government's functions.

Type	Function	Characteristic
Night-watch government	*Small functions*: to maintain the market order and serve as the market monitor.	Market economy
Active government	*Medium functions*: to actively overcome the market defects and change the market structure.	Mixed economy
Proactive government	*Comprehensive functions*: covering all aspects.	Planned economy
Service government	*Proactive functions*: coordination, promotion, allocation, re-distribution, and public service.	Knowledge and public economy

further emphasize on the provision of elementary education service, environmental protection, regulation of the monopolistic enterprises, and overcome of incomplete information in addition to the scope of small functions; the scope of proactive functions extends further on the basis of small and medium functions, and pays particular attention to the coordination, promotion, allocation, re-distribution, public service, protection of the disadvantaged, and promotion of social impartiality. This type of transformation in the government's functions refers to the transformation of the governmental organization's philosophy, structure, system, functions, and methods from one type to another. It is a process that the government adapts to the social environment so as to maintain balance through the systematic reform in order to meet the demand of political, economic, and social development. Transformation of the government does not refer to the simple revision of the existing government administration mechanism; neither does it refer to the general adjustment of the government's functions. Instead, it is the establishment of a modern government mode through systematic improvement to fit in the economic transformation and social transformation. The transformation of the government's functions is a continual process, and as long as the economic and social development demands, this process will never stop. The fundamental reasons behind it include: (i) the administrative functions of the government, as the superstructure, need to adapt to and benefit the social and economic development and (ii) improper administrative functions will generally cause disharmony to the government's work, primarily reflected in the poor applicability of the rules and systems formulated by the government which cannot meet the demand of social activities and social development.

Public affairs management is an important function of the government in the new century. In the 21st century, the international economic order is undergoing profound changes and the world economic pattern is experiencing significant adjustments along with the accelerated development of the economic globalization. The governments are all re-examining their role and position in the economic development. In spite of the large difference in development level and development environment, there is a common view in the international community that the government must perform the important functions and correctly play its role in the economic and social development. An important function of the government is to manage public affairs, including the economic regulation, market supervision, social management, and public service. This function is reflected as a special public power.[1] In the new century, the public power of a country's government shall have the capability (1) to exercise macro-control, i.e., to maintain the macroeconomic stability; (2) to build market rules and maintain the economic orders; (3) to coordinate the social distribution and organize the social guarantee; and (4) to strengthen the international cooperation and jointly respond to the global issues. The government's work in the 21st century should be strategic, scientific, sustainable, and accountable; and the government in the 21st century shall serve as the advocator, planner, guide, public service worker, and judicator.

The government shall first serve as the advocator of the scientific approach to economic and social development, introduce the social cost concept to its work and the administrative management process, strengthen the education and publicity on social cost and social

[1] The *Selected Works of K. Marx and F. Engels*, Vol. 4, published by the People's Publishing House in 1995, P94.

benefit, enhance the government staff's awareness of social cost and their consciousness of responsibility, reinforce the awareness of social cost management, and strive to reduce the social cost.

The government shall serve as a planner for the social and economic development. Before exercising the economic intervention functions, the government shall carry out budgetary analysis in advance on the intervention behavior pursuant to the cost-benefit principles. Only when the benefits derived from interventions exceed the cost, the government's intervention is efficient, and the behavior to reduce social cost is feasible.

The government shall serve as a guide and actively point out the directions. Through formulation and implementation of the laws, regulations, policy documents, and development plans, the government shall guide and regulate the behaviors of various entities, reduce the social cost, promote the comprehensive advancement of society and economy, and boost the substantial improvement of social welfare.

The government shall serve as a servant of public affairs, utilize its legislative power, judicial power, and executive power to actively provide public service and assistance for the social development.

The government shall serve as a judicator in the social and economic activities, define the boundary of rights of various economic organizations and individuals as well as the boundary of property rights on natural resources, gradually improve the definition of power boundary, transfer the external burden into internal cost, and effectively control the social cost.

As proven from the experiences and trend of transformation of governments worldwide, the public service function of the government is still developing and has become the core function. The core of the government transformation is to properly deal with the relationship between the market and the government, effectively overcome the government's and the market's respective inherent defects, bring into play their irreplaceable functions, and realize the favorable interaction between functions of the government and the market. This is the fundamental prerequisite and the system foundation of the modern public service system.

8.3 Transformation of the Chinese government

In the 21st century, China faces the following two major tasks.

(1) To accomplish the structural transformation from an agricultural economy to an industrial economy, i.e., the transformation from the primary industry to the secondary and tertiary industries, from the medium/low end of the secondary industry to the high end, from the secondary industry to the tertiary industry, and from the low end of the tertiary industry to the high end. Simply speaking, it refers to industrialization and urbanization, which is very hard to be attained.
(2) To accomplish the system transformation, i.e., the transformation from planned economy to market economy, and build a relatively advanced socialist market economic system with Chinese characteristics. This is also an arduous task.

The dual tasks put forth special requirements on the government's functions as follows:

(1) *The function of development strategy planning*. The government needs to formulate the development strategies and policies on industrialized development, such as the agricultural development, the population migration, and urbanization.

(2) *The function of market system reform*. The government is the designer and dominator of the market system reform, and only by exercising the government's organizational advantages, can we speed up the pace of market system construction.

(3) *The macro-control function*. The Chinese government adopts much greater macro-control efforts relative to other countries due to the huge urban–rural difference and regional difference; and the government needs to properly carry out the macro-control and create an impartial, competitive, and orderly market environment.

(4) *The social function*. The government assumes more responsibility on the protection of ecological environment, narrowing of the income gap between the rich and the poor, protection of the disadvantaged groups, and provision of public goods.

(5) As a developing country, as the role and influence of the Chinese government in the international community enhances, the Chinese government's responsibility will also increase.

It should be noted that the prevailing market system of China is still not complete and efforts should be extended to cultivate more growth points and boost development of the economic entities. The Chinese government should unleash the advantages in organization and coordination, properly build and cultivate the market, and boost the development of market economy. First, the Chinese government needs to weaken the functions of microeconomic management, and strengthen the functions of macro-control. China adopts a progressive method to accomplish the transformation from a planned economy to a market economy. Given that it is still in the primary stage of transformation, the Chinese government's functions still bear many features of the planned economy. This is primarily reflected in the following: the government pays excessive attention to the detailed construction projects; and the government fails to perform the due functions in time, which leads to unreasonable allocation of resources. This is inconsistent with the general pattern of macroeconomic management. The government needs to further clarify its functions. In addition, it should transfer those matters to the market and the microeconomic entities that can be effectively handled by them. Second, the government needs to accelerate the building of systems to support the economic development. Institutional arrangement is a kind of public goods, and the supply of systems should be a fundamental function of the government. Governments at all levels should further improve and develop the characteristic medium/long-term strategic plans, formulate corresponding rules and systems, create a benign economic environment, guide, and protect the healthy development of society and economy. Third, the government needs to further unleash its organizational advantages, and step up the guidance to, supervision over, and cultivation of various industry organizations and economic entities. A successful market economy is bound to be backed by a batch of successful industry associations and economic organizations, and these industry associations and economic organizations may serve as an important "bridge" between the market and the enterprises, enterprises and other enterprises, and the enterprises and the governments. Fourth, the government should bring into play its unique credit advantages and actively support the building of market credit system. A basic characteristic of the government credit is transparency, impartiality, and justice. The transparent government administration is an important component of the government credit, and the acceptance of supervision and audit from the People's Congress is a symbol that the government administration comes under the external supervision, a basis for the open and transparent administration of the government, and a basis for development-oriented finance to extend cooperation with the government on financial affairs and credit. The government credit plays a vital role in improving the enterprise credit, the individual credit, and other social credit, and the improvement of government credit generally means the improvement of overall social credit standing. The role of the government is particularly important, especially in the context of a still imperfect individual credit, enterprise credit, and social credit system in China.

The transformation of the Chinese government is the inherent requirement of social and economic development and it is rooted from the objective rules of social and historical development. Since its opening up and reform, the Chinese government has undergone two revolutionary transformations with the economic transition and social transformation: (1) it has successfully accomplished the transformation from a political leadership government before the opening up and reform to an economic construction government and (2) it has successfully accomplished the transformation from an economic construction government in the market growth period to a public service government in the market maturity period. These transformations produced certain achievements, because the government gave up direct pursuit of efficiency by handing the efficiency mechanism to the market, and shifted the focuses of its work to the improvement of market environment and protection of fair competition, rather than because the government instated on the "efficiency" principles. In this sense, it should be the fundamental value orientation of the market deepening and the government transformation that the market creates efficiency and the government guarantees fairness and justice.

Compared with the government transformation of countries implementing the market economy system, the transformation of the Chinese government follows different paths in terms of the starting point and the direction of transformation, although there is commonality on adjustment of the relationship between the government and the market. Transformation of countries with a market economy has high starting points that also emphasizes on the comprehensive functions, thus showing strong elasticity. The functional transformation of Chinese government, however, has a lower starting point, pays much attention to the management by industry, and is prone to "distort the market due to excessive adjustment". In certain circumstances, the government has overstated the market's role. Over the past 30 years, China was exposed to the imbalanced and inharmonious economic and social development, although it has created an "economic miracle". The emergence and development of many imbalance issues are, in essence, closely related to the social and economic development strategies formulated by the government, the guidelines and policies, the government's administration methods and administration measures in different stages, and are directly related to or even determined by the government's macroeconomic control capability and public administration capability. The prominent conflicts and problems in the economic society all have direct or indirect relationship with the government's reform. Only by correctly dealing with the issue of government transformation in the new stage, can China realize the benign interaction between government transformation and the transformation of economy and society. China is experiencing the economic and social transformations driven by economic system reform, and the transformation of economy and society will cause profound changes to the social structure and people's life and will decide whether our national revitalization and our modernization undertaking will be successfully accomplished.

Looking back to the past 30 years since the opening up and reform, China has been promoting the reform in the first 15 years and transformation in the last 15 years. In the first decade, the government has been promoting the reform in a top-down manner; while after 1994, China has been maintaining development largely on back of the bottom forces. At present, the economic transformation is gradually changing toward the political transformation and the overall transformation of society. The government transformation occupies an important position in the process of overall transformation, and the success of government transformation will inevitably improve the harmonious development of economy, society, and politics. But imbalance issues also occurred to China's transformation. The imbalanced development is caused by the different rhythm of transformation: in some cases, the policies have been transformed, while the related mechanisms have not; or the mechanisms have been transformed, while the laws were not timely revised; or the laws were updated, while the philosophies were not changed in time. In particular, the credit system construction of China was greatly imbalanced, and the backward credit system was not in line with the financing demands arising from the fast development of economy and society. In order to redress the imbalance, the government forces should be aligned with market forces. The Chinese government boasts important advantages in accelerating the credit system construction and promoting the financial market development. Apart from the organizational and political advantages, the Chinese government also enjoys great advantages on resources and policies, including the government credit and the State's financial control measures. The economic and social development of China is reliant on the powerful support of the government.

The government's role may be brought into better play through a transmission mechanism. The government cannot address all kinds of imbalance issues directly and comprehensively, and a modern credit system cannot emerge spontaneously in China as a big developing country. It is necessary to set up an effective intermediary transmission mechanism between the government and the market, i.e., the third kind of force. The government and the market should develop through mutual interactions and mutual promotion; and growth of the government and the market should be driven and promoted by both external and internal forces. The effective functioning of the government is a necessary condition for the sustainable development of the economy and society, and will catalyze and promote the market economy and individual activities and thus upgrade the efficiency and utility of the market. The market, financial institutions, and the public may also energetically boost the economic development and cover many fields that are previously driven by the government. China may utilize and strengthen its resources in this respect, combine such strength with the great energy of national credit to develop the third kind of force, utilize it into the micro systems and the financial infrastructure construction, promote the market building, and realize the government's objectives. In the past, we had been relying completely on the government in social and economic development, and now, we need to combine the government with the market forces and promote the comprehensive, harmonious, and sustainable development of economy through market building. This is unprecedented in the traditional fiscal financing methods. The development of the intermediary transmission mechanism is rooted from the market defects and the government defects. The government defects are shown in many aspects: incomplete or asymmetric information acquired by the policy-makers leads to erroneous decisions; objectives of the public institutions or government officials are primarily for pursuing of the departmental or individual benefits and cannot always represent the public interest; the interest groups influence the government's decision-making through rent-seeking and get indirect productive profits; the government departments abuse their legislative right and the discretionary power; the organizational institutions of the government are unreasonably established and maintain low efficiency; the decision-making, implementation, supervision, feedback, and coordination processes of the government administration mechanism are poorly linked with low efficacy; the assessment of the government's operating efficiency may be distorted and cannot produce incentives on the related organizations; and the long-term "organ culture" prevents the supervision and restriction mechanism from playing their role, etc. The market defects make the government's intervention possible, but the existence of government defects urges people to establish an intermediary transmission mechanism between the market and the government. The intermediary transmission mechanism may effectively overcome the market defects and the government defects, and boost the social advancement and the economic development. Systems and the market will not take shape spontaneously, and their formation needs the efforts of active establishment. The establishment of a developed market economy system in western countries has experienced a process of blindly and long-time evolvement by extremely high costs and considerations. China will neither wait for the spontaneous and natural formation of the market. It needs to and must bring into play the latecomer advantages, integrate the resources of the government, financial institutions, and enterprises to actively build the market, credit, and systems in an efficient and systematic manner, and realize frog-leaping development through voluntary and active building of the credit system.

8.4 Development-oriented finance bridges the gap between the government and the market

It is a strategic route for initiative construction of system and market to exert the government's organizational advantages, strengthen cooperation between the government and the development-oriented finance, and provide necessary organizational credit enhancement to redress the imbalances between the backward credit system and the growing financing demands derived in the process of rapid economic and social development. Organizational credit enhancement is a kind of cooperation means between the development-oriented finance and the government; and under it, both parties prevent risks through joint building of credit system and institutional system. It is also a kind of common sense, joint construction, coordination and cooperation, and an effective form of the exploitation and utilization of government credit. At present, in the process of building the socialist market economy, China can hardly realize the self-optimization of factor portfolios capitalizing on the spontaneous flow and blind collision of various factors. Instead, most of the factor portfolios are optimized leveraging on the government's organizational advantages. Even these portfolios are not the most desirable one, as long as a majority of these portfolios are optimal or sub-optimal solutions, they will represent a remarkable progress in social and economic development and will help China build a more economically efficient market system with a higher starting point and at a faster speed than the western economies. In our economic life, the various project flows, fund flows, expert teams, and risk control networks rely closely on the various organizational systems. This is a unique advantage in China's social system, and proper use of this advantage will produce huge productivity and help promote the social development. Development-oriented finance attempts to seize the major tasks of the government organization, make full use of the existing organizations, and carry out work in line with the government's path. Development-oriented finance takes the national credit as the foundation and the market performance as the support, realizes the government's development objectives through market building, and promotes flow of the social fund and development of other financial institutions through the "road-paving" and "bridging" intermediary transmission mechanism. It helps boost the development and prevent risks, attains the national strategic objectives, and plays an important role in the State's key fields and many of the traditionally backward domains. Development-oriented finance highlights the financing advantages and the government's organizational and coordination advantage, pays special attention to the cooperation with local governments in market construction, and transforms the government's force into the market force through organizational credit enhancement. In market building, an important aspect is to use the market-oriented method to build the credit system. In this process, financing projects of the development-oriented finance regulate and restrict the platform enterprises, integrate the scattered resources and institutions, promote the healthy, harmonious, and overall development with an aim of building healthy fiscal system and sound financial system, thus realize the market building and risk mitigation and promote the market stability and financial asset security. As the extension and development of policy finance, development-oriented finance improves the market and promotes the financial development through "redressing the systems", and provides an efficient financial deepening mechanism in a certain period. On the one hand, development-oriented finance greatly enhances the availability and reliability of financial information and resources through credit building, cultivation of lenders and introduction of government coordination and guarantee, lowers the market information cost and transaction cost, and promotes the improvement of the financial market; on the other hand, development-oriented finance serves as a bridge and a tie between the government and the market in the process of system and market building, and changes the government's macro policies and overall guidelines into feasible plans through certain specific financing system.

The core philosophy of organizational credit enhancement is to establish a risk control mechanism and a credit system so that the party with enhanced credit can effectively prevent risks and minimize losses, thus creating conditions for micro fundamental system building and development of the market. To be specific, it should help the government clarify the ways of credit resource collection, organizational promotion, fiscal subsidy, marginal coverage of the ultimate-guarantor risk, and the credit guarantee fund with government background.

(1) Fiscal resources, as an important part of the government credit, are generally segmented by the various government levels and departments. China needs to collect her fiscal available resources as much as possible and deliver great efforts on centralization of the major resources.
(2) The fiscal subsidy of the government generally sets many different restrictive conditions and has a relatively small scale. Through development-oriented finance, China may put forth the methods on how to establish and build the financing platform entities, gradually shift the limited and scattered resources with restrictive conditions to provide credit support for the platform projects, boost the development, and create conditions for channeling the social resources into related fields in the future.

(3) In view of the scarcity of the government credit resources, it is necessary to include the market cash flow into the construction of public projects and create various reasonable tax mechanisms to realize sustainable and recycling mechanism for public resources input. For the gap between the market fund flow and the actual investment of public projects, the government may cover it in a proper form by promising to provide fiscal subsidy or write-off the loss on the cash flow circulation gap. This will make full use of the leverage effect of the government credit.

(4) Development-oriented finance, through organizing and participating the nationwide re-guarantee system building, includes the credit guarantee fund established by local governments into the scope of cooperation, assists in building an internal organizational structure that is in line with the modern corporate governance standards, actively supports the active involvement of social resources (such as private guarantee), and thus promotes the system design, input of first fund installment, and the building of credit organization and credit culture.

The organizational credit enhancement of the government proposed by development-oriented finance is different from government guarantee. Government guarantee assumes civil responsibilities, while the organizational credit enhancement of government enhances the credit relying on the organizational advantages of the government and the government credit to meet the market demand. There is much operating room for the system building and credit building from the organizational credit enhancement to the assumption of loss by fiscal departments, monetary authorities, and institutions. The risks ultimately assumed by fiscal departments, monetary authorities, and institutions are closely related to the level of system building and credit building, and directly hinge on the level of credit risk control and organizational management. The limited financial strength or risk provision, no matter in the form of finance or an institution's self-owned fund and bad debt provision, tries to assume greater risks through a type of arrangement that is similar to insurance in nature. The arrangement provides merely a final reserve and is not necessarily used. Should the credit building and system building be both relatively complete, the part of loss that is eventually borne by the fiscal departments, monetary authorities, financial institutions, and local government is very low. In this respect, the organizational credit enhancement merely applies the law of large numbers of the insurance compensation. The organizational credit enhancement advocated by development-oriented finance does not require the government to provide guarantee, and its effect and significance may be far more meaningful than the guarantee provided on individual credit business. It helps to enhance the mutual understanding, appreciation, and trust, wins the right of active market development, and achieves the dual success on project construction and system building. The government relies on the financing advantages and market operation capability of development-oriented finance, changes development-oriented finance into a "visible hand" of the government, and thus realizes the government's policy intents. Development-oriented finance, meanwhile, capitalizes on organizational credit enhancement to intensify the risk diversion and expand the support to national infrastructure construction, thus meeting the customers' demand. In other words, development-oriented finance is the government's extension in the market, enhances the "visible hand" function, reflects and realizes the government's purposes and policy intents; and from the market perspective, development-oriented finance expands the scope and efficiency of market resources allocation through market building and improvement, thus making up the "market failure" and avoiding "government failure".

The organizational credit enhancement of the government proposed by development-oriented finance and credit enhancement are credit enhancement activities at different levels. The former primarily offsets the system defects and is an important mechanism that China uses to offset the market defects in the certain economic development stage, strengthen the credit system and risk control capability of the financial crisis in the context of system transformation, extend the government's functions, and strengthen the macro-control in the times of economic system transformation. The latter, however, sets up control measures in response to the various types of credit risks in the process of financing projects, which are primarily in the form of guarantee, security, insurance, cash control mechanism (reserve account or suspension of dividend distribution etc.), standby facilities, letter of credit, and debt upgrade, in a bid to improve the reliability and security of cash flow used to repay debts. Development-oriented finance brings into full play the government's organizational and political advantages through organizational credit enhancement, integrates the political resources, economic resources, and management resources of the government and provides talent, monetary, and materials support tangibly for the project construction as well as the system and rules support intangibly for the credit system building. Besides, organizational credit enhancement also promotes integration of the government's functions from the following four major aspects to boost improvement of the credit system:

(1) It combines the government credit with that of development-oriented financial institute. By combining the credit construction and financing advantages of development-oriented financial institute with the organizational and coordination advantages of the government, it builds a horizontal credit relationship between the various economic entities, shapes a diversified organizational system with complementary functions, and promotes the dissemination of the credit concept between the government officials, governmental departments, banks, enterprises, and individuals.
(2) It integrates the assets. It operates the government's assets and resources on cooperative terms, and authorizes the lender to run the state-owned assets generated from the urban fiscal investment.
(3) It integrates the supervision mechanisms, promotes the establishment of fundamental systems such as strict separation of financial revenue and expense, bid-invitation and tendering, supervision and inspection, and effectively supervises the use of funds.
(4) It integrates the institutions. The government will usually integrate the fiscal department, the planning commission, the urban construction department, planning and land reserve centers in organizing the urban infrastructure project lenders, abide by the sustainable development between urban planning, land reserve,

and urban facility construction, and ensure that the government completes the urban infrastructure construction in a systematic and centralized manner.

In the theoretic framework of development-oriented finance, the government is a necessary link, while banks and governments mutually depend on each other. The organizational credit enhancement by the government is a basic system arrangement for the establishment of a risk control mechanism and a credit system and for the maintenance of financial security and economic safety. In practice, development-oriented financial institute sign cooperation agreements with the local governments to implement organizational credit enhancement, reach the common view on credit, jointly build the legal person platform based on the market terms, and promote the building of governance mechanism, legal person, cash flow, and credit. It should be pointed out specially that development-oriented finance creatively establishes the credit entities under the coordination of the government, and this is an innovation of the financing mechanism. The innovation of legal person construction creates favorable conditions for the building of urban construction financing platforms. From the perspective of development, the financing platform should participate in the planning and the credit system building itself, and should be a management platform with great vitality and organizational advantages in the development-oriented finance practice. At present, the means realized by development-oriented finance include the following: requiring the government to include the loan funds into the fiscal budget, build a credit structure on the basis of government credit, and make use of the government credit in cash flow construction; requiring the People's Congress of corresponding level to approve or confirm that the repayment fund has been listed into the fiscal budget and taking it an important content of the government credit building; and requiring the financing platform construction projects to accept audit and supervision from the people's congress and the public. This is an important part of credit building (Figure 8.1).

Figure 8.1: Organizational credit enhancement.

Development-oriented finance promotes the interconversion between government forces and market forces by building a government-backed credit platform. In the past, the government regarded money of the financial system as money of the fiscal departments and had little understanding of finance. It took a certain period of time before the government gradually improved its understanding of the market. In the first stage, i.e., in the mid/later stage of the "cultural revolution", China mistook the market as capitalism. Later on, it deemed the market as small peddlers and a rural marketplace, emphasized little on the market construction despite requirement to open up the market. It, in fact, refused or did not recognize the difficulty and importance of market building, deemed the market as a small marketplace in the beginning, and wished to "relax the restrictions on" the market later on. This was the second stage. Now, the understanding of the relationship between the government and the market and of the market is further deepened. The public has come to a deeper understanding that the market should be developed through construction, and "relaxing the restrictions on" the market is merely a process in the market construction progress. This is the third stage. During these three stages, development-oriented finance unleashes the government's advantages in organization and coordination, and combines the government and the market with development-oriented finance to transform government forces into market forces. In the fourth stage, market forces will be changed into government forces. After the market construction is improved, the government may capitalize on the market to accelerate the development and meet new objectives. Instead of simply observing, supervising, and formulating the rules, the government makes use of the financial strength, coordination capability, legislative power, and ideological education to accelerate the market building. In this process, the role of development-oriented finance will come into the best play.

To promote the interconversion between government forces and market forces is the essence of development-oriented finance. Development-oriented finance converts government forces and other forces into market forces through financing projects. Integration of the market forces may enhance the market efficiency, eliminate the bubbles, and accelerate the sound development of economy and the market construction. On the other side, once the market is matured, it will be driven by the government's financial strength. Both the gross market capacity and the market structure may be regulated through macro-control. Seen from the evolvement history of the fiscal, credit, and securities financing mechanisms, these three financing mechanisms bear different functions, and with the evolvement of financing mechanism, the efficiency of resources allocation will gradually improve. Besides, the financial strength of the government has also multiple types of expressions. If the government puts the limited financial strength into the social public-good projects, it cannot promote the market development; moreover, the market construction will be deprived of the inherent driving force. It is the most scientific approach that the government invests the financial resources into market building and attains the government's objectives through it. Development-oriented finance involves three kinds of financing means and serves as a bridge between the government and the market. It converts the government's financial strength into the forces of market building, and uses the means of organizational credit enhancement to strengthen the government's financial strength, enhance the coordination between the three financing mechanisms through system and market building, build a new platform and support for the market resources allocation, and boost the market development through promotion of the individual projects. This represents a Chinese-characteristic way of market building.

8.5 Conclusion

In this chapter, we have elaborated on the innovative theories and practices on correctly handling the relationship between the government and the market, on the basis of correctly understanding the government's functions and the bridging role of development-oriented finance (Figure 8.2). In the 21st century, China will transform from agricultural economy to industrial economy and from a planned economy to a market economy. It is a major concept of accelerating China's development to bring the organizational advantages of the government and the role of development-oriented finance into full play, combine resources of the government, financial institutions, and enterprises, actively build the market, credit, and systems, and boost the transformation in a market-oriented method. Development-oriented finance extends its cooperation with the government closely,

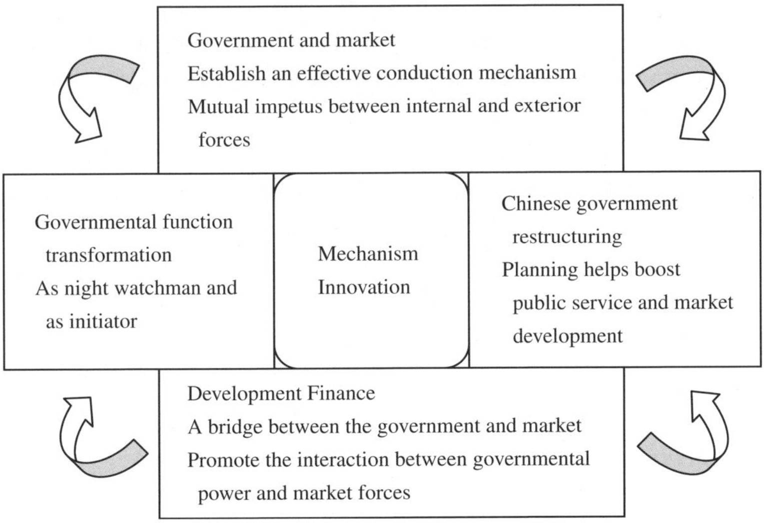

Figure 8.2: Credit enhancement helps accelerate credit system building.

serves as a "visible hand" of the government through organizational credit enhancement, and thus effectively converts the government forces into the market forces. Development-oriented finance creatively builds a government-coordination-guided credit platform, promotes the interconversion of government forces and market forces, and energetically quickens China's urban infrastructure construction and urbanization. The government credit platform is a creative achievement of China's investing and financing mechanism reform. Local governments, as the executor of the regional fiscal policies, build effective investing and financing platforms, and make up the market failure in public investment by capitalizing on the controllable resources and the foreseeable revenues in the process of regional infrastructure construction, thus enormously boosting the urbanization process under the leadership of the government. The government credit platform is new in China's economic development process and needs to be further improved and regulated in practice. In the process of responding against the financial crisis, the government credit platform has played an important role, but there are also some problems that were reflected in the over fast and nonstandard development as well as the poor management capability of the county governments' platforms. Going ahead, we need to regulate the county governments' platforms in line with requirements of the No. 19 document of the State Council in 2010 to ensure the stability of finance and economy. The policy intentions of the No. 19 document of the State Council in 2010 are, in essential, highly consistent with the principles of development-oriented finance. Standardization and clearing of the platforms aim at urging the platform entities to comply with the requirements of development-oriented finance and become normalized and healthy entities with sustainable development potential in line with the principles and methods of development-oriented finance. On the whole, the government credit platform is not only a strategic approach for the active construction of markets but also an important carrier of mixed financing and reflects the strategic concept of hedging risks through comprehensive utilization of resources. We will make an in-depth discussion on this topic in Chapter 9.

Chapter 9

Portfolio Financing, Banking's Efficient Two-Edged Tool

China Development Bank (CDB) has extended Markowitz's Modern Portfolio Investment Theory into a concept of portfolio financing that simultaneously lowers systemic risk and aids in credit market construction. As practiced by CDB, portfolio financing allows us to prudently lend for projects which others would spurn as excessively risky and so build a solid economic foundation in the financial backwaters of developing countries. As we have developed its principles and procedures for use, what we call portfolio financing means both the concept and the detailed financing mechanism. We use it to pool resources, clip financial peaks, and fill financial valleys in an efficient strategy that hedges risks and achieves steady and balanced development. Created for China's financially disadvantaged areas, CDB's portfolio financing adheres to a structured development approach and is a creatively practiced tool for urban infrastructure construction, drawing on advanced international portfolio investment theory. To support the development of small enterprises in China's county economies, CDB has actively pushed forward the organizational construction of community credit associations, putting forward portfolio financing thinking and portfolio financing methods with appropriate Chinese characteristics. These ideas as implemented have allowed us to take great strides in the building of modern credit market systems in such areas. At the same time, we make this effort because we find it effective in preventing systemic financial risk.

This chapter summarizes the practices of CDB in portfolio financing, rigorously analyzing the concept of resources and market scope, and reveals the relationship between portfolio financing and medium- and long-term development. It describes the functions and effects of portfolio financing, as it supports the integrated use of various resources of governments, banks, enterprises, and other objects within the credit market system, and takes into account differing financial plans based on the credit structure and overall cash flow. This chapter expounds on CDB's dynamic monitoring and adjustment of the risk concentration degree of portfolio financing, risk status of on and off-balance-sheet business, and risk limit implementation, as well as the expected loss on portfolio financing, i.e., not only supporting the economic and social development but also carrying out effective risk management. Practice proves that both the concept and mechanism are essentially viable and popular with various governments, and conform to the requirements of the development banking arena. There is no doubt that our procedural regime is continuously optimized, improved and advanced with changing times and circumstances, but the concept is fixed. In this age of economic globalization, we envision more and more governments and financial institutions in developed countries adopting the concept and mechanisms of portfolio financing in order to take advantage of various resources, hedge possible risks, and attain the objective of stabilizing markets and achieving comprehensive development. This is a non-traditional development strategy and an important lever in support of sustainable economic and social development in the 21st century.

9.1 Risk management is a key task of financial system stabilization

Risk management is a key topic that must be taken into account in both enterprise financial endeavors and the broader field of development-oriented finance. Markowitz, a Nobel laureate, and some other economists discussed various securities investment methodologies theoretically and developed the concept of the relatively systematic balanced portfolio that is the centerpiece of Modern Portfolio Investment Theory. They stressed risk diversification management and interest rate, and maturity structured management in order to achieve benefit maximization under the specified risk levels or risk minimization under the specified return levels. Such theories are of guiding importance at the micro-level, and may guide enterprises in reducing financing cost, optimizing capital structure, and improving business performance. These theories serve as a key component of the development strategy from which institutions, such as CDB, must draw learning lessons that could be applied to financial practice. Meanwhile, we also consider that these theories, as refined, will further enhance the core competence of financial institutions and help mitigate systemic risk at the macro-level. Systemic risk is closely related to market maturity, economic management, and the distribution of medium- and long-term economic development.

Development-oriented finance mainly involves financing for medium- and long-term infrastructure construction and for socially "hot" agenda items. It is generally recognized that risks arising from financing for these fields are relatively considerable. Apart from the unsystematic risk arising from general commercial bank financing and closely relating to internal factors of enterprises, there are systemic risks associated with social and economic management system — we can summarize these special risks as the risks of pioneering. Management of such risks needs innovation and new measures. Development-oriented finance has consequently researched the risks of pioneering in depth.

By definition, development-oriented finance accords top priority to the national strategic interest, which is closely centered around the hot and thorny topical issues that are addressed by governments and the general public. In China, development-oriented finance supports the construction of key state projects of infrastructure, basic and pillar industries, and business development, especially in relation to small and medium-sized enterprises (SMEs), energy conservation, emissions reduction, environmental protection, education, medical treatment, moderate, and low-income housing and "going global". These particular business areas as prioritized for development-oriented finance are consistent with our country's economic and social development needs, but we find ourselves funding immature public infrastructure projects in the majority of instances. These immature public infrastructure projects are the strategic core business of CDB's development-oriented finance, and a large number of them belong to pure public products or quasi-public products with remarkable, very positive, social benefits but poor economic benefits.

Consider some of those "worthy" but traditionally "not creditworthy" projects that are addressed by CDB. These include renovation of the shantytowns in Liaoning, as well as non-profit roads and bridges, sewage treatment, storm water drainage, and urban flood control. We have also addressed infrastructure schemes that would be unable to repay loans if they are solely reliant on the income from a single project — the ones that traditionally depend on government assistance as a matter of policy support. For such projects, with their huge required investment and long construction periods without positive cash flow (or even any cash flow), ordinary commercial banks flinch at the early stage, and are unwilling to provide financing. In the face of such difficult banking challenges, development-oriented finance boldly innovates and actively builds credit, cultivates markets, and manages risks based on a government institutional role in credit enhancement. For instance, in order to accelerate urban infrastructure construction, CDB learned lessons from the financial crisis and creatively put forward its earliest "portfolio financing mode" in 1998, in response to the imperfect credit market system. The mode was to integrate two or more financing projects into a portfolio of a certain manner in order to provide the necessary credit support for the loan projects that were affecting several differing public infrastructure modalities. This was done in order to overcome the temporary cash flow problems associated with one or more funding needs of our customers. This effectively removed a bottleneck to certain public product/project financing. CDB's portfolio financing mechanism also adopts the build-transfer (BT) and build-own-transfer (BOT) methodologies and is gradually normalized and standardized by continuous improvement.

One of the most outstanding contributions made by the portfolio financing mode is that it elegantly solves issues of "long, drawn-out" projects and "zipper roads" in urban infrastructure construction. Before the financing mode was launched, urban infrastructure construction faced the phenomenon that one project would be built if there was enough money for such a project, without regard to other projects. Accordingly, we would see a new road built only to see it almost immediately torn up to lay pipelines, or a project with a short construction cycle that had to be deferred due to a temporary shortage of financial institution funds. The portfolio financing mode can solve financing problems for infrastructure construction such as these and greatly promote the process of urbanization.

In order to tackle the financing difficulties of county-level economies and meet the needs of SMEs, CDB has actively promoted the establishment of credit associations in villages and towns, adopting the law of large numbers in their governance and adhering to the practice of "giving a rose and leaving behind fragrance in the hands". By the latter, we mean that CDB has been devoted to the pooling of various resources for the development of county-level economies, giving play to the democratic advantages of public financing and peer pressure, developing family credit, neighborhood credit and friends and associates credit, optimizing portfolio credit elements, coordinating the management of upstream, midstream, and downstream products, and effectively controlling the risks so as to efficiently support the development of county economies and SMEs without reliance on slender individual financial endeavors.

The construction of portfolio financing modalities and community credit associations does not simply bind two or more services, nor does it simply bind some enterprises. Instead, it is a system that combines various resources, manages all projects as a whole, and creates overall funding operation rules in order to minimize financing cost, maximize funding efficiency, facilitate credit system building and operation, and speed up economic development. Of course, such a mode also needs to be monitored and improved in practice over the course of time, as we learn from experience optimization techniques and ineffective approaches. Especially in the immature fields of "social hot spots, government hot spots, and market gaps", development-oriented finance needs to be further improved and a systematic portfolio financing mechanism should be established. CDB is committed to refining its portfolio financing forever.

9.2 Portfolio financing, a boon to risk management

Traditional portfolio investment means diversified management of assets by investment managers according to asset selection theory and investment portfolio theory, so as to diversify risks and improve efficiency. Drawing from the advanced international financial theories and summarizing the practice of development-oriented finance, we further extended the implications of traditional portfolio investment, and put forward new ideas on portfolio financing, centering on system innovation, promotion of credit market system building, and prevention of systemic risk (Figure 9.1).

The portfolio financing of development-oriented finance means that all constituents grasp and pay attention to the concept of the overall situation, portfolio development, integration of resources, uniform arrangement and assessment, and coordinated operation in line with a structured development approach. With awareness on their part, we then promote the idea and mechanism as to medium- and long-term sustainable social and economic development, in order to mitigate risks, save resources, and improve efficiency. The fundamental difference between the traditional portfolio investment and the portfolio financing of development-oriented finance is that the former is a microcosmic behavior centering on investment

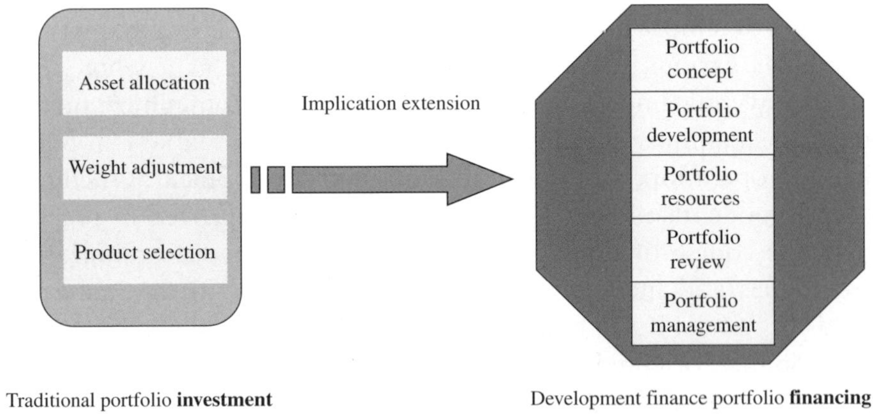

Figure 9.1: Implication of development.

managers and independent product selection, while the latter is a macrocosmic endeavor centering on the building of a credit market system that takes various rights and interests into coordinated account. Portfolio financing especially stresses that construction and development should be subject to uniform planning, and should be built around the advanced concept of integrated resource and project planning, promoting credit market system building through financing, meeting customers' overall funding demands, and attaining the objective of greatly supporting economic and social development while effectively managing the pioneering risks inherent with development-oriented finance. Portfolio financing, as an innovative financing mode, is interpreted via the following five perspectives:

(1) *The portfolio concept.* This builds up the concept of resources and the portfolio embracing the larger market scope, i.e., the awareness of the overall situation. It combines an advanced concept developed internationally with an advanced concept developed domestically, traditional concepts with modern concepts, and commercial financial concepts with policy bank financial concepts, and develops a new portfolio concept, i.e., the concept of the development-oriented finance portfolio. Through innovation, such a new portfolio concept has drawn upon the essence of various economic and financial theories but differs from any previous separate concept. CDB's portfolio financing is indeed an innovative concept. The new concept can guide our development action and direct its operating mechanism. The portfolio products of "investment, lending, debt, leasing, credit, and guarantee" that we put forward are the specific applications within the portfolio concept of financing, with a view to our marketing it as improving our comprehensive risk management capability. Economic globalization provides us with a broader action space to take advantage of domestic and overseas knowledge, funds, and technology. We should have a concept and mechanism to effectively mobilize various global resources to ensure China's sustainable development.

(2) *The portfolio development.* We advocate aggregation approaches to the development of domestic and foreign markets; development of

upstream, midstream, and downstream projects; development of large strategic projects and small and medium-sized projects; coordinated development of for-profit and non-profit projects; development of urban and rural projects; and development of China's eastern and western projects. Aggregation means that we consider the formation of project clusters, project chains, and project networks, and arrange for clustering projects as a whole. Such portfolio development reflects the requirements on project clustering, project flow, and comprehensive project funding distribution, which helps improve the efficiency of project financing, promotes the building of credit market systems, and controls project financing risk. Based on an analysis of portfolio development, Project Management Institute of the US (PMI) considers that portfolio development and/or a collection of projects and other work grouped together can reflect effective management and meet strategic business objectives.[1] The remark makes sense and reflects the essence of management science. Development-oriented finance takes into consideration the many individual construction projects of China, with the aim of promoting industrial restructuring, accelerating the development of industrial clusters, and attaining China's medium- and long-term development objectives by grouping of projects.

(3) *The resource integration.* We advocate large-scale integration, i.e., integration of the resources of governments, market, enterprises, and financial institutions, integration of domestic and international resources, and integration of social and natural resources to form a new resource, i.e., the development-oriented finance portfolio resource. Wider optimization and integration of resources help us to solve the major contradictions within China's macroeconomic operation and allows us to speed up and boost the scale of development in the Chinese economy and society.

(4) *The portfolio review.* We conduct credit and project reviews by combining various projects within a region in order to examine the

[1]The original text runs as below: "A portfolio is a collection of projects and/or programs and other work grouped together of facility effective management of that work to meet strategic business objectives".

comprehensive quality and scope of a prospective market. With the wide application of IT and continuous development of the market economy, traditional credit analysis divides credit products into good and bad products and thereby makes decisions of "lending" or "not lending". Such a limited perspective cannot meet the requirements of modern credit management, not to speak of the needs of development-oriented finance business.

Development-oriented finance assumes the obligation to turn bad assets into good ones, turn projects not qualified for loans into projects qualified for loans, and turn immature markets into mature ones. Therefore, CDB has continuously innovated its review measures and enriched the content of "uniform review, classified approval, separate signing, and management of risk". For instance, CDB combines general guarantees with innovative guarantees to support the start-up of pioneering technological enterprises and the development of high-tech and new technology industries.

(5) *The portfolio management.* We should take into account the actual conditions of industries, regions, and customers, and the characteristics of short- and long-term loans, domestic and international loans, as well as loans for public products and non-public products. We should also incorporate the existing loans and loans for businesses to be explored into a uniform plan, consider the relevance of compounded risks and various risks from the perspectives of portfolio financing, and establish a coordinated management mechanism. We should substitute objective risk standards for subjective judgments in categorizing and acting on specific risks and improve the transparency and democracy of leadership decisions. In recent years, the regulatory efforts that are aimed at the development of the financial industry have unfortunately and belatedly highlighted system deficiencies. The frequency and severity of recent risk events in the international banking industry have clearly demonstrated that stand-alone credit-risk management is increasingly unsuitable in today's financial environment. The blending of endogenous and exogenous risks objectively requires the uniform and coordinated operation of financial institutions. The basic concept of the coordinated operation and management of credit asset risks by development-oriented

finance is as follows: on the premise of making capital adequacy ratios come up to international standards, we should reasonably define the risk limit of industries, regions, and important customers in a certain period within the control target for the credit risk concentration degree, introduce portfolio limit management for different industries, different enterprises and different services, and achieve the coordinated development of on and off-balance-sheet business.

Development-oriented finance combines the following: (i) related concepts, related resources, related customers, related projects, and related talented people; (ii) government competence with market competence; (iii) financing capability with risk management capability; (iv) R&D capability with application and promotion capability; (v) production capability with marketing capability; and (vi) creativity with willpower to develop a new power to solve new issues in the future. That is the full measure of the power of portfolio financing to promote credit market system building and the prevention of financial system risks. Under the guidance of national strategic plan, portfolio financing of development-oriented finance must take advantage of all resources available, giving play to its features and capability to effectively integrate various resources, continuously expand portfolio elements, and improve the quality of the portfolio level.

We at CDB have demonstrated that well-executed portfolio financing greatly promotes the building of credit markets and prevents financial system risks. Of course, such a process is complicated. Figure 9.2 illustrates the relationship between the portfolio level step-up and the development of the credit market system.

Portfolio financing is a combination of art and science that applies knowledge, resources, skills, and tools to financial fields in order to support economic and social development. Portfolio financing is an amalgam of inspiration, wisdom, and toughness. The portfolio financing process can be considered within either top-down or bottom-up planning, internal to external development, and external to internal utilization. It is truly a new system arrangement. We believe that in the field of finance, the sum of the transaction fees on separate operations of a specified number of loans will be higher than the transaction fees on the combined operation of these loans,

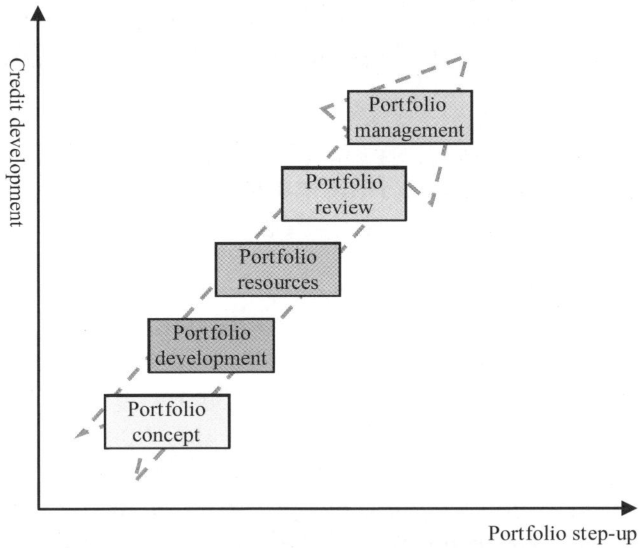

Figure 9.2: Portfolio financing and market.

so there is an inherent economy of scale beneficial to all parties. Portfolio financing will become a natural system choice for financial institutions to maximize the marginal utility under market-oriented conditions. Depending on the system arrangements, such as integration of concepts, resources, projects and reviews, and coordinated operation, development-oriented finance scientifically classifies projects with different risks, different cash flows, and different maturities, so as to achieve comprehensive balance of benefits and hedge risks. Based on the maximization of economic and social benefits of a totality of sub-projects, development-oriented finance effectively eases the restraint of serious shortages of resources on the economic operation at the highest level, facilitating the building of credit market systems by financing, giving play to the role of investment and construction in stimulating economic growth, and increasing the supply of public products.

The portfolio financing concept we put forward has extended the portfolio investment theory of Western countries. It helps us to broaden our ideas on financing for urban infrastructure construction, and enhance credit system building for economically weak areas. More importantly, portfolio financing has been further expanded and helps meet the principle of "risk minimization under a specific return".

9.3 Building a portfolio financing model with Chinese characteristics

Based on the portfolio financing concepts we put forward previously, we can obtain a logical and mathematical underpinning of the portfolio financing model in practice by referring to advanced Western investment theory. Such a new portfolio financing model obviously improves the benefit room under risk management representation diagrams. According to the principle of risk minimization under a specific return, we understand that portfolio financing has expected loss/return similar to other financial activities. Just as the occurrence of an event associated with a random probability, the occurrence of loss and return of each credit asset in a portfolio must have its own probability of default and recovery. By multiplying default/recovery probability of each credit in a portfolio by the loss/return at the time of default, we may deduce the expected loss/return of such credit asset. Such an expected loss/return is not risk, but the amount of loss/return that we forecast. Risk is the deviation of actual loss/return from our expected loss/return, that is, the loss that we fail to forecast, unexpected loss, and failure to reach expected return. Briefly speaking, the risk of portfolio financing refers to the fluctuation severity of deviation of actual loss/return from expected value. The fluctuation severity comes from two aspects: (1) the fluctuation of deviation of each credit asset in a portfolio from its expected value; and (2) the impact of fluctuation relevance between any two credit assets on the fluctuation of financing portfolio. The severity of such deviation expectation is denoted by σ_p^2. Under the guidance of portfolio financing, we integrate not only various credit assets but also various resources, and thus greatly diminish the severity of deviation of actual loss on portfolio financing from expectations. In other words, the possibility that the actual financial return of portfolio financing is significantly lower than the expected return will decrease. We are aware that such a possibility may be deduced by weighting the variance of return on the funds in a portfolio and their covariance, i.e.,

$$\sigma_p^2 = \sum_{i=1}^{n}\sum_{j=1}^{n} x_i x_j c_{ij}$$

(where, C_{ij} is a covariance and x_i and x_j are theproportion of each credit in the portfolio); the expected return in the portfolio financing R_p means the weighted average of expected rate of return of various credit funds in the portfolio r_i (expected return estimated according to statistical data), i.e.,

$$E(r_p) = \sum_{i=1}^{n} x_i r_i = R_p.$$

Thus, we draw on conventional textbook notation to use the following expressions to reflect the basic conditions that financial institutions adhere to the principle of portfolio financing, provide financing, reduce risks, and generate a given rate of return:

$$\min \sigma_p^2 = \sum_{i=1}^{n}\sum_{j=1}^{n} x_i x_i c_{ij} \tag{1}$$

$$\begin{cases} \text{s.t } E(r_p) = \sum_{i=1}^{n} x_i r_i, \quad i = 1,2,\ldots,n \\ \sum_{i=1}^{n} x_i = 1, \quad i = 1,2,\ldots,n \\ x_i \geq 0, \quad i = 1,2,\ldots,n \end{cases} \tag{2}$$

where, expression 1 means the portfolio financing risk is minimized and the proportion of each credit will obviously decrease under the concept of the broadened portfolio, and therefore σ_p^2. is smaller than the value in its usual sense; expression 2 means the two constraint conditions for generating stable return: the first is stable loan input $\sum_{i=1}^{n} x_i = 1$ (we denote the total amount by a unit); the second is stable return brought by credit in portfolio financing to financial institutions. Similarly, under the broadened portfolio, effectively controlled resources will increase and the stability of input will be enhanced. The two constraint conditions may be effectively improved, thus indicating that the credit funds and project number *n* actually experiences a quantum leap. That is to say, portfolio financing can considerably reduce the possibility of failure to recover principal and interest. That is because the sum here is not a simple sum but a portfolio optimization strategy, i.e., effectively hedging various risks by way of the broadened portfolio.

Then, how does the broadened portfolio effectively mitigate risks? We understand that an effective boundary curve of a set of traditional financing arrangements *E*1 may be deduced according to the functional solution based on a specific return and minimized risk above. Our portfolio financing theory further expands the content and structure of existing textbook investment portfolio theory, as it relatively reduces the uncertainty facing financing institutions, improves, and moves the effective boundary curve from right to left, yielding a new effective boundary curve *E*2. In addition, different economic subjects have different risk control principles (risk aversion). That is to say, different economic subjects have different requirements on return by assuming a specific risk, i.e., their indifference curves of risk and return substitution are different. Assume the indifference risk curve that reflects the risk control principle (risk aversion) of a financial institution is Curve C: when Curve C is tangent to the new effective boundary curve *E*2 of portfolio financing, we obtain the best portfolio financing return. Since we have improved the effective boundary curve of portfolio financing, the effective zone of portfolio financing under the new effective boundary curve is obviously larger than the effective portfolio zone in traditional banking theory, thus creating more opportunities for lowering risks under the specific return *R*0, i.e., the point of risk moves from *S*1 to *S*2 in Figure 9.3.

The above figure shows that the expected loss of a portfolio is only the average of expected losses on various assets in a portfolio, and its risks may be diversified and hedged. The risk or loss after

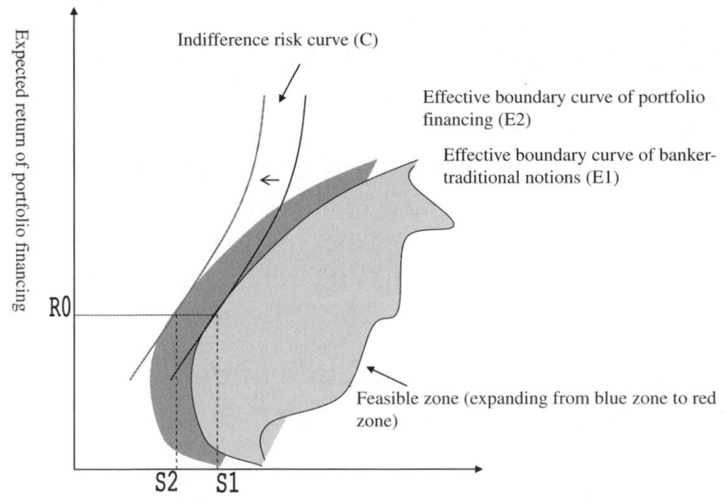

Figure 9.3: Improvement diagram of effective boundary of portfolio financing.

portfolio is far lower than the weighted average of various credit risks before portfolio financing. In other words, the loss on the whole portfolio is smaller than the aggregate losses on various credits in the portfolio. Therefore, portfolio financing is an effective way to tap markets and turn red ocean (previously infeasible financing opportunities) into blue (clearly feasible) ocean (financing opportunities), embodies systematic overall strategy, and helps optimize resources and prevent systemic risks. Portfolio financing management can be deemed to actively exploit resources and achieve high-level management at a certain development stage.

China's credit market system is imperfect, and the major risk facing its banking industry is credit risk. Under circumstances of uncertain credit risk, a certain asset can be deemed to have a known modal possibility of default. This is its default probability. Once default occurs, a portion of the value of such an asset will be lost, and banks will correspondingly suffer financial losses. From this perspective, the loans extended by banks may be regarded as the selling of put options, or banks buying risky assets. If we develop and design strategic options and correctly apply financing concepts and mechanisms to financial work according to actual conditions, we may mitigate risks and support development. That is, we actually develop a call option for the market. Summing up practical experience, building a portfolio financing decision model by taking into account the financing return and risks, and computing call options will help banks make scientific decisions by quantified computation, improving credit quality of their assets, preventing systemic risk, and promoting smooth, rapid, and healthy economic development.

9.4 Portfolio financing in practice under development-oriented finance

The portfolio financing model of development-oriented finance, which is designed in line with the features of financing for public infrastructure and county-level economies, operates by way of continuous innovation, repeated refinement, and the collective wisdom of the CDB staff. It has been tested and recognized by society and the market. The outstanding performance of development-oriented finance as practiced by CDB over the past years also reflects the great contribution of portfolio financing to the dispersion of micro-credit risk and improvement of the bank's rate of return on its assets. As of the end of the second quarter of 2009, the quality of assets has maintained a dynamic steady state: the NPL ratio was only 0.83%, below 1% for the 17th consecutive quarter; the cumulative recovery ratio of principal and interest stood at 99.57%, maintaining a high percentage for the 38th consecutive quarter. By employing the financial principle of investment portfolio management with a consistent positive cash flow objective, portfolio financing allows CDB not only to realize a neutral to positive balance of cash flows but also to lock upside risks, thus improving the number of performing projects that offset non-performing ones. Over the past 10 years, CDB has been a leader in portfolio asset quality management, domestically and internationally. Long-term practices have proven that it has developed financing modes and mechanisms that can effectively offset the side effects of backward systems and credit deficiencies and break through financing bottlenecks in social and economic development.

The concept and mechanisms of portfolio financing of development-oriented finance are under continuous improvement and development. In practice, we have explored new portfolio financing channels in a broad sense, including jointly guaranteed credits, joint loans, direct syndicated loans, indirect syndicated loans, and interest rate swaps, in addition to portfolio financing for urban infrastructure construction and village credit associations, all of which have been improved comprehensively over time. Our practices demonstrate that these portfolio financing innovations, which are aligned with the specific economic and financial circumstances of China, have played a positive role in the allocation of financial resources, support to economic construction, and enhancement of risk prevention in the following respects:

(1) Portfolio financing has been beneficial to the channeling of social capital into the structural adjustment of our national economy and the construction of major projects. In implementing portfolio financing, development-oriented finance selected some superior electricity, road, and urban infrastructure projects as pilot projects for commercial banks to involve themselves in and share the fruits of development-oriented finance. Commercial banks, especially small and medium-sized ones, have been attracted in order that their capital can also be channeled into the construction in key sectors, bottleneck sectors, and key regions, which has assured funding commensurate with the demands of the affected sectors and regions and contributed to the strategic targets of China's economic structural adjustment. Besides, portfolio financing has promoted the centralized planning and integration of resources by regions to avoid redundant construction and blind investment and therefore brought regional economic construction back onto track.

(2) Portfolio financing has helped to disperse the risks of credit assets. Generally speaking, loan concentration is correlated with the risk level of loans, namely, the higher the loan concentration, the bigger the loan risk. Under portfolio financing, the underwriting of syndicated loans, credit asset securitization, and credit derivatives are appropriately used to attract capital from one or more investors to

collectively satisfy project financing needs. Apart from effectively dispersing risks from loan concentration, this approach efficiently optimizes the structure of credit assets from different sources. It structures assets of different risk-return ratios by weight so that the risk from market fluctuations is essentially avoided and the investment return obtained is not lower than the average rate of return on the market.

(3) Portfolio financing has contributed to closer cooperation among domestic financial institutions, improvement of asset structure of small and medium-sized financial institutions, and collectively enhanced China's financial institutional competitiveness. Development-oriented finance, by way of portfolio financing arrangements, has enhanced collaboration among domestic commercial banks, allowing commercial banks to share in the achievement of development-oriented finance and reap the benefits, thus turning inter-bank relationships from competitive to cooperative, assuring common and further optimized development. Since development-oriented finance shows obvious competitive strengths in terms of loan marketing and project review, the strengths are used for developing superior customers and projects, designing the structure of credit systems, and enhancing inter-bank cooperation.

(4) Portfolio financing has deepened the channel for inter-bank credit asset circulation and efficiently addressed matters of credit asset liquidity. Effective asset liquidity management is the most effective means for banks to avoid the pitfalls of financial system risk and for maximizing institutional risk immunity while increasing the average rate of return. It has become a significant concept and topic in banking risk management, particularly in the wake of the subprime mortgage debacle. In the backdrop of no credit assets market in China, development-oriented finance took the lead in developing an indirect syndicated loan product by referring to the common practices of first-class international banks and obtained the approval of the regulatory authorities for marketing the product. Since the launch of the indirect syndicated loan service, it has solved the problem of long maturity and poor liquidity of development loans; furthermore, it

opened a new way for the banking sector to liquidize principal assets, dredged the exit channel of banking assets, created conditions for liquidizing earned assets, added a new tool of credit liquidity management, and contributed to the construction of a healthy and safe financial system for China.

Portfolio financing under development-oriented finance has been practiced based on four understandings:

(1) In the background of China's incomplete credit market systems and an increasingly complicated international financial situation, portfolio financing is a robust and flexible way of breaking through the bottlenecks in the country's medium- and long-term construction financing.
(2) Portfolio financing creates opportunities to find new strategic credit spaces in the portfolios of resources, markets, and projects and further deepens the medium- and long-term development strategy plan.
(3) Portfolio financing offers diversity of capital sources to assure the stability of capital supply and diversification of capital demands and lowers the cost of financing.
(4) Portfolio financing realizes risk hedging in a better way to avoid undue credit risk and thus is an efficient tool for obtaining reasonable returns against well-evaluated and controlled risks. The starting point for promoting portfolio financing under development-oriented finance is effectively managing systemic risks while supporting the rapid but healthy social development of the economy and society.

Case Study 2: Solving the problem of small enterprise financing with portfolio financing

I. *Background*

SMEs are playing an increasingly important role in the national economy. According to the statistics in 2009, the number of SMEs in China exceeded 40,000,000, representing 99% of total Chinese enterprises. Besides, over 75% workforce in urban and rural areas was employed by SMEs. The added value and service value created by them contributed 58.5% of GDP. Taxes paid by these enterprises accounted for 48.2% of total taxes. And the import and export value made up more than 70% of total import and export. Nevertheless, the financial resources that SMEs, especially small enterprises, had access to did not match their role in the national economic and social development. Big enterprises which only accounted for 1% of total Chinese enterprises obtained more than 50% loans, while the proportion of loans to small enterprises which represented 88% of total Chinese enterprises was less than 20%. Thus, the financing problem is the primary bottleneck that restricts the development of small enterprises as well as economic and social development. In recent years, China has done a lot to address such problem, but the fundamental problem has not been tackled yet. Reasons lie in the following:

(1) The inherent restriction of small enterprises. In contrast to big enterprises, small enterprises have smaller scale, without standardized financial and internal control systems, and they cannot disclose information on a sufficient basis. Therefore, lending conditions cannot be met.
(2) The restriction of commercial banks when providing financial support to SMEs. In the credit activities of commercial banks, the principles of safety and soundness are always stressed, and differential treatment is applied to different borrower groups.
(3) The tardy development of credit guarantee and rating agencies, failing to fill the credit gap for SMEs.
(4) The restriction of government when offering financing assistance to SMEs. Despite of huge funding gap, it is hard for SMEs to obtain financial subsidies. Therefore, the SME financing mode needs innovation. CDB actively explores and creates its financing service mode for small enterprises to energetically prop up their healthy development.

II. *Solution*

CDB has proposed the mixed mode of "four in one, four platforms and one association, and four constructions".

The concept of "four in one" refers to the fact that advantages and resources of government, banks, intermediary agencies, and enterprises are all integrated organically to form a credit structure which is conducive to the development of vulnerable groups and small enterprises. By positively relying on competent departments of district (city) and county governments, small and medium-sized commercial financial institutions, and social forces (including guarantee institutions, credit promotion association and accounting firms), CDB redesigns its business processes, and works out an innovative risk and interest sharing mechanism to facilitate the credit construction of small enterprises, and provide them with all kinds of assistance, instead of the "one-to-one" relationship between banks and enterprises.

The mechanism of "four platforms and one association" refers to that, organization platform, borrowing platform, guarantee platform, announcement platform, and credit association coordinate and undertake different responsibilities in order to commonly improve the financing environment for small enterprises. The organization platform means that the development-oriented finance cooperation offices established by governments at city and county levels push forward the cooperation with CDB in the grassroots financial areas. The office is not a branch of CDB, but a coordinated institution of local governments. The borrowing platform means that the small enterprise platform companies (corporate) solely funded or controlled by municipal and county governments should be responsible for the acceptance of loan application submitted by small enterprises, selection, and preliminary review of projects. In addition, as the borrower, such company is also responsible for unified borrowing and repayment of funds as well as related managerial work. The guarantee platform means that the guarantee institutions which have established stable cooperative relationship with CDB are able to provide guarantee for loans of CDB undertaken by municipal and county platform companies within the guarantee limit approved by CDB. The institutions are responsible for providing guarantee and review opinions for loan projects by issuing a letter of guarantee. Besides, joint and several liability security should be provided by them. The announcement platform is the generic name of social announcement channels and a mechanism established by cooperation office and borrowing platform for the announcement (announcement on acceptance, disbursement and repayment) of loans granted by CDB to small enterprises. The purpose of such platform is to fully utilize social forces, to supervise CDB's disbursement of loans on an open, fair and justified basis, and to commonly prevent risks. The credit association refers to the SME credit association (or industry association) established in accordance with law. Generally, enterprises should join local SME credit association before applying to CDB for loans. The association is responsible for self-discipline management, information collection, and credit rating for its members.

The characteristics of "four constructions" refer to the following:

(1) *The construction of governance structure.* Before corporate is established or improved, the management and coordination of cooperation office, credit association, and guarantee companies will be relied on to make up the deficiency in corporate governance structure.

(2) *The construction of cash flows.* Cash flows of SMEs vary according to different industries, scales, and seasons. Matching credit products should be created to increase cash flows of SMEs and boost their development.

(3) *The credit construction.* The advantage of government in organization and that of credit association and industry association in management, the peer pressure from member institutions, guarantee, and counter-guarantee measures adopted by guarantee institutions will be fully utilized to improve various systems, enhance SMEs' credit intent, and reduce credit risks.

(4) *The system construction.* Market rules and enterprise systems will be established and improved to enhance information transparency, strengthen market supervision, improve service means, and advance healthy development of enterprises.

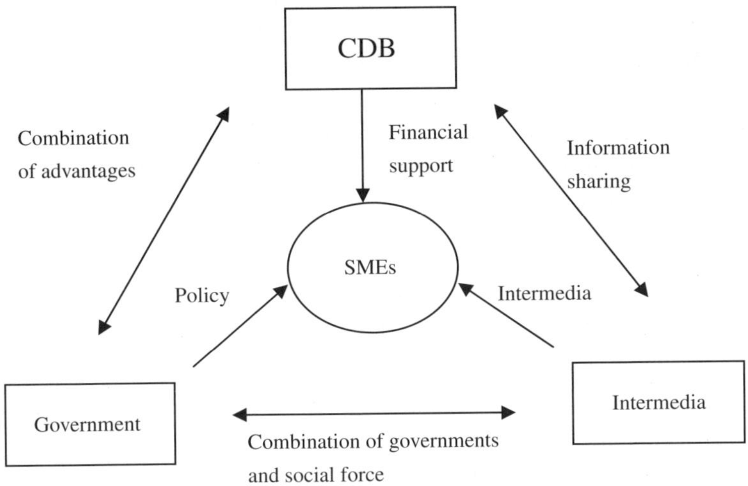

Figure 9.4: Portfolio financing mode solves the problem of small enterprise financing.

III. *Comments*

(1) The portfolio financing mode (Figure 9.4) has far-reaching significance. The problem of small enterprise financing troubles the world and is particularly serious in China. The guiding ideology of "four in one" and lending mode of "four platforms and one association" proposed by CDB are designed to tackle the problem that loans to small enterprises are usually high in costs and risks. By means of standardized access threshold and approval procedures, equal financing right is given to vulnerable groups, so that more small enterprises can obtain financial support, and the concept of "finance socialisation" can be achieved step by step.

(2) The formation of portfolio financing mode supports resultant force of small enterprises. CDB has made great efforts to cultivate partnership institutions, and actively promotes the cooperation between market-based businesses and government, investment and financing companies, guarantee companies, micro-finance companies, and other professional institutions. In addition, a risk sharing and compensation mechanism with "support from the government, sharing among institutions, and mutual guarantee by customers" as

core is established, so as to construct socialized, marketized, and professional institutions and system arrangements, and fully exert the function of grassroots democratic financing mechanism. A large number of small and medium customers are gathered, so that "organized, systematic, and professional" batch operation could be applied, to effectively boost the growth of loans to SMEs.

(3) The portfolio financing mode brings more profit-making opportunities to small enterprises. Under such mode, member enterprises need not provide their assets as guarantee for repayment when applying for loans. Instead, portfolio guarantee is provided by guarantee platform, which offers lending banks a second stable and effective source of repayment and preservation measures, and reduces the risk exposures to SMEs. In the meantime, as the specialized service institution for SMEs, the borrowing platform can act as a counterbalance in the negotiation between enterprises and banks. Besides, it can even strive for more favorable lending conditions in terms of interest rate, fees, and maturity, so as to further increase the profits of enterprises. The platform can effectively enhance the security of loans to SMEs and reduce approval procedures and formalities.

(4) The portfolio financing mode needs to be further improved. The pre-loan investigation methods should be innovated, contents to be reviewed in the lending should be ameliorated, and post-loan examination should be improved, so as to raise the flexibility in the review of earmarked funds and use of funds by enterprises, optimize lending methods, solve the problem of information asymmetry, and raise return on loans. At the same time, the evaluation mechanism should be improved, so that employees who are responsible for loans to small enterprises can be appraised in the same manner as other employees in terms of fulfilling strategic targets, workload, contribution and remuneration, and employees' enthusiasm toward work can be motivated.

9.5 Summary

This chapter analyzes the connotation of portfolio finance and its relations with economic development. The financing portfolio is a general idea of risk management, reflecting the holistic strategy of the system and conducive to the overall optimization of resources and the effective prevention against systemic risks (Figure 9.5).

The financing portfolio proposed by the development-oriented finance institution is a development-friendly and risk-averse business model based on international portfolio theory as well as China's conditions and the development-oriented finance's practice. This business model reflects the financing idea that uses the portfolio concept to guide development practice and uses the wholesale method to manage systematic risks and is committed to integrating resources, hedging risks, levering peaks and valleys, and coordinating development, so as to guide social funds to better support economic and social development, alleviate the bottleneck and weaknesses hereof and promote the formation of diverse investment and financing systems. In the meantime, it can improve the assets structure, assets quality, and risk prevention ability of financial institutions and enhance the overall efficiency of their business operations. To date, financing portfolio has become a powerful tool for

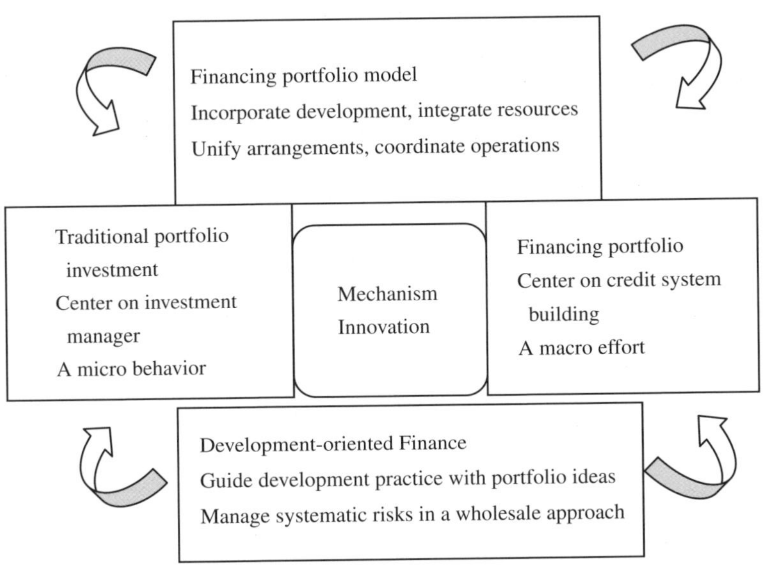

Figure 9.5: Financing portfolio guards against systematic risks.

development-oriented financial institute to implement national macroeconomic policies and accomplish the mission of strengthening national strength and improving people's living standards, and it is enjoying broad prospects. The reason development-oriented finance institution stresses financing portfolio lies in their expectation for establishing a development philosophy and financing mechanism based on a comprehensive hedge to guard against systemic risks and promote the steady, rapid, and healthy economic development. Of course, this is a long-term, arduous task. Development-oriented finance institution will continue to test, modify, and supplement such model, motivate collective efforts and strive to boost the sustainable economic and social progress.

Chapter 10

Perceptions on Financial Socialization

10.1 Introduction

The four important parts of development-oriented finance theories are (i) to unveil the relationship between financial socialization and the medium- to long-term development, (ii) expound the rule that sustainable finance supports social development, (iii) social development is conducive to the finance's prevention of risks, and (iv) financing helps realize the equal financing rights among individuals.

To build a harmonious society and carry out the scientific approach on development is the fundamental requirement for the socialist construction with Chinese characteristics. It is also the inherent demand for China to realize the rapid yet sound development of economy and society. The objectives of the Chinese Communist Party and the Chinese government in the 21st century as well as the fundamental interest of people of all ethnic groups are to reach the level of preliminarily developed countries by 2020, build a moderately prosperous society on all fronts by 2050, and attain the living standards of medium developed countries by 2100.

Through more than 30 years of opening up, reform, and construction, China has made astonishing achievements in all aspects. However, China's development is largely imbalanced, and the growth of social undertakings apparently lags behind the economic development. Against the huge development room and great financing demands in China's social fields, it is impossible to resolve the two world-class difficult issues of "huge capital gap" and "low efficiency" concerning social undertakings merely relying on the fiscal income of the government and to improve the people's living standards completely based on the market means, given that China is still in the primary stage of socialism and its market systems are still less efficient.

Development-oriented finance actively supports the development of various social undertakings on the principles of "national, strategic, and development" and in accordance with the national development strategies and policies as well as the strategies of persisting in the "two wheels" while continuously supporting development of the "infrastructure, fundamental industries, and pillar industries", with an aim to consolidating the national strength and improving people's livelihood. Development-oriented finance summarizes historical experiences, and makes active exploration in the social and livelihood-related financing mechanism in line with the unique characteristics of each social field with reference to international advanced practices. It boosts the comprehensive development of the society with a focus on employment, housing, education, health care, environmental protection, endowment, culture, and other fields that closely bear upon the improvement of people's livelihood. In recent years, development-oriented finance has attained remarkable achievements on supporting construction of the "infrastructure, fundamental industries, and pillar industries" and has created a solid foundation for the expansion of financial services in social fields, the energetic support to the construction of a harmonious society, and the active response to the ordinary people's appeals. In accordance with requirements of the scientific approach on development, the Strategic Plan on Business Development in Social Fields under the development-oriented finance program was formulated with reference to various research achievements and in line with the social development rules, in a bid to uniformly plan the direction and emphasis of the development of financial businesses in social fields, explore the social and people's livelihood-related financing mechanism, drive forward and guide the social resources in supporting development of the social undertakings through financing projects, and facilitate the risk control and growth of development-oriented finance with social development.

10.2 Trend of financial socialization

The financial socialization concept was formed during the practice of development-oriented finance supporting construction of the bottleneck fields in the society. On the one hand, it reflects the development philosophies of "people-oriented", "development for the people, development with support from the people, and development achievements shared by the people", emphasizes that financial services should serve the building of a harmonious society, and that financial means should be actively adopted to remove the various bottlenecks in social development and to promote the common prosperity of the people. On the other hand, we should realize that, financial socialization represents an important trend in the social development of the 21st century.

10.2.1 *Development environment*

The factors dominating development of the international society are transforming from material capital to human capital. In such a context, it will become a mainstream phenomenon in the social and economic fields that top priorities of investment are being placed on human beings, and this will serve as a powerhouse for the development of modern civilization. Influence of the eco-friendly development philosophy and the social responsibility on the economic development is increasing; high technology is deepening its influence on people's demands, and the trend of economic globalization is strengthening. China, as an important growth pole of Asia, or even the world, economic development, is maintaining rapid growth in macroeconomy, but an impartial, open, reasonable, and stable modern social structure is still far from being built. The population issue, environment issue, and resource issue are imposing heavy pressure on the social and economic development of China. In this sense, scientific planning, optimization of structure, uniform arrangement of rural–urban development, energy conservation and emission reduction, environmental protection, and financial socialization are becoming the foundations for China's sustainable development.

10.2.2 *Development trend*

The building of a harmonious society has become the main theme of development in the 21st century, and the comprehensive development of human beings becomes an important characteristic of the social civilization. Caring for the disadvantaged groups, paying close attention to the aging population, and highlighting social impartiality and justice are the critical issues of the national development strategy. In the critical period for building a moderately prosperous society, the key tone of China's development has been shifted from the GDP-centered economic growth to caring about the people, scientific approach on development, harmonious development, and peaceful development. The government's governance focuses on the improvement of people's welfare and the building and maintenance of a harmonious society.

10.2.3 *Ways of development*

The economic growth pattern of China is changing from extensive growth to intensive growth, from investment-driven growth to consumption-driven growth, and from large projects-driven growth to private business-driven growth. Before the opening up and reform, China's economic growth was primarily driven by the major industrial projects; yet afterwards, big projects in the agriculture, forestry, water, energy, transportation, and materials fields played a crucial role in the economic development. Entering the 1990s, especially after 1998, the driver of China's economic growth gradually changed from investment in major projects to the investment in infrastructure facilities, in particular the construction of infrastructure in townships, which laid down a solid foundation for China's sustained and rapid growth. When the economic development level reaches a certain stage, the weighting of grain, other farm produce, energy, and materials in economy will gradually decline, although their importance and strategic position will not weaken. The growth of macroeconomy will be primarily bolstered by consumption, including the consumption of housing, medical care, and education services, and the weighting of culture, entertainment, and information industries will gradually increase. Seen from the future development trend, the consumption of housing, medical care, culture, and education will develop in the directions of "market, finance, and society orientation" in a step by step manner.

10.2.4 *Financial reform*

More and more social attention are paid to the livelihood-related finance. There appears a clear trend of financial socialization and more finance-oriented society. Finance plays an increasingly fundamental role in economic and social development. In such a context, to protect and ensure the financing right and supervisory right of citizens becomes the fundamental value pursuit of financial reform. With the gradual diversification and decentralization of financing entities, the service targets of financing programs are changing from the big projects and enterprises to individuals. On the one hand, it offers financing support to the individuals; and on the other hand, individuals begin to participate in the financing projects. The social finance, which serves primarily the individuals, is an important component of the financial system. The financial system of the United States has completed such a transition, while in China, social finance has only emerged. In spite of the blankness and weak strength, social finance does represent an inevitable trend for the financial service development. Finance, in essence, is to provide funding support for the people's production and living, and thus maintains the people's livelihood. But in China, it is extremely difficult for the ordinary people to get financing support, and the lack of funds has been the most important barrier to the individuals' production and operation. In particular, the financing issue in rural areas has severely restrained production activities and the increase of farmers' income.

10.3 New requirements of social development on finance

The trend and characteristics of social development put forth new requirements on finance. Financial socialization, in line with the requirements of social development, strives to combine the following:

(1) The goals of financial development with the goals of social development properly. During the period of a planned economy, China's financial service industry did not have a development objective. It was merely a "cashier" helping the government realize its economic and social development objectives. As a result, huge financial risks were accumulated. After the Asian financial crisis, financial enterprises began to strengthen the risk control and highlight the maximization of their own benefits. Consequently, the financing business at the grassroots level was marginalized, and the social development objectives and social responsibilities were played down. Now, the market gradually reaches a consensus that only when the social responsibilities are taken as an important component of the financial development, can we realize simultaneous development in the financial service, economy, and society.

(2) The "offering fuel in snowy weather" with "adding brilliance to splendors" in the provision of financial services. Financial enterprises need to "add brilliance to splendors" for the fields with sound economic benefits, and meanwhile, "offer fuel in snowy weather" to the social bottleneck fields. The financial service industry should provide vigorous support in helping the government remove the financing difficulties troubling the bottleneck fields, and facilitate development of central/western China, "agriculture, rural areas, and farmers", county economy and small to medium-sized enterprises.

(3) Financing right with supervision right in financial work. We need to diligently push forward the construction of a financing system so that the individuals can enjoy equal financing rights. Financing right is also a kind of basic human rights. It is the due right of various social classes, especially the medium- to low-income groups, to get the credit fund support through normal financial channels to become rich. This is the necessary requirement of impartial, just, and equal development. In a socialist society, the financial system is a component of the social public resources, and its public goods nature should be

highlighted by extending the justice and impartiality to the financial and economic fields, i.e., providing services for all the different types of labor with labor capacity, pioneering capability and development capability, and make sure that they enjoy the same chance of social development. This is reflected as the impartiality and justice of society, the impartiality and justice of finance, and the equality and impartiality of opportunities. The current construction of financial markets attaches close importance to the building of basic systems. In order to bring into play the role of finance in promoting social impartiality, it is necessary to build the socialist finance into a new instrument that allows everybody to enjoy the same financing right, covers all people, and promotes the social stability and prosperity, in addition to the realization of public participation and public benefit. While extending efforts to build a financing system for everybody to enjoy the same financing right, we need to take social supervision as an important means to prevent, control, and mitigate the financial risks. In a highly organized society, social supervision may coordinate various social parties, including the government, special organizations, and enterprises, in building the financial market, the credit system, and the various mechanisms, effectively control the credit and operational risks in banks' operation, and create a favorable situation for relying on the whole society to construct financial services, and preventing financial risks at low cost.

Financial socialization is of rich connotation of times.

(1) Financial socialization reflects the interdependence between finance and society. In Chinese, "Jin" refers to gold, and "Rong" refers to facility. The financial services were derived from the currency circulation, credit transaction, and other economic activities between social members. Its development should also take into account the specific national and global circumstances. The long-term development of the financial services should be attained in boosting the social development. Financial industry, instead of being isolated from, is closely related to the social development. The goal of "socialized finance and finance-oriented society" means that we should use the objectives and methods of social development to step

up growth of the financial industry, and meanwhile, apply the achievements of financial development to provide strong inherent growth power for social development.

(2) Financial socialization is the inevitable requirement to implement the scientific approach on development and build a harmonious socialist society. The core of the scientific approach on development is people-first. Financial socialization integrates the "people-first" ideas of China (enriching the people, benefiting the people, etc.) since the ancient Qin Dynasty. Through construction of the financial socialization, we may support the comprehensive and coordinated development of the economy and society, gradually narrow the income gap between various social classes, especially the income gap between rural and urban residents, weaken the effect of the Mathew effect, and support the realization of a harmonious society.

(3) Financial socialization points out an important direction for financial development. At present, the toughest issue and the biggest constraint facing China is the backward market mechanism. We need to use the socialized method, combine various forces, including government, enterprises, finance and social parties, and promote the benign interaction between development of finance, economy, and society. We need to combine international advanced financial theories with the practical situation of China and select a China-characteristic path of financial development.

10.4 Development-oriented finance and financial socialization

Development-oriented finance actively supports the realization of financial socialization and has strategic considerations of the working principles, objectives, and thinking as follows:

(1) *Clarify the working principles*: to abide by the principles of comprehensive, coordinated, and sustainable development. Guided by the scientific approach on development and centering on the comprehensive development of human beings, to strengthen the expansion of business into the social fields, and promote the construction of a

harmonious society while continuing to support the development of traditional businesses to the "infrastructure, fundamental industries, and pillar industries", development-oriented finance closely cooperates with and implements the national development strategy, insists on analysis of the globalization trend and characteristics, proactively explores for the key tasks of development-oriented finance in the various social fields, and promotes the building of a social and livelihood financial mechanism with a view to accelerating development of the social undertakings. Besides, development-oriented finance abides by the principles of "planning innovation, mechanism innovation, organizational innovation, and method innovation", improves the way of thinking and the working method, builds dynamic analysis models, combines theories with actual conditions, extends the depth of planning, upgrades the quality of planning, and ensures that scientific and feasible plans are implemented. Development-oriented finance abides by the principles of "overall planning with all factors taken into consideration, combination of business points with business aspects, space-time expansion, dynamic optimization, and comprehensive encouragement", uniformly arranges for businesses, periodic priorities, systems, and measures and organizational structure for the development-oriented finance in various social fields. Development-oriented finance follows the principles of "by region, level, category, and stage", actively explores the financing plan for the social and livelihood projects in accordance with demands in the specific stages of social development and from the different regions and the different groups of population, in a bid to provide powerful financial support to the development of social undertaking.

(2) *Define the working objectives*: *long-term objectives*: in accordance with the goal that China should reach the level of moderately developed countries in this century, development-oriented finance will take the scientific approach on development and the harmonious development of society as its long-term strategic task, strive for making great contributions in driving forward the comprehensive development of human beings and the coordinated and sustainable development of society and economy and in building a harmonious society in China, and contribute to the healthy development of

China's social undertakings. This is reflected in the earnest and continuous fulfillment of social responsibilities by development-oriented finance. *Medium-term objectives*: in accordance with the requirements that the construction of a moderately prosperous society should be carried out in three stages, development-oriented finance should actively guide the allocation of social resources, proactively promote the building of a Chinese-characteristic financial system to support the development of social undertakings, comprehensively prop up the construction of social and people's livelihood projects, realize the financial socialization and finance-oriented society, and create a favorable employment environment to continuously satisfy the people's demands, effectively improve the working and living conditions and comprehensively upgrade the people's livelihood. Development-oriented finance should play a dominating role in some important social fields so as to greatly boost the improvement of people's livelihood and the growth of national strength. *Objectives for 2020*: to actively push ahead the establishment of a Chinese-characteristic social and livelihood-related financial mechanism, organically integrate the government resources, the private sector resources, the resources of CDB, and other resources, adopt effectively financing models to facilitate the urbanization, and accelerate the building of inexpensive residential houses in accordance with the social development demands at different stages and from different fields and people. To give top priority in supporting the comprehensive compulsory education program and promote the impartiality of education; to promote the implementation of "science education revitalizes a nation" strategy and sharpen the social innovation capability; to support the building of community or village health-care service system and improve the people's health condition; to support the energy conservation and pollution discharge projects, expand the environmental protection projects, and improve the living environment; to support the protection and development of historical or cultural cities, towns, and villages, carry forward the ethnic culture, develop the cultural undertaking, and satisfy the cultural demands of the public; to support the implementation of positive employment policies and improve the employment service system; to promote the employment and re-employment, strengthen labor protection, develop harmonious labor relationship, and realize the favorable interaction between economic development and increase of employment rate; to support the building of an endowment mechanism and strive for solving the basic living problems of the poverty-stricken population. Development-oriented finance should serve as a pioneer in promoting the harmonious development of the society. In order to achieve the above-mentioned objectives, development-oriented finance should collect and guide use of domestic and foreign capital with an emphasis on supporting the development of social undertakings and the construction of livelihood projects while continuously providing support to the development of "infrastructure, fundamental industries, and pillar industries". By 2020, the development-oriented finance businesses in the social fields of CDB should account for 40% of the total from the current 20%, and take an important position in the similar businesses of other Chinese banks.

(3) *Clarify the thought of working*: to clearly understand the actual situations, grasp the rules, plan in a uniform manner, highlight important tasks, forecast the demand and supply, renovate the mechanism, and drive economic development forward with financing support. In accordance with the requirements of the scientific approach on development and centering on the comprehensive development of human beings, to prepare the medium- to long-term plan for the support of development-oriented finance in social undertakings based on scientific analysis and calculations, in line with the trend of population development and urbanization and with reference to the experiences of leading countries. Place top priority on population, housing, education, medical care, environmental protection, employment, poverty alleviation, endowment, and culture issues, and in particular, attach great importance to the population such as migrant farmer workers, the old, the disabled, and the poverty-stricken children in rural areas. In line with the logic of "livelihood issue → livelihood projects → livelihood finance → livelihood strategies", to innovate the business concept and expand the Blue Sea project in social fields; to innovate the development strategy while taking into account the social and economical projects; to innovate

the business system and enhance the social and livelihood financing function of development-oriented finance; to innovate the financial mechanism and boost the harmonious and sustainable development of the society; to innovate the financial products and faithfully solve the social hotspot issues; to innovate the credit structure, build and improve the risk prevention system; to actively explore the financial mechanism to support development of social undertakings, promote the financial socialization and finance-oriented society, create an impartial and fair financing environment to support development of the weak links in social development, including small and medium-sized enterprises, education, medical care, environmental protection, and construction of housing for low-income groups, and thus push forward the construction of a harmonious society in the 21st century.

In order to actively explore the establishment of a livelihood finance mechanism, the following measures should be taken:

(1) *Build a livelihood finance mechanism.* To closely seize the hot and tough issues in the social fields in line with the national strategies and policies, we must accurately find the breakthrough points of CDB, innovate our financing mechanism and working method, and realize the coordinated development between the society and development-oriented finance businesses (Figure 10.1).

— To analyze the social development objectives of China during the various stages under the constraint conditions, as well as the strategic tasks in the crucial fields, establish a dynamic analysis model for the population, environment, and resource constraints, analyze the utilization and development potential of various resources.

— To further improve and implement the social development plan of the State in accordance with the various plans and research results and with reference to the international leading experiences, plan the development directions, philosophies, and emphasis of the development-oriented finance in various social fields as well as the financing mechanism

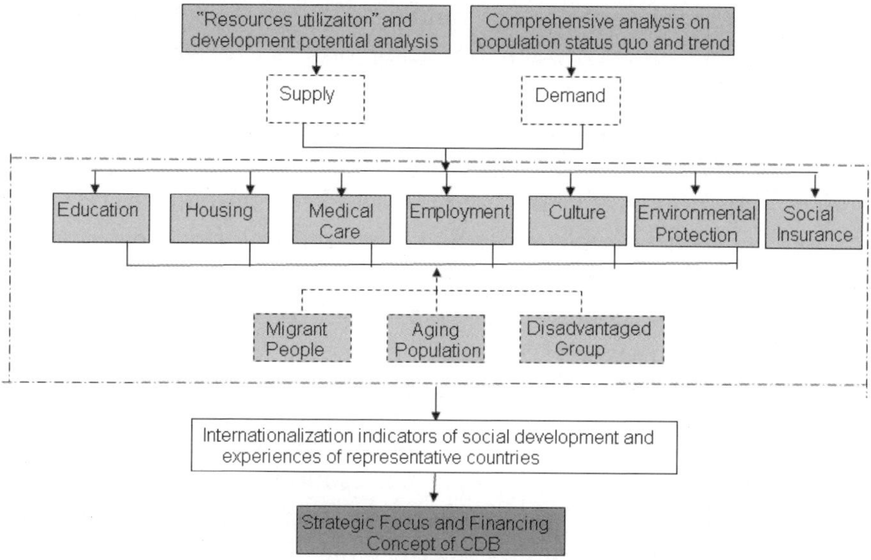

Figure 10.1: Working mechanism of financial socialization.

design, actively explore the new concepts of social undertaking development, scientifically analyze the utilization and development potential for various resources, and drive forward and guide the social resources in supporting the development of social undertakings.

— To actively explore the establishment of a four-dimensional strategic development framework that integrates the strategies by region, population group, social level and stage. Adopt different supportive strategies in line with the unique demands and characteristics of different regions, population groups, social levels and stages.

— To actively build a livelihood finance mechanism, stimulate the strength of social development, guide and optimize the allocation of public resources, and vigorously support the development of various social undertakings such as housing, environmental protection, education, medical care, employment, poverty alleviation, culture and social insurance.

— To actively explore the building of a social livelihood finance mechanism. Through financing projects, drive forward the building of a harmonious society, carry forward the effective use of the nearly 20-years of "population bonus" and related resources, and accelerate the transition from a country with huge population to a country with huge human capital.
— To actively explore the building of a township development fund and promote the reasonable flow of population and accelerate the urbanization through the financing projects.

(2) To actively explore the financing model to support the livelihood undertakings. To launch the financial innovation based on the hot issues and the characteristics of social livelihood projects, make use of and integrate the various types of resources in the government, CDB, and the private sectors, build its own financing model for social undertakings. To utilize the dynamic analysis model for influence of population, resources, and environment, study and build an eco-compensation mechanism, and a "rewarding the society" mechanism after the people's living standards are improved. To organize a series of livelihood business development funds in CDB, including the natural ecology construction fund, the venture capital fund, the cheap-rent housing development and management fund, the protection and development fund for national well-known cities, towns, and villages, and the technological innovation fund. To build and improve the review and management rules for the businesses in relation to various social fields, and advise the government to further improve and build the related policy system and service platform. To renovate financial services, realize market-oriented finance, and finance-oriented society.

(3) To steadfastly regulate and push forward development-oriented finance-related work. In recent years, development-oriented finance has established the operating concept of "big projects and large enterprises enrich the nation; small projects and small enterprises enrich the people", and has taken "transformation toward the livelihood with an emphasis on 'enabling people to get rich' projects" as its obligatory mission and social responsibility. It takes the

livelihood projects as a "Blue Sea", insists on continuous market construction under the guidance of various plans, establishes a financing mechanism that is "based on the city-county cooperation, and realized through the means of platform and partnership institution construction with the guarantee of multiple-level risk sharing and compensation mechanism" through innovation of the organizational model and working methods, successfully addresses the risk control issue and the credit standing construction issue. Development-oriented finance has not only fulfilled its social responsibility but also achieved sound performance. It made significant breakthrough in supporting the development of livelihood undertakings and achieved notable social and economic benefits. By the end of 2008, CDB has cumulatively issued RMB201.5 billion worth of loans to the grassroots operations. Of which, the loans granted to rural infrastructure projects and agricultural leading enterprises amounted to RMB106.7 billion; those granted to the construction of farmer worker training bases were RMB1.91 billion; those to the small and medium-sized enterprises were RMB36.8 billion; the unsecured education loans granted to the native provinces of students (24 provinces and regions) were RMB2.96 billion; the housing loans granted to medium- and low-income households were RMB47.58 billion, which were used to build 1.13 million units of welfare houses. Besides, RMB5.5 billion worth of emergence loans were granted to help fight against the snow disaster affecting South China, the Wenchuan earthquake and the storm in Hainan. The non-performing loan ratio of development-oriented finance has been kept below 1%. Practice shows that development-oriented finance, on the basis of national credit, starts with the building of credit standing system, the market construction and rule construction brings the advantages of a highly socialized and organized structure in China into play, builds a risk-sharing mechanism through close cooperation with the government and the various social parties, explores a sustainable development-featured livelihood finance business model, and achieves the balance of risk and income in the construction of livelihood undertakings.

Case Study 3: Addressing the "Taihu Lake Dilemma"

I. *Background*

1. The economy develops at the cost of the environment. As the third freshwater lake in China, Taihu Lake covers a basin area of 36,900 square kilometers. In terms of the administrative division, the lake covers some parts of the Jiangsu Province and Zhejiang Province as well as most the Shanghai Municipality. The lake has been a major drinking water source for the surrounding cities for a long time. Besides, it plays a significant role in guaranteeing water for industrial and agricultural production including regulating water supply to meet the tourism and shipping demands along with its storage for flood prevention. Such measures contributed to regulating climate, and maintaining ecological balance. In the last 30 years and more, the cities around Taihu Lake have developed rapidly; however, such fast economic growth with high energy consumption and pollution levels have finally led to an environmental crisis, seriously affecting the quality of water in ponds, rivers, and lakes. The Taihu Lake blue algae event in May 2007 sounds a warning.

2. Taihu Lake dilemma brings about a difficult problem. First, cities around Taihu Lake belong to different administrative divisions. Each division thinks about promoting local economic development by means of the lake, but does not want to be responsible for the environmental improvement of the Taihu Lake. In general, water conservancy departments manage the quantity of water, environmental protection departments are responsible for the quality of water, while construction departments undertake sewage disposal, presenting decentralized duties and responsibilities. When pollutant sources flow into the rivers and lakes, no department could assume the responsibility. Second, the river network turns into a sewerage discharge network. Great efforts have been undertaken by the cities around Taihu Lake to improve water environment in recent years, such as implementation of sewage discharge standards and control of industrial pollutant sources, achieving certain effect. But the concern is that some low-tech industrial enterprises with severe pollution levels are gradually moving to the countryside under comparatively weak regulation causing a great amount of industrial pollutants to flow into the Taihu Lake. Third, immediate interests are pursued with negligence of environmental protection. Annual GDP has been the primary target of local governments, and no one lays stress on the environmental costs. Enterprises just seek profit maximization and vandalize surrounding environment without any sense of social responsibilities. Citizens are not concerned about environmental pollution. When pollution directly threatens their lives, they begin to realize its seriousness.

CDB has promoted comprehensive improvement in Taihu Lake's environment by means of early planning and innovation of financial instruments.

1. **CDB actively implemented the General Plan on Comprehensive Improvement of Water Environment in the Taihu Lake Basin issued by the State Council and provided financing support for the preparation of the improvement plan.** In August 2007, CDB signed cooperation agreements on improvement of Taihu Lake with provinces and cities including Jiangsu. It provided RMB20 million of class A technical assistance loans to shore up the preparation and implementation of Taihu Lake improvement plan. At the same time, CDB participated in the project in advance to propose an overall financing plan.
2. **Financing bottlenecks were to be removed by guiding social funds.** According to the General Plan, RMB111.3 billion would be needed for the improvement of Taihu Lake in which Jiangsu's contribution would account for 52%. Such huge funding needs give rise to obvious financing difficulties. Nevertheless, by taking into the actual situation that such funding needs last long with large amounts, CDB made innovation in its financing plan for the improvement of Taihu Lake by combining its advantages in development-oriented finance. It fully utilized various funding sources, arranged fiscal financing and market financing in an overall manner, and raised sufficient funds at the least financing cost to meet the funding needs of projects involved in the prevention and control of water pollution in the Taihu Lake basin.
3. **A financing risk prevention mechanism was set up to facilitate a virtuous cycle.** First, a reimbursement mechanism for public welfare

water environment projects was established. For a public welfare water environment improvement project, CDB, after disbursing loans to related platforms, established a fiscal sharing mechanism for provinces, cities, and counties according to local situations to urge the timely transfer of related funds. Second, a reimbursement mechanism was established for market-based water environment improvement projects. For water environment improvement projects operated in pursuant of the mechanism, the market conditions for debt service would be made out of the earnings on completed projects in order to push forward sewage discharge trading so that enterprises that discharge sewage could buy such rights. In this way, a virtuous cycle will gradually form, containing inputs in water environment improvement comprising earnings on environmental improvement i.e., improvement funds replenished with earnings — re-input in water environment improvement.

4. Administrative barriers were removed by financing to build a new economic pattern in the Taihu Lake area. First, a follow-up planning work was promoted to elaborately determine key processes for long-term improvement. Second, development and construction were closely combined with environmental protection to explore a long-acting mechanism for the option of "Taihu Lake Dilemma". Third, the multiplier effect of development-oriented finance was intensified to further accelerate the comprehensive improvement of Taihu Lake environment, and realize benign development for economic, social, and environmental improvement in the Taihu Lake Basin.

II. *Comments*

The "Taihu Lake Dilemma" is typical in the economic development and environmental improvement of China. First, Yangtze River Delta is an area that developed first in China, and the transformation from extensive economic growth to low-carbon economic growth is distinctive. Second, the development course of "improvement after pollution" is typical in the regional economic development in the country. Third, Taihu Lake improvement covers two provinces and one city. The solution of property right ownership problem and transformation of public land system are typical. In addition, CDB attaches importance to people's livelihood, cares about important issues of the government, and actively explores the role of development-oriented finance in improving the environment. As the above-mentioned case suggests, generally, environmental improvement could be regarded as the supply of quasi-public goods, and reasonable credit system and incentive measures on investment and financing can only form after systematically combining the advantages of the government and market. From the socioeconomic perspective, investment and financing for environmental improvement could be defined through environmental property rights such as the right to discharge sewage, to achieve the consistency of investment, and environment. In the meantime, relevant authorities of the State should re-design regional environment and economic policies to strengthen regional air pollution control, improve regional environmental regulation and emergency linkage mechanism, and ameliorate regional environmental information release system, so as to build a new economic pattern in the Taihu Lake area (Figure 10.2).

Figure 10.2: Beautiful Taihu Lake and blue algae in Taihu Lake.

10.5 Summary

This chapter analyzes the connotation and far-reaching significance of the financial socialization and social financialization, two significant trends of social development in the 21st century that reflect the symbiotic relationship between finance and the society and indicate the direction of financial development.

A financial enterprise can achieve the ultimate mission of modern financial enterprise only when it realizes the synchronous development of the pursuit of wealth, the commitment to social responsibility, and the self-discipline of corporate ethics. It is out of such sense of responsibility that development-oriented finance comes up with the work ideas of "financial socialization and the financialization of society" and commits to do its utmost to give back to the community, serve the community, and boost the harmonious development of finance, economy, and society. It concentrates on the financing need of entrepreneurship and employment of disadvantaged groups, strives to accelerate the establishment of socialized, institutionalized, and standardized credit system, reflects the principles of fairness, justice, and transparency, and guarantees the universal access to the right of financing. The core of development-oriented finance is to actively create or develop markets where there is no market or where there is a lack of a sound market instead of passively waiting for the market to emerge naturally by itself. The

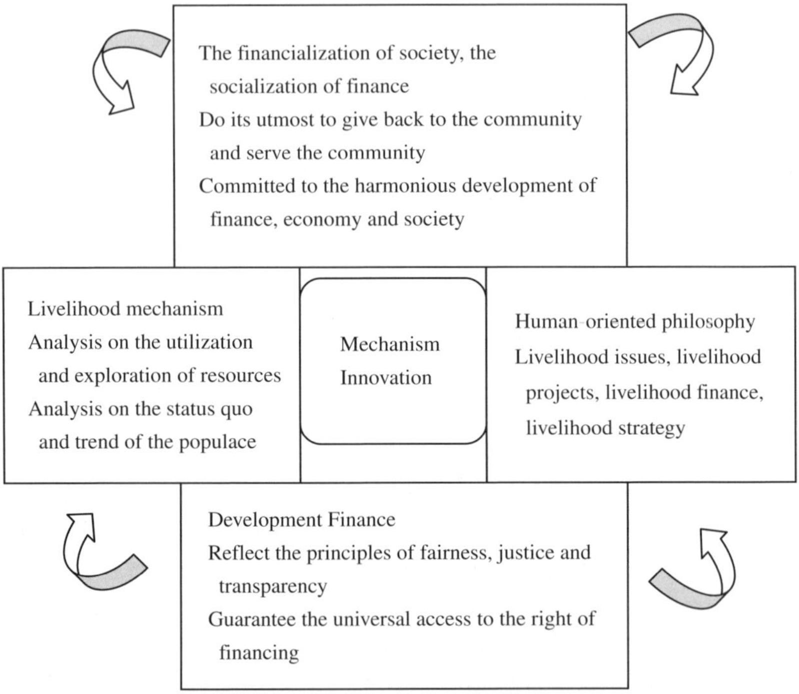

Figure 10.3: Financialization of society and financial socialization.

socialization of finance not only relies on the government but also on the market and society, requiring the organizational strength of the government and the enthusiasm of all sectors of society to accelerate the market development and system building. Market development aims to advocate the market-oriented development concept and ensure the returns and efficiency of capital investment while system building aims to ensure the control, compensation and balance of risks. Important measures to attain the smooth progress of the financialization of society and financial socialization include credit education, moral constraints, ethic assistance, mutual guarantee system, compliant operations, government guarantees, and intergenerational risk-benefit offset. Development-oriented finance institution should bring out the best of the advantages in market development, system building, and credit management and leverage financing to promote the financialization of society and financial socialization, boost the advance of market-based livelihood financial businesses and facilitate the overcoming of bottlenecks to meet the immediate needs of the mass, satisfy the demands of economic and social development, and support the building of a harmonious society (Figure 10.3).

Part III

The Operation Mechanism of Development-Oriented Finance

The operation system of development-oriented finance is a system arrangement in order to meet the restrictions of capital, market, and mechanism, enhance the ability of financial institutions, and support our economy and society to develop sustainably. Development-oriented finance is a strategic measure to implement the scientific concept of development, which aims at safeguarding national security, financial security, and enhancing international competitiveness. With the goal of attaining the first-class services in the international market, development-oriented finance makes full play of its creativity, changing theoretical thinking into action to make solutions to the bottleneck of China's mid- and long-term capital raising and promoting the economy to develop in a sustainable way. China's infrastructure building, integrated urban and rural development, livelihood finance, and "going out" all form the "one system three domains" of long-term development. In order to make full play of the dominant role of development-oriented finance institutions to support capital raising, we think the following: in the aspect of the sources of fund, development-oriented finance should mostly be based on financial bonds so as to guarantee the stable funding sources; in the aspect of operation mechanism, it should insist on the principles of "government entrance, finance supporting, market exit" and fulfilling the goal of government through market; in the aspect of corporate governance, we should insist on innovation of business model, cooperation model, and management model. In the process of the construction of socialism with Chinese characteristics, we should make full play of the role of development-oriented finance and depend on the advantages of China's high organizational efficiency. Furthermore, we should not throw away any sources and should form a good situation that finance serves social development and society helps finance to avoid multifarious risks. The operation mechanism of development-oriented finance demonstrates the combination of the theory and practices of development-oriented finance. In this part, we will analyze the operation mechanism of development-oriented finance, trying to answer the question of "how to do", including sources of capital, management mechanism, and operation mechanism.

Chapter 11

The Operational Mechanism: Government Entrance, Financing Process and Marketing Exit

The development-oriented finance should always adhere to the operational mechanism of "government as starting point, finance as incubator, and market as outlet", which aims to achieve the government's objectives by adopting market-based approaches, facilitate development, and prevent risks through the operational mechanism that is both effective and characteristic.

11.1 Introduction

In practice, development-oriented finance has clearly defined guiding ideologies, which include "determining priorities, giving timely assistance, planning first, constructing credit, and propelling by financing". "Determining priorities" means that hot issues and difficulties faced in the economic and social development should be taken as work priorities for development-oriented finance, including bottlenecks in materials and systems. "Giving timely assistance" means that market-based approaches should be adopted to explore financing sources to help meet the needs of government and achieve the government's development objectives. With respect to "planning first", as economic bubbles and repetitive construction are liable to occur due to inefficient planning and market building, it is necessary to combine the advantages of development-oriented finance with the advantages of government organization at a higher level, and strengthen regional planning, industry planning, social planning, market planning, and corresponding financial planning. Efforts should also be made to vigorously promote overall planning for urban and rural development, regional development, social and economic development, harmonious development between human and nature as well as domestic development and opening up to the outside world. "Constructing credit" means that the credit construction in development-oriented finance should penetrate the entire credit process and all related business areas including project development, review, loan extension, and recovery of principal and interest, to greatly boost the construction of credit system, prevent financial risks, and guarantee asset quality. As for "propelling by financing", development-oriented finance, with individual loans as carriers, helps develop corporate construction, cash flow construction, credit construction, and project construction. Based on quality assets and virtuous circle of funds, it can enable the financing service to realize unprecedented size and best ever efficiency. To embody and implement such guiding ideologies, CDB has developed the operational mechanism of "government as starting point, finance as incubator, and market as outlet" based on the experience accumulated in a continuous manner, in which, all the three stages link with one another and constitute an organic whole. Figure 11.1 shows the relationship between them.

Without an efficient operational mechanism, no idea could come into true. Next, the operational mechanism is analyzed.

11.2 Government as starting point

11.2.1 *Implication*

It means to take the cooperation with the government as starting point in development-oriented finance. The main implications of development-oriented finance are as follows:

(1) Development-oriented finance will take the development objectives of the government as its working basis by fully comprehending the general thought of the government for economic development, determining medium- and long-term business orientation, and continuously regulating its priorities, which will help it to survive the intense market competition.

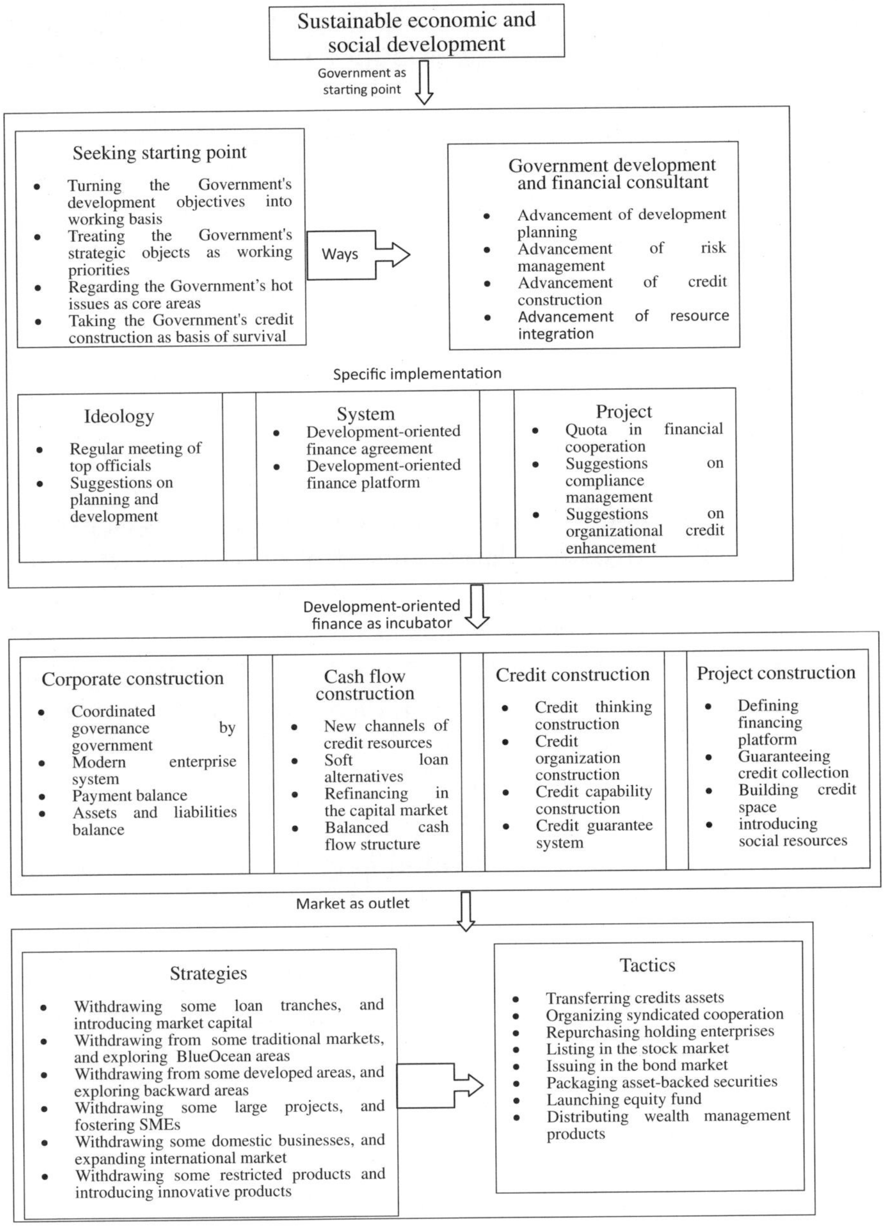

Figure 11.1: Operational mechanism of development-oriented finance.

(2) Development-oriented finance will take major strategic projects of the government as its working priorities by timely providing various services in a comprehensive and meticulous manner, ensuring essential supports, and building up core competitiveness for national development.

(3) Development-oriented finance will take major concerns of the government as core support areas by focusing on the breakthrough of bottlenecks in related sectors, accomplishing outstanding results, and shouldering social responsibilities.

(4) Development-oriented finance will take government credit as its strategy of survival, thus, it will fully utilize and maintain government credit to create favorable internal conditions for its development. Since it plays a certain role in social and economic development, the government is familiar with regional economic and social situation and usually possesses a large amount of information, precious resources, projects to be constructed, and all kinds of talents. Besides, the creditworthiness of the government directly reflects its financial payment capability. Particularly, China's financial budget, with its rigid feature, can be a direct source of cash flows on debt service.

(5) The development planning of the government and CDB should be incorporated in the construction of credit system for financing platform in order to fully exert the rights of the National People's Congress to decide, supervise, and review with respect to planning preparation and financing development, effectively realize the development potential for government credit, and ensure the scientificness and effectiveness of planning in the medium- and long-term development. The cooperation with the government in development-oriented finance aims to combine the advantages of the two sides, as well as realize win–win cooperation and strategic development objectives of the State.

Development-oriented finance mainly strengthens its cooperation with the government through development consultants. As an important part of the intermediary business of the bank, development consultants constitute a main strategic method and means to expand the space for development. The World Bank is highly effective in terms of financial consulting service for governments. Based on in-depth analysis and assessment on the financial, fiscal, and economic positions of some countries, the World Bank proposes advices that are of great significance to the development planning and policies of the countries, which are highly valued by governments. JP Morgan, a top-class international financial consulting institution, is experienced in providing financial consulting service to companies, especially in the design of M&A plans for companies. Development advice is the fruit of an international developed market, with established technologies and products. As China lies in an initial stage, different kinds of credits will be involved, with possible intentional interference. Along with the integrated development of international economy, China accelerates the development of market-oriented economy, as a result, economic activities, especially financial activities, become more and more complicated. In the meantime, there are higher requirements for expertise and more demands for development consultants. Government agencies, enterprises, and individuals have increasingly recognized that scientific consulting service will greatly boost development. Development consultants assume duties that are both challenging and creative. Different customers and requirements need different methods and starting points. A good suggestion may lead to a new market, new source of supply, new form of organization, new balance, new development strategy, and new hope. Without a doubt, development consultants, with unprecedented growth potential and a huge market, constitute an important part of the consulting industry. In this connection, an earlier starter with favorable performance will occupy an advantageous position in the competition. Some important enterprises in China, including those listed overseas, primarily receive consulting service from overseas consulting institutions. In this way, the quality of consulting services can be enhanced but some significant trade secrets cannot be kept any more, which explains why information about some issues is more accessible overseas than in China. Besides, some government agencies of China also rely on the development consulting service offered by international institutions, which may threaten China's economic security. Therefore, it is necessary to put great efforts into the development of the domestic consulting industry, which is of special significance to China's economic security. In this sense, development-oriented finance is well positioned to undertake such responsibility. As an important innovative business in development-oriented finance, having development consultants is an essential way to realize the objectives of development-oriented finance and survive fierce competition in financial sectors home and abroad.

Development-oriented finance enjoys certain advantages in brand, performance, financing, talents, and comprehensive financial services for offering development consultant services. Brand advantage means that development-oriented finance enjoys a credit rating that is the same as a country's sovereign credit rating, thus fostering a good image in international and domestic capital markets. Such advantage will help enhance customers' image and creditworthiness and reduce their financing costs by providing development consulting service to them. Performance advantage means that development-oriented finance has boasted world-class market performance. Financing advantage means that a development-oriented finance institution can issue financial bonds backed by government credit, and the loans granted by it have the features of long maturity, large amount, and fast transfer after review. Talent advantage suggests that a development-oriented finance institution, with the support of a batch of high-quality financial management personnel and technical experts across all industries, owns a high-level professional team in terms of project technologies, improvement of financing structure, asset, and debt restructuring as well as the design, issue, and underwriting of corporate bonds. A development-oriented finance institution is required to have the following qualifications: experienced in acting as a development consultant for key national construction projects as well as large and medium-sized projects; successfully organizing indirect syndicated loans and joint loans, and carrying out umbrella asset management business in cooperation with commercial banks; ranking among the best domestic bond underwriters; participating in the sponsorship of Sino–Swiss Partnership Fund, China–ASEAN SME Investment Fund, and China–Belgium Direct Equity Investment Fund; being able to manage and dispose of equity assets of debt-to-equity swap program. A close cooperative relationship with relevant competent departments of the State Council, local governments, companies in different sectors, media, commercial banks, and securities companies will help develop, launch, approve, promote, and distribute financial products. Besides, the development-oriented finance institution establishes favorable partnership with foreign investors, which can lay a sound foundation for the introduction of foreign capital. By fully utilizing various conditions and exerting comparative advantages, the development consulting business will be developed successfully, provided there are definite and practicable measures. After years of practice, development-oriented finance has strengthened its cooperation with the government through development consultants, developing some effective measures in regard of ideology, system, and project.

11.2.2 *Measures on ideological building*

In terms of ideology, first, regular meetings are held with top officials of the government. The constant communication between development consultants and top officials of the government, including exchange of ideas on development and analysis on situations, provides a good opportunity for development-oriented financial institute to integrate market demands with the government's goals. On the one hand, the basic views and overall considerations of the government on current hot issues can be learnt. On the other hand, the latest experiences in propelling the market by development-oriented financial institute can be shared with such top officials, to clarify the focus of cooperation between the two sides and set down corresponding measures. A team led by CDB's leaders will hold one or two meetings every year with top officials of relevant ministries and commissions, provincial and municipal governments, discussing major proposals and cooperation framework covering national and regional development strategies, and defining corresponding joint propulsion mechanism. The results are encouraging.

Second, the principle of planning first is prioritized. As the organizer and coordinator for national or regional economic and social development planning, the government has the right to approve the final planning scheme. Development-oriented financial institute will actively take part in the government preparation and organization of planning, so as to understand the whole picture concerning regional economic and social development from the source, work out countermeasures against bottlenecks in projects and financing for medium- and long-term development, and accelerate the early initiation of major strategic projects. Focusing on social development and financing rules, development-oriented finance also take cash flow balance and break-even of projects as major indicators to study, analyze, and formulate financing plans from long-term, comprehensive, and objective perspectives, which will help supplement the government's planning scheme. In 2009, CDB completed 1,030 items of regional, social, and industrial market planning, with the emphasis on regional planning for Yangtze River Delta, Beijing, Tianjin, Hebei, and Beibu Gulf Rim, Yangtze River protection and development planning, as well as planning on major energies, mineral, and agricultural resources in the world. Besides, medium- and long-term consulting service was provided for government planning to properly solve the potential irrationality related to government planning and administrative management cycle, and maintain the consistency and continuity of planning implementation. Planning first is an important method and business mode for development-oriented finance, by means of which, development sources could be traced, projects could be developed, and constructed in batches on a systematic and efficient basis, so as to extend risk prevention and improve financing quality and efficiency. Such principle, being regarded as a long-term concept in the development-oriented finance, is incorporated in various works, aiming to achieve more scientific, comprehensive, objective, sustainable, and reasonable layout, strengthen information transparency, and provide a definite, convenient, and practicable blueprint for the subsequent project construction, cash flow construction, credit construction, and system building.

Third, research on policies is intensified. Policy guidance exerts long-term influence on economic and social development, involving structural layouts of areas, industries, markets, and society. Development-oriented finance attaches importance to the research on policies, which will help provide comprehensive, objective, and practicable strategic suggestions for the preparation of policies by the government. For example, supporting suggestions related to financing for industrial restructuring and M&A, financing for the strategy of "going global", long-term financing arrangements for strategic industries including large aircrafts and space flights are proposed to respond to the "Top Ten Industry Promotion Planning" of the State, assisting the government in establishing an efficient development mechanism for the preparation and direction of industrial policies. In another instance, suggestions on policies and rules for the collection of financial resources and construction of credit culture system by the government were proposed according to the financing rule for the construction of medium- and long-term projects, which will help the government establish a more scientific and effective internal support and restriction mechanism. Another example was that similar suggestions were put forward for supporting financial policies on major strategic reforms in the social development areas, including employment, education, medical care, housing, and pension, to help the government build a revolving and regenerative cash flow mechanism and avoid heavy financial burden on the government in the long run.

11.2.3 *Measures on system building*

In terms of system building, the first is to sign cooperation agreement on development-oriented finance. To define specific framework and contents regarding the cooperation between the two sides, concluding the agreement on development-oriented finance with the government indicates the cooperation at the system building level, which is an important link to involve the government at the starting point.

(1) The government will recognize that such a agreement, different from general financial cooperation agreement, is an institutional arrangement for turning the ideological consensus between the two sides into specific cooperation mechanism and framework, which could effectively avoid uncertain risks caused by the replacement of top officials of the government.

(2) The agreement itself must be a scientific evaluation on the overall strategic credit space for a region, industry, or enterprise, which should clearly define the general institutional arrangements for the construction of credit structure, and suggest preliminary plan of

over-financing for regional development program in the next five years or even longer.

(3) The agreement should decisively promote the operational platform and connection mechanism for in-depth cooperation, and point out the direction and coverage of further exploring efforts, as well as deepening institutional innovation and mechanism reform in the future. In practice, CDB has signed corporation agreements on development-oriented finance with relevant ministries and commissions of the state as well as provincial governments, which have been renewed by adding new provisions to reflect new requirements. In fact, the conclusion of agreement itself is a process of publicizing development ideas and promoting credit construction.

The second is to establish a cooperation platform on development-oriented finance. The cooperation platform on development-oriented finance is the core carrier for realizing propulsion by financing, collection of resources, and supporting polices, which plays a significant role in the regional economic and social development.

(1) From the perspective of resource integration, efficient system, and standard management, the government should choose or establish a qualified entity as the investment and the financing platform for effectively carrying out the intentions of the government, providing all kinds of credit resources and quality assets as possible as it can and ensuring stable and positive cash flows in the future.
(2) Such a platform should be defined as the cooperation platform of development-oriented finance. Great support should be given in terms of labor, corporate governance, and financial standards. Assistance should also be provided by development-oriented financial institute to cultivate the abilities in project selection, planning, and organization as well as risk prevention in the financing.
(3) Sufficient power on organizational credit enhancement and motivation should be given to the platform. Particularly, efforts should be made to guarantee the communication ability of the

platform with competent authorities responsible for the construction of public projects of the government (such as National Development and Reform Commission (NDRC), bureaus of finance, and construction commissions), and development-oriented financial institute should provide assistance in an active manner.

(4) By focusing on long-term development, the group enterprise management framework of the platform should be established and standardized steps, to develop main business modules with clarified business lines, and strengthen the credit space for market-based financing. At the same time, a development-oriented financial institute should assist in the expansion of market-based financing channels. Such platform construction pattern could also help expand international development-oriented finance business by exploring credit resources of local governments according to local conditions. In addition, with the deepening of financial system reform and national economic development, it is necessary to extend the cooperation platform on development-oriented finance to cities, counties, and townships, expanding the credit coverage for grassroots financial system, and providing strong fundamental support for new countryside construction and urbanization development strategy of the State.

The third is to set up external service-oriented technical consulting systems. The government will need a senior government consultant in the processes of planning preparation, project selection, organizational credit enhancement, and propulsion by financing. By means of personnel exchange and technical training, a development-oriented financial institute can set up various external service-oriented technical consulting systems for the government.

(1) Experts will be organized and an expert database management system be established, providing the most authoritative consulting service for the government.
(2) Assistance will be provided for the government to prepare a series of project selection standards and dynamic tracking,

management, and evaluation mechanisms which are more specific and are based on long-term benefits.

(3) Regular meeting and personnel exchange mechanisms will be established to strengthen the timeliness and effectiveness of services.

11.2.4 *Measures on project construction*

In terms of project construction, the first is to define cooperation quota on development-oriented finance.

(1) The key projects will be selected in a scientific manner and various credit structures will be built pursuant to concepts of development-oriented finance, which will help define a reasonable quota range for financial cooperation, and advance major projects in a substantive manner.
(2) The overwhelming advantages of the government in financing infrastructure and pillar industry project construction will be brought into play, and the strength of development-oriented financial institute in integration and large-scale financing will be incorporated into the investment and financing platform backed by the government.
(3) Reasonable evaluation will be conducted for significant hidden risks suggested by uncertainties, existing cooperation quota will be adjusted and improved in a planned manner, risks will be mitigated through the organization advantage of government and subsequent market-based financing efforts, and basic supporting systems and credit culture construction will be accelerated.
(4) Through improving various specific management systems, sustainable strategic credit space will be created, and different strategic options be available, offering over-financing supply chain for major projects, in which, the credit resources in the credit and capital markets are covered.

The second is to provide financial consulting service for projects. The basic financing demands and disposable financial resources for development will be analyzed for projects. Sufficient communication will be conducted with the government and departments related to projects, to obtain the information on potential organizational advantages and credit resources available for development, and straighten out government assets or resources with idle features. By taking into consideration the macroeconomic trends and direction of financial market reform and development at present and in the future, the solutions on portfolio financing will be put forward, covering fund sources, cash flow features, financing subjects, financial products, and connection mechanism, and targeted measures will be proposed toward key issues in the specific project and credit construction.

The third is to stick to project selection and compliance management.

(1) Bottleneck problems in the regional economic and social development will be evaluated in an objective manner, and the unique information advantage of development-oriented finance will be exerted to cover all the information of major strategic projects.

(2) Assistance will be provided for the government to prepare corresponding selection standards, determine priorities of projects to be initiated, straighten out sources of cash flows for project construction, excavate various potential credit resources, internal and external, and conduct scientific rating for projects recommended by the government.

(3) Suggestions on compliance operation will be provided for the projects in progress and to be progressed by the government, including approval documents for projects, qualifications of financing subjects, requirements on profitability, risks in connection with environment assessment, and policy red lines, which will help exert the advantages of development-oriented finance in the information, organization, and resource allocation, and eventually provide strong assistance for the government's project construction.

In short, a typical pattern has gradually taken shape in the practice for development consultants in development-oriented finance, which integrates "financing" with "wisdom" based on the government's objectives and with market-based approaches as means, to provide advice for the governments at all levels and important customers. The cooperation with the government could be regarded as the starting point of development-oriented finance, which includes two respects: the first is to develop development consulting service according to the needs of the government by integrating "financing" with "wisdom", helping the government define objectives and clarify thinking, providing all-round and professional suggestions on development strategies, preparation of planning, financing credit, risk prevention, and supporting policies. The second is to propel development by financing in an active manner, coordinate and guide various resources, assist the government in integrating internal resources pursuant to national industrial policies and regional strategic planning, select and confirm projects, as well as determine aggregate financing according to regional economic development level, financial revenues and expenditures, performance of contracts, and credit review. The working objectives include: on the one hand, helping government departments further improve development strategies and plans of regions, cities, and industries, giving timely assistance with respect to the hot issues of the government, "liquidizing remnant assets and expanding increments", and increasing limited resources of the government, to push forward governance structure construction, corporate construction, cash flow construction, and credit system construction, promote coordinated development of society and economy in the regions, and reflect the responsibilities and functions of development-oriented financial institute; on the other hand, providing plans and suggestions on development strategies for the government and enterprises by actively participating in various preparatory works and communicating with related markets and enterprises, which will help the government and development-oriented financial institute to establish a mutual trust and interactive mechanism as well as develop a new pattern of "bank–government cooperation and bank–enterprise combination". In addition, there are three purposes in this stage: the first is to advance development planning, to incorporate the objectives and demands of government in plan preparation, seize development opportunities, define basic development direction, and make clear staged development objectives; the second is to advance risk management by preparing prevention plans according to potential uncertainties in the stage of plan design, and reserving policy room for countermeasures, so that the government can consider the issues related to project construction and regional development on a long-term basis; the third is to advance credit construction. While working out development strategies and project planning, practicable suggestions will be proposed for specified credit construction framework of the government, emphasizing the importance of credit resource integration by the government in the development of strategies and financial consulting service. In 2006, the cooperation between development-oriented finance institution and the government in terms of RMB50 billion policy loans in Liaoning Province just reflects the above-mentioned issues. A basic framework is defined through the cooperation with the government to quickly designate and replenish some construction platforms. In this way, subsequent projects will be easily implemented with approval. When commercial banks are still looking for an appropriate way, development-oriented financial institutes have established and integrated financing systems from top to bottom. In the reconstruction of shantytowns, CDB and Liaoning Provincial Government, based on the scientific outlook on development and people-first approach, initiated the loans of CDB after realizing the inevitable trends, which finally brought about the input of financial funds of the state. Overall, it was much better than the effect of reviewing projects one by one. Therefore, in early stages, the cooperation between development-oriented finance institution and the government could be strengthened, and scientific development planning could be performed, to realize resource integration and information exchange, which will help reinforce the construction of basic credit system at the strategy level, and facilitate sustainable development of economy and society.

11.3 Finance as incubator

The "finance as incubator" means that, development-oriented financial institutes actively enter the blank financing areas beset by system defects and market failure, and practice the concepts of development-oriented finance as coordinated by the organization advantages of the government, so as to drive credit system construction by financing and improve four construction processes including corporate legal person, cash flows, credit, and project. Its foothold is to establish projects and market systems which meet commercial operation standards and financial risk management requirements. Table 11.1 summarizes the incubation process of development-oriented finance.

In terms of corporate construction, it is key to build a modern enterprise system. As we know, corporate construction aims to build and improve corporate governance structure with liquidity balance as means and starting point, to turn the corporate with balanced cash flows into the one with balanced balance sheet, and eventually set up modern enterprise system and corporate governance mechanism meeting the standards of listed companies. The building of corporate governance structure covers organizational framework of the management, decision-making mechanism for projects, coordination mechanism for government projects, government credit resource collection mechanism, and financial management standard mechanism and so on. First, before the establishment of corporate legal person, development-oriented financial institute will make up the deficiencies in the corporate governance structure with the structure under the coordination of government, to facilitate various management policies and system arrangements on development-oriented finance in the initial stage. Second, after the establishment of corporate legal person and in the stage of financing platform and project collation window, development-oriented financial institute will assist the government in fostering basic abilities in project selection and management and intensifying the ability of planning preparation. Such institutions will provide guidance and suggestions for prior works in the project development, to develop a legal person with basic balanced cash flows. Third, when the corporate lawyer develops a management team with independent experience and decision-making mechanism under the Board of Directors, the development-oriented finance institution will work to transform the financing platform from a legal person with balanced cash flows into the one with balanced balance

Table 11.1: Incubation process of development-oriented finance.[a]

Indicators Stage	Corporate construction	Cash flow construction	Credit construction	Project construction
I	The government coordinates and dispatches personnel Pure financing window Several project proprietors fail to establish corporate governance structure	No cash flows. Rely on government subsidy	Complete government credit	Determine basic management standards by adopting project construction agent system Strengthen capability of selecting projects Fostering capability of preparing planning
II	Be able to establish primary corporate governance structure according to the operation, of enterprise, and adopt break-even method	Convert some government subsidies into cash flows of enterprise	Reveal some market credit and government balance credit	Guarantee capability of allocating resources for project construction in terms of policy; collect various government credit resources for unified management
III	Independent market player improve cooperate governance structure; corporate with balanced balance sheet	Own large cash flow sources	Government's organization credit enhancement by focusing on market credit	Develop a holding conglomerate; intensify project operational ability; take risk prevention and control measures
IV	Establish modern enterprise system Corporate governance meeting the standards of listed companies	Basically develop sustainable cash flows	Complete market credit	Become a holding conglomerate engaging in multiple areas; operate project finance pursuant to principles

[a]See the *Outlines on Development-Oriented Finance*, written by the joint research group of China Development Bank and Renmin University of China, Renmin University of China Press, 1st edition in March 2006, p. 102. Further collation and modification are made.

sheet. In this stage, financing will be used to help the legal person develop certain real assets (such as transferable land, right to charge, and right to operate) with cash inflows. Such assets will serve as the credit basis and source for further investment and expansion (mortgage or pledge), to accumulate original capital, increase owner's equity on the balance sheet, establish enhanced supplementary free cash flow mechanism, and push the legal person into the market as a player with independent operation. Fourth, after the corporate legal person turns an independent market player, development-oriented financial institute will intensify the collation of corporate asset structure by means of early planning and financial consultancy, which will help develop a corporate management entity with two projects coexisting, that is, public welfare project and self-reliance project. In the meantime, efforts will be made to help the corporate legal person to establish modern enterprise system, and engage top-level talents from the market, to gradually develop some collective holding subsidiaries meeting the management standards of listed companies by way of capital operation, transit into a corporate legal person that could be listed step-by-step through M&A, and develop full financing functions in the capital market.

With respect to cash flow construction, the key element is to ensure relative balance of construction funds. As we know, cash flow construction aims to adopt corresponding methods to increase cash flow sources for projects in line with medium- and long-term strategic development objectives and the features of cash flows from less to more and from instability to stability, which will help ensure relatively balanced cash inflows and outflows in the entire cycle from project construction to operation, and avoid the risk of cash flow shortage. Cash flows in the development-oriented finance construction projects include two ways: the first is to balance cash flows by means of credit construction, which includes short-term and long-term channels. For the former, land transfer, government subsidy, and pledge of right to charge will be regarded as the sources of cash inflows. While for the latter, cash inflows after the completion of project or government subsidy after taxes increase will be the emphasis. Besides, refinancing in the capital market including bonds, trust, and listing will be taken as an important supplement to cash flows, so as to gradually turn government credit into enterprise credit in the development of enterprise. The second is to adapt to the unbalanced feature based on unbalanced cash flows by constructing special development-oriented finance products, for example, soft loan — a sort of cash flow loan product featuring "higher first and lower later". In the beginning, sufficient capital will be replenished in a lump sum for financing platform, reasonable loan grace period will be granted (only paying interests, without repayment of principal), and corresponding risk guarantee and sharing mechanism will be defined. In the later period, the right to select will give lenders certain risk premium compensation opportunities. Anyway, in general, the cash flow match mode of being "higher first and lower later" will be formed by means of standard capital and loan management mechanism.

Nevertheless, from the perspective of standardized development, China's capital loan management mechanism must follow its own unique road by fully drawing on foreign mature experiences, to ensure that sufficient resources could be used to provide sustainable capital loans by commercial banks or policy financial institutions in a long term. Such mechanism includes the following three respects:

(1) To determine stable bond issue mechanism for capital raising in the specific projects (major strategic projects), to ensure that qualified commercial banks or policy financial institutions can raise comparatively low-cost (lower than stock market) quasi-subordinated debts or capital financing bonds on a regular basis, and the size should not be smaller than the core capital of financial institutions (or a certain proportion of entire capital).
(2) To determine certain project financing standards for capital loans, define which level of governments will have the authority of verifying financing projects, and make clear the risk control boundary for financing size in the capital loans (such as project cycle, internal rate of return (IRR), principal source of repayment, risk compensatory mechanism, and credit enhancement conditions of the government organization).

(3) To give financial institutions sufficient right to innovate on the types of capital loans and structural design, so that they could be allowed to set up risk premium compensatory mechanism and instruments in accordance with laws (such as the right to select project, right of debt-to-equity, preferential right of financing and preferential right of capital market service, and corresponding compensation measures could be taken in case of risk losses).

With respect to credit construction, it is of most significance to exert the advantage of government organization. As we know, credit construction is to organically combine government credit, including financial credit and coordinated credit of government organization, with the advantages of development-oriented finance in the credit and financing, which will be used to foster and improve enterprise credit in a centralized manner after the management, use, distribution, evaluation, and final conversion, helping bring it into full play to the maximum extent. Credit construction, the highest level relative to system building and market construction, is a process of incubating, cultivating, and building enterprise credit (or personal credit) starting from national credit, development-oriented finance credit, local government credit, and grassroots social credit. It includes three development stages: (i) the first stage is ideological building. The problem of understanding should be solved and credit awareness should be intensified. (ii) The second stage is organization building. The advantage of development-oriented finance institution in financing, that of government organization in coordination, and that of the masses in democracy should be combined, so as to turn the demand for funds in the social and economic development into a major force driving economic development. Credit construction could be sped up, which plays an irreplaceable role in the financial credit system construction of grassroots institutions, including individuals, SMEs, and county-level economies. (iii) The third stage is the construction of sustainable development ability. Through credit resources from individuals, families, enterprises, and governments, the building of cash flows, tax source basis, credit network, and micro-system should be reinforced, which will help generate sustainable financial resources in enterprises and the government, and develop ever increasing government credit. In the meantime, with the credit or mortgage security in the form of balance credit of the government and packaged enterprise credit, bigger project risks could be covered, and government credit could be gradually converted into market credit in a continuous manner, realizing the credit development course from nothing to existence and from weak to strong. With regard to fund size, development-oriented financial institutes are inferior to other commercial banks. However, such institutions must be better in respect of planning and credit construction to have the initiative in hands.

In respect of project construction, it is of key importance to work out a project management system. As we know, project construction aims to gradually make previously unqualified projects meet commercial principles through development-oriented finance, and develop a project construction mechanism in line with commercial financing standards based on various risk prevention and sharing measures. It can be regarded as a process of operation and management within its own system framework. First, in the initial stage, the government selects specific financing platform through a project construction agent system, defines corresponding construction subjects, determines basic management standards, intensifies the capability in project selection, and fosters the capability in planning preparation for financing platform. Second, in order to straighten out channels, development-oriented finance urges the government to guarantee the allocation of project construction resources from the perspective of policies, and gradually collect various government credit resources for centralized management in an orderly way. Third, to further intensify the capability of project in operation and management, development-oriented financial institute, acting as financial consultants, assist the government in collecting and sorting out the assets generated from existing investment, which will also help build a holding conglomerate with strategic credit development room. Besides, various risk prevention measures are adopted to standardize project construction, including diversified shareholding, mutual-guarantee as well as introduction of operational mechanism for build-operate transfer (BOT) and public private-partnership (PPP) projects. Fourth, under the assistance provided by development-oriented financial institute, all sorts of market-based financing methods are explored step by step, to build up certain market credit standing, expand financing room in the capital market, develop a holding conglomerate oriented for multiple areas, and establish a mature mechanism for the operation of project financing in accordance with commercial principles.

In short, in the incubation process of development-oriented finance, the construction of corporate legal person, cash flows, credit, and project is an organic unity evolving and developing according to the space-time conversion principle, each one being affected by one another. In which, corporate construction is a carrier to establish a corporate legal person with reasonable governance structure through incubation of development-oriented finance. Cash flow construction could be taken as a basis to ensure a sustainable cycle including financing process, input, and output. Credit construction should be treated as a core objective, which, ideologically and organizationally, set up the risk prevention and control network with huge potential for the incubation of development-oriented finance and create basic conditions for market outlet. As the foothold, project construction can only establish a favorable project development and management process, with benign inherent quality of corporate legal person, cash flow, and credit basis. Only in this way can it be truly favored by market. Theoretically, development-oriented finance combines its advantage in financing with the advantage of government organization, pushing national credit, bank credit, and local government credit to convert into enterprise credit, and improving development financing mechanism.

11.4 Market as outlet

The "market as outlet" means that development-oriented financial institutes make some adjustments to strategic credit space according to the changes of situations, to embody its functions of market construction and system building. This is the last process after "government as starting point" and "development-oriented finance as incubator". Without a good withdrawal strategy and mechanism, everything will be eliminated gradually along with historical development. In a sense, taking the market as outlet is the key to ensure smooth withdrawal of development-oriented finance arrangements, and it also reflects the functions of development-oriented finance in terms of market construction and system building. As a result, we could consider from two levels including strategies and tactics. Strategic withdrawal, from the perspective of macroeconomy, seeks financial projects backed by the government and based on society, market, and finance, which is a dynamic process with continuous evolvement and development. Tactic withdrawal is relatively simple, which is reflected as all kinds of mature or immature instruments and channels in the financial market. Here, the concept of market is quite extensive, which not only includes tangible financial markets but also covers those that have not drawn attention or been fully developed.

With respect to strategic withdrawal, the following measures are to be taken:

(1) To withdraw some loan tranches and introduce market capital. Through transfer of credit resources, trust, insurance investment plan, and launching of bank's wealth management products, a development-oriented financial institute can introduce some market funds into existing project construction to meet the financing demands of existing and additional projects, and enhance liquidity efficiency of long-term financing activities.
(2) To withdraw from some traditional markets and explore Blue Ocean areas. Due to special advantages in financing structure, development-oriented financial institutes have maintained a high market share in areas of infrastructure, basic industries, and pillar industries for a long time. Nevertheless, with the increasing financial strength of local governments and maturing investment and financing platform, commercial financial institutions start to get involved in these traditional markets previously occupied by development-oriented financial institute. Thus, development-oriented financial institutes need to conduct necessary strategic conversion in order to actively enter some Blue Ocean areas of

people's livelihood, county-level economy, international cooperation and new countryside construction, and make all kinds of attempts in financial innovation. It is not only a process of turning credit construction mechanism of traditional markets into market credit but also a process of creating a new-type credit structure construction mechanism for new Blue Ocean areas, preparing for the next mature opportunity of market as outlet.

(3) To withdraw from some developed areas and develop backward areas. With continuous development and improvement of credit system in the entire society, breakthrough has been made in some areas which could not be easily accessed by commercial financial institutions previously, and social capital has gained outstanding growth in these areas. However, in most backward areas, lots of infrastructures, pillar industries, and potential resources are still waiting for development. By means of withdrawal from some developed areas, development-oriented financial institutes could acquire new funds and human resources and introduce emerging resources into the backward areas, thus achieving unexpected results. Such a move not only contains mature experience of previous developed areas but also introduces some social capital under innovative attempts into backward areas, for joint cooperation and development.

(4) To withdraw some large-scale projects and foster SME projects. Once complete market credit is determined for financing subjects of large-scale projects, a huge amount of funds could be obtained through capital market and commercial credit. However, the SME area has been short of sustainable financing sources for a long time. According to historical data, the SME is the most important force driving economic and social development in a country or region, which not only constitutes the entire social credit system but also realizes sustainable growth of national income. In addition, the SME is an important carrier to ensure the solution of unemployment. By withdrawing the financing processes in some large-scale projects, development-oriented financial institute, as the financing service provider, can provide subsequent value-added services. In the meantime, new financing

forces which have been systematic with a certain scale can be extended to the bottleneck areas for SME financing beset by insufficient market credit and market failure. By setting up nationwide re-guarantee system, SME credit security fund of governments at all levels, lending institutions backed by the government in the form of batch and financing assistance platform, venture capital guidance fund and venture capital fund, grass-roots credit mutual assistance and guarantee association, village banks, micro-finance companies, and other micro-finance institutions, development-oriented financial institutes have constructed a complete set of social credit financing system oriented for SMEs.

(5) To withdraw some domestic businesses and expand international market. With the gradual improvement of domestic financial system, development-oriented financial institutes may consider withdrawing some domestic businesses and expanding international businesses. Strategic horizon should be extended to developing countries in the world, as well as areas with market failure and credit defects in the developed countries, which will help seek more long-term strategic interest objectives for the country. In many developing countries and less developed regions, infrastructure, pillar industries, and potential resources have not been fully developed due to historical, ethnical, political, and social reasons. But, more importantly, there are no fair, just, and equal financing opportunities in these countries or regions. Consequently, development-oriented financial institutes can play a utilitarian role in such areas.

(6) To withdraw some products and launch innovative products. The products without market advantages and export potential should be abandoned resolutely. Breakthrough should be made according to customer's demands and new macroeconomic situations. A series of innovative products should be launched to ensure market competitiveness and tackle bottleneck problems. From the perspective of strategy, first, innovation should not be made for the sake of innovation; instead, customer's demands should be taken as the starting point and the concept of service

as the basis. Under the guidance of theories on development-oriented finance, new strategies, mechanism, products, and services should be developed and designed from the perspective of medium- and long-term development of the State. Second, existing products and systems of other financial institutions should not be imitated. Instead, internal product development and operational mechanism should be modernized, and comprehensive consideration should be conducted in terms of process, pricing, risk control, and settlement. Third, the study of economic development and financial theories should be intensified, and targeted research on existing domestic financial regulatory system should be conducted, to find out the development course of financial products, and create a reference system for domestic financial products. Fourth, the construction of product research and development team should be reinforced, and analysis should be applied from the perspective of macroeconomy, microeconomy, and industries instead of one single product, which will help fully understand the historic opportunities implicated by times. For example, CDB has provided soft loans to support the implementation of national strategic projects for a long time, including the Three Gorges Project, South–North Water Transfer Project, the Olympics, World Expo, and large airplane project. Nevertheless, due to the implementation of commercial reform strategies, soft loans cannot be provided for original major infrastructure projects, hence new alternatives must be introduced. The "capital loan mechanism" under the background of "special project loans of the government" was a good try, in which, CDB actively assisted NDRC in preparing management measures, providing previous experience, proposing suggestions, and sharing concerns of the government. In the meantime, the bank could also consider taking the investment system reform of insurance companies as a major opportunity, to introduce insurance funds by means of convertible debts and replace original soft loans. In this way, not only the anti-periodic fluctuation feature of insurance fund in the long-term allocation can be fully exerted but also reasonable and effective market outlets can be found for the application of increasing insurance funds. During this process, development-oriented financial institutes can serve as financing leaders. On the one hand, overall plan on capital raising for the government's projects can be formulated. On the other hand, arrangements can be made for insurance funds and capital from other sources, achieving win–win situation.

With regard to tactic withdrawal, according to the progress of four construction projects in the stage of incubation of development-oriented finance, the bank has designed different fund repayment mechanism for market outlet pursuant to financing natures, purposes, and use, covering transfer of credit assets, organization of syndicated cooperation, repurchase of holding enterprises, introduction of private capital, listing in the stock market, bond issue in the bond market, packaging of asset-backed securities, launching of equity fund, and distribution of wealth management products.

11.5 Summary

This chapter introduced the operation mechanisms of development-oriented finance, covering three links, government entry, financial incubation, and market exit. These three links are intended to promote the maturity of market entities and establish an efficient financing platform by virtue of project construction and system building (Figure 11.2).

The three processes of "selection of projects by government, incubation of development-oriented finance, and realization of market outlet" are the operational characteristics of development-oriented finance. The central point is to promote the maturity of market player, and construct efficient financing and credit platforms through project construction and system building. Selection of projects by the government means that local governments select and recognize projects, as well as recommend and apply for loans from development-oriented financial institute according to national industrial policies and regional strategic planning, and integrate internal resources. In the meantime, a development-oriented finance institution will determine aggregate

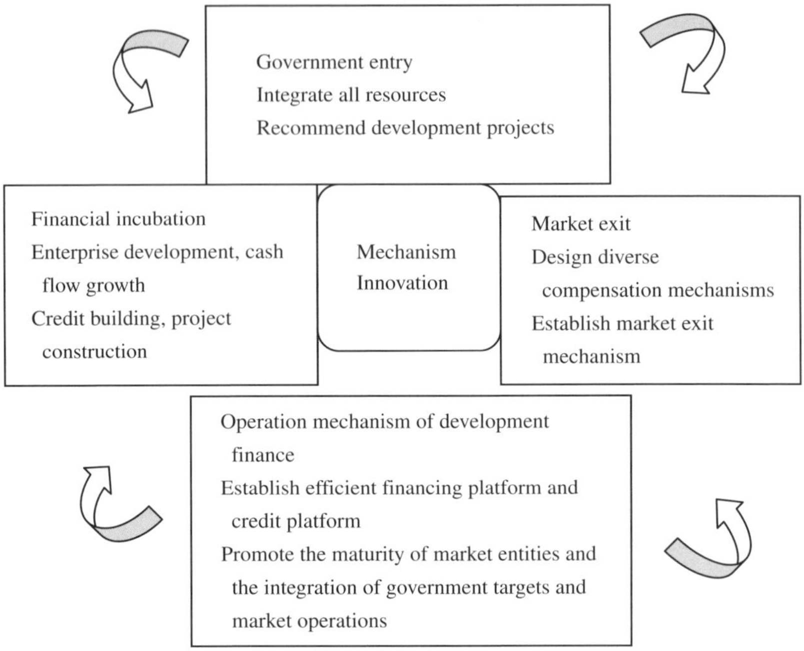

Figure 11.2: Operation mechanism of development-oriented finance.

loans according to regional economic development level, financial revenues and expenditures in the region, performance of contracts, and credit review. The incubation of development-oriented finance means that, under the coordination of the government, project construction and system building will be facilitated by financing, so that the corporate legal person with balanced cash flows can be gradually converted into the one with balanced balance sheet. Selection of market outlet suggests that, according to the development trend of cash flow construction, different market-based repayment mechanism will be designed in line with loan nature, purpose, and use, including the repayment of normal loans, repurchase by parent company, and capital market outlet, as well as financial repayment mechanism adopted for some public welfare projects including the repurchase by the government.

The three-staged operational characteristics constitute an inseparable and organic whole in development-oriented finance. Taking the government as starting point aims to deal with the starting point when development-oriented financial institutes implement national strategies. Finance as incubator emphasizes being guided by the concepts of development-oriented finance, to integrate resources from various sides, direct a large amount of social capital, incubate the areas with system defects and market failure, construct a credit system with Chinese development characteristics, as well as strengthen the ability of borrowers to prevent risks. Seeking market outlets considers strategically the targets and outlets for financial environmental improvement of less developed areas, to seek sustainable project construction pattern, and inject new energy into such areas in a continuous manner. In a word, the operational mechanism of development-oriented finance attempts to establish a stable bridge between government objectives and market demands, which will help provide service for medium- and long-term construction in China.

Market performance is closely connected with the government. Therefore, in pushing forward economic and social development, it is also very important to boost development-oriented finance. Besides, innovation should be made in terms of management system, and the decision-making process for the areas of capital, finance, customer, risk, and audit should be strengthened and be more democratic, to establish an effective incentive and restrictive mechanism.

Chapter 12

Sources of Funding: Financial Bonds Supplemented with Other Raised Funds

As a national development-oriented finance institution, China Development Bank (CDB) issues financial bonds that are based on government credit to raise funds for the mid- and long-term construction and social and livelihood undertakings, which is a vital achievement of the economic system reform. It is imperative for CDB to strengthen its operations as a bond bank and establish diversified financing mechanisms in which issuing financial bonds is a principal means of financing, supplemented with other financing sources in order to raise funds for the mid- and long-term development of the country.

12.1 China calls for bond bank

China's mid- and long-term advances and social and livelihood undertakings demand long-term funding support from development bonds. This type of bonds, which can be considered as financial bonds of policy banks to some degree, is issued to designated subscribers. Also, based on the specified procedures and on the premise of approval of the State Council for the purpose of collecting credit funds, these bonds are also issued through public bidding by development-oriented financial institutions. They are also known as silver-edged bonds as the credit rating of such bonds ranks second only to treasury bonds. The characteristics of financial bonds are as follows:

(1) The funds raised through such bonds are mainly used for directed loans.
(2) The bonds are issued in a centralized way and in a certain amount.

(3) The collected funds have long maturities and are thus conducive to long-term loans.
(4) Financial bonds cannot be redeemed in advance, but can be traded and transferred on securities market.
(5) Financial bonds have high interest rates and the financing cost is relatively high.

For these reasons, it is suitable to invest funds raised through such financial bonds into large and medium infrastructure sectors, basic industries, and pillar industries which are closely related to mid- and long-term development of the State. Development bonds were first introduced in China in 1994. As a primary issuer, CDB has distributed over 90% of all financial bonds. The funds of CDB mainly come from financial bonds and above 90% of its loans are extended by means of bond funds. Thus, CDB is known as a bond bank. Development financing mainly invests its funds raised through financial bonds in large and medium infrastructure sector, basic industries, and pillar industries, and has intensified support for county economy, livelihood undertaking, and "going global" activities of enterprises in recent years, thereby playing a significant role in adjusting industrial and regional economic structure, helping economic growth of China's western regions, and promoting the healthy and sustainable development of the national economy.

China's mid- and long-term advances and social and livelihood undertakings, which financial institutions are generally unwilling and unsuitable to engage in, are in urgent need of support of development financing of bond banks. Investments in areas such as infrastructure and basic industries usually involve enormous capitals, long period, high risk, and uncertain returns; especially, capital flows are remarkable at the early stage of investment and it may take a long time to obtain investment income. These are the basic features and dilemmas of financing for mid- and long-term constructions. As the market economy is still in its infancy after a long period of planned economy and the current economic system reform is dominated by the government, China is faced with serious problems in relation to system deficiencies and lack of market development.

In other words, despite the achievements, the market system is still backward and remains as the Achilles' heel of China's mid- and long-term development. Specifically, at the micro level, corporate governance is defective and credit of market actors is still missing; at the macro level, there exist notable regional imbalances, urban–rural differences, and social disparities, the basis for infrastructure and its construction is still weak and pressures in social security, employment, and environmental protection are huge while there is serious shortage of funds available for public causes. Issues such as large population, limited resources, and imbalanced development have become increasingly prominent; restrictions of resources have existed and will exist for a long time; the task of developing infrastructure sector, basic industries, and pillar industries remains arduous and accelerating urbanization needs a large amount of funds. To resolve all these problems, it is imperative to improve the financing mechanism for mid- and long-term infrastructure construction.

In March, 1994, the State Council approved to establish CDB, and allowed it to issue China's first development bond by means of assigned purchasing and use the funds collected for the development of infrastructure sector, basic industries, and pillar industries. In September 1998, the State Council then permitted CDB to issue financial bonds on the inter-bank market through public tendering, which is considered as a crucial achievement in the reform of China's investment and financing system and the financial system, and a revolutionary breakthrough for resolving mid- and long-term financing dilemma. With the deepening of reform and opening up, China's financing system and financial market have made significant progress. At the early stage of reform and opening up, the financing system focused on fiscal financing and attracted foreign investments, and in recent times, it has developed into a diversified system in which financing operations of commercial banks, capital market financing, policy financing, and development financing also contribute to the rapid social and economic development. With regard to the financial market, the liquidity of China's capital market has increased and financial resources available for economic development are more abundant than ever before, which are reflected in the growth of residents' deposits and the remarkable change in the structure of national savings. In 1979, the savings of residents, businesses, and the government accounted for 23.55%, 33.63%, and 42.82% respectively, and the figures became 40%, 40%, and 20% in 2009; China's foreign exchange reserves increased to US$2.64 trillion in September 2010 and financial assets climbed to more than RMB60 trillion in April 2009, accounting for 4–5% of the global total. However, it has been well recognized that considering the low financing efficiency and the status quo as an immature primary market, China's financial market is, despite the large total amount, still lagging far behind that of developed countries and unable to meet the demands for the rapid, steady, and sustainable economic development. On the whole, what China is short of are not funds, but the effective mechanism for motivating funds, especially a sound financing mechanism for ensuring the needs of mid- and long-term growth and "bottleneck" areas in social development.

12.2 Issuing development bonds is an efficient financing mechanism

The issuance of financial bonds by CDB is an effective mechanism for ensuring the financing needs of China's mid- and long-term advances and social and livelihood undertakings. As the national development-oriented finance institution, CDB possesses characteristics of a policy bank, has the nature of a financial enterprise, and also takes responsibilities as development-oriented finance institution. The features of a policy bank refrains credit expansion driven by for-profit purposes; instead, CDB must prepare and implement credit policies as a macro-control authority according to the macroeconomy and industrial policies and reflect governmental intentions. As a financial enterprise, CDB must operate independently as a market entity, focus on the efficient use of funds, and guard against financial risks. Moreover, as a national financial institution, CDB should earnestly undertake responsibility for promoting market system building and creating conditions for the sound and sustainable economic and social development while providing financing services for national strategic projects. The essence of development-oriented finance is to, by utilizing policy resources conferred by the country through market-based instruments, connect the bank's performance in infrastructure construction and hot areas in need of development closely with governmental goals and ultimately reflect strategic objectives and policy requirements of the State. Therefore, the issuance of financial bonds by CDB constitutes a unique bond financing mechanism for China known as the development bond financing mechanism. In this mechanism, the financial bonds are issued based on government credit to centralize commercial banks' short-term funds and the social funds and to effectively allocate idle social capitals to support the mid- and long-term infrastructure construction and social and livelihood undertakings. Meanwhile, it mitigates systematic risks of the financial sector by cutting off the direct relations of investments in the mid- and long-term construction with the monetary base. The reason that the mechanism can play such a role lies in its vitalizing of government credit in the following three aspects:

(1) It expands the financial credit of government. Financial credit, generated by tax and budget regulations, derives from economic development and tax revenue growth and is related to fiscal incomes. For now, China's financial credit mainly plays a role in the treasury bonds issued by the fiscal system itself and besides, provides certain guarantees for international financial institutions such as the World Bank. Thus, there is a large room for improving the capacity and using efficiency of financial credit. As a special organization of the government, the development-oriented finance institution issues financial bonds based on the particular credit conferred by the government. Such financial bonds are considered as quasi-treasury bonds and an extension of the government's financial credit. Issuing financial bonds can bring ample funds to areas such as the infrastructure sector, basic industries, and pillar industries, and is conducive to stepping up the aggregation and industrialization process of investments and expanding the multiplier effect and acceleration effect of investments in treasury bonds. The development bond financing mechanism opens up a channel linking the government and the capital market. Compared to the mere financial pattern of loans, it

can bridge shortage of fiscal construction funds and can realize the efficient use of government credit and improve the financial system's efficiency of resources allocation by lessening the "crowding out effect" where fiscal capitals could squeeze out social funds.

(2) It strengthens the currency credit of government. Currency credit is generated from the issuance of legal tender by a country or a region. It is based on a country's or a region's macro performance and represents certain economic sovereignty. Currency credit, a typical government credit, is directly associated with the amount and liquidity of the legal tender issued by a state or an area. Development-oriented finance securitizes some monetary assets and manages these securities. It also transfers commercial banks' short-term funds into long-term centralized and large-amount funds to improve the efficiency of shifting savings to investments, which is helpful in guiding commercial banks and social capitals to invest in proper areas and achieving the objectives of macro-control.

(3) It makes rational use of the government's institutional credit. Institutional credit arises from the position of a statutory financial institution. As CDB is such an institution, it was granted with RMB50 billion by the State as capital funds at the start and conferred with quasi-sovereign government credit, which is a vital basis for the market-based operations of development financing and the credit enhancement by virtue of the state and governmental organizations. Applying the credit of statutory financial institution, CDB propels economic growth by focusing on market development and nurturing borrowing units into efficient market entities.

These three types of government credit are interrelated and differ from each other, and at the same time, are not subordinate to each other. Immune from fluctuations on the market, government credit is the basis for stabilizing the market and finance and can maintain the system steadiness of the market and the overall benefits. Through effective use of particular type(s) of government credit, the development bond financing mechanism connects government credit and the market. Besides, the mechanism also connects government credit and institutional performance credit by proactively relying on the support of its institutional performance. Through the two "connections", the mechanism ultimately reflects the benign interactive between the national economic strength and the market.

The development bond financing mechanism is a core mechanism of the bond bank. As a major carrier of government credit and a bridge between government and the market, development-oriented finance institution is an integral part of the financial system and plays a crucial and unique role, no matter whether we are enjoying steady economic development or coping with financial crisis.

12.3 Development bonds and macro-policy transmission mechanism

Development bond is an effective transmission mechanism of national macro policies. It has turned out to be such a big success that CDB issues development bonds by relying on national credit to raise funds for the country's mid- and long-term infrastructure construction and social development.

The following characteristics prove that development bonds act as an effective transmission mechanism in China:

(1) Development bonds have become a magnifier of China's fiscal policy. By bond financing, development-oriented finance institution steers a large amount of social funds to support key projects of national infrastructure, basic industries, and pillar industries. According to the 2011 Annual Report of CDB, more than 76% loans were extended to the above-mentioned sectors by CDB.

(2) Development bonds have become a conductor of China's monetary policy. As a significant type of open market operation of the central bank, development bonds provide a vital instrument for the monetary policy operations of the central bank. For example, by March 2009, the inventory of such financial bonds amounted to over RMB2.7 trillion, of which above RMB2 trillion were held by commercial banks. The issuance and innovation of development bonds has transformed the short-term, decentralized funds worth trillions into long-term, large-amount funds, effectively mitigated

the systematic risk of financial market and played a crucial role in implementing national macroeconomic policies and collaborating in the enforcement of fiscal and monetary policies.

(3) Development bonds have become a booster of China's industrial policies. Development bonds have provided strong funding support for industrial restructuring and technological upgrading, and propelled industrial development policies to put into practice and yield positive results.

(4) Development bonds have become a vital instrument for brand and asset management on China's bond market. With innovative and pricing power, development bonds have significant influence on the bond market. They not only serve as important instruments for Chinese financial institutions to optimize asset structure and liquidity management but also provide new funding sources for institutional investors. At present, commercial banks and insurance companies are major investors of development bonds, and they hold 78% and 14% of total development bonds respectively. China Insurance Regulatory Commission (CIRC) gives full policy support to insurance institutions' investments in financial bonds and subordinated debentures, exempting them from credit ratings and allowing them to independently determine the investment proportion according to asset allocation needs. Development-oriented finance and life insurance funds have supplementary advantages in terms of assets and liabilities structure and can forge long-term strategic cooperation.

(5) Development bonds have beefed up the development of China's bond market. As the second largest bond issuer only after the Ministry of Finance, development-oriented finance takes up a share of 27% on the bond market and 75% of policy financial bonds, and has laid a foundation for the bond market's system building, product development, and the cultivation of rational market. As a key development-oriented finance institution, CDB is the exclusive bank in China qualified as lead underwriter of long-term corporate bonds, mid-term notes, and short-term financing bonds simultaneously. By the end of 2009, CDB participated in underwriting 148 bonds in total, including 55 bonds (41 corporate bonds and 14 short-term

financing bonds) worth RMB152.8 billion (RMB125 billion of corporate bonds and RMB27.8 billion of short-term bonds) as the lead underwriter.

(6) Development bonds have become industrial criteria and provided significant reference for the pricing of the bond market. Development bonds have a wide range of varieties, including fixed-rate bonds and floating-rate notes, as well as standard bonds and optional bonds specific for different types of investors. In terms of duration, development bonds have various maturities from 3 months to 30 years, which is a vital foundation for the complete yield curve of policy financial bonds on the Chinese bond market, and provides pricing basis for many other products such as corporate bonds, short-term financing bonds, and commercial banks' financial bonds. Development-oriented finance is committed to the serialization and standardization of bond issuance and is conducive to determining benchmark yield of China's bond market.

(7) Development bonds have improved the financing efficiency of CDB and optimized the structure of its balance sheet. Bond financing has advantages such as intensive issuance, large scale, and high efficiency. As a key development-oriented finance institution, CDB once set a record of issuing RMB60 million bonds in half an hour. According to the 2007 Annual Report, the per capita volume of bond financing of CDB was 21.53 times that of deposit-taking commercial banks. To date, CDB has maintained reasonable asset-liability structure, in which mid- and long-term bonds maturing in more than five years account for 95% of total bond inventory. This avoids maturity mismatch between assets and liabilities prevalent in deposit-taking banks and provides fundamental guarantee for CDB's issuance of mid- and long-term loans.

According to the 2008 Annual Report, by the end of 2008, CDB issued RMB4,362.28 billion of financial bonds, in which RMB494.21 billion were assigned bonds and the other RMB3,868.07 billion were issued in a market-oriented approach, and the inventory of financial bonds stood at RMB2,706.375 billion. As a major funding source of development-oriented finance, financial bonds have effectively supported the development of large and medium infrastructure sector, basic industries, and pillar industries, and have made significant contribution to mitigating bottleneck restrictions, adjusting industrial and regional economic structure, and promoting the healthy and sustainable development of the national economy.

12.4 CDB needs to uphold the positioning of a bond bank during commercialization

From the end of 2008, under the leadership of the State Council and other authorities, CDB ushered in the stage of commercialization. According to the CDB Reform Program of the State Council, CDB will be transformed from a policy financial institution into a commercial bank; after the reform, it will support significant mid- and long-term development strategies of the economy by providing financial services such as mid- and long-term credit loans and investments. In other words, CDB will become a multi-purpose bank with credit and investment functions; at the same time, its foremost focus in mid- and long-term businesses will distinguish it from other commercial banks. The reform is arduous and needs ample exploration and practice. When engaging in mid- and long-term businesses under the framework of commercial bank, CDB is bound to be confronted with some new problems and situations. The most crucial issue is the source of funding, which is subject to factors such as indefinite nature of bonds, the constraint of capital adequacy, and the variation in risk weights of bonds. The key to CDB's steady transformation is to maintain the continuity of existing mid- and long-term businesses. To well serve mid- and long-term development strategy of the economy, it must optimize the funding source for medium- and long-term development. To date, there have been the following three categories of contradictions in the composition and source of funding:

(1) The contradiction between small capital funds and rapidly expanding business.
(2) The contradiction between limited sources of funding and the growing demand for funds. With the expansion of bond

issuance, given that CDB can only issue bonds to institutions through inter-bank market, the difficulty in bond issuance and risk of pass will be mounting.

(3) The contradiction between the market-based interest rate of bonds and the non-market-based lending rate.

As CDB has adopted a market-based bond issuance, the financing cost is largely affected by market fluctuations while there is still a regulatory upper limit for lending rate; thus, it has no other alternative but be passively exposed to market risk. In contrast, commercial banks, whose deposit interest rates are statutory, can collect funds at a relatively low cost and bear no market risk. The combination of new problems emerging from the commercialization of CDB and existing issues may render the issue of funding sources extremely complicated. In response, it is advisable for CDB, under the principle of persisting in mid- and long-term businesses as a national development-oriented finance institution, to uphold the basic positioning of bond bank and follow the strategy of raising funds mainly through financial bonds and via supplementary means (Figure 12.1).

12.5 Summary

This chapter describes that development-oriented finance relies on government credit to float financial bonds and raise funds required for medium- and long-term construction and social welfare undertakings. Development financial bonds, serving as the macro-policy transmission mechanism, convert the short-term and scattered funds of commercial banks into large-amount and long-term funds, mitigate the systematic risk of financial market, and promote the effective implementation of industry policies.

Faced with the grim situation of the international financial crisis and economic downturn as well as the increasing uncertainties in domestic and global environments, China should concentrate on maintaining her social stability while dealing with diverse challenges and address any problem that may arise by relying on her successful experiences and good practices. During its commercial

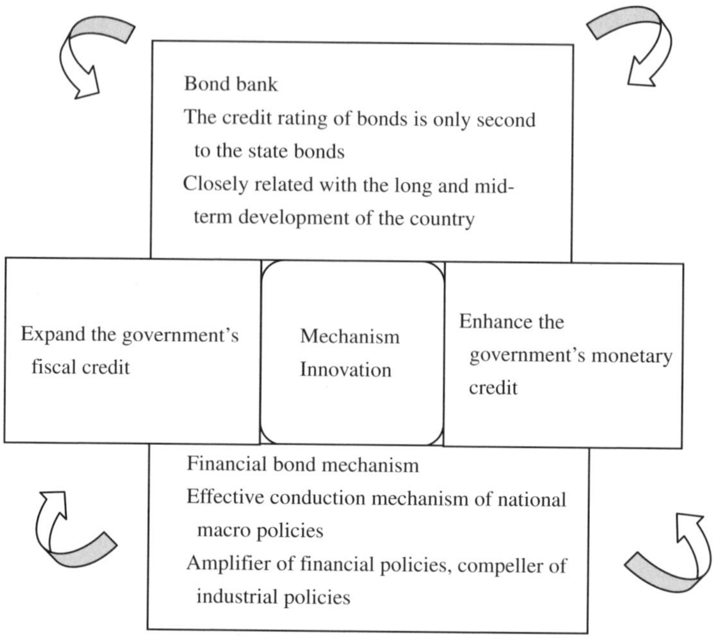

Figure 12.1: The commercialization of CDB should uphold its role as a bond bank.

transition, CDB still needs to uphold its role as a bond bank and its main features of bond issuance and long-term credit, take a development path different from traditional commercial banks, avoid weaknesses, and give full play to the strengths in medium- and long-term business to achieve competitive differentiation against other commercial banks.

Chapter 13

Governance Structure: Democratic Funds and Financial Management

Development-oriented finance should constantly refine governance structure, coordinate and regulate the relationship with all stakeholders, manage funds and financial affairs in a democratic style, and strengthen supervision and restraint so as to ensure rational decision making, improve financial efficiency, achieve world-leading performance, and facilitate the objectives of macro policies of the government.

Governance structure is a concrete reflection of an organization's operating style and strategic ideas, and also serves as the basis and precondition of effective management. The success of international financial institutions can first and foremost be attributable to their efficient governance structure. In recent years, as a national development-oriented finance institution, CDB has constantly reformed its governance structure, which has yielded a few positive results. Nonetheless, it still needs to deliberate upon issues such as how to reflect the particularity of development-oriented finance in the reform and meet the specific needs of commercialization.

13.1 Specific characteristics of the governance structure of development-oriented finance

The unique characteristics of development-oriented finance determine the particularity of the governance structure. The most special feature of development-oriented finance derives from its specific task of fundraising and risk management of medium- and long-term construction of the state. In this sense, the governance model of development-oriented finance falls into the category of public governance. Development-oriented financial institutions are special financial entities belonging to the country with state credit and empowerment. They mainly provide financing services for mid- and long-term national development such as infrastructure sector, basic industries, and other public undertakings, and support for the country's "going global" strategy. In essence, such institutions are an instrument for the government to realize strategic objectives through market-based means. Different from commercial banks whose operations are profit-oriented and also different from policy banks which merely engage in policy financing service, development-oriented financial institutions, as special financial enterprises, render financing services in some immature areas in need of support in line with the requirement of the government while urging the mid- and long-term development of the county with their own sustainable growth. Owing to the distinctive attribute of governance structure, development-oriented financial institutions should, based on the governance pattern of common companies, commercial banks, or policy banks, take full consideration of the functional particularity so as to determine the governance model consistent with the features of development-oriented finance.

The governance structure of development-oriented finance should meet the following eight requirements: (i) clear strategic objective and values are established inside the bank; (ii) effective work mechanism for serving the national strategy is developed; (iii) responsibilities of internal units are well defined so as to share information and resources and improve efficiency; (iv) ensure that the members of the Board of Directors and the Board of Supervisors are qualified, work independently, and fulfil their duties; (v) ensure the smooth progress of internal audit and inspection; (vi) ensure the remuneration system is consistent with the bank's ethnics, its goals, strategies, and control environment; (vii) conducive to cultivating sound financial culture; and (viii) practice corporate governance in a transparent environment. These requirements are based on the market positioning, intend value, business characteristics, marketing model, and risk management of development-oriented finance, which are described in detail as follows:

(1) *Market positioning*: Development-oriented financial institutions are long-term lending banks and wholesale financing institutions, and mainly provide financing services for key projects and sectors that are crucial to national development strategy and involve long period and large uncertainties. In this respect, development-oriented financial institutions are clearly distinct from commercial banks which generally provide short- and mid-term loans and working capital loans and stress the self-liquidity of loans to ensure the security and timely recovery of assets. It is the mission of development-oriented finance to provide financing services in immature areas and, at the same time, ensure the safety of funds.
(2) *Intended value*: As financial intermediary, development-oriented financial institutions carry out risky transactions to realize the efficient allocation of financial assets and promote economic growth. In other words, development-oriented financial institutions mainly engage in long-term, uncertain transactions, which involve much larger risk than that of commercial banks and have systematic influence on financial and economic security. If successful, these transactions will bring fruitful results — this is exactly the intended value of development-oriented finance.
(3) *Business characteristics*: The wholesale business has determined the intensive feature of development-oriented finance; however, with the reform and advance, development-oriented finance business will become diversified and development-oriented financial institutions should innovate accordingly.
(4) *Marketing model*: In this regard, development-oriented financial institutions should learn from commercial banks, strengthen market-based functions, and establish marketing mix including brand marketing, service marketing, price marketing, advertising, and comprehensive marketing to integrate all available resources and enhance competitiveness.

(5) *Risk management*: To ensure the virtuous circle of funds and avoid risks, development-oriented finance needs to not only follow the general principles of commercial finance in business operations but also develop policy supporting system like the compensation mechanism subsidized by public finance and a governmental debt service fund to guarantee the recovery of loans.

13.2 Experience of governance reform from foreign financial institutions

There are two governance models in international commercial banks: (i) horizontal governance model with the branches as operational center and (ii) vertical governance model with the head office departments as the command center. For a long period, whether in the Europe, the Americas, or Asia, the banking sectors have unanimously adopted the geographically based governance model dominated by branches. But over the past four decades, this trend has greatly changed to emphasize on banks' system management with businesses as the main line, thus significantly weakening the functions of branches and strengthening the functions of banking departments of the head office. In this aspect, the US banking sector stands out with such transformation that was brought in 50 years ago. One case in point is Citibank, whose organizational structure went through three transitions between the 1960s and 1990s, and each transition turned out effective in responding to competitive pressures. In the 1960s, adopting the recommendations of McKinsey & Company, Citibank replaced the geographical organizational structure with product division structure and established personal banking, commercial banking, corporate banking, and international banking departments, in addition to the department of investment managers and the operations department which was designed to provide support for the other sections. In the 1980s, Citibank had three banking departments: (i) the institutional banking, (ii) personal banking, and (iii) investment banking departments; two supporting departments: (i) the finance and information service and (ii) legal and external affairs; and several committees. In the early 1990s, to streamline the levels of decision making, it further reformed the organizational structure and established a group with 15 members which later was reduced to 12. In recent years, Citibank has introduced the concept of organizational design, regard customer demand as a key principle of organizational reform, and attach more importance to internal coordination. It can be concluded that the success of Citibank partly lies in its efficient organizational structure. However, as economic and financial development and political regimes, traditions and the like vary from country to country, commercial banks in different countries have their particular organizational forms and systems. Thus, in theory, there is no such organizational structure that is applicable to banks of all countries. While learning from the governance of foreign commercial banks, China should reform the development-oriented finance governance based on its particular conditions.

The international experience — both positive and negative, in development-oriented finance governance models, is illustrative. For example, KfW Entwicklungsbank, a development-oriented finance institution intended to revitalize the German economy in coordination with the European Recovery Program, was jointly funded by the state and federal governments according to the KfW Law in 1948. The sustainable development capability of KfW, whose capital was provided by the federal and local governments, lies in the combination of state credit and the rules of market economy, independent operations under protection of relevant laws and regulations, as well as the dual-layer operation and supervision structure within its organization. For another example, the Development Bank of Japan (DBJ), previously known as Rehabilitation Finance Corporation, was established in 1951 to supply long-term funds for industrial development, social and economic advance and supplement the insufficient long-term funds of private financial institutions. In the 1950s and 1960s, the Bank played a vital role in Japan's industrialization and the later economic revitalization. However, the excessive intervention of the government in the bank's operations entailed various defectives and thus posed a huge risk.

Under the impact of the Asian financial crisis in 1997, the Japanese government had to reconstruct it and established the DBJ in October 1999, also known as Japan Policy Investment Bank. After restructuring, the DBJ, with funds provided by the government pursuant to law, has developed the "planning-implementation-feedback" supervision mechanism and internal operation assessment system, which overcame the previous drawbacks of excessive administrative intervention and improves the management-dominated governance model. As can be seen from the above, the governance models of KfW and DBJ share the following characteristics: (a) the models are conducive to the realization of the government's objectives; (b) the government provides full capital to ensure the bank's funding source; and (c) the combination of external supervision and internal governance restructuring enhances the operating efficiency. Therefore, based on the inspiration from the aforesaid features, the governance reform of China's development-oriented finance should give full consideration to its particular circumstances, which is conducive to improving operating efficiency and realizing the State's strategic goals.

13.3 Basic ideas of governance reform of development-oriented finance

Considering the particularity and fundamental philosophy of development-oriented finance and the industry's requirements for it, the basic ideas of its governance reform are proposed and summarized as one main line, two focuses, three systems, four characteristics, and open structure as follows.

(1) *One main line — "serving the national mid- and long-term development strategy"*: We should make full use of the unique advantages of development-oriented finance, collaborate the domestic and overseas markets, build efficient work mechanism, and rationally allocate strategic resources of national development to support the financial security, economic security, and national security.

(2) *Two focuses — strategic customers and strategic projects*: We should strengthen relation management and strategic cooperation with customers, improve bank governance, and lay a solid foundation for the expansion of development-oriented finance. Maintaining important customers is essential to achieve first-class business performance and has significant influence on the quality of credit assets and on the operating results of the bank. Without customers and projects, banks are like water without a source, or a tree without roots. As the customer's value grows with time, it is a long-term strategic task for development-oriented finance to maintain sound customer relations and fortify organic, co-dependent relationship with key customers. Highlighting customer relation management is not only related to product prices and quality but also to the transparency and service quality of the bank. It is far from enough for a bank to maintain its advantages in satisfying product demands of the customers by merely reducing the interest rate. Instead, the bank should endeavor to provide innovative, customer-specific services, and increase transparency so as to develop strategic projects and consolidate market share. The bank needs to nurture new financial service ideas, take quality and value as its core, guarantee the growth via integrated financial services and supply chain, strive for projects and positive performance by enhancing customer satisfaction, and realize development goals through customer lifetime value. Development-oriented finance should focus on strategic customers and strategic projects to strengthen relationship management and strategic cooperation with customers, and may consider the four dimensions with respect to governance structure. First, CDB should improve the marketing structure of financial services, including the organization's core advantages, value communication, value delivery, and performance evaluation. Specifically, the essentials of the four above-mentioned aspects are to: (a) analyze market environment and competitive situation, and prudently forecast development scale and capabilities; (b) recognize customer value and understand customer satisfaction and the voice of the customer; (c) provide customized and integrated services based on market segmentation and differentiated disadvantages; (d) establish evaluation criteria which takes customer value

into full consideration. Second, we should develop differentiated service strategies for old and new customers, namely, to win new customers and maintain old ones. We will attract new customers by increasing market share, expanding market occupancy, and the like. Meanwhile, to retain customers, we need to improve customer satisfaction, know the dynamics of rivals, and promptly adjust service strategies. Third, the Customer Asset Management System (CAMS) should be developed. As an important part of the financial service strategy, CAMS entails developing key features of customer service quality, designing understandable and satisfying response languages, and establishing a complete set of customer asset and resource model. Fourth, we should launch teamwork-based model for customer and project services. The customer- and project-centered financial system is an essential part of modern finance. Thus, we will further improve the system of customer and project managers, clarify responsibilities of the front, middle, and back offices, select appropriate customers and project managers based on personal traits, and work characteristics and set up account manager and project teams. With ever-increasing competition on the financial market, it is imperative for development-oriented finance to systematically study the customer- and project-centered financial service system, develop financial service marketing strategies, standards, methods, and performance appraisal system suited to the particular conditions of China and determine market segments and target markets, and the customer relationship strategy conducive to market objectives.

(3) *Three systems — business expansion, risk control, and supporting departments*: First, business departments can be divided by customer segments so that a certain department specific for particular customer group, as the front office of overall business procedures, can provide direct service for customers. At present and in the near future, the customers of CDB can be classified into six categories: (i) government departments, (ii) large state-owned enterprises, (iii) large private businesses, (iv) small and medium enterprises, (v) vulnerable groups, and (vi) international customers. Business expansion lines should be set up according to different customer segments, which is conducive to the provision of customer-specific services and the development of

corresponding management measures. Second, from the perspective of risk control, we need to develop a risk management system which integrates internal and external resources and combines business sections and general administration departments. To facilitate regulatory interactions, we should proactively set up the joint supervision mechanism in coordination with regulatory authorities, local governments, and all circles in the society. Party committees, audit department, and business sectors should control potential risks before, during, and after their occurrence from different perspectives. Meanwhile, the comprehensive risk management concept should be advocated in the whole bank to implement relevant requirements of the Basel Capital Accord (Figure 13.1).

(4) *Four features — flat, flexible, outsourcing, and professional organization internally*: First, flat organization means reducing intermediate hierarchies, expanding control coverage of management, and promoting the transmission and communication of information. The finance and the industrial sector are co-independent, and the governance structures of them influence each other and are

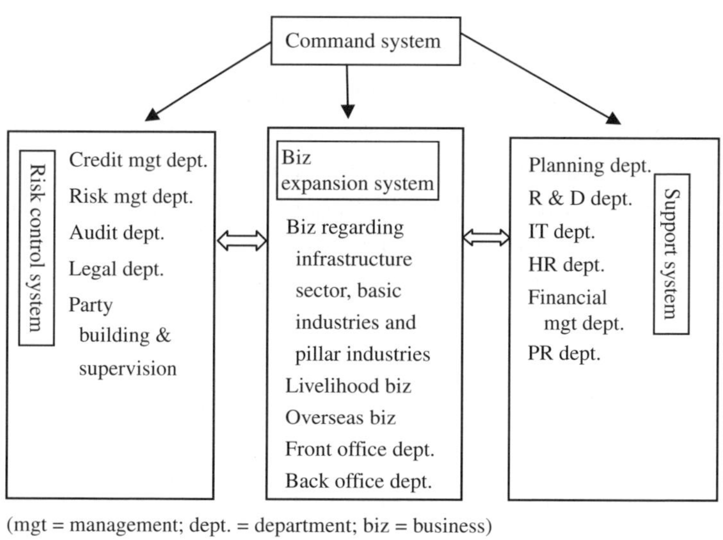

Figure 13.1: Development-oriented finance institution.

inter-related. Consistent with the top-down pyramid organizational structure at the early stage of industrialization, the financial organization also took on a vertical hierarchy at that time. In the 21st century, the knowledge-based economy relying on information technology has promoted the industrial sector to shift from the previous vertical organizational structure to the new flat structure change, and accordingly, the governance reform of financial institutions is also showing a trend toward a flat structure. The traditional management theory believes that each manager can control only 7 to 9 people, and beyond this range, it will lead to inefficient management, but thanks to the development of information technology, the span of control has been expanded to 20 to 25 people, and even up to hundreds of people in some service industries (such as the financial sector). Second, flexible organization means that it can respond rapidly to changes and make timely adjustment according to the consequence of change. Based on customer needs and the priorities of business, we should form the appropriate team by breaking out of the limitation of functional departments and hierarchies to efficiently allocate the talents with different expertise to arouse the collision of knowledge and fusion of ideas, which is conducive to solving complex problems such as the R&D of financial products and the marketing of large projects. For the purpose of rapid response to external changes, timely adjustments of the relevant team can be made if necessary so as to maintain the competitive edge. Third, through outsourcing, CDB can draw support from social forces by contracting with them and providing them guidance like professional training, so as to extend some of CDB's businesses and internal functions to external community while maintaining its core value. In this way, CDB can reduce transaction cost, improve operating efficiency, and serve the society. Specifically, CDB should retain knowledge-intensive activities that reflect its own competitive edges, and should outsource non-core businesses that will require high technology and substantial resources if operated by itself, and outsource other mature, standard, and non-advantageous activities as well. Fourth, professional organization means embodying characteristics of an expert bank. We should concentrate on providing professional services in terms of team building and organizational setup, determine positions and units according to business needs, and realize the organic combination of the departments which independently fulfil their own duties and cooperate with each other. Moreover, we should unify the allocation of resources, facilitate the access to information, and provide integrated services. Specifically, we will ensure the resources are rapidly motivated and allocated to the needy business, no matter where they are or when they are demanded. CDB will ensure that the leaders, according to the need of decision making, are able to gain multi-channel, timely access to internal and external information, especially the international information; and that employees can quickly receive top-down information and professional information based on the need of business operations. Meanwhile, CDB will build an efficient service system which integrates all the resources of the Bank to provide one-stop services for strategic customers and projects.

(5) *Open structure — the business-oriented matrix structure based on divisional organization*: With the expansion of the CDB and the diversification of businesses, its organization form also calls for corresponding adjustments, and one appropriate choice for this may be the divisional organization, in which several divisions are set up according to the businesses of development-oriented finance institution, or in other words, according to products, regions, or customers. Currently, the branches are set up by geography and the subsidiaries are divided according to products. We may consider establishing divisions in line with customers and strategic fields and grant them with independent internal accounting and decision-making right of their operations. Thus, the division responsible for vertical management and regional branches for horizontal coordination will together constitute a matrix structure. Moreover, CDB will, based on the organizational structure of "four platforms and one association" (management platform, lending platform, guarantee platform, supervision platform, and credit association), motivate the resources of all circles of the society to extend the grassroots network of development-oriented finance and fortify an open system. To this end, the following preparatory work must be accomplished: First, a clear and

well-defined strategic development plan must be formulated. The adjustment of organizational structure should be made step by step under the direction of explicit strategic objectives and the responsibilities of relevant departments should be clarified according to the tasks they undertake. Second, a unified database and smoothly-operating information system must be developed. The Head Office needs a centralized database and advanced data processing system as technical support to control the operations of branches and departments. Meanwhile, the departments and organizations at all levels also need a smooth information delivery system to communicate timely and manage and share information through digital, network-based approach. Third, a sound accounting system and employee performance evaluation system must be in place. Only under the support of such an accounting system of internal management, can we scientifically verify the cost-efficiency of products, evaluate the business in an all-round way, and precisely measure the contribution of the employee. The open matrix structure is a crucial trend of the transformation of bank governance structure, and the essence of matrix structure is to minimize hierarchies in structure design and form a complementary relationship between departments and between individuals, so that the entire organization is similar to the "UFO" in shape and can conduct activities in the economic sphere with minimal friction coefficient.

13.4 Governance reform of development-oriented finance is a progressive process

It is a progressive and innovating process for the aforesaid envisagement to come true. And whatever comes up in the process, development-oriented finance will not be impeded by any challenges. Only with innovation can an institution maintain advantages in the fierce competition and realize its reform and development objectives. As a national development-oriented finance institution founded in 1994, CDB comprises 37 branches, 2 representative offices, and 2 wholly-owned subsidiaries. Compared to the giant organizational structure of ordinary commercial banks, CDB has a small number of staff, outlets, and hierarchies. With the deepening of commercialization reform and the expansion of business, CDB needs to refine its organizational structure through the following measures:

(1) The decision-making role of the Board of Directors and the management and the supervisory function of the Board of supervisors should be brought into full play. With the deepening of commercialization and the establishment of cooperation, the key to the reform of CDB is to build sound governance structure and transform the operating mechanism. CDB needs to step up the development of a mechanism of effective communication and the checks and balances between the decision-making body based on the Board of Directors, the executive body led by the President, and the oversight body led by the Board of Supervisors, and form a modern financial corporate governance structure with Chinese characteristics. In such a governance structure, the Board of Directors is primarily responsible for determining the overall development plan, risk management objectives and market positioning, and developing incentive and restraint mechanism and internal control mechanism based on the targets; the management is responsible for independent and efficient operations and management; and the Board of Supervisors plays an irreplaceable role in decision making and risk control. Based on the sound corporate governance structure, a mutually independent, vertical risk management structure will take shape.

(2) CDB will actively transform management philosophy. On the one hand, we need to build the management philosophy of creating value for shareholders and take steps to infuse the concept of value management into business operations and management to realize sustainable business development; on the other hand, we need to shift the constraint management philosophy from funds constraint to capital constraint so as to propel the optimization of economic capital allocation. To guide the direction of business development and accomplish the optimal yield-risk portfolio, we should take into consideration both the immediate interests and the long-term strategic targets and allocate the economic capital among various risks, management levels, and products in a reasonable way.

(3) The corporate governance structure will be constantly improved. On the one hand, we will promote the reasonable diversification of ownership structure, propel the strategic restructuring and mergers by introducing strategic investors, steer insurance funds, and social security funds to development financial projects, steadily and rapidly expand the assets under management, and rationalize and standardize decision making and benefits distribution with diversified and reasonable ownership structure. On the other hand, we should energetically advance the building of a "process bank". Under the customer- and project-centered and market-oriented principles and for the purpose of lean, efficient, and flat organization, we will launch organizational structure reform to boost the connection between product departments and customer departments, integrate business processes in an all-round way, and establish strict and clear internal system of rights and responsibilities and transform the inefficient extensive business model with overlapping of functions and business items, so as to realize flat organizational system, comprehensive business functions, centralized information processing, and globalized operations and management.

(4) Multiple forms of social organizational structure will be expanded. Livelihood undertaking is a strategic focus of national development and also an important "blue ocean" business of development-oriented finance. Owing to limited staff and institutions, CDB is bound to take a new path rather than distribute outlets throughout the country — a route that has been taken by commercial banks when promoting grassroots businesses of livelihood. On the basis of "four platforms and one association" (management platform, lending platform, guarantee platform, supervision platform and credit association), CDB will make best use of its advantages by relying on government credit and the support from all sectors of the society to extend the grassroots network, urge county-level financial organizations to operate in line with the concept of development-oriented finance, and support rural economic development. When time is mature, it may launch pilot programs to set up county-level branch offices in selected areas with solid foundations and broad

cooperative prospects and then make use of such experience to explore the social structure applicable to a wide range of regions.

(5) A new structure of scientific management of modern financial corporation will be framed. First, we will introduce category management based on the characteristics of products and service targets, tighten authorization, refine the orderly, flexible, and efficient internal operating mechanism, constantly improve market adaptability, resilience, and core competitiveness, and grow into an organization capable of standing up to any test. Second, we should energetically introduce innovative decision-making talents, aspiring management personnel, farsighted financial faculty, and market-adaptable compound talent, adopt the talent competition mechanism, provide equal opportunities throughout the process of recruiting, employing, nurturing, promoting, and retaining talents, and establish the employment mechanism of the survival of the fittest. Third, we should enhance the CDB's new image of high quality and diversified services and formulate a systematic service plan concerning service philosophy, service methods, services technology, service channels, service team, and the like while streamlining business processes, reducing intermediate processes, and improving service efficiency under the premise of effective management. Convenient, efficient, value-added, and high-quality services will be delivered to the customers via the internet and other advanced means. Additionally, we will firmly stick to our credit commitment and strive to win customers' respect and trust with high-quality services.

13.5 Summary

Based on the particularity of the governance structure of development-oriented finance, in this chapter, we have devised a governance framework which can be summarized as "one main line, two focuses, three systems, four characteristics, and open structure", the essence of which is to minimize hierarchies, make the entire organization similar to the "UFO" in shape, and form a flat, flexible, and specialized structure (Figure 13.2).

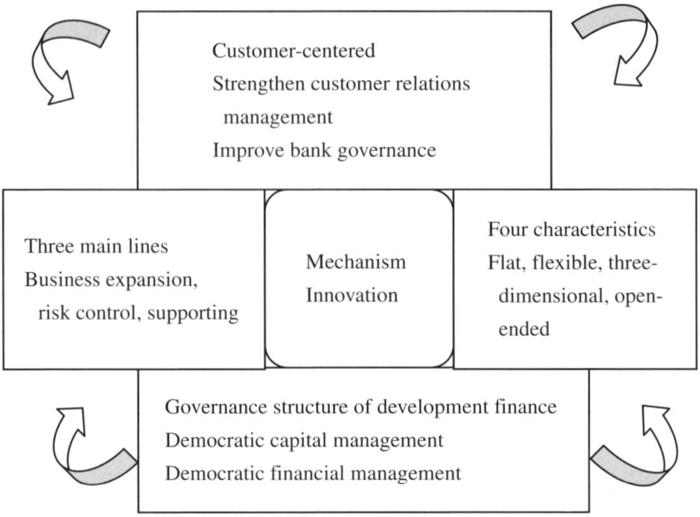

Figure 13.2: Governance structure of development-oriented finance.

As a development-oriented finance institution, CDB should constantly improve bank governance and build a governance structure featuring democratic management. Thus, the following measures can be taken:

(1) CDB can implement financing democracy. Through establishing systems such as the electronic road shows of independent committee members and the deliberation of loan projects by the Lending Committee, the Bank can make loan decisions in a more scientific, democratic, and socialized manner, free the loan granting from complex administrative procedures, and avoid the over-centralized decision-making approach that a small number of people determine whether to extend large-amount loans.
(2) CDB can strengthen financial democracy. CDB should introduce a transparent regulatory system for fund allocation and expenditure, optimize the centralized procurement system, and invite well-known domestic or foreign accounting firms to conduct audit on its operating results and financial conditions.

(3) CDB can strengthen operation democracy and allow staff of various levels to participate in the decision-making process such as setting up major objectives, formulating measures, and determining business solutions.
(4) CDB can establish an independent information investigation system, implement a vertical audit system, and strengthen the supervision and control of decision making. The commercialization of CDB has placed new demands on the governance structure. The governance model of CDB should, according to the planning of national economic and social development and the requirements of macroeconomic policy, embody the concept of development-oriented finance, serve national development strategies, help raise long-term large development funds mainly used for basic facilities, basic industries, and pillar industries, the high-tech sector and priority development areas, as well as the "go global" strategy projects, and help improve the level of professional management to effectively deal with all kinds of complex problems and enhance competitive edge. Through governance reform and strategy and business innovations and through nurturing new core intermediary businesses like custody, guarantees, and securitization, CDB will progressively develop into a globalized development-oriented finance institution with comprehensive strengths, distinctive competitive advantages, and sufficient capabilities to better accomplish national strategic objectives.

Chapter 14

The Management Style: Market-Based and Standardized Management Mode

To strengthen the operational efficiency and core competitiveness, development-oriented financial institutes should constantly improve their mode of management and strive for diversified services, market-based operation, and standardized management.

With the deepening of China's reform and opening up, development-oriented financial institutes are experiencing changes in the operational environment, approaches, and tasks, and accordingly their management modes need constant improvement. It is essential for development-oriented financial institutes to actively carry out innovation in management practices, and strive to tap their own potential, stimulate the inherent vitality, and enhance the capabilities for grasping market opportunities, perceiving financial risks, and integrating resources.

14.1 Innovation of management mode

Development-oriented financial institutes should persist in the innovation of management mode and endeavor to create increasing market value and social value while satisfying the financing needs for medium- and long-term development of the state.

To cope with the global financial crises, financial institutions have generally stepped up reform and innovation. In the key stage of reform to commercialize its operations, development-oriented financial institutes are faced with an even more arduous task of management mode reform and innovation. On the one hand, such reform and innovation is driven by the ever-changing situations. From a macro perspective, to reconstruct a new international financial order is an irresistible historical trend, and major financial institutions should take this opportunity to make a difference. At the meso level, financial markets are experiencing a new round of restructuring characterized by large scale, all-round functions, globalization, network-based approaches, and diversified means, thus placing new demands on the management mode of financial institutions. At the micro level, financial concepts are changing. For example, a growing number of financial institutions are looking for development opportunities in market segments, and believe that information is the basis of the bank's security and there is an upper limit of loan proceeds and lower limit of loan losses. These ideas to some extent reflect the trends and characteristics of financial development, and development-oriented financial institutes should advance with the times. On the other hand, the necessity for reforming the management mode is determined by the function of CDB. As a national development financial institution, during the commercialization, CDB should, based on the reality and in line with the market-oriented principle, concentrate on the medium- and long-term national development strategies and unify the financial reform and economic development to avoid homogenization. It is essential for CDB to sustain financial innovation on medium- and long-term businesses, stabilize economic cyclical changes with medium- and long-term investment and financing, and develop into a distinctive commercial bank rather than a traditional deposit-taking bank. Also, CDB needs to persist in financial innovation with the characteristics of development-oriented finance. To fill gaps in the market and in the availability of credit, it should incorporate system development, market construction, and credit building into financing promotion, build the market microfoundation and transmission mechanism for financial operations, and transform non-financial, non-market, and non-credit areas into financial and market fields that commercial banks can have access to, and enable these areas to be an integral part of the market economy. As a development financial institution engaging in the wholesale business, CDB has stretched its presence across the capital market and credit market, and as explicitly specified by the central government, the risk weights of credit and bonds should remain unchanged during the transition. The regulatory authority is likely to adjust this based on the particular situation after the transition, but it is believed that no significant change will take place. The State Council's program on the reform of CDB approves it to set up wholly-owned or controlled investment subsidiaries and investment banking subsidiaries, which provides favorable conditions for development-oriented financial institutes to expand investment business. Development-oriented financial institutes should make full use of such important institutional advantage and seek for further advances based on the new situation by carrying forward previous good practices.

14.2 Innovation of risk management mode

Development-oriented financial institutes should constantly renovate the risk management mode and develop a long-acting risk management mechanism to minimize credit risks of medium- and long-term national development.

Banks are enterprises specialized in risk management. According to Basel III, by January 2015, the lower limit of tier-1 capital adequacy ratio (CAR) of global commercial banks will be raised to 6% from the current 4%, the minimum proportion of the core tier-1 capital constituted by ordinary shares in the bank's total risk assets will be increased from 2 to 4.5%, and the bank shall also set capital conservation buffer, whose total amount may not be less than 2.5% of the bank's risk assets. Therefore, to build a long-acting risk management mechanism for development-oriented finance is not only an important part of CDB's reform and development but also the requirement of implementing the regulatory rules of Basel III. Such a mechanism, based on a comprehensive understanding of the bank's risks and capability of self-improvement, is an organic combination of risk management mechanism, decision-making mechanism, transmission mechanism, and operating mechanism, with a view to ensuring the timely adjustment and optimal effects of risk management. As an integrated development financial institution, CDB has always taken prudent risk management as a principal policy. During 2007, CDB made significant adjustments in its risk management system, namely, from credit risk management to an enterprise-wide risk management system. The Credit Management Department was renamed as the Risk Management Department and its roles and responsibilities redefined as the enterprise-wide risk management department of the Bank. The Risk Management Department is responsible for managing bank-wide credit risk, market risk, and operational risk. While sustaining support for infrastructure and other major projects, development-oriented finance has been expanded to the county economy, grassroots business, livelihood projects, and "going global" business, and is faced with growing diversified credit risks; in addition, with the acceleration of market-oriented reforms of interest rates and exchange rates and the expansion of international business, there is also a great challenge of market risk management and operational risk management. In response to the new situations, CDB should concentrate on the innovation of risk management system, method, technology, and culture to improve the overall capabilities for risk prevention and control.

14.2.1 *Innovation of risk management system*

First, we will highlight compliance and fortify the institutional foundation for risk management. We will strictly follow the over 60 regulations and normative documents such as the Law of the People's Republic of China on Banking Regulation and Supervision and the Management Measures for Capital Adequacy Ratio, develop relevant implementation rules and measures in accordance with our own situation, ensure compliant operation, and base the long-acting risk management mechanism on a solid legal foundation.

Second, a socialized risk management mechanism will be established. We will develop an all-round, whole-process risk management system led by the Risk Management Committee and shift the focus of risk management from real risks to potential risks, from post-risk rectification to pre-risk control, and from the management of risk assets to the management of asset risks.

Third, we will improve risk analysis and early-warning mechanism. On the one hand, we will establish the early-warning system for risk monitoring and evaluation covering all business risks to prevent and resolve risks including credit risk, market risk, and operational risk by promptly forecasting and identifying risks and accurately quantifying and scientifically estimating risks with the measurement model. On the other hand, we will develop an effective capital constraint, asset-liability proportion management, and risk management constraint mechanism, and enhance the capacity for risk prevention and control.

Fourth, we will develop the accounting information management and disclosure system featuring group synergy to improve the transparency and effectiveness of information disclosure and ensure the accuracy and completeness of the information disclosed.

Fifth, we will establish a socialized risk prevention and management system at the grassroots level. To boost the development of county areas, new countryside, and SMEs, we will adhere to the grassroots business management mode in which government cooperation is the basis, building a platform for lending-banking institutions is a measure, and risk sharing and compensation serves as a guarantee. We will also take measures such as staff extension, centralized promotion, and front-office handling of businesses to develop a risk control mechanism covering the whole process of grassroots lending business.

Sixth, we will refine the credit management system and improve post-lending management in an all-round way. A set of detailed operational rules for key matters of post-lending management will be designed. For example, considering a region as a whole, we will formulate corresponding rules for the implementation of internal control throughout the process of lending management, and incorporate pre-lending verification, lending review, and post-lending inspection into the systematic credit management standards.

14.2.2 *Innovation of risk management measures*

First, adjust the product pricing approach. Commercial banks determine the pricing based on two aspects: (i) the customers' own profitability and the adequacy of their own funds; (ii) the customers' ability to raise funds and the adequacy of external cash flow. In the case of capital surplus, the fundamental factor determining pricing is no longer credit risk, but the competition and market price. Thus, it is necessary for CDB to shift from credit risk pricing to competition-driven pricing. Evidently, the market-to-market pricing method also entails cost pricing and risk-based pricing.

Second, loan supervision should be strengthened and guarantees and collaterals should be inspected. We will, on the one hand, closely oversee the qualification changes of guarantee platforms and loan guarantee agencies to prevent misconducts and, on the other hand, strengthen the government's supervision over financing platforms and stringently implement the separated management of income and expenditure to ensure the payment and rational use of risk compensation and eradicate improper retention and misappropriation of funds and malicious evasion of debts.

Third, a safeguard mechanism for the growth of syndicated businesses should be developed. We will concentrate on syndicated loans, strengthen business coordination, standardize syndicated business operation, and refine the performance evaluation and incentive mechanism.

Fourth, a scientific risk management mode should be established. We will strive to (a) implement the key concept of "risk compensation" throughout the credit approval and management process; (b) separate credit policy formulation, implementation, and supervision in terms of institutional setup to ensure the adequacy and effectiveness of the mechanisms of checks and balances and constraint; (c) optimize the asset structure and improve the overall return on assets based on the combination of loan issuance and post-lending portfolio management and through active portfolio management; (d) effectively prepare the ground and focus on risk management at the grassroots level, relieve the burdens of front-line credit personnel, and allow them to gain in-depth understanding of customers and make technical credit risk analysis; and (e) establish a credit risk management qualification system and a continuous learning mechanism to ensure the smooth operation of risk management in terms of human resources. It is essential for CDB to comprehensively and effectively manage various internal risks by applying scientific risk management mode; achieve the whole-process risk management through advanced risk identification, judgment, monitoring, control, and transfer technologies; and realize effective coordination and linkage between different levels of business units and staff by clarifying risk management functions and responsibilities to establish a risk management system aimed at credit enhancement.

14.2.3 *Innovation of risk management technologies*

First, an information-based risk management system should be accelerated. By making full use of modern information processing and communication technologies, we can establish sensitive information collection, processing and feedback mechanisms, and complete information exchange channels covering risk management dimensions like risk monitoring, risk analysis, and non-performing assets disposal, and build a whole-process risk management information network system as technical support to optimize risk management and take decision-making and management activities in a proactive and well-targeted manner.

Second, the development of risk measurement model should be stepped up. We should, on the basis of risk management information system, develop highly operable risk control and management methods which can be easily quantified, explore risk measurement models regarding loans, financial transactions and other investment activities, and integrate the risk management information system and the risk measurement system to enhance the early warning function of risk monitoring.

Third, the improvement of the internal rating system should be accelerated. We will launch efforts to (a) establish an appropriate internal rating approach in accordance with the credit personality of CDB's customers and the large amount and long maturity of single loans; (b) develop the underlying database of internal rating; (c) increase the proportion of front office-based risk management in internal rating system; and (d) validate the rating system on a regular basis and improve the consistence between the whole system and details.

Fourth, the measures for stress test management should be further improved. We will strengthen the sensitivity test on significant risk factors and the scenario test on multiple risk factors changing simultaneously to ensure that the stress test can be carried out in a regular, institutionalized, and standardized way.

Fifth, a special analysis on material matters influencing the Bank's profits and losses should be reinforced. We will (a) closely keep track of and analyze the influence of market changes and force majeure events on the Bank's profits and losses, such as the exchange loss caused by the exchange rates of US dollar and British pound against RMB, the book loss caused by impairments of equity and bond investments, the interest income decrease caused by the reduced interest rate of RMB, and the decline in asset quality caused by earthquake; (b) rationalize the allocation of profitable resources and support the expansion of foreign exchange credit and international businesses by utilizing domestic resources; (c) strengthen the operational efficiency analysis on special businesses, particularly the analysis of income from business derived from loans, the analysis of inter-bank non-interest income, and the analysis of return on investment; and (d) accelerate the development of profitability analysis system, provide product profitability analysis statements on credits, bonds, and other mature products with large asset-liability ratio, and measure the promotional effect of technical assistance loans through management accounting method to realize the optimal balance between scale, risk, and efficiency.

14.2.4 *Innovation of risk management culture*

Risk management culture, an important part of the bank corporate culture, is a fusion of elements like operating philosophy, risk management concept, risk management behavior, risk ethical standards, and risk management environment of modern commercial banks. CDB needs to enhance the employees' sensitiveness and understanding of risks by delivering a wide range of risk education and highlighting risk assessment all through the business processes, emphasize risk awareness throughout the conscious action of all employees, establish an all-round risk management concept covering all departments, business lines and products, and advocate the whole-process risk management culture which includes risk monitoring, management, and disposal before, during, and after the occurrence respectively. Banks' risk management is a systematic project and requires long-term planning, support, and convergence; in other words, business processes, credit decision making, and internal restructuring should complement each other whilst the development of business system and the adjustment and training of banking professionals need to be carried out simultaneously. Only with a long-term mechanism for credit risk management can the bank ensure the sound and sustainable growth of development-oriented finance.

14.3 Innovation of business management mode

To strengthen the service brand and provide quality services to customers, development-oriented financial institutes should persist in the innovation of business management mode and build an integrated service system.

In recent years, China's economic and financial environment has witnessed significant changes:

First, with the progression of market-oriented reform of interest rates, the loan-deposit spread has a growing tendency to narrow down and it is difficult for banks to maintain long-term growth by simply relying on the income from interest rate spread.

Second, with the rapid development of capital markets, it is an irresistible overall trend where a lot of bank funds are flowing directly into the financial market leading to the emergence of financial disintermediation. Thus, the banks which rely on traditional businesses are unlikely to maintain stable source of funding and find themselves under increasing pressure to survive.

Third, the competition among banks is increasingly fierce. State-owned commercial banks, joint-stock commercial banks, and urban cooperative banks have become major players in the financial competition; in particular, after China's entry into the WTO, foreign banks with advanced management ideas and mature management methods are swarming the domestic market, smashing the traditional pattern of the banking sector. In terms of the business scope, the geographical and industrial restrictions have been broken, replaced by overlapping business, and all-round competition. With the market-based transformation of areas like the infrastructure, basic industries and pillar industries, their financing modes have been progressively mature and thus the traditional business space of development-oriented financial institute will shrink. From the perspective of business management, as development-oriented financial institutes have limited varieties of products and source their profits mainly from issuing bonds and granting loans, it is of urgent and realistic significance for them to strengthen innovations on assets, liabilities, and fee-based businesses.

14.3.1 *Innovation of assets business*

First, the innovation of lending business should be steadily promoted. The measures include strengthening financing support for hi-tech industrialization, launching pilot program on consumer credit, exploring derived business, and renovating new forms of loans like syndicated loans, mergers and acquisitions (M&A) loans, and factoring loans (with accounts receivable as collaterals).

Second, equity investment businesses should be developed. Development-oriented financial institutes can, by making use of the favorable policy of being permitted to set up equity investment companies after the transformation into joint-stock company, concentrate on the initiation of projects, make direct investments, and hold corresponding shares of the enterprise to increase the ratio of investment income and open up a new pattern of the sources of profit.

Third, overseas credit business should be energetically expanded. Amidst the economic globalization and international economic governance reform, China's economic development mode is shifting from relying on "bringing in" to focusing on both "bringing in" and "going global". As a development financial institution, CDB has vigorously expanded international business by emphasizing international cooperation, actively implementing the "going global" strategy, and seeking for business opportunities on a global scale. By January 2012, CDB had reported a foreign exchange loan balance of more than US$200 billion, stretched its coverage over 113 countries, and became the largest foreign investment and financing bank in China. Apparently, overseas credit business has just come to the fore, ready to embrace the ample opportunities waiting ahead.

14.3.2 *Innovation of liabilities business*

Liabilities business, to a large extent, is a business about weighing the risks and returns and entails four links of identification, measurement, operation, and monitoring. We can identify liquidity and interest rate risks through measures such as gap analysis (maturity gap), re-pricing, and maturity re-determination, identify credit risks by loan rating, recognize foreign exchange risks through exposure positions, and measure risk positions, short-term gains, and long-term returns based on indicators such as interest rate spread, net interest margin, return on assets, and net assets market value. As a development financial institution engaged in wholesale business, CDB needs to maintain sustainable growth of capital and shareholder value during its commercialization.

First, capital replenishment mechanism will be developed. After the capital injection of US$20 billion by Central Huijin Investment Ltd. in 2007, the CAR of CDB increased to 12.77%, but it will demonstrate a downward tendency year by year due to the expansion of loans. To ensure its compliance to the 8% CAR requirements, CDB is in urgent need of establishing a sustainable capital replenishment mechanism. Specifically, it may increase the core capital by injecting funds into the expanding share capital, enlarge the supplementary capital by expanding the issuance of medium- and long-term financial bonds, and increase the share capital through capital operations like going public or injecting funds.

Second, the innovation of deposit-taking business will be energetically stimulated. Development-oriented financial institutes can develop new varieties of deposit-taking business and focus on the convertibility of deposits under the premise of security, mobility, and efficiency; launch a pilot program of deposit securitization and issue large-amount of negotiable certificates of deposits to increase customers' revenue and mobility; and diversify the source of funding via deposits and other channels.

Third, the securitization business will be vigorously renovated and expanded. For example, a close cooperation mechanism with large and medium commercial banks can be established to transfer their scattered, short-term savings into long-term securitized funds to open up long-term, stable, and cost-controllable source of funding for development-oriented finance. Also, in order to steer funds in Central China to support its development, western assets can be securitized to serve as a bridge for funds in the central area to flow into the western region.

14.3.3 *Innovation of fee-based business*

The integration of traditional credit business and the capital market has been trending in the banking sector. Development-oriented financial institutes can, by leveraging their own advantages and based on lending, actively steer their focus to security financing while maintaining credit financing; develop diversified financing portfolios associated with capital market operations like corporate bonds, convertible bonds, equity, and asset securitization; and provide comprehensive services such as financing planning, loans, underwriting, guarantees, and direct investments for the enterprises. In particular, to just name a few examples, development-oriented financial institutes can (a) energetically promote the securities underwriting business and enhance their functions in underwriting domestic and overseas government bonds, especially corporate bonds based on the good relations with the government and large enterprises; (b) engage in M&A business by looking for the objects of M&A, offering consultancy on trading price and non-price terms, and helping to arrange financing and bridge loans, corporate restructuring, asset restructuring, and other activities; (c) vigorously carry out project financing business, sustain close relationships with related government departments, financial institutions, investors, and project initiators, coordinate project feasibility study with lawyers, accountants, and engineers, and arrange financing for the project through bonds and shares issuance, inter-bank borrowings, auctions, mortgages, and other means; (d) offer corporate wealth management and investment consultancy, and help enterprises develop contingency measures, prepare development strategies and reconstruct financial systems, and asset reconstructing programs; (e) actively get involved in funds management as funds initiator, manager, or underwriter.

14.4 Innovation of strategic cooperation mode

To strengthen customer confidence and loyalty and constantly improve competitiveness and services, development-oriented financial institutes need to sustain innovation of the strategic cooperation mode and reinforce cooperation with the ministries, local governments, industrial authorities, and enterprises to establish a win–win mechanism.

14.4.1 *Cooperation with the government*

Cooperation with the government is the core concept of development-oriented finance. To further advance such cooperation, CDB needs to put the concepts of development-oriented finance into practice and accomplish the following four transformations regarding bank–government cooperation: (i) it should shift from providing funds to proposing advice for local economic development and serve as a think tank of the government; (ii) it should shift from specific project cooperation to all-round economic cooperation based on the overall economic development; (iii) it should shift from closed cooperation to open cooperation so as to fully tap the market potential, look for new cooperation areas, and proactively foster high-quality customers; and (iv) it should shift from short-term cooperation to long-term cooperation to avoid bank–government cooperation being manipulated by some government officials as immediate achievements during their term of office.

14.4.2 *Cooperation with commercial banks*

CDB should fully tap the potential and areas of cooperation with commercial banks by applying the competitive cooperation strategy. Given that the commercialization of CDB will intensify the competition with other commercial banks, we need to strengthen the linkage between the head office and branches and develop a rapid response mechanism to improve the overall competitiveness; meanwhile, we can learn good practices of other commercial banks through competitive cooperation to further improve market functions and fix our own weaknesses. More importantly, to maintain the role of development-oriented finance in guiding the market and building systems, we need to launch extensive cooperation with other commercial banks through the following measures:

(1) *Forming syndicates*: CDB should proactively call upon local governments, regulators, and commercial banks to form syndicates, facilitate orderly competition, and build a new regional financial environment together while maintaining its domination over financing. Furthermore, CDB may develop Head Office–branch linkage mechanism for the syndication of major projects to enhance its leading bank image and brand effect in the field of syndicated loans.
(2) *Strengthening wholesale business*: The wholesale approach will be adopted to support the growth of SMEs, and the funds and risks incurred will be shared by CDB and other commercial banks according to certain proportions.
(3) *Reinforcing entrusted loans*: Loans can be directly granted to the borrowing platform through signing of loan contract; the borrowing platform, after commissioning commercial banks to relend to qualified SMEs, is responsible for the recovery of principal and interest and the post-lending management. The two platforms are jointly responsible for project acceptance, screening, approval, and recommendation.
(4) *Boosting inter-city cooperation*: Development-oriented financial institutes can sign cooperation agreements with commercial

banks located in the same place as the project and authorize them to provide the project with liquidity, revolving loans, temporary loans, settlement agency business, and services like principal and interest recovery from settlement account.

It is understandable that development-oriented financial institutes and commercial banks, as different market entities, are rivals to some extent and distinct from each other in terms of business philosophy and operational procedures. However, development-oriented financial institutes should, from the long-term and overall perspective, establish different forms of strategic alliances and long-term cooperation mechanism with commercial banks on the premise of obtaining long-term benefits and supporting national economic growth and financial system development — this is where the fundamental interests of development-oriented finance and the responsibilities of development-oriented financial institute both lie in.

14.4.3 *Cooperation with corporate customers*

Bank–enterprise relationship is a type of reputation capital and can compensate the deficiencies of the contract and expand the scope of transactions to the extent far beyond where the contract explicitly defines and the legal enforcement can reach. In a modern economy, banks and enterprises are like two sides of a coin, which are inseparable from each other. Good bank–enterprise relationship not only means that the banks have sufficient understanding of the enterprises and have adequate capacity to acquire and analyze information about them but it also means that the banks are able to supervise the misconduct of enterprises and hence significantly reduce the cost of services arising from asymmetric information and moral hazard. With the development of market economy, the interests of banks and enterprises are increasingly definite and clear. Meanwhile, on the market of supply and demand of financial resources and financial services, banks and enterprises are having their own choices, and their statuses are also constantly changing — from overpowering superiority of banks to increasing equality and mutual benefits.

For these reasons, it is imperative for development-oriented financial institutes, in line with the market-oriented principle and based on efficiency and credit, to build new bank–enterprise relationship for the purpose of win–win results.

Considering the imbalance of regional economic development, development-oriented financial institutes should adopt different strategies for establishing bank–enterprise relationships in different regions. For example, in economically developed areas, when practicing the development-oriented finance theory, CDB needs to consider how to establish sound relationship with the enterprises on the basis of improving efficiency and how to consolidate such relationship by providing integrated, high-quality services. In underdeveloped regions where enterprises are weak and financial development is relatively backward, bank funds are a major source of funding for these enterprises and even the only source of medium- and long-term financing. Thus, development-oriented financial institutes should function as the pioneer and engine by providing a relaxed environment and strengthening cooperation with the government and all sectors of society to establish the credit system suitable for local situations and support the growth of enterprises in backward areas. Such an approach is not only conducive to the establishment of solid bank–enterprise relationship but also to the prevention of fund outflows from these areas. Under the growing impact of the financial crisis on the real economy, strengthening bank–enterprise cooperation based on the particular situation of different regions is a crucial measure to promote coordinated economic and financial development and also a practical choice to jointly overcome challenges and achieve a win–win situation.

14.5 Innovation of credit building mode

Development-oriented financial institutes should constantly renovate the credit enhancement mode, improve the credit appraisal system, build a transparent, fair, and institutionalized management mechanism and accelerate the development of credit system.

First, the system of credit portfolio review should be continuously improved. Neither equivalent to independent credit rating nor equivalent to the general project review, credit portfolio review comprises credit rating, assessment of credit development, and credit risk portfolio management. For example, on the basis of analysis of customers' credit intention, credit capacity, credit demand, and credit cooperation conditions, the credit structure can be put in place through the signing of development-oriented finance cooperation agreement, and dynamic risk regulation can be realized by strengthening credit management in the front-office process.

Second, further efforts will be launched to build a transparent, fair, and institutionalized credit management mechanism. Traditional risk control, based on the identification and quantification of credit risk, is a passive risk control designed to restrict credit risk within a bearable range through risk hedging, prevention, transfer, dispersion, compensation, and other means. In contrast, the credit management mechanism of development-oriented finance is an active and dynamic risk control system concentrating on credit building. The core of such system is to realize credit management at front-office level and shift the leader-driven credit management to mechanism-driven management. First of all, we can urge the government to set up a credit-building working group, appoint the credit building contacts, and establish a credit building joint conference system. Then, we will define the subject of credit according to the requirement of modern enterprise system, promote democratic and scientific debt decision making by formulating procedures such as feasibility study, expert consultation, and panel deliberation, emphasize institutionalization and standardization, and ensure the compliance of work processes such as bidding, project supervision, engineering insurance, budget audit, and project completion acceptance. Moreover, branches of development-oriented financial institute can establish corresponding leading groups for credit building and originate contact mechanism with the local government to obtain and supervise the dynamics of credit building of the government. Through the development of institutions and mechanisms, the task of promoting credit building can be effectively fulfilled in the work procedures and mechanisms.

Third, the debt-service mechanism should be introduced and optimized to ensure the virtuous cycle of construction funds. To standardize the sources of funding for government loans and promote the building of local financial system, development-oriented financial institutes can launch the pilot system for government debt service reserve fund in some areas. To protect the virtuous cycle of construction funds and ensure stable and healthy development, local government should, based on sound planning, prepare the necessary financial resources to cope with potential losses and emergencies. The local government's authority and responsibility for urban construction determines its repayment obligations for the financing, and its urban construction income and expenditure analysis are crucial considerations for development-oriented financial institutes to decide whether to grant urban construction loans. Thus, to establish a special debt service reserve fund system according to the government's financial situation is not only a necessity for the government to regulate financial management, improve financial system, and rectify institutional deficiencies, but also an effective means for development-oriented financial institutes to prevent credit risk and improve the efficiency of credit management. For the innovation of credit system, it is a crucial attempt to encourage the government to clarify the sources, financing methods, purposes, and management system of debt-service reserve fund and incorporate these into government administrative provisions or local laws and regulations.

14.6 Innovation of performance appraisal mode

To sustain the growth of development-oriented finance and provide sustainable financial services for the medium- and long-term infrastructure and social development, development-oriented financial institutes should persist in the innovation of performance appraisal mechanism and mobilize internal and external resources.

As a product of the reform and opening up, development-oriented finance has, during nearly two decades of exploration, vigorously supported and witnessed significant changes in the Chinese economy. Strictly complying with the guidance and policies of the central government and applying advanced principles of international finance based on the conditions of China, CDB has, thanks to the collective efforts of all staff, transformed from a traditional policy bank engaging in fiscal financing into a market-based development financial institution integrating national credit and market performance. The Bank has proactively adapted to macroeconomic development needs, actively supported the development of medium- and long-term infrastructure and weak social fields, and opened up financing channels to ensure funds chain for key projects influencing the country's overall development, thus embarking upon a path of development-oriented finance fit for China's particular situation. While promoting the market credit system and economic advance of China, development-oriented finance itself has reported satisfactory business indicators and demonstrated impressive results from the perspective of its own or compared with domestic and foreign financial institutions. Such achievements are attributable to the creativity, courage, and dedication of all members of CDB and deserve strong affirmation.

To mobilize the internal and external enthusiasm, sustain the growth of development-oriented finance, and provide sustainable financial services for China's medium- and long-term construction and social development, it is essential to encourage innovation of the performance appraisal mechanism. On the one hand, China should establish the stimulus mechanism and risk-return mechanism to mobilize development-oriented financial institutes to engage in development-oriented finance. For example, the government can grant a certain percentage of risk sharing or compensation to development-oriented finance operations, provide patent protection and financing concession for the innovation of development-oriented finance business mode, or allow lead arranger of considerable fee in syndicated operations; and give policy support to development-oriented finance in terms of risk assets measurement, concentration supervision, ROC evaluation, and taxes, etc. On the other hand, to keep the shareholders and all sectors of society informed of the operational status of development-oriented finance and allow them to supervise the operations, development-oriented financial institutes should work together with them to establish and improve the development-oriented finance performance reporting system. This is essential to regulate management and mobilize all stakeholders, and should be incorporated into relevant laws of the state. Furthermore, on the basis of summing up existing appraisal methods and drawing on good practices, development-oriented financial institutes should introduce a scientific performance appraisal system in which front-line workers with excellent performance and staff with outstanding contributions will be rewarded. Such appraisal system constitutes the core section of internal management and control, and is of great significance for development-oriented financial institutes to strengthen management, standardize operations, and improve governance. As special financial entities of the country, development-oriented financial institutes should enhance capabilities to facilitate their ultimate goal of supporting socioeconomic development, which includes enhancing national competitiveness, improving the government's ability, promoting the building of a harmonious society, and helping realize the national macro-strategic objectives as soon as possible. Accordingly, it is necessary for the government departments concerned to establish qualitative and quantitative indicators to evaluate the contribution of development-oriented financial institutes to the socioeconomic development, so as to enhance the intensity and effectiveness of reform, promote participation in, and support for development-oriented finance and encourage development-oriented financial institutes to make further contribution.

14.7 Summary

In this chapter, we have discussed the management mode of development-oriented finance and emphasized that management model innovation is the foundation of development-oriented finance institution, including the innovation of risk management model, business management model, strategic cooperation mode, credit development model, and performance assessment model.

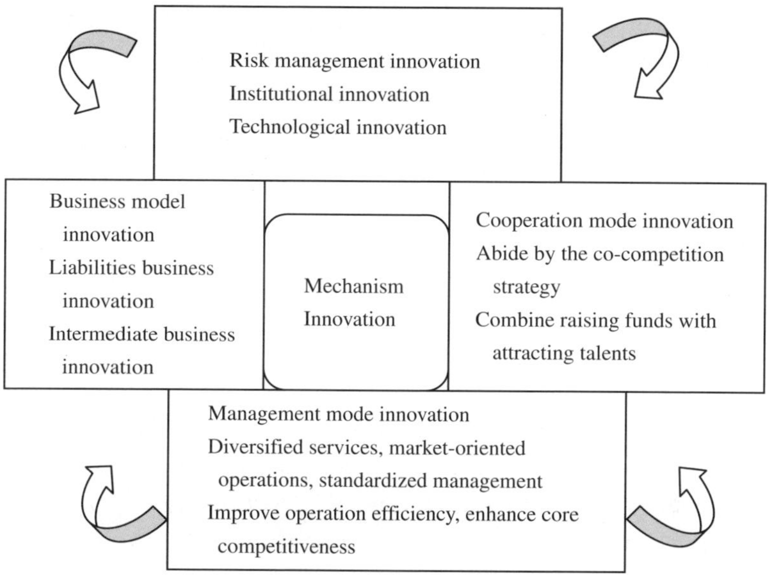

Figure 14.1: Management model of development-oriented finance.

Development-oriented financial institutes should persist in market-oriented operations to achieve the government intentions and their own sustainable development (Figure 14.1).

Management innovation and mechanism construction are long-term tasks of development-oriented financial institutes (development-oriented financial institute), which should not be content with what has been achieved or indulge in the seemingly satisfying data, but rather acknowledge the imbalance, have a sense of crisis, and strive to accelerate the establishment of advanced banking system and promote the reform of the macro-management system. The imperfect system, defective market mechanism, and credit defects have resulted in the considerable imbalance of China's economic development and protruded a series of difficult problems and widespread concerns, including issues concerning agriculture, farmers, and rural areas, SMEs financing, the county economy, employment, public health, and environmental improvement. Development-oriented financial institutes should adhere to the management model innovation, rely on government credit and institutional credit to raise funds from the bond market in a market-oriented way and based on national interests to serve the financing needs of the national mid- and long-term projects, and focus on addressing institutional constraints and system bottlenecks while conducting large-scale, in-depth financial behaviors in close cooperation with the government, integrating domestic and overseas resources and making rational use of credit, investment, investment banks, and other financial instruments to serve the significant mid- and long-term development strategy of the state and boost the sound and rapid socioeconomic development. Faced with competition from domestic financial institutions and more importantly, the severe challenge from foreign banks that stride into China's financial sector, development-oriented financial institutes have no alternative but endeavor to secure a pioneering position in the financial market through constant innovation and courageous exploration of new approaches and new ideas. Only in this way can they obtain broad scope of development, accumulate competitive advantages, and push the undertaking of development-oriented finance further forward. The essence of a development-oriented financial institute's business is to deliver financial products and services to meet the needs of mid- and long-term socioeconomic advance and create market value when identifying needs (opportunities) and satisfying the needs. As a national development-oriented finance institution, CDB will, after completing the commercial transition, boast more functions and more dynamic operations, and make greater contribution to the comprehensive, healthy, and sustainable development of the economy.

Part IV

The Reform of Development-Oriented Financial Institute

The imbalance and diversity of China's economic development determines that China should build a financial system of good operation, complete range, and a reasonable division of labor. Not only should China have short-term and retailing saving bank but also a mid- and long-term and wholesale bank. The developing model of development-oriented financial institute with some commercial characteristics is feasible and necessary. CDB should absorb the advantages of some commercial banks and improve the function of market so as to form an advanced mechanism to break the bottleneck of development. CDB should make full play of the role of a bridge linking the government with the market to better avoid risks and realize the intention of the government and self-sustainable development.

Under the shock of financial crisis, the inside and outside economic situation has become more and more complicated, making the relationship of international finance a vital content of international relationship. We would like to make some thoughts about the development of financial reform under the background of great history, great reform and great challenge, and try to answer the question of "how to further our development", including financial development strategy, financial diplomacy strategy, going out strategy buttressed by development-oriented finance, and the correct handling of the relationship of recent recovery and long-term sustainable development.

Chapter 15

Global Financial Crisis Promotes World Order Change and International Strategy Adjustment

The world is undergoing profound changes. While the financial crisis in the 1930s changed the world order in the 20th century, the global financial crisis triggered in 2008 by the US subprime loan problem sent the world economy into recession and will likely change the world order in the 21st century. In this situation, it is vitally important to China's sustainable development in the 21st century that the country clearly sees the direction of the change of the world order and seizes the opportunity to overcome difficulties and make sustainable arrangements.

15.1 21st century features globalization and multi-polarization

Economic globalization is a "double-edged" sword. While it has strengthened the link and dependence between different countries, it has also had serious impacts on national sovereignty and on the national industry in developing countries. In the course of growing conflicts between new concepts, new technologies, and new products on the one hand and traditional concepts, national ideologies, and group interests on the other hand, economic globalization can force a country to advance or deprive it of a foundation for development.

Economic globalization is a historical process. Due to different historical conditions and development environments, different countries and regions cannot have the same speed in globalization.

Different countries, nations, and economic groups can both cooperate with each other and have conflicts of interest between them. On the one hand, the international community may gradually converge on same standards in economic, environmental, and public health sectors. On the other hand, regional issues tend to become characterized global ones and the international community places greater emphasis on the tapping of geopolitical and geo-economic advantages. Furthermore, all countries and nations continue to emphasize their unique local cultures. Multi-polarized politics and diversified cultures make the world more colorful: Western brands versus oriental products, scientific thoughts versus religious cultures, materialist philosophy versus idealist history, and realistic literature versus romantic art. Things exist in comparison and develop in competition.

Economic globalization has expedited the internationalization of production and consumption. The extensive use of Internet technology has led humanity to a more open world. The globe is experiencing a revolution in energy technology and biological technology. Despite economic downturn over the past four years, global investment in developing wind power, solar energy, and other renewable energies has been relatively stable, totaling US$110 billion yearly on average. All countries and regions are doing all they can to develop energy-saving technologies, new-energy technologies, biological technologies, and new material technologies. This is bound to lead to greater economic and social changes in the world.

The global economic recession arising from the US financial crisis has further exposed the deeper contradictions in economic globalization and international financial order, and further promoted world changes. The coexistence between one superpower and diverse forces is likely to become a basic pattern before a multi-polarized world order is formed. The multi-polarization of the world order is a requirement of the times, and serves the interests of the people in all countries. It brings all forces in the world into a situation, where they rely on each other and contain each other. This situation can help contain hegemony and power politics, establish a just and rational new international political and economic order, realize the beautiful pursuit of all people for a new peaceful, stable and prosperous world, and help developing countries to seize opportunities and develop themselves. World multi-polarization is a long, tortuous, and complex process, in which the contradiction between unipolarization and multi-polarization, the struggle between hegemony and the fight against hegemony, the competition in cooperation, and the cooperation in competition will exist for a long time.

Economic, technological, and military strength is a fundamental prerequisite for a country or region to become a pole of the world. It is the inherent support for a country or region to strive for world strategic initiative in the 21st century. Whether the multi-polarization of the world order can become a reality depends, in the final analysis, on whether all major economic powers can develop fast and on whether developing countries can realize leapfrog development. In order to address the global financial crisis, environmental change and other challenges facing humanity, all countries hope that new world outlooks on development will appear to steer the advance of human civilization and that unilateralism will be overcome, development be diversified, and national rejuvenation and development be realized.

15.2 21st century features innovation, competition, and democracy

Innovation, competition, and democracy will be the central themes of the 21st century, which will be a century of innovation, a century of competition, and a century of democracy. Innovation, competition, and democracy will be the forces to drive development in the 21st century. There will be no development without innovation, no cooperation without competition, and no progress without democracy. He who makes major breakthroughs in innovation will have the initiative in competition and development in the 21st century; he who occupies the highland in competition can become the economic center in the 21st century; and he who truly taps the roles of democracy will be able to mobilize countless innovative forces and make greater contributions to the building of a harmonious, healthy, fair, and just society.

The innovation in the 21st century calls for the innovation of ideas, the innovation of systems, and the innovation of technologies that represent the higher levels of civilization. Innovation is an inherent force to continuously drive social development forward and to advance social productive forces from the industrial revolution to the information revolution. The financial crisis calls for a review of financial innovations and a reform of the existing systems, both the international monetary and financial systems and the regulatory systems in various countries. Innovation in developing countries is too little, instead of being too much.

The competition in the 21st century is competition against the backdrop of deeper economic globalization and competition in pursuit of cooperation, development, and win–win result. Competition embodies the "survival of the fittest" law on social development, and has even higher demands for cooperating partners. Accordingly, developing countries will face more difficulties and challenges.

The democracy in the 21st century is democracy in pursuit of healthy, harmonious, and sustainable development, and also democracy with which developing countries strive for independent development and role playing. Democracy is both a tool and even an endogenous demand of human civilization and progress. While emerging countries should boost their own strength, they should put forward their views and positions on the current world order and rules. The democratic status of the latecomers is equally an important condition for their progress and development.

Without innovation, competition, and democracy, the Chinese economy will allow bad money to drive away good money, fail to retain talents, and lose its true competitiveness.

15.3 21st century features rise of new nationalism

On surface, the economic competition between countries against the backdrop of modern globalization is a competition between enterprises or between markets. In fact, it remains and must be a centralized competition between countries. Countries are the organizers and promoters of institutionalized international competition.

The international competition in the 21st century is both an economic competition and also a competition in overall national strength. Moreover, it is a political struggle, because national interests are a form of politics.

Currently, new nationalism is rising in the world. This nationalism is more popular and prominent among the younger generation. The political pressure arising from new nationalism on the internal and external policies of a country or region should not be neglected. It will have major impacts on the world community in the 21st century.

Although new nationalism is in reflection, anxiety, and resentment, it has a new height and a new vision in the sense of national recognition. While free trade agreement has become more possible within regions and between countries and can help shorten the distance between countries and improve their relations, it will not weaken the pursuit for state and national interests.

New nationalism is characterized as "remembering national concerns despite humble status". It is expressed in spontaneous action politics. It tends to make radical reactions to the gains and losses of national interests, rejoicing at the slightest national gain, and saddening at the slightest national loss. When the citizens of a country, especially the youth, discover that their own destiny inter-grows with that of their country, they tend to make action-based reactions. New nationalists take pride in their own countries and nations, emphasize the greatness of their countries and the outstanding of their nations, and have a strong sentiment toward their countries and nations. They hope from the bottom of their heart that their countries can have a firm foothold in the world, free from foreign control, enjoy peace and prosperity, and stand out among advanced nations.

New nationalists are the main force on the Internet. They rely on the Internet to acquire the latest information and issue all sorts of mobilization orders. The Internet provides an advanced channel for new nationalism to spread and a stage for new nationalism to show its strength. In the cyberspace, new nationalism is growing rapidly in all parts of the world in the course of economic globalization.

We may say the electoral victory of US President Barack Obama was a victory of the main forces in cyberspace; the Russian youth who grew up along with the growth of the Internet and hip hop songs constituted the firm shield for Vladimir Putin's tough foreign policy; the Chinese youth born in the 1980s were a lucky outcome of the times, carried a distinct mark of the times and grew up closely along with China's reform and opening up, China's economic takeoff, and the interaction between China's modern civilization and world civilizations. The siege of Carrefour Supermarket staged by Chinese youth in the spring of 2008 after the Olympic torch relay was obstructed in France was a full reflection of the spirit of the modern Chinese.

Modern youth are much stronger than the old generations in terms of patriotism and national cohesion. They have no historical burden but have the courage to do what they want. If this force is properly guided and utilized, it will be the hope of a country. But if it is not properly considered and handled, the growing self-confidence of new nationalism may harbor a radical nationalist tendency. Unlike the positive social changes desired by the youth, this type of radical actions is more of a nihilist nature and a form of hatred and anger against social reality, which makes the world anxious and fearful. For example, the London Turbulence on August 9, 2011 was mainly staged by youth. Some of the participants wore the brand-name sportswear they looted and vowed to get back every penny taken away from them. This type of actions suggests they are a perplexed generation and also a worrisome one. Therefore, unofficial forces and emotional burning points may foster social turmoil and disputes in the 21st century. This we must take into account when we consider the development strategies for this century.

15.4 21st century remains American century

Under the impacts of the global financial crisis, the world order has shown more visible changes. While the United States begins to feel some pressure and challenges, the world also has many expectations and predictions. But the 21st century will remain a century of the

United States. This is not only because the United States will continue to be the number one country in the world for a long time to come, and continue to be a country with the greatest innovation capacity, the greatest consumption-driving force and the influence of monetary sovereignty. Every action taken by the US government will have major impacts on the world order. Besides, the policy and strategy-formulating mechanism of the United States is quite elastic and energetic and can make timely adjustments in light of the changes of the world situation and the requirements of development.

In addressing the global financial crisis and the new world situation, the number one country in the world has accelerated the adjustment of its international strategy. The US administration headed by President Obama coincided with the most volatile age of the global economy since the Great Depression in the 1930s. Holding high the reform banner and emphasizing national interests, President Obama has demonstrated a ruling style with drive and sweep, a ruling concept of using both the carrot and the stick, and a ruling tactic with flexibility. Being determined to reform, pursuing coordination and making balanced consideration constitute the embryo of "Obamaism", which contains many important strategic thinking and new measures.

In the economic field, Obama urged Congress to swiftly approve the 787-billion-dollar economic stimulus package, the largest ever in the US history, which focused on energy conservation, environmental protection, infrastructures, education support, medical service, and broadband networking. Universal tax credit was introduced to implement the Making Work Pay program, and the outdated industries would be resolutely eliminated, such as declaring Chrysler Motors bankrupt. In mid-July 2010, President Obama signed the Financial Reform Act, which, along with the Medical Insurance Reform Act signed in early 2010, constituted the most important economic legislation since the 1930s. The Financial Reform Act summarized the lessons of the global financial crisis in time, contained further legal regulation of financial derivatives, and requested that banks must establish independent subsidiaries to exclusively handle the business of financial derivatives. It expanded financial regulation to include hedge funds and private-placed funds.

The Federal Reserve, the US Treasury, and the United States Securities and Exchange Commission set up a joint committee to oversee systematic financial risks. The Consumer Financial Protection Bureau newly designed by the Federal Reserve is in charge of regulating the consumer businesses of credit card, housing mortgages, and student loans. In light of the inaffordability and gross wastes associated with the medical insurance system since World War II, the Medical Insurance Act made legal reforms and adjustments to emphasize the government responsibility and obligation in basic medical security, restrict extreme charges and consumption, and provide necessary subsidies for small and medium-sized enterprises and individual operators to purchase basic medical insurance. These measures can help reduce the waste of medical resources, increase the coverage of basic medical security, promote the mobility of wage earners, and enhance the efficiency of government work. However, the above two new acts are all of a basic nature and cannot produce immediate and direct effects on current unemployment and dwindling investment and productivity. Nevertheless, these reforms are generally regarded to have long-term historical significance. Like the financial reform and the reform of the social insurance system in the 1930s, these reforms will have major impacts on the sustainable and healthy development of the American economy.

In the field of foreign affairs and national security, Obama declared that US troops would be pulled out of Iraq within 18 months of his administration. He also made gestures to ease relations with Cuba, Iran, and other "hostile" countries so as to build a new diplomatic image featuring multilateralism, cooperation, and dialogue. It tried to improve relations with major powers, strengthen cooperation with China, Russia and other countries, emphasize the use of "smart power" in handling international relations, and show a "modest posture" unlike in the past. In his speech at the West Point Military Academy in May 2010, President Obama further explained the country's new national security strategy and made a major adjustment of the preemptive unilateralist international policy adopted by his predecessor George W. Bush. The new national security strategy seeks to establish, at the initiative of the United States, a new international order in the interests of the United States. He said the United States cannot act unilaterally in the world, emphasizing his preference for diplomatic tools. Mainly through diplomatic tools, it will unite historical allies and new strategic partners including China, distinguish terror organizations from religious values, distinguish ideologies from national economic interests, crack down on violent extremisms and rebellions, stop nuclear proliferation, and prevent hostile organizations from acquiring nuclear materials. The new policies of Obama indicate that in order to continue to play leadership roles in the 21st century, the United States has clearly sped up internal reforms and strategic adjustments. His reforms conform to the changes of the situation, have a fairly strong appeal, and are of major significance to the further improvement of the country's strategic thinking in the 21st century. But Obama's reforms were mainly of a tactic nature, instead of a strategic one. In other words, the United States has not changed its strategic goal of dominating the world in the 21st century. It is the strongest country in the world today, and it will continue to be in the 21st century. There is no visible change in the general principles. What has changed are tactics. The international tactics have become more tolerant and elastic, emphasizing the importance of alliance and common action. The internal tactics emphasized infrastructure, innovation, and education. The voluntary and timely adjustments and reforms by the United States reflected the elastic and strategic nature of the American economic policies and mechanisms and indicated that the US systems and economy remain very dynamic.

In particular, the innovation capacity of the United States is fairly dynamic in tools, technologies, and concepts. This is a major source of continued American strength. American universities constitute a source to drive sustained social development, accounting for two-thirds of the world's top 50 universities. Population growth in the United States is fairly healthy. Among developed economies, the United States is only country that can maintain the 2.1% aggregate fertility rate required to surpass simple population reproduction. Besides, the age structure of the population has been rational for a long time. Each year, the country attracts about 1 million new immigrants, of whom many are talents with cutting edge and are effective labor force. This is something no other country in the world can achieve.

Therefore, the United States will undoubtedly continue to be the strongest country in the world in the 21st century.

15.5 21st century features rebuilding of new global financial order

The recent global financial crisis has further exposed the inherent defects and potential systematic risks of the current international financial system. After the currency of a country becomes the pricing currency for primary products around the world, the currency for trade settlement and the currency for foreign reserve, economic globalization both benefits from the universally-accepted reserve currency and is affected by the defect of the system to issue this currency. This systematic global financial risk does not vary simply because of the geography and boundaries of various countries. The speed, width, and depth of this crisis indicate that the systems of various regions and regions are closely linked with each other. As a member of the global community, the link and dependence between different countries and regions have become ever closer. So they must strengthen intergovernmental cooperation and deepen cooperation at different levels and between different interests.

Currently, seeking the change of international organizations is an indispensable step.

(1) The global political summit mechanism should introduce new participants, expanding from the former G8 group to the current G20 summit with China, Brazil, India, and other developing countries becoming important members.
(2) In order to prevent crisis, all countries while injecting liquidity should commit themselves to the expansion of the International Monetary Fund and increase the voting rights of developing countries and especially China.
(3) The IMF, the World Bank, and other international organizations should reform their management systems so as to cope with the new situation of globalization and multi-polarization.

In order to address global complex risks and their challenges, the international community should establish a new international order above national sovereignty and existing systems. The leadership in formulating the programs and rules of the new international order has become the focal point of competition between major powers. The process of abolishing the old rules and establishing the new ones is full of the games of interest and the contest between major powers, and it naturally has conflicts and friction. What the new international financial order needs is an integrated and long-term strategy instead of frequently-changing reforms. This strategy is designed to ensure the sustained, healthy, and coordinated development of the global economy and emphasizes the use of wisdom and problem solution, rather than capricious political contentions. The adjustment of the new international order should be progressive, with the main expression being the continued existence of American leadership.

The new international order should have a panoramic blueprint for global cooperation, provide a brand new thinking for global cooperation systems and mechanisms, publicize and enhance the awareness of working together to deal with global systematic risks, and elevate the levels of existing international cooperation and global governance so that the whole world can more effectively address the challenges in the 21st century. The new international order should be creative in many aspects. It is an overall and globally integrated way for cooperation, which can reflect different views and different demands and embody inclusive and interregional multilateral cooperation. It should be a cross-disciplinary development strategy and solution, which can reflect the inherent links of global risks and challenges and is highly forward-looking. It should be a sustained action for generations, which can fully realize the decisions now made will have far-reaching significance to future generations. It is a method for coordination and consultation, which can use the latest communications technology and media tools to allow all members to participate and speak freely in an interactive way. The design of the new international order should aim to seek support for the improvement of global governance so that world leaders can participate and consult with each other, all countries can mobilize their cross-disciplinary information networks to address global challenges and the international community can use global risks evaluation and analysis and their interregional and inter-industrial platforms for dialogues and actions. As a neutral and independent economic organization, the global agenda council of the World Economic Forum boasts of the most authoritative and most intelligent talents and aims to improve the state of the world. Therefore, it should make contributions to the design and implementation of the new international order.

In the 21st century, the status of various countries may encounter major changes. China has all opportunities to rise in peace and development. This will not be a spectacular piece of news, because China has all along been among advanced countries except in the past couple of centuries. It should be something only too natural that a major country like China surpasses Britain, Germany, Japan, and even the United States in GDP. But China must realize that even if its GDP surpasses Japan and the United States tomorrow, it still lags behind developed countries in the quality and soft strength of its economy, enterprises, and society. China's per capita GDP will remain very low, and the country as a whole will remain in the initial stage of socialist market economy and still has a lot to learn from developed countries in the rule of law, creation, invention, environmental protection, and the improvement of civic qualifications. Besides, while developed countries will be surpassed by China in terms of GDP, this does not necessarily mean that these countries will inevitably "sink". They will remain strong in many aspects and are highly likely to continue to lead the world for a century to come. China needs to fully seize the opportunities arising from the change of the international order and integrate ideological culture, strategic planning, system change, policy making, and micro execution so as to enhance the country's capacity for competition and development.

15.6 Summary

While the financial crisis has exacerbated global pattern changes and international strategic adjustments, the 21st century is believed to be a century featuring globalization and multi-polarization, a century embracing innovation, competition and democracy, a century seeing the prevalence of neo-nationalism, and a century witnessing the reconstruction of a new international financial order. For a long period to come, the United States will remain as the world's biggest power and the most innovative country, with the greatest consumer power and the most influential monetary sovereignty. The US has a flexible and dynamic policy and strategy development mechanism which can be adjusted timely according to the changing situation and development requirements. Amidst the spectacular international economic and financial transformation, China should clarify the objectives, tasks, and measures of its financial development in the strategic layout of national economic and social stability and long-term development strategy, because a country having no say in international financial affairs is not a big power in the real sense. To put it briefly, China's financial development model should be a government-led, market-based financial model (Figure 15.1).

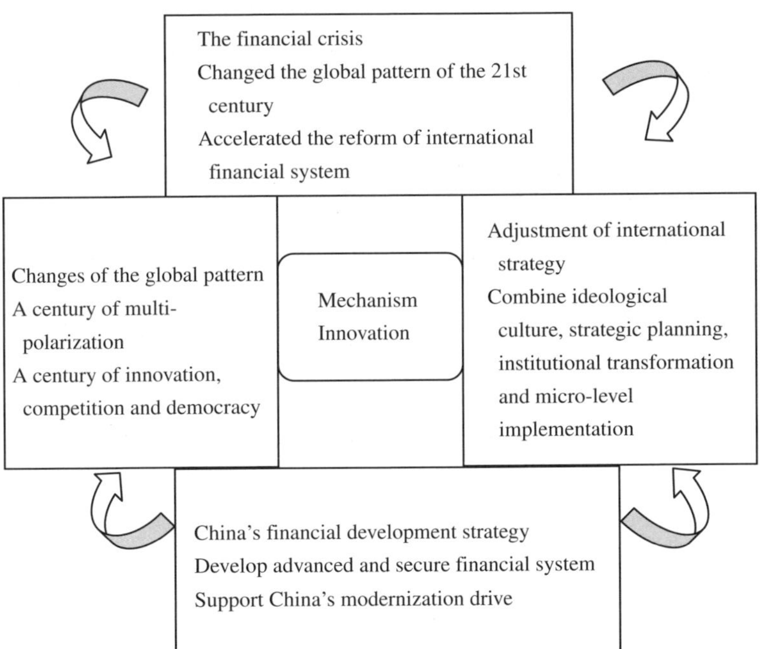

Figure 15.1: New international order.

Chapter 16

China's Finance under the Background of Global Changes

Finance is the core of modern economy. A country without developed and advanced finance cannot become a truly strong power. In the international economic system, a country without financial say cannot claim to be a major power in the real sense. In major international economic and financial changes, China needs to further define the goals, tasks, and measures of its financial development in light of its economic and social stability and its long- and medium-term development strategies.

16.1 Basic information

Shortly after the People's Republic of China was founded in 1949, due to the international blockade and the deviation of domestic policy, China's economy and financial industry was basically under a state of closed operation. In this case, Chen Yun, a top official of the first-generation central leadership of the CPC, proposed to adopt a single currency, centralize financial spending, and unify material scheduling, a guiding ideology that helped to effectively improve the fiscal and financial situation at that time. The system of unified state control over income and expenditure was then introduced, under which the state turned part of the income due to urban and rural residents into mandatory savings through measures such as agricultural and industrial products price scissors and low wages, centralized the profits of state-owned enterprises (SOEs) that were turned over to the state treasury, and then allocated funds to sectors and fields in need of investment. Such a system played an indelible role in coordinating limited resources to speed up the industrialization initiative and infrastructure construction. During that period, the banks only assumed the function of fiscal cashier instead of financing intermediary, and their credit activities almost had no effect on social financing scale and financing decisions.

Since the reform and opening up policy was implemented in 1978, China's planned economic system has gradually transited to a market economy, in which profound changes in the distribution of national income began to take place, household savings increased while the proportion of government revenue in national income declined. Consequently, financial capital alone was difficult to support economic growth. In 1985, China began to shift the method of investment in infrastructure from allotting funds to granting loans, to transform the finance-centered financing system into a bank-centered system. Thus, banks of various types recovered their genuine functions and no longer served as government cashiers; commercial banks began to extend loans to enterprises, but mainly to government-designated SOEs. With the decline of fiscal appropriation and the replacement of profit delivery by taxes, the enterprises gradually resumed autonomy as players in the market economy. However, the SOEs still depended on fiscal appropriations to a large extent, and as the market was extremely underdeveloped, the rigid demand of economic development for long-term funds made SOEs the main financing tool of the government responsible for public and policy financing, thereby exacerbating the capital supply pressure of banks and the deformation of the use of funds. Under government control, the banks, which were essentially the government's bureaucracy rather than independent enterprises, actually had borne the huge cost of reform in China's economic transition. Many SOEs occupied the banks' credit funds for a long time and evaded bank debts through various measures such as merger, division, acquisition, false bankruptcy, or other forms of reform. Thus, the high rate of non-performing loans, high risk, and low efficiency rendered the banks to financial difficulties. Despite their monopoly in China's financial system, the banks were in severe difficulty which was covered up by the continued growth of savings.

After over 30 years of reform and development, China's financial sector has made substantial progress. The functions of the central bank, policy banks, and commercial banks have been distinctive and separated gradually: the commercial features of the four major commercial banks (The Agriculture Bank of China, the Bank of China, the China Construction Bank, and the Industrial and Commercial Bank of China) have become increasingly clear; the central bank has gradually built its role as the lender of last resort and monetary policy began to take effect; the municipal commercial banks, with a total of over 300, began to flourish in almost every prefecture-level city; the modern banking system and modern enterprise system have been highlighted and the role of policy banks has been further strengthened. By the end of 2010, the banking sector had reported total structural assets of RMB95.3 trillion and total liabilities of RMB89.5 trillion. A preliminary modern financial system has taken shape, but it is far from perfect and is still very unstable. Besides, China's financial industry remains highly vulnerable. The satisfactory performance in the Asian financial crisis of 1997 and the global financial crisis in 2008 does not mean that China's financial system has sustained ability to resist risks. To achieve modernization in the real sense, China's financial sector still has a long way to go. Well aware that financial instability will plunge the country into chaos, the central government, in an effort to maintain financial stability, once spent as much as RMB 5 trillion to pay for the non-performing assets of bankrupted financial institutions and commercial banks. Nonetheless, such transitional relief still failed to solve the core problem of the financial industry. This can be explained from two aspects. First, the financial risk remains high. Although the banks' non-performing loan ratio dropped considerably from 33.37% in 2000 to 2.4% at the end of 2010, not because the banking system was fundamentally improved, but because the rapid expansion of the loan base and the long-maturity trend of loans made the denominator of the non-performing asset ratio even greater. Second, the structural deficiencies of the financial system remain serious, which is primarily represented by the imbalance between credit financing and capital market financing. Among the total financing, the bank credit financing has an overwhelming proportion whilst the direct financing only takes up a small proportion. In 2010, the bank credit financing made up a disproportionately high share of 92% in total financing whereas the capital market financing accounted for only 8%. China's financial sector still lags behind that of developed countries. The reasons mainly include the following:

(1) The lack of a sound credit system and advanced, applicable credit rating system, which is the basis of the financial modernization drive.
(2) The lack of scientific and standardized bank credit management rules and methods, which are irreplaceable measures for the prevention and control of risks.
(3) The lack of stringent risk constraint and management mechanism, which is a must-have for effective prevention of financial risks.
(4) The lack of high-level, professional intermediary service agencies, and brokers and correspondent industry self-regulation behaviors, which are the basic elements of financial modernization.
(5) The lack of necessary policy environment and incentives to encourage innovation, which is a breeding environment for the financial modernization.
(6) The lack of advanced computer information disposal and management network system, which is a basic condition for modern bank management.

For these reasons, China's financial reform is more arduous than ever and it is imperative to sum up experiences, learn from lessons, and make elaborate plans to push forward the reform. As global competition is increasingly fierce, the efficiency of the allocation of resources in the capital market has a significant impact on a country's core competitiveness.

16.2 Strategic goals of China's financial development

China should establish an advanced, developed, and secure financial system to support its modernization drive and to become a moderately developed country in this century. In conjunction with the national economic development strategy, China's financial development should also proceed in three stages. In the next two decades, China should establish a fairly sound modern financial corporate system and a preliminarily developed financial market and realize preliminary financial socialization. In the next four decades, China should establish a fairly developed market credit system and realize a fairly high level of financial socialization so that China's share in the international financial market will be visibly higher. In the third stage, China should truly become a major financial power and a strong financial power by the end of the century so that China will have fairly large influence on the international financial market and the Chinese currency will have a fairly large liquidity and become an important component of the world monetary system.

16.2.1 *Main current tasks of China's financial development*

The first task is to support the building of the domestic market. It should provide financing support for growth assurance, domestic demand expansion, structural adjustment, upgrading, and raising the employment rate. It should provide financing support for the building of innovation systems and the boosting of the country's innovation capacity. It should provide financing support for the construction of infrastructures and the development of basic and strategic industries. It should provide financing support for the healthy development of urbanization. It should intensify support for county economies, livelihood undertakings, and corporate overseas operations, and play important roles in adjusting industrial and regional economic structures, supporting the development of the west region, and promoting the healthy and sustained development of the whole national economy. It should intensify the building of a modern financial system and the integration with the international financial market. It should boost the capacity of financial policies for overall adjustment and coordination.

The second task is to support Chinese enterprises to pursue overseas operations. It should provide financing support for Chinese enterprises to pursue overseas development strategies and international financial development strategies. It should provide financing support for the transnational allocation of resources by Chinese enterprises and for the strengthening of the joint development and integrated utilization of overseas resources. It should provide financing support for the development of international market so as to drive China's economic growth. It should provide financial support for the cultivation of multinational companies so as to boost their international competitiveness.

16.3 Models of China's financial development

China's financial development model should be a government-led financial marketization model. Government leadership is manifested in government planning, government regulation, and government service, which is an indispensable important factor for the integration of resources and the proper handling of diverse relations in a mixed economy. It can also embody China's unique strength in government organization. Market-based finance means that market tools are fully used for financial operations. This is also an indispensable important factor for the enhancement of financial efficiency and the aversion of market risks, and conforms to the requirement of financial activities. At a time when global economy and finance become increasingly open, there are diverse models for financial development, including the European and American model, the East European model, and the Japanese model. And these models are also in the course of continuous adjustment and improvement. The formation of a financial development path is subject to the limitations of a country's cultural and economic bases and the historical stage the country is in. The European and American model featuring the natural evolution of market is not applicable to China. A simple "transplant" and imitation of this model will be harmful instead of being beneficial. In face of the current global financial crisis, the "market first" doctrine of the mainstream economics is actually being challenged. The government-led economic and financial development strategy (or the East Asian model) adopted by the East Asian countries of China, Japan, and South Korea is gradually receiving the attention of the economic community. One major feature of the East Asian model is that the government exercises active intervention in the financial system and establishes policy-oriented financial institutions to implement the government's financing intention.

Since the beginning of reform and opening up, China has upheld a government-led market-based economic development model, which has effectively promoted fast economic growth. In the course of financial development, the government and its policy-oriented financial institutions act as the fosterer and promoter of market mechanisms when markets are undeveloped and when market mechanisms cannot fully meet the demand of financial resource allocation. Here, government and market are in a relationship of integrated combination and mutual complementation instead of a "one or the other" relationship. Under government leadership, China's finance observes the rules of market economy and emphasizes rational layout, resource integration, priority breakthrough, phased implementation, and financial ecological improvement so as to establish a Chinese-style modern financial system. We may say that the "Chinese financial development model" is a major-power model in which government promotes market efficiency. Facts prove that this model can both better avert the time cost arising from the natural evolution of the market and overcome the effect of unacclimatization arising from reforms. In a major mixed economy like China, an effective combination of government and market factors in the course of financial marketization is all the more important. A government-led financial marketization model is an effective model for China's financial development.

China's financial development model should be a government-led financial marketization model. Government leadership is manifested in government planning, government regulation, and government service. This is an indispensable important factor for the integration of resources and the proper handling of all relations in a mixed economy. It can tap China's unique strength in government organization. Financial marketization requires that market tools are fully used for financial activities. This is also an indispensable important factor for the enhancement of financial efficiency and the aversion of market risks. It conforms to the requirement of the law of financial activities. The China Development Bank (CDB), which has actively explored Chinese-style development financial theory and practice, is a specific form of the government-led financial marketization model. Taking national development goals as its own mission and through market operation, CDB has improved the strained operation of macroeconomy and removed the financing bottleneck to long- and medium-term construction. It has vigorously supported the development of national infrastructures, basic industries, strategic industries, and society, actively participated in global economic governance and regional cooperation, promoted the leapfrog development of industrialization and urbanization, and expedited the process of modernization.

16.4 Summary

After over 30 years of reform and development, China's financial industry has made great strides (Figure 16.1). A preliminary modern financial system has taken shape, but is far from perfect and still very unstable. Besides, China's financial industry remains highly vulnerable. The satisfactory performance in the Asian financial crisis of 1997 and the global financial crisis in 2008 does not mean that China's financial system has sustained ability to resist risks. To achieve modernization in the real sense, China's financial sector still has a long way to go. A country without developed finance can never become a real power. Increasing efforts need to be launched to build an advanced and secure financial system in support of China's modernization drive. The path of financial development is subject to the restrictions of a nation's cultural and economic base and historical stage. The Western model characterized by the natural evolution of the market is inapplicable to China and it will be harmful, let alone useful, to China's financial sector if we copy or borrow indiscriminately from the west. In contrast, the government-led model of market economy development that China has followed since the implementation of the reform and opening up policy has energetically bolstered rapid economic growth.

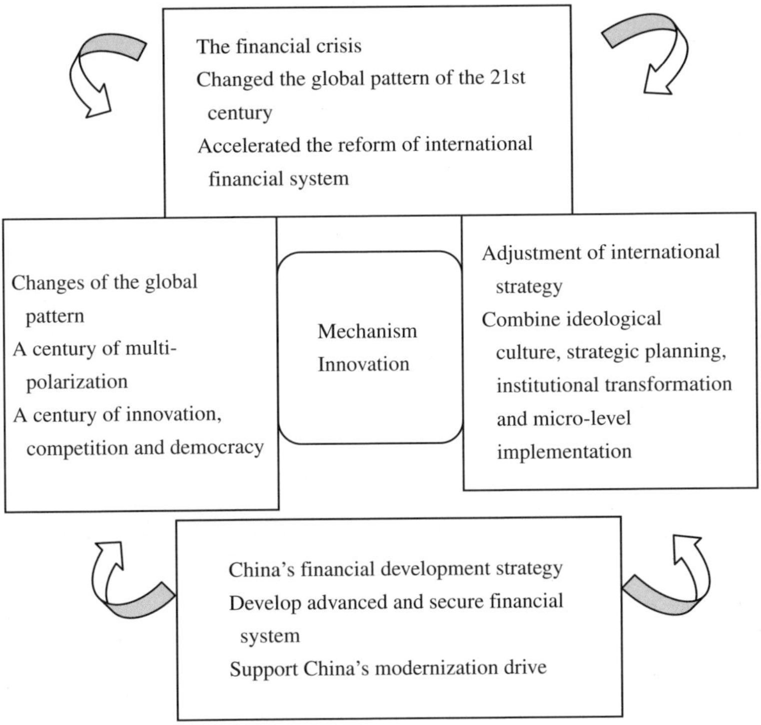

Figure 16.1: China's financial sector in the changing world.

Chapter 17

The Study of How A Development-Oriented Financial Institute Functions as a Commercial Bank

Ever since the establishment of the China Development Bank (CDB), remarkable efforts have been made and great achievements have been realized in accelerating urbanization, promoting the coordinate development of varying regions, ensuring the safety of the national economy, strengthening the competitiveness of the national economy, and stimulating the development of causes concerning public welfare. Some new problems revealed themselves in the process of strategic restructuring of the China State Bank into a commercialized financial institution. These problems affected the purposes of policy financing. Much attention needs to be paid to these problems and effective measures must be adopted to promote the healthy development of the CDB.

17.1 Commercialization of the CDB is different from reforms in commercial banks

The CDB puts heavy emphasis on the new situation in the process of strategic reforms. Since its early establishment in 1994 as a state policy-related comprehensive financial institution, the CDB has been conscientiously performing its duties and playing an important role in promoting the realization of significant national strategies. For instance, the CDB has provided very important and strong support to the construction and development of national infrastructure, basic industries, and "pillar" industries, and the development of the western regions, strategies for the revival of old industrial bases in north-eastern China and the rise of central China, the strategy of "going global" for international business, and enabled the cooperation between mainland China and Taiwan in finance and emergency loans for earthquake relief work. In recent years, the Bank has strengthened its efforts in the construction of rural infrastructure, the development of medium and small enterprises, the provision of housing loans to medium- and low-income families, and creating scholarships and training programs for migrant workers, thus playing an essential role in alleviating the restrictions of "bottlenecks," adjusting the economic structure of industries and regions, and promoting stable and relatively rapid economic development to become an important means by which the government can regulate the economy.

In December 2008, the CDB made its first step in strategic restructuring by turning itself into a commercialized financial institution, renamed the China Development Bank Corporation, thus embarking on the road to its development into a commercialized bank. Nevertheless, some new problems appeared that merited concentrated attention. These problems are discussed as follows:

(1) *The nature of bonds*: The nature of the bonds, issued by the Bank after the transition period, was not clear. The investing institution was worried that because of the change in the nature of the Bank, the bonds might possibly remarkably reduce investment in the Bank. A situation of this kind did appear during the transition period. Take the CDB financial bonds that were issued on December 3, 2008 for example. Although the amount of subscription was 8.19 times that of issuance, there was a minor change in subscribing entities. Instead of being the national commercial bank with the largest number of subscribing entities, it dropped to the third, while they maintained the largest number of subscribing entities of financial bonds issued by the other two policy-related banks. It is certain that if great changes ever occur in the nature of bonds after a transition period, chain reaction is bound to take place in financial institutions, thus forming potential system-related risks.

(2) *The problem of capital abundance ratio.* In the third quarter of 2008, the capital abundance ratio of the CDB was 10.68% (including foreign exchange open-ended risks) and the net capital was RMB332.328 billion. With the completion of reform, in its initial development of banking business of various kinds, it will further increase demand for capital. Capital restriction will become one of the most important issues related to development of the financing for the CDB.

(3) *The problem of bond risk weight.* The Detailed Plan for Implementation of the Reform of the CDB, approved by the State Council, points out that "the risk weight of RMB stock notes issued before the establishment of the China Development Bank Corporation is 0% until they are due. The risk weight of bonds to be issued after 2010 in the name of the Corporation will be adjusted gradually according to market principles. It will be decided later by the China Banking Regulatory Commission and other relevant departments through negotiations". After the transition period, the change of bond risk weight directly affects reorganization of credibility of the institutions of the CDB by markets, both at home and abroad, and the cost of capital-raising, thus such a change has a lot to do with the existence and development ability to develop financially.

(4) *The problem of concentrated rate of loans.* The Guidelines for the Regulation and Relevant Supervision and Management of State-Owned Commercial Banks stipulates that the ratio of loan balance amount to the same credit receiver should not be over 10% of the bank capital balance amount. The Guidelines for Risk Management of Credit-Giving to Group Clients by Commercial Banks stipulates that the total credit-giving amount to a single (and the same) group client should not be over 15% of the risk bearing ability of the capital balance amount of the commercial bank; the Directions for Operation of Trial Regulations for Internal Control Assessment of Commercial Banks stipulates that the ratio of credit-giving balance amount to the top 10 clients to the net capital amount of the bank in question should not be over 30%. Yet as far as present credit-giving is concerned, the concentration rate of the

CDB is over the policy provision. Take the Aluminum Corporation of China Limited for example. The loan balance amount with the CDB to it was US$15.158 billion. Both the loan balance amount and the loan of US$25 billion for the oil pipelines project in cooperation with Russia were over the limited amount to the same credit receiver. During the 10th Five-Year Plan period, the CDB gave credit to the Ministry of Railways in an amount of as much as US$25 billion. The credit-giving rate was as high as 75% for an individual group client, over the 15% index of supervision and regulation. At the end of the third quarter of 2008, the ratio of loan balance amounts of the top 10 clients to the net bank capital was as high as 76%, far over the 30% index for supervision and regulation.

(5) *The problem of the deposit loan ratio and the liquid ratio.* Article 39 of the Law of Commercial Banks stipulates that the deposit loan ratio and liquid ratio should not be over 75%. Items 1 and 3 of Article 8 of the Core Indexes for Risk Supervision and Regulation of Commercial Banks (For Trial Implementation) stipulate that liquid ratio is the ratio of current asset balance to current liabilities, which is used to assess the general level of liquidity of commercial banks. The ratio in question should not be lower than 25%. The CDB is mainly engaged in raising capital through the issuance of bonds; it focuses on large-sum and mid- and long-term loans. There are obvious differences in the deposit-loan structure from commercial banks.

(6) *The problem of capital return rate.* Item 1 of Article 13 of Core Indexes for Risk Supervision and Regulation of Commercial Banks (For Trial Implementation) stipulates that ROA and ROE should not be lower than 0.6 and 11%, respectively. In 2008, the ROA of CDB was about 0.62% and ROE about 5.97% — the latter fails to meet the requirements of supervision and regulation. Under the serious situation of the international financial crisis and the worsening of economy, the external environment is unfavorable and uncertain factors are increasing, problems that appear in the transition process are likely to become even more complicated.

17.2 How the new situations are addressed relates to financial security and economic security

If the new situations in strategic reforms are not properly dealt with, if the nature of bonds changes from the current financial bonds policy to become institutional bonds for instance, it is possible that there may be certain negative impacts as follows:

(1) *A negative impact might be felt on the credit rating of the CDB.* Credit of CDB has been rated over the years as A, A2, and A by the three rating corporations: Standard and Poor's, Moody's, and Fitch. Their results are the same as those of Chinese rating organs. After commercialization-related reform, the possibility that CDB's credit rating go down is relatively great.

(2) *The negative impact upon depository debts of the CDB.* First of all, if there is any change in the policy of zero-risk bonds of the CDB, in order to reduce capital occupancy, in all likelihood, commercial banks will dump a large number of bonds issued by the CDB, thus producing a relatively large impact in the financial market. Furthermore, there are clear and refined illustrations of terms for bonds issued abroad as well as the nature and position of the CDB. In terms of contract breaching, in addition to stipulation for being unable to pay interests and perform other obligations under the contract, more often than not, there are no other terms and conditions related to the nature of the CDB or the termination of governmental support. If reform of the Bank is carried out, and there is the occurrence of cases as mentioned above, some of the bond holders may declare that their bond capitals are immediately due and ask the Bank to make payments without delay. Finally, in some of the foreign exchange loan agreements prepared by the CDB, there is a provision that the Bank should make an announcement to the public about matters of importance. Hence, after the reform of commercialization is achieved, first of all, an announcement should be made to credit-givers to inform them of the impact of reform on the CDB. If the Bank loses the support to liquidity, part of the loan agreements may lead to breach of contracts and credit-givers may ask to

have their capital returned in advance, thus causing a chain of unfavorable reactions in bond markets at home and abroad.

(3) *The negative impact on domestic credit-giving.* Along with lowering the credit rating of the CDB, investment capitals in the Bank will be unavailable and in need of credit-giving management. Consequently, the investment amount of commercial banks will be restricted and the CDB will run into more difficulty in bond issuance, the increased rising cost of capital and risks of aborted bidding will be augmented. Furthermore, according to the current stipulation of the Central Bank, when an exploration-related financial institution issues RMB bonds, it is required to submit only its annual plan at issuance for examination and approval — credit-rating is not required. However, when a commercial bank issues bonds, it is required to submit every issuance and its credit-rating for examination and approval. Once the CDB is commercialized, when the Bank undergoes the same procedures as a commercial bank does, its effectiveness to raise capital will be influenced and issuance expenses will be increased.

(4) *The negative impact upon bond issuance abroad.* As the CDB is no longer a policy bank, it is also no longer able to undergo registration formalities abroad as required for bond issuance application. For instance, at present, the CDB is issuing bonds in the United States. It can use the B form for government-issuing bonds for registration at securities and exchange commission (SEC), but when it is commercialized, it will undergo procedures for registration as an ordinary corporation. The impacts of these requirements may be intertwined or overlapped, interacting with each other, and seriously affecting the present and future business of the CDB.

From a large-scale point of view, if the new situation within the strategic restructuring is not dealt with properly, the following two major problems might appear:

(1) The stability and development of the financial market will be affected. When the three-year transition period is over, it will be difficult to keep CDB's traditional channels for raising capital and it is very unrealistic to build a new commercial saving network. Consequently, there may be a shortage of capital sources.

The Bank will not only lose the ability to support its national policy projects but also the ability to pay back matured policy bonds, thus augmenting bad debts of the state-owned Bank of Industry and Commerce of China and other state-owned commercial banks, igniting systematic financial risk in China.

(2) There will be something missing in national policy financing. Since commercialization was achieved through strategic reforms, although great efforts have been made to conduct policy financing, commercialization is restricted by reform targets. The CDB has to develop toward the goals of a commercial bank. As a result, China's ability of policy financing has been greatly weakened. No support has been obtained for policy financing of projects for public welfare. It is increasingly difficult to promote the coordinated development of regions, providing assurance for the security of the national economy, strengthening the competitiveness of the national economy, and promoting public welfare causes, projects that are related to national long-term strategies to obtain the support of credit funds. In particular, while the international financial crisis continues and the global economy is worsening, the state-owned CDB is playing a leading part in implementing the State Council's policies of "expanding domestic demand, guaranteeing economic growth, adjusting economic structure," raising capital to support state-assigned fields and also playing an irreplaceable role in stimulating a stable and relatively rapid development of the economy. After the strategic restructuring is completed, if fund sources are blocked, the loan-granting capability will be affected and the CDB's promoting function of implementing national policies toward a macroeconomy will be weakened. In all likelihood, the mid- and long-term development of China will be unfavorably affected.

17.3 Causes and understanding of the aforementioned problems concerning the current set-up

Upon analyzing the guiding principles for commercialization in strategic restructuring, we will find two confusing concepts: First, the concept of commercialization is confused with that of a market-oriented economy. The CDB is market-oriented, employing market forces to realize the government's goals. While supporting the development of mid- and long-term construction and the foundations for people's livelihood, the Bank effectively controls bad loans. Like commercial banks, the CDB itself gets "big-leap" developed. Right here, a problem related to commercialization in an ordinary exchange and market-oriented economy that causes confusion appears. In fact, there is an essential difference between commercialization and a market-oriented economy.

Commercialization is a goal for regulation, requiring the giving of priority to commercial profits. Thus, a commercial bank sets profits as its first and foremost aim. Trying one's utmost to avoid various risks is a principle of heaven and earth. Commercialization is an operation mode or means. A certain goal may be achieved by way of market means. With a view to both realizing the government's goals and enhancing fund effectiveness, the CDB has earnestly conducted quite a number of explorations and attained successful experience. A summary will be complete in order to continue to keep up the meaningful work.

Second, the concept of policy financing is unclear. Because of this, some governmental departments have come to the conclusion that, among all the financing of the CDB, policy financing accounts for only 10–20%. Truly, policy financing included financing projects that did not bring obvious commercial benefits to commercial banks but needed financial support when national mid- and long-term development strategies were practicing in a market that was not mature at all. During the initial stage of socialism, most infrastructure facilities, foundational facilities of strategic industries, foundational facilities for social development, and foundational facilities for tertiary industry ought to have been included in policy financing. For instance, there are a large number of "bottlenecks" and weak links in socioeconomic development. They are beyond the power of government financing, commercial banks are not willing to get involved, and the capital market is not able to cover them, but they need development. This is when policy financing should step in. This kind of financing has much to do with the security of national politics, diplomacy, and economy. For another example, financing related to "go global" projects of national energy resources, mineral resources, sophisticated technologies, and the capacity export is also policy financing. Policy investment projects approved by the governmental department are only part of it. Financing these projects is based on their background — both policy-wise and strategy-wise. They cannot be judged by commercialization and it is improper to carry out financing in the name of commerce. Nor can they be supported by way of financial subsidy or by administrative orders. The major characteristics of this kind of financing are as follows: (i) the financing amount is large and concentrated; (ii) investment for the initial development is big; (iii) the cost is high; (iv) great efforts are needed for construction, consolidation, and integration; (v) low benefits are seen at the beginning but high benefits will be seen in later stages; (vi) and it is difficult to control risks. The financial morphology of the aforementioned financing, promoted by fundraising, is development-oriented finance, which is generally seen to by mid- and long-term financial institutions of development. Certainly, the in-depth cause for confusion is the imperfection of the market set-up and regulation set-up in which the macroeconomy was operating during the initial stages of socialism in China. If the market is imperfect, not normalized, and not standardized, it is difficult to bring the market function of allocating resources into full play. A capital market finds it difficult to effectively satisfy the demand for funds on its own. Therefore, the leading role of the government is still required. While the government is playing its leading role, many policies may not be flexible enough and there may be no "going-with-the-time" mechanism for adjustment and coordination. Possibly, there are no necessary legal guarantees for policy for financial institutions that are closely related to the government, when they are playing their roles as tools of the government. This is probably where the shoe pinches most tightly. The reality of the current set-up and efforts to reform it should be taken into consideration in order to achieve a satisfactory solution to these problems.

17.4 Joint efforts by the CDB and supervision-regulation departments to address the new situation

While the Bank is conducting stable strategic restructuring, it must retain its financing continuity, at the same time overcoming difficulties and solving new challenges which it may come across during the process of strategic reforms. The most essential and urgent task of the reforms is to set up a mechanism for guaranteeing financing funds. To achieve this, the CDB should explore new approaches with the spirit of reform. On the other hand, relevant supervision and regulation departments are required to consider current realities, hold a far-sighted view, and equip themselves with overall planning procedures to help solve the problems the Bank finds difficult to deal with alone and they must plan jointly with other departments to ensure a smooth transition for the strategic restructuring of the Bank.

The specific requirements for the mechanism to guarantee financial funds are as follows: Amount-wise, the demand for funds for the CDB to conduct financing should be satisfied; time-wise, funds should be raised quickly and on time; cost-wise, the cost of fund-raising should be controlled within a certain range; channel-wise, fund sources should be diversified; procedure-wise, the less supervision and regulation over fund-raising the better, and the more simplified procedures for examination and approval the better; term-wise, the capital term should match the asset term as closely as possible to reduce unnecessary risks.

To meet the requirements of capital guarantees, the CDB, as its main task, should persist in the policy of organizing its functions as a bond bank and its other financings are only complimentary tasks. This discrepancy is due to the essential difference between the operating modes of the CDB as a financial institution of development and other traditional commercial banks. The following are the characteristics of the CDB:

(1) *The interest rate differentials are small.* After its strategic restructuring, the CDB continued to conduct mid- and long-term credit-giving and investment and to serve the mid- and long-term

development strategies for the national economy for overall and long-term national interests. The loan earning rate and interest rate differentials are low for national strategic projects, especially for "going global" strategic projects. According to the 2008 Annual Reports of commercial banks: the Industry and Commerce Bank of China, the Bank of China, the China Construction Bank, and the Bank of Communications, their average loan interest rate differential was 4.69%, while the RMB loan interest rate differential of the CDB was 2.76% and its foreign exchange loan interest rate differential was only 0.35%, far lower than that of commercial banks.

(2) *The cost of capital-raising is high*. Being different from commercial banks that mainly depend on accepting deposits of residents and enterprises, the CDB is mainly engaged in capital-raising through issuing bonds. It is not yet able to accept deposits of residents and its scale of bond issuance is under unified management with the Central Bank. When the Central Bank adjusts the interest, the bond interest rates and basic interest rates of the CDB cannot be adjusted synchronously. Therefore, the cost of bond issuance is somewhat fixed. The average term for bonds issued in 2008 by the CDB was 7.94 years and average cost was 4.11%; this is 0.51% higher than the cost for five-year fixed deposits.

(3) *The ratio of risk assets is high*. The ratio of risk-weight assets of the CDB is about 90%, approximately 34% higher than the average ratio of 56% for commercial banks.

(4) *The revenue structure is unitary*. As a wholesale bank, revenue of the CDB depends mainly on loan interests, while commercial banks have an extremely large service network and a large number of employees working to oversee the "retailing", financing, and operation of the banks' intermediate products. According to the measurement of revenue structure results, the intermediate products of commercial banks take up 14.3% of the average business income, while that of the CDB is only 5.1%. In particular, in recent years, there has been rapid growth in the asset scale for loans to support national projects of strategic importance. Consequently, asset-scale growth is likely to lead to capital consumption and a profit rate of net worth that is inevitably lower than that of commercial banks.

Therefore, its development financing is somewhat unusual. It needs to be backed up with policies and government credit; it has to persist in being a "bond" bank. When the transition period is over, its nature of being a bond bank cannot be altered and bond risk weight cannot be changed.

When the strategic restructuring of the CDB is completed, apart from its continuance as a "bond bank" and raising capital by way of issuing bonds, the Bank will be required to make many efforts to explore diversified ways of raising capital, strengthen and improve its market functions, expand capital sources, control capital-raising costs, further improve the mechanism for capital-raising, and widen the range of investment by learning whatever good practices are used by commercial banks. In doing so, stable and long-term capital sources can be guaranteed for the CDB. This is instrumental to promote the development of a capital market in China. It is not only necessary but also possible to broaden diversified capital-raising channels. Where there is will, there is a way. For instance, expansion of deposit scope and the many efforts used to develop depositing operation, the introduction of strategic investors, striving to turn accumulated profits into capital in accordance with legal procedures, the issuance of necessary junior bonds, striving to employ foreign exchange reserve funds, strengthening all-over cooperation in negotiated deposits with other financial institutions, merging or acquisitioning financial institutions to procure capital, conducting the business of trust administration for social security funds and enterprises' annuity funds, raising funds for project investment through fundraising, and raising capital by way of interim transactions. Reform can also be carried out in the area of financial bonds. The following practice should be continued: issuance of financial bonds should be gradually transited from the inter-bank market to public-market-oriented issuance; ideally issuing them to the public at stock exchanges and bank counters. The market-oriented issuance of bonds can further bring into play and improve the function of adjusting and allocating the social capital of financial bonds, enhance capital-raising effectiveness for mid- and long-term development capital, and further deploy inactive social capital to support construction. Market-oriented issuance will help promote the healthy development of the financial market and support mid- and long-term infrastructure construction and other social causes.

17.5 Summary

In general, the reform of CDB is different from that of commercial banks (Figure 17.1). The restructuring of development bank is to transform it from a policy bank into a development-oriented finance institution in a commercial form. If transformed to a traditional commercial bank, the development bank would encounter new problems with respect to credit stability, major project concentration, and risk regulation and have to address challenges like determining future business development model, increasing outlets, expanding the variety and scope of bond issuance, and improving settlement and

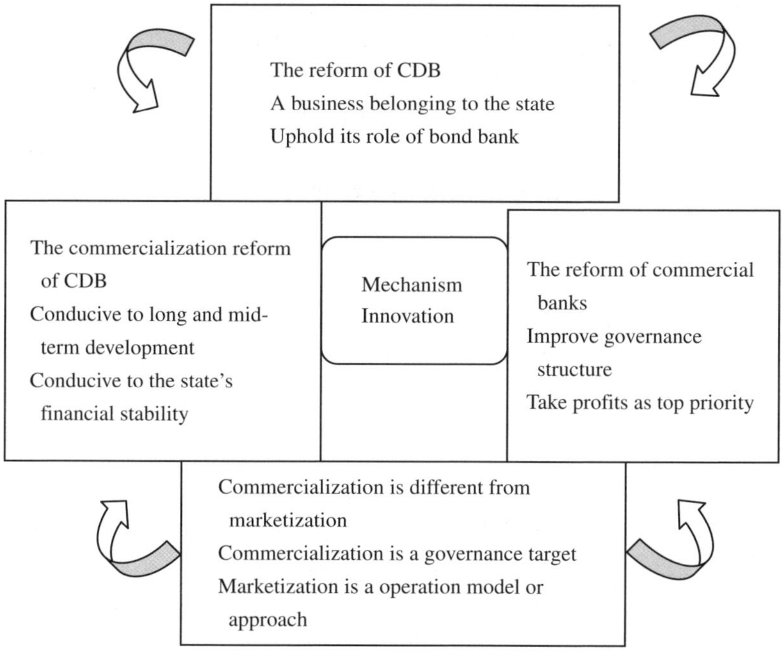

Figure 17.1: The reform of CDB is different from that of commercial banks.

deposit-taking functions. CDB's financing model and medium- and long-term credit positioning should be different from those of commercial banks. After the reform, CDB will turn into an enterprise, but more importantly, a state-owned enterprise. Instead of pursuing the indicators of commercial banks such as the yield, CDB should carry forward the good practices, maintain its own characteristics, distinguish itself from commercial banks in its advantageous areas, and avoid vicious inter-bank competition to form a differentiated development pattern and develop into the largest and most influential bank in the field of loans but not foolishly "picking sesame" in favor of the pursuit of yield and other commercial banks index. For a very long period to come, CDB still needs to uphold its role as a bond bank, maintain its characteristics of retreating back in a booming market and coming forward to boost the sluggish market, and strive to play a greater role in the overall initiative. Regulatory policies should take into account multiple factors, and should be conducive to the country's financial stability as well as mid- and long-term development. In any case, China should have an effective financing mechanism to address the financing bottlenecks in the macroeconomy and provide necessary financial support for national strategies, medium- and long-term infrastructure construction, and social progress.

Case Study 4: America national infrastructure bank

I. *Background*

After the American financial crisis led to a global economic depression, America, like many other countries, has seen the infrastructure building as an important strategic move to resume the economic growth, create job opportunities, and enhance the national competitiveness.

Infrastructure has always been an effective way to ensure the sustainable economic development. In the beginning of the past century, an American congressman submitted this proposal to prevent the economic downturn. In response to the current economic crisis, Christopher J. Dodd, a Democratic congressman, Chuck Huge, a

Republican congressman, and other congressmen submitted the proposal again to construct a "National Infrastructure Bank". In early September 2010, Obama said he would join hands with Congress to carry out the proposal. Now, the proposal stays at the stage of documentation and technical procedure.

II. *Contents*

Purpose of the Bank: Guide the direction of the national infrastructure investment; support the construction of high-speed railways and other strategic traffic facilities, and support the building of energy, water conservancy, electric power, and other infrastructures; and support strategic large projects across industries.

Governance of the Bank: The Bank will act as an independent operating entity like the Federal Deposit Insurance Corporation in nature. It will be managed by the board of directors consisting of relevant experts not assigned by the government.

Mechanism of the Bank: The funds of the Bank mainly come from government appropriations and credit products. The Federal government will contribute US$50 billion as the capital of the bank, which can also issue US$60 billion of long-term bonds with a term of 50 years. The funds will be used for direct loans, loan guarantee, and long-term tax support. The Bank will support projects with a minimum investment of US$75 million.

III. *Comments*

The establishment of the National Infrastructure Bank is now the hottest political topic in the American economic life, and indicates that America also pays much attention to the role of the government in guiding the medium- and long-term loans, though the country is a market economy.

China will still stay at the preliminary stage of the market economy in the period of the 21st century. China does not lack money, but lacks the effective mechanism to raise money, so it will need to exert the high efficiency of national development.

Chapter 18

Promoting the Healthy Development of the Financial Institution to a State of Commercial Operation

According to the requirements of the reform plan for the China Development Bank (CDB) approved by the State Council, the CDB will change into a commercial bank. When the reform is complete, the Bank will mainly depend on conducting the financial operations of offering mid- and long-term credit loans and investment to serve mid- and long-term strategies in national economy. Under the grave circumstances of the international financial crisis and worsening economy, the CDB will not only reform its business systems but also its strategic structures. Therefore, it is facing augmenting risks. Its reform is a process of arduous exploration. There is no firm experience to learn from in transitioning a policy bank into a commercial bank focusing on mid- and long-term credit loans. The Bank is expected to break free of its fixed and customary concepts, move with the times, and continually make breakthroughs. Once it is successful, it will create an approach for a policy bank to restructure its strategies under China's actual conditions.

18.1 Characteristics and functions of different financial forms

In the past 30 years of reform, remarkable changes have taken place in China's financial set-up, thoroughly transforming the situation in which central financing (governmental financing) used to be the only way out for construction. A pattern of "a cart drawn by five horses" has been formed: central financing, commercial banks, capital market, policy finance, and development-oriented finance (a financial institution of development). They have jointly raised capital to support mid- and long-term construction and development. Investment for central financing takes up a certain percentage in mid- and long-term infrastructure construction and, in the future, it will continue to play its leading and promoting role, especially in infrastructure construction projects of pure public welfare and bottleneck fields that obstruct social development, governmental financing should be augmented. However, generally speaking, this kind of financing is a far cry from satisfying construction requirements. Besides, the effectiveness of governmental investment is relatively low and it is liable to be blindly expanded, thus causing losses and waste. Excessive direct governmental investment is detrimental to the growth and the building-up of a capital market.

It is encouraging to see that commercial banks are involved in relatively mature mid- and long-term construction fields. This is a very rewarding progress. However, objectively, the deposit- and-loan structure of commercial banks requires them to not make too much effort in capital-raising for mid- and long-term construction projects. Otherwise, it is liable to bring about a "misfitting of deposit and loan terms", in other words, a set-up related risk that might become a potentially unstable factor in the finance market and for economic development. Besides, there are quite a few markets that are immature in mid- and long-term construction fields and bottleneck fields that obstruct social development. The tendency of commercial banks, more often than not, makes them separate themselves far from those markets.

Remarkable achievements have been realized in that construction departments are able to make some use of capital market to raise funds needed for the mid- and long-term construction projects. However, China's capital market is still in the "infancy" stage, meaning that the support to mid- and long-term construction is limited. There are certain resources and driving forces in the society, but due to the lack of an effective mechanism and regulatory systems, these resources and driving forces have not been fully utilized to serve mid- and long-term construction.

As matching capital of the government policy, policy finance serves national strategies, expands fundamental capital-raising means, and service functions, but policy finance also expects certain financial compensation, as its ability to achieve sustainable development is relatively weak.

The outstanding trait of development-oriented finance is that it introduces the concept of a market constraining force and of capital cost into policy financial activities, thus completely eradicating the traditional ideology of "policy finance can go without economic accounting or without considering principles of a market economy", adopting basic principles of effectiveness and profits, and placing policy financial activities and commercial financial activities not only within the same market principles but also integrating them. The CDB is an important financial institution for the development of this country. It made its appearance in a unique financial form and also, in its own growth, has gradually developed a unique capital-raising mechanism and it has become a principal force in mid- and long-term infrastructure construction. The Bank has deeply enriched the financial ecology in China. These are all significant fruits of the policy of reform and opening up, symbolizing a new stage for financial development and for a socialist market economy with Chinese characteristics. It is worthwhile to make a conscientious summary for further development. Table 18.1 shows the comparison, analysis, and summary of five different financial modes.

18.2 The essences and characteristics of a financial institution of development with the functions of a commercial bank

As the title implies, development-oriented finance with the functions of a commercial bank is a finance form with capital-raising for mid- and long-term construction projects and bottleneck projects for social development as its major task. Development-oriented finance with the functions of a commercial bank closely follows national mid- and long-term strategic aims and policy demands. On the one hand, with government support, it makes up for the "ineffective

Table 18.1: Comparative features of five financial modes.

	Government financing	Commercial bank	Capital market	Policy finance	Development-oriented finance
Orientation	Seed capital; guiding social investment	Capital provision and acting as a loan intermediary	Raising of private capital and providing an investment platform	Serving national strategies as government's matching fund	Basing itself on national strategies, recognizing government intentions; acting as a bridge between government and market
Service objectives	Raising capital for public goods; promoting social fairness	Providing commercial activities with accomodation, payment convenience, and value-added service	Raising capital for enterprises; realizing maximized value for investment share Holders and creditors	Raising capital for public goods and quasi-public goods; realizing national strategic aims for each stage	Raising capital for public goods, quasi-public goods, and bottleneck fields; realizing mid- and long-term national strategic aims

(Continued)

Table 18.1: (*Continued*).

	Government financing	Commercial bank	Capital market	Policy finance	Development-oriented finance
Market value	Improving infrastructure environment; promoting social and market development	Promoting production and consumption; satisfying public demands on multiple financial services	Providing capital raising channels; providing mid- and long-term sources for wealth accumulation of private investors	With government guidance providing matching service; expanding foundational capital raising means, and service functions	Providing market sectors that fail to work properly with proposals related to set-up construction and credit environment; improving defective credit
Commercial pursuit	Not expecting direct commercial return, promoting realization of comprehensive development	Commercial operation; expecting return; providing mid- and long-term capital-raising; avoiding risks	Seeking relatively high return; being able to bear risks and a certain amount of loss	Seeking certain finance compensation	Market-oriented operation; providing capital raising for mid- and long-term investments; seeking certain commercial return and finance compensation

(*Continued*)

Table 18.1: (*Continued*).

	Government financing	Commercial bank	Capital market	Policy finance	Development-oriented finance
Sustainable development	Depending on government financing	Depending on sustainable growth of depositing; developing along with economic development; being able to realize "survival of the fittest"	Depending on accumulation of private capital and social wealth; slow development; restricted by national policies and environment of foundational credit	Depending on finance subsidiaries and continuous commitment of investment	Has relatively strong ability to survive, adapt itself, and develop in markets; good achievements in markets and exportation; able to go against economical cycles
Defects	Depending on macroeconomical environment; project performance assessment; project performance restrictions and not enough supervision	Influenced by cycles of macroeconomy; sensitive to market fluctuation; having higher demand on credit environment	Almost no desire to raise capital for bottleneck social projects; no patience to promote market construction	Policy burden relatively heavy; commercialized means limited; inadequate internal motivation; sustainable development limited	Restricted by macro-policies and market environment; will not be able to meet expectations of investors in the near future

market" with government credit, such as the "missing" of market credibility, imperfect set-ups, and ineffective channels for deposits to become investments. On the other hand, basing itself on the principles of commercial finance, it conducts policy financial activities, trying as much as possible to weaken the administrative hues of traditional policy finance to avoid "ineffective government". In short, development-oriented finance is the employed mode of commercial banks or market-oriented means to realize government aims.

A financial institution of development functioning as a commercial bank has its own regulation structure, but is a bond bank of the government. It possesses the qualities of a financial enterprise, but it attaches more importance to government intentions. It has policy tasks, but they are not extensions of financial policies. It has market functions, but it does not set profits as its purpose. Therefore, it is a new financial form. It is a renovation in the financial system. It has drawn on the practices of similar international financial institutions such as the World Bank, Fannie Mae, and Freddie Mac, summarized its own and other financial institutions' experiences and taken into full consideration the impact of the international financial crisis. All this encompasses the requirements of China's mid- and long-term development strategies.

A development-oriented financial system with functions as those of a commercial bank is composed of the following four parts: (i) strategic finance, (ii) supporting finance, (iii) compensatory finance, and (iv) poverty alleviation finance. By strategic finance, what is meant is the provision of financial service to "two foundations; one branch" and "conducting financial activities abroad" that national mid- and long-term development activities needed in a unique development-oriented financial institution like the CDB (or a financial institution of development); supporting finance means the way by which activities of development-oriented financial institutions give full reflection to policies toward specific components in economic systems that the government intends to develop and bring into realization the government's inclination to gain profits from socioeconomic development. According to the experiences of other countries and the actual conditions in China, supporting finance focuses on importation and exportation and on the development of medium- and small-sized enterprises. Compensatory finance means that through the efforts of various activities of policy financial institutions, to compensate certain industries and social groups which are at a disadvantage, especially focusing on compensation of effectiveness loss caused by imbalance of industrial structure. At present, this kind of finance is employed to promote the development of agriculture and agriculture-related departments in rural areas. Poverty alleviation finance means that governmental policy financial methods will narrow the difference between regions, urban areas and rural areas, the rich and the poor, promoting a general enhancement of living standards for all residents so as to lay down a foundation for common wealth. Poverty alleviation finance lays more emphasis on fairness in social-economic development, or by way of policy, financial means compensating for the loss of social welfare as a result of market competition. For example, providing fund support to re-employment of the unemployed or encouraging starting an undertaking which will alleviate pressure on the basic social security system. Table 18.2 is a comparison, analysis, and summary of financial institution developments.

Characteristics of a developmental financial institution with the functions of a commercial bank lie in its "strategization", well-roundness, institutionalization, and scale. Its "strategization" finds its expression in serving national strategic aims; its well-roundness is revealed in its promotion of the enhancement of overall economic

Table 18.2: Development finance structure of an institution with functions of a commercial bank.

Structure	Major feature
Strategic finance	Serving infrastructure construction and strategic tasks
Supporting finance	Getting rid of bottlenecks in social development
Compensatory finance	Compensating for differences arising from the development of various industries
Poverty alleviation finance	Narrowing the gap between the rich and the poor

effectiveness through financial development means; its institutionalization is shown by not only emphasizing the raising of capital for its projects but also by advocating the promotion of market construction through capital-raising; and its scale can be seen in its concept of large-scale collectives and its means of combined operation. It is important to emphasize that a reform of policy finance should be oriented toward the functions similar or identical to that of commercial banks, simply because we are determined to utilize the aforementioned characteristics of development-oriented finance, to bring into full play functions and roles of a market-oriented operation of development-oriented finance, to promote the organic combination of strategic finance, supporting finance, compensatory finance, and poverty alleviation finance so as to establish a developmental financial set-up with Chinese characteristics.

The progress and development of capital-raising for mid- and long-term construction and the government's "hot spot" means of capital-raising is stamped with the brand of reform and opening up. Progress in finance, especially in capital-raising for mid- and long-term construction and for overcoming bottleneck obstacles, is extremely obvious. Urgency for further reform and development of finance is also of the utmost importance. As far as the financial ecological balance in China is concerned, there is no lack of outstanding retail-related commercial saving banks, but this country is short of mid- and long-term bond banks with commercialized operation that serve mid- and long-term development strategies. What merits serious consideration for reform in finance and its development is to adapt finance to the needs of accelerating urbanization, industrialization, and to the building up of a well-off society in an all-round way and to maintain the diversity of financial ecology.

18.3 Actively exploring the growth mode for a financial institution of development with functions of a commercial bank

Under the situation of addressing the financial crisis, there are the following three choices for the CDB.

(1) To take the commercial bank road with absolute, genuine resolution and direct the CDB with stipulations and regulations for a commercial bank.
(2) To lay emphasis on policies, also, re-play the part of a policy bank and undertake national policy financial business, bad accounts, and bad assets of which will be covered with subsidiaries and support from governmental financing after submitting applications.
(3) To actively explore the development mode of a financial institution of development with functions of a commercial bank, summarizing successful experiences in market-oriented operation over the years, learning actual and specific practices from commercial banks, further strengthening capability of market operation and continuing to realize the government's aims with market-oriented means. The CDB should conscientiously strengthen its sense of responsibility and sense of history to choose the third choice, a road full of hardships and difficulties to be sure, but worthy of exploring. It should engage in development financing within the framework of a commercial bank. Specifically, the CDB is a whole state-owned bank, a mid- and long-term bond bank with commercialized operation, a financial institution of development with the functions of a commercial bank, a bank engaged primarily in capital-raising and investment for mid- and long-term projects, as well as a bank serving national development strategies through commercialized operations. This kind of orientation is identical with the reform plan which was approved by the State Council and in compliance with the reality of the situation in China and the needs of socio-economic development. First of all, China is a large developing nation with heavy development tasks. On the one hand, there are many bottleneck fields and weak links in the national economy that are in need of the support of mid- and long-term capital-raising. On the other hand, flawed creditability and an imperfect market make it difficult for bottleneck fields and weak links to obtain commercial funds. Development means the stimulation of the construction market through capital-raising, the building-up

of creditability, the establishment of systems, and the building-up of healthy markets are absolutely needed. Furthermore, to realize national development strategies, it is necessary for development-oriented financial institutes to continue to display their unique advantages for mid- and long-term capital-raising and intensify their market-oriented operations while avoiding the "misfitting" risk in credit and debt terms.

(4) To improve financial ecology and the financial system, it is necessary for a financial institution of development to discover development approaches which are different from those for saving banks. The imbalance and diversity of socioeconomic development require the strengthening of financial systems that are healthy and orderly and are able to provide multiple services and with a reasonable division of work. This is needed not only for short-term and retail-like saving banks but also for mid- and long-term wholesale-like bond banks. All these various kinds of banks are able to increase operating efficiency of financial systems and the capacity for supporting development.

(5) The in-depth reform in economic systems requires creative ideas and remodeled set-ups and mechanisms. As long as the requirements of mid- and long-term development strategies can be met, active exploration and experimentation of this sort are worthy efforts. Promoting the healthy growth of development-oriented finance, with the functions of a commercial bank, is instrumental not only to accelerating the building-up of a modern finance system in China but also to stimulate the improvement of government functions and its ways of governing, thus helping to find a means to further reform in the political system.

It is feasible for the CDB to have the functions of a commercial bank, mainly because it is able to control risks related to mid- and long-term capital-raising. With the long-term support of national creditability, the Bank continues in being a bond bank, raising capital for sustainable development, and maintaining a balanced cash flow. After strategic restructuring is completed, a modern corporation system will be established and its market functions strengthened; this is instrumental to its adaptation to international practices. Thus, acting as a commercial institution, it will establish unique relationships with other markets, both at home and abroad, and it will also further expand its financing operation. The CDB has made great efforts in creating modes for risk management and establishing a long-term mechanism for risk regulation, thus ensuring that there are as few risks as possible when giving credit for mid- and long-term construction.

(1) *Renovation in the set-up*: Establishing and improving the forewarning mechanism for risk analysis, an all-round risk management organizational system for the entire process, and an organizational system at a grassroots level for the prevention of socialized risks.
(2) *Renovation in management*: Adopting a means of "consortium loans" and "loaning before selling" to gradual retail loans of significant amounts to other commercial banks to share loan risks.
(3) *Renovation in technology*: Accelerating mastery and popularization of information technology and the development of quantification for risk management.
(4) *Renovation in management culture*: Cultivate a sense of prevention of risks among bank employees and implement a culture of risk management that covers fore-monitoring before taking a risk, management during the risk period and dealing with the results if ever a default occurs. The CDB's practice speaks for its achievement. By the end of March 2010, the Bank's reclamation rate of principal and interest was 99.23% for 41 quarters and its rate of bad loans was only 0.85%. The CDB has been engaged in mid- and long-term financing for over 10 years. Its practice has proven that its measures for controlling risks are good and effective. In the past 10 years or more, its capital has topped RMB150 billion. Note that it was only RMB35 billion when the Bank was established. It has handed over tax revenue upwards of RMB100 billion and its asset scale is over RMB4,000 billion. The CDB is confident that as time goes by, it will do a better job in running itself, to embody the ability of the governing Communist Party.

18.4 Inspirations from international development-oriented finance

The concept of a financial institution of development is not something new. The World Bank and the Asia Development Bank are both well-known financial institutions of development established after the Second World War. These institutions provide long-term and low-cost loans of significant amounts for infrastructure construction, foundational construction and key projects of many countries and regions, thus playing an important role in economic development. Apart from internationally well-known financial institutions of developments, many countries in the world attach great importance to development-oriented finance. They regard it as an essential tool for realizing their national economic and political strategies and fully make use of its functions of compensation in an "imperfect market", its maintenance of stability of economic finance, and its promotion of socioeconomic development. There are corresponding financial institutions in the United States for agriculture, housing, small and medium enterprises, import and export and student loans, and long-term financial support is given to them. In Germany, there are 18 policy financial institutions focusing on development tasks, of which the Kreditanstalt für Wiederaufbau (KfW) that was established in 1948 provides long-term credit support for small and medium enterprises, rural construction, and large-size public projects. The Development Bank of Japan (DBJ), a policy investment bank, has played a significant role in post-war economic restoration and in the promotion of high-speed economic development. The Korean Development Bank has played an important part in implementing national policies toward industries. Their experience demonstrates that policy finance is an important regulation measure in order to compensate for the imperfectness of the market.

Internationally, there have been precedents of carrying out development-oriented finance in the form of commercial banks. For example, though Fannie Mae and Freddie Mac in the United States have become commercial institutions and gone public, they are still financial institutions of developments, responsible for the policy mission of "residents shall have their own dwelling places" and continue to play an important role in construction, development, and stability of the secondary market of housing mortgage loans in the United States and they also continue to get support from the government. Fannie Mae and Freddie Mac still enjoy bond creditability at a quasi-sovereign level and the bonds they issue are still regarded as bonds of those of American governmental institutions and their standard mortgage loan bonds are still regarded as zero risk weight. Fannie Mae and Freddie Mac were in great trouble in the sub-prime crisis, mainly because the American financial set-up had gone wrong. In a long-term view, the system of Fannie Mae and Freddie Mac was successful, which conducted policy financing in the form of a commercial bank. What deserves mention is that the Federal Reserve also does so. Its operational structure is almost the same as that of a commercial bank and it covers its operation costs, but it performs the function of the central bank.

Besides the acceleration of globalization and the rapid development of commercial finance, direct capital-raising market is becoming increasingly mature. Since the 1990s, remarkable changes have taken place in the operation environment for a financial institution of development.

(1) Relatively speaking, there has been less desire for long-term capital-raising.
(2) Financing fields which financial institution of developments used to be well versed in have been challenged by commercialized financial institutions.
(3) There are increasingly more capital channels that a financial institution of developments may employ. In order to deal with the new situation, some financial institution of developments go with the time, constantly adjusting themselves, re-orienting themselves in the market, and speeding up reform. Nevertheless, although some commercial institutions have undergone strategic restructuring, they are still responsible for certain policy missions and also enjoy the government's powerful creditability support. Especially during the process of strategic reform, they can neither change their loan creditability nor so easily maintain a relatively

long transition period. For instance, it took the Dexia Bank of France 10 years to transit from a policy bank into a private one. During the entire transition period, the French government was continuously giving it quasi-sovereign-level creditability support. KfW of Germany separated from its commercial financing through setting up affiliated companies. After reform, the essence of the KfW Group as a policy bank remained unchanged because of this separation. Its original financing and operation modes were maintained and the government's preferential policy, credit rating, and ways of capital-raising remained the same. Although the DBJ has set the goal of privatization, it still maintains its policy financing and enjoys the government's creditability support. International financial institution of developments, represented by the World Bank, are intensifying their development function and making new breakthroughs in the development field and in the objectives of development. Their financing covers Europe and the "four small dragons" in Asia, ranging from infrastructure to environmental protection, poverty alleviation, disease control, and foundational education.

Since the recent international financial crisis, there have been some changes in the reform of international financial institutions of development. First, countries in Europe and the United States now set great store in governmental creditability intervention and market rescue. They invest in financial institutions, increase creditability, and add liquidity to the market to stabilize market confidence and the financial system. Second, the role of policy financial institutions is demonstrated even further. For instance, German KfW provided €12.2 billion to financial institutions in crisis and was responsible for the management of the German government's €100 billion for relieving enterprises. Third, some countries adjusted the direction and pace of policy finance. For example, the Japanese government, on the one hand, reconsidered reform-related privatization of the DBJ; on the other hand, it adjusted the reform plan, postponing the deadline for reform from October 2008 to April 2012. Even after 2012, there will be another 5–7 years for transition. If necessary, the government will continue to provide capital to ensure that DBJ will receive enough support. On the other hand, DBJ, centering on aims of the Japanese government, has expanded and increased loans to medium- and large-sized enterprises, purchasing commercial invoices, investing in assigned enterprises, provided medium- and large-size enterprises with liability guarantee, and is now held responsible with other policy financial institutions for the prevention of financial risks and maintaining market stability.

18.5 Great importance shall be attached to the position and role of financial institutions of development in the new situation

Under the grave situation of the international financial crisis and the decline of the world economy, there are more uncertain factors for China in this unfavorable external environment. As a large developing country, China has long been in the initial stage of socialism. It has a large population but is short of resources. Its development is rather unbalanced. In the near future, China will be at a key stage for the industrialization, urbanization, and modernization of the national economy. This country must earnestly strengthen and improve macro-controls and carry out the development modes of a market economy under the guidance of the government. The roles of development-oriented finance are of great importance because they are irreplaceable. In summary, they are as follows:

(1) Development-oriented finance is the implementation means of a coordinated operation of national monetary policy, financial policy, and industry policy in order to eradicate the gap between urban and rural areas, narrowing the gap between rich and poor, as well as between production and resources, solving imbalances between regions, industries, development levels, and environmental protection, setting up a credit system and improving market mechanisms.
(2) Development-oriented finance provides loans for reconstruction of slums and for the construction of low-rent dwellings,

small-amount loans, loans for beginning an undertaking, loans for alleviating poverty and for development and scholarship loans to improve social security, promote development of people's livelihood and stimulate the right to equal capital-raising. Development-oriented finance is an important force in solving livelihood-related issues.

(3) Development-oriented finance provides capital-raising for long-term and significant amount projects and also capital-raising for importation and exportation to support important military-industry-related projects, emergency projects, projects of tackling key problems in science and technology, and projects related to regional deployment of strategies. Development-oriented finance is an important tool for maintaining national security strategy and increasing international competitiveness.

Infrastructure, infrastructure construction, strategic industries, environmental protection, poverty alleviation, disease control, and the development of rural areas are matters the government will forever be concerned about, and they are also long-term tasks for the CDB as a national financial institution of development. Its reform transition from a policy bank to a financial institution of development requires tremendous efforts for exploration and trials. The essential transition cannot be expected to be completed in one morning. It requires trial-and-error practice over a long period of time.

18.6 Recommendations to support healthy and sustainable growth of a financial institution of development functioning as a commercial bank

In order to fulfill the reform aims put forward in the reform plan for the CDB, approved of by the State Council, having combined the actual conditions in China and the characteristics of security banks, for the purpose of making the CDB better serve national strategies and prevent risks, the guiding ideas for reform are as follows: (1) Continuing to carry out strategic restructuring and to support the sustainable and healthy growth of the CDB as a financial institution of development functioning as a commercial bank. (2) Being fully aware of the reality that the reform of the CDB still requires a lot more exploration. It is arduous and it takes time. The Bank should combine its strategic restructuring, its features of a bank for issuing mid- and long-term bonds, and its ability to serve national development strategies and make constant improvements in its practice. (3) At present, the urgent solution expected is the establishment of a regulation policy, a mechanism for encouragement and legal assurance for a differentiated financial institution conducting financing with all the functions of a commercial bank. Our specific recommendations are the following:

(1) Defining the CDB's orientation and guiding thoughts for its development. A financial institution of development that shoulders a lot of policy tasks plays a very important role in socioeconomic development. Even if the CDB turns into a commercial financial institution, its function of exhibiting comprehensive policy financing, position, and role are irreplaceable. We recommend that the CDB, as a national financial institution of development, continue to maintain its important function of providing service of comprehensive policy financing through market means. For its future development, the Bank should continue in focusing on mid- and long-term policy financing, taking a road different from traditional commercial banks for development, avoiding its weaknesses while exploiting its strengths, continuously improving market-oriented mechanisms for development-oriented finance, and realizing differential development from commercial banks.
(2) Keeping unblocked capital channels of the CDB. We support the CDB in remaining a "bond bank". It should focus on raising capital in the form of security by relying on national creditability. In addition to original capital-raising channels, we recommend expanding and widening capital sources and further improving capital-raising mechanisms.
(3) Improving laws and statues and assessing set-ups. The current Law of Commercial Banks and other statues are mainly for

commercial banks that raise capital by drawing deposits. They are not accurate for capital-raising through bonds and neither are they applicable to financial institutions conducting a lot of policy financing. We recommend that regulations be formulated for the CDB, defining its place in national finance, development orientation, service strategies, supervision standards, and accessing mechanisms.

18.7 Summary

At the primary stage of socialism, China needs the government-led model of market economy development and the vital role of development-oriented finance. To achieve the objectives defined in the State Council's CDB Reform Program, we hereby propose the following recommendations for the healthy and sustainable growth of development-oriented finance institution in a commercial form (Figure 18.1).

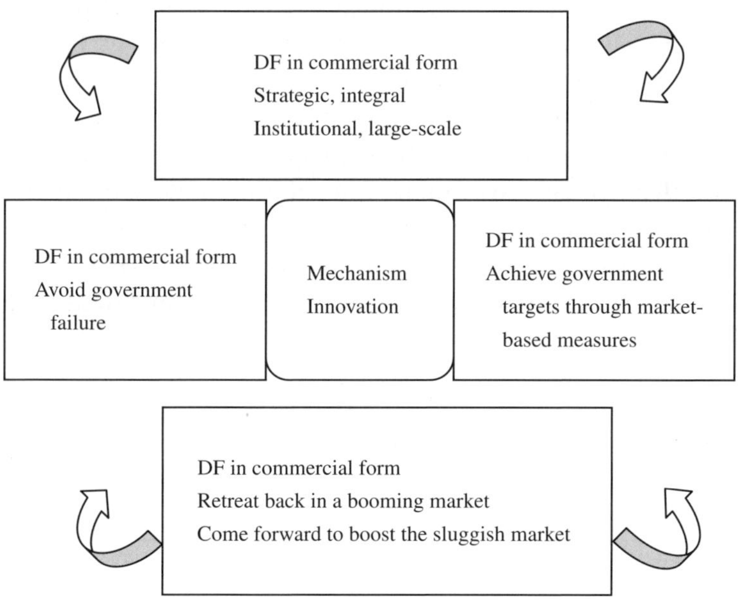

Figure 18.1: Development-oriented finance institution in a commercial form.

(1) Clarify the positioning and development ideas of CDB. Development-oriented financial institute assuming a number of policy tasks play an important role in the economic and social development of China. In spite of the transition to commercial financial institution, CDB still has irreplaceable functions, status, and role as an integrated policy financial institution and the state needs to retain the critical functions of CBD as a national development-oriented finance institution to provide comprehensive financial services through market-based operations. For further development, CDB needs to persist in the medium- and long-term businesses, take a development path different from traditional commercial banks, avoid weaknesses, and give full play to the strengths so as to achieve competitive differentiation against other commercial banks.
(2) Ensure the sound funding channel of CDB. While upholding its role as a bond bank and relying on the state credit to raise funds, CDB is recommended to broaden the sources of funding and further improve the funding mechanism.
(3) Improve the legal and appraisal system. The existing Law on Commercial Banks and other laws and regulations for deposit-taking commercial banks do not apply to financial institutions that issue bonds for financing and assume a large number of policy-related businesses. It is proposed that relevant government departments formulate the National Development Bank Ordinance to define its target, positioning, development direction, service strategy, regulatory standards, and assessment mechanism and provide legal support for the sustainable growth of CDB.

Chapter 19

A Preliminary Study of Financial Diplomacy

Finance is the nervous centralis of a national economy. With the development of globalization, international financial relationships have become an important component between national partners. Influenced by the global financial crisis, the focal point of a relationship between world powers is no longer the competition or cooperation of military strength; the leading powers of formulation for planning and rules for international finance have replaced it. If China expects to develop into a world power, it not only needs superb strategies for political diplomacy and military diplomacy but also brilliant strategies for financial diplomacy. Great importance should be given to financial diplomacy because it is part and parcel of state affairs.

19.1 Essence and tasks of financial diplomacy

Financial diplomacy refers to international financial activities for national financial security, which means that, with the prerequisite possession of a national sovereign economy, the nation's fields of finance are in dynamic balance. This kind of balance is not only influenced by domestic factors but also by international ones. The tasks of financial diplomacy are the following:

(1) Serving domestic socioeconomic development and maintaining national financial security.
(2) Strengthening domestic financial strength and elevating the international position of domestic finance.
(3) Establishing and developing the international finance system, coordinating international financial relationships, solving

international financial disputes, conducting international financial operations, resolving international financial crises, and improving and reforming the international financial order.

The following are the two forms of financial diplomacy:

(1) Conducting diplomatic activities with a view to realizing financial targets, or seeking after financial interests for the state with diplomatic approaches.
(2) Conducting financial activities for the purpose of realizing diplomatic goals. (For example, a goal for the creation of a good external environment, this is able to raise the state's international position.) Or, seeking after interests in foreign relationship with financial means.

The following are the two traits of financial diplomacy:

(1) The first trait is soft, manifesting itself in soft strength, mainly devoted to finance design and financial mechanisms, and playing its role of a lever.
(2) The second trait is speciality, reflecting the state of the virtual economy. Its chain of relations is very long and not easy to comprehend. Its operational forms are relatively unclear, definitely not easy to be seen. With knowledge and practice related to various aspects, it is still relatively complicated.

Following the deepening development of economic globalization, the position and the role of financial diplomacy are becoming increasingly strengthened. After the end of the Cold War, especially since the 1990s, finance has been a basic factor with an increasing impact on the social and political life of all nations. In some developed countries, it is also the direct cause of political crisis and social turmoil. At the turn of the century, great changes took place in world economic patterns. For example, a gigantic and unified market was realized in Europe and the relationship between countries was developed through transnational financial operations. This has become an important option for many countries in adjusting their international political and economic relationship. Likewise, in comparison, financial strength has become a new and more effective weapon of diplomacy for modern powers and an important means for realizing national strategic targets. Financial diplomacy is as important as political diplomacy and military diplomacy. Financial diplomacy is able to better reflect the essence of economic globalization than political diplomacy and military diplomacy.

The United States and other Western countries are fully aware of the great role of financial power, especially because it holds more value of application than do nuclear weapons. Under the prerequisite of non-violation of the basic standards of international relationships, they utilize the development of the international financial system to consolidate their hegemony and utilize their own powerful financial strength to challenge the economic sovereignty of other nations, in order to control the destiny of most other countries in peaceful times and to establish a stable global hegemony. The United States' position as the overlord of the Western world is closely associated with the Bretton Woods system based on a strong US dollar. Professor Samuel Huntington of Harvard University lists the main points of strategies for Western countries to control the world in his book, *The Clash of Civilizations and the Remaking of World Order*. Of Huntington's main points, there are three points relating to finance: (i) control of international banks; (ii) control of global hard currency; and (iii) seizure of international capital markets. Obviously, the United States has been excellent in accomplishing these things. In present days, financial diplomacy has become an important diplomatic means for powers to vie for the international arena. If China expects to realize its targets for modernization in the 21st century, the nation will have to strive to become a financial power and have its own way of thinking about financial diplomacy.

19.2 British and American financial diplomacy in review

The significant impact of finance on international relationships can be traced back to 19th century. Since 1870, Britain and other industrialized countries accumulated a large amount of capital. In order to show, as much as possible, the insignificant effect of capital, they vigorously exported capital abroad, adding a new dimension to their international relationships. At that time, the power of Britain did not lie in its enormous number of colonies, or in the British fleet whose prestige had spread far and wide or in its vigorous industrial production, but in the international finance system under its control for already almost 100 years. Britain managed the world finance system through its government and the Bank of England. It practiced the gold standard system to exchange between sterling and gold. Pound sterling became a major international reserve currency. Over 40% of international trading was settled in sterling. As illustrated by British scholar Susan Strange's analysis, nearly 100 years of rapid development, supremacy, and prosperity of the 19th century British Empire had a great deal to do with the stable, sterling-supported, gold standard system. On the eve of the First World War in 1914, Britain's overseas investment was as much as four billion pounds, accounting for half of the total investment of all Western countries. About one-fourth of its national wealth was invested in railways, seaports, and other urban infrastructure facilities abroad and in the purchasing of bonds issued by foreign governments. British investors and financiers obtained tremendous profits from investment abroad. Britain became a nation dependant on investment. Its economic system suffered a great deal due to the two World Wars and its treasury was nearly emptied by them. Britain thus fell from its dominant position of world hegemony.

In 1945, Britain's overseas assets suffered a loss of US$4 billion. Its export trade was only one-third of the pre-war export volume, its debts were as much as US$12 billion, and its gold reserve was only US$1 million. Obviously, Britain was hard up, and so unable to continue to support its powerful position in the international community. Naturally, Britain began to phase out from the center of the international arena, giving up its seat of world domination. Then, another world authority made itself up and went on stage.

After World War II, when planning for its position in the international system, the United States was well aware that it could not rely on military strength alone to achieve world hegemony. The Soviet Union was then as strong as the United States in military strength. The United States' trump card was utilizing accurate strategies, combined with military authority and powerful economic strength, to create an international financial system with it and using this system for the purpose of financial hegemony, in order to simultaneously realize political and military domination. Since the Bretton Woods conference, the United States has been an enormously powerful leader in the battlefield of international financial diplomacy, by way of controlling international financial institutions such as the International Monetary Fund and the World Bank. The Marshall Plan that the United States put forward, also known as the European Recovery Program, provided US$13.15 billion between 1948 and 1951 in economic aid to Western European countries. The purpose and effects of this move are obvious. Politically, the United States intended to advance the consolidation of regional range of the capitalist system through capital-raising and to bring about the union of Western European countries in order to resist the expansion of socialism in the former Soviet Union and Eastern European countries. Economically, the United States intended to export surplus post-war production capacity in order to realize its domestic economic targets and its overseas economic expansion. Stimulated by the Marshall Plan, shares of American grain on the world market rocketed from a pre-war of 10–50% in 1950. After the 1970s, the Bretton Woods system disintegrated. The leading and dominating power of the US weakened for a while not only because the European Community emerged strong from the war years, but especially because of the soaring development of Japan. However, after drawing a good lesson from this bitter experience, the United States exploited whatever usable conditions were available to it and applied various adept control methods to effectively complete a major encirclement campaign on the battlefield of financial diplomacy. When the financial crises of the end of 20th century hit the world, Mexico, East Asia, Russia, Brazil, and other countries involved were cowed into turning to the International Monetary Fund for assistance. In a certain sense, they became victims of "financial colonialism", their economic sovereignty being gravely "injured". The United States actively participated in the aid plan of the International Monetary Fund and provided large amounts of funds, thus becoming a "Savior" of sorts, and reaped exorbitant profits from the crises.

At the turn of the century, as "the only and also the last all-mighty global superpower," the United States made its journey everywhere around the world, and especially in the field of finance. In Asia, it proved its tremendous energy in guiding the international financial order. In Latin America, it snapped at the "Samba whirlwind", avoiding the danger of a fire in its own backyard. In Russia, it conducted its financial diplomacy, vigorously pressuring Russia to abandon its "cold war ideology". The United States' huge virtual economy and enormous energy consumption depend heavily on the world market. That is the exact and deep-rooted cause of why it is anxious to ensure its monopoly interests by establishing world hegemony and exercising control over world funds, resources, and directing the supply of energies. The goals of the United States have caused it to coerce other countries to open their financial markets. With its financial diplomatic skills and strength of financial diplomacy and in order to market its value system to the rest of the world through its formulation of "game rules", the United States has established a financial order under its hegemony and expanded its monopoly interests.

Due to the impact of the global financial crisis, the situation of the world is changing at a fast speed. The United States feels some pressure and has several challenges. There are quite a few expectations and sayings about it. Nevertheless, it should be said that the 21st century still belongs to the United States, not only because it will remain for a long time to come the leading superpower in the world, it is also a nation that is the most creative, has the most currency-sovereignty influence, and has the highest level of global consumption. No matter what the US government does, it will wield a significant impact on the shape of the world. Additionally, US policies and strategy formulation mechanisms are relatively flexible and changeability in their ability to make alterations according to the changing situation and other corresponding adjustments in accordance with what the new development requires.

19.3 The essence of China's financial diplomacy

The core essence of China's finance diplomacy is "to demonstrate good faith for achieving comprehensive understanding and co-development". On the basis of the core role and regular patterns of finance in a national economy, financial diplomacy brings into full play various resources concerning finance and build-up credit cooperation relationships needed for national mid- and long-term development, thus manifesting mutual trust and mutual benefit while also realizing national development targets.

Undoubtedly, financial diplomacy is an important component of China's overall diplomacy. Together with economic globalization, especially with the deepening of financial globalization after each passing day, competition between countries is shifting to become the competition of comprehensive national strength with economic interests at its core. The central position that finance holds in international economy is becoming increasingly obvious. Objectively, financial diplomacy is required to play a larger role in maintaining national interests.

The relationship between financial diplomacy and overall diplomacy is like the difference between uniqueness and generality, individuality, and commonness. When we consider international finance, we should maintain the consistency of financial diplomacy with overall diplomacy, while focusing on the uniqueness of financial diplomacy.

The consistency of China's financial diplomacy, as well as its overall diplomacy, lies in three things.

(1) Its diplomacy lies in actively advocating three general principles: the principle of respect for national sovereignty, the principle of mutual benefit, and the principle of general development.
(2) It strives to establish a fair, rational, and highly efficient new international financial order in the global financial field.

(3) China is a large, responsible, international financial nation. How China administrated itself during the financial crisis in East Asia, and the actions it took during the current international financial crisis, have shown the world that China is a large and responsible nation. This is precisely consistent with what China's overall diplomacy represents.

Compared with the entirety of diplomacy, financial diplomacy's uniqueness lies in this: financial diplomacy is conducted by centering around the establishment, adjustment, and formation of an international financial arrangement. The international financial arrangement includes mainly the coordination and management of financial affairs, such as the organizing of exchange rates, by the regulation of international revenue and expenditures, as well as international reserve assets and international currencies, of which the arrangement of exchange rates is most important.

19.4 Reform of the RMB exchange rate and financial diplomacy

In recent years, reform of the RMB exchange rates has drawn worldwide attention. It is also the most important issue of priority when considering China's financial diplomacy.

RMB exchange rate reform is China's internal affair. However, because an exchange rate has external effect, when a nation makes known its exchange rate policy, it has to consider the responses of other countries. "Responsible to the international community, while persisting in maintaining independence and keeping initiative in our own hands" is the main principle which is upheld by reform of the RMB exchange rate.

Reform of the RMB exchange rate depends on three factors: (i) the needs of national mid- and long-term development; (ii) the needs of present economic balance; and (iii) compliance with laws concerning financial activities. A strong RMB is good for China's mid- and long-term development. When a decision for the appreciation or depreciation of the RMB exchange rate is made, consideration should be given to the impetus and the needs of domestic economic development. Meanwhile, consideration should also be given to external factors, as exchange rate serves as the price of a transaction. To promote the adjustment of economic structures, and also to consider the growth of China's actual wealth since the beginning of reform and the opening up of the country, it is necessary to appreciate the RMB eventually, although it may exert a certain negative bearing on present economic development. Consider, for instance, the negative impact on export. The Chinese government has actively committed itself to the reform of the RMB exchange rate mechanism; this is recognized by the international community. Currently, Western countries frequently express their expectation for China to substantially appreciate the RMB exchange rate. These countries do so, totally out of their own national interests, thus violating the basic principles of the exchange rate mechanism. In response, China should persist in the highest national interests, be prudent in making decisions, and steadfast in maintaining a correct policy for financial diplomacy as follows:

(1) A gradual and comprehensive advancement of reform in the exchange rate system. At present, according to the degree of opening up of Chinese finance and the stages of economic development and financial market development, it is good to maintain a fixed exchange rate between the RMB and the USD. Taking the most principal reserve currency as the standard for monetary policy is instrumental to the stability of the Chinese currency, trade growth, direct foreign investment, international settlement, and overseas investment with domestic capital.
(2) The proper management of foreign exchange reserves. Foreign exchange reserve is an important means for the adjustment of macroeconomy and for the realization of internal and external balance. Large amounts of surplus invite risk, just as a huge balance payments deficit does. As long as the current foreign exchange reserve is well-managed, it will not only become an

enormous economic resource but also an important instrument for financial diplomacy. Excessive purchasing of American national bonds might not be the best solution. We should seize the opportunity to buy petroleum, mineral products of noble metals (including gold), large tracts of forests, and other commodity brands, so as to scatter the investment risks of foreign exchange reserve assets, while appropriately increasing in Euros and other currencies as reserve assets.

(3) Controlling the dynamics and tempo of the opening up of China's finance to the world. Financial development should first of all give priority to our national security and our financial security. Overall design should be adopted and development should be achieved by following logically and advancing step-by-step and the financial system should be opened up in an orderly manner, focusing especially on the dynamics and tempo of the financial market (including foreign exchange, stocks, and derivative financial instruments). In the opening up of China's finance to the world, the attention should be on guard against international "hot" money, or a sudden coming and going of investment capital, to maintain the dynamic balance in both the economic and financial fields. As China's finance and financial markets are not yet fully developed and their supervising capacity is somewhat backward, they are insufficient to endure the speculative impact of international "hot" money. What matters most is that China does not need the hyperbole of international "hot" money; it needs essential investing in the construction of enterprises to provide more employment opportunities and the introduction of advanced management and technology to boost China's technological level and accumulate an assembly of human resources.

(4) Further improving China's financial development strategies. In order to improve the national financial supervising system, China should first draw upon the experience of other countries and guard against the financial risks experienced by them by purposefully creating a national financial risk pre-warning

system. Next, China should establish and improve the conduction mechanism of monetary policy and raise our capacity to address external pressures and deal with "games". Then, China should further improve our foreign exchange management. For example, setting up and improving basic social security funds, funds for stabilizing the stock market, and national innovation fund with part of the assets in USD foreign exchange, changing the current foreign exchange settlement system to reporting and filing systems to leave part of foreign exchange behind, the part that enterprises need with them. After that, further improvements to the strategy of "going global", great efforts should be made to advance qualified domestic institutional investor (QDII) and encourage investment in overseas industries. China should learn from the experience of Japan the following: constructing overseas production bases and establishing a trans-border payment system, controlling the direction of flow for short-term capital and allowing the flow of current accounts, encouraging swapping transactions of RMB and other currencies, encouraging the establishment of overseas branches of financial institutions and the strategic acquisition and ownership of some key stocks, internationally distinguished brands and enterprises when opportunities arise. Finally, being meticulous in designing a Chinese-version plan for governing international finance: actively participating in the revision of global rules and standards, while expressing China's requirements for national interests and the desires of other developing countries, advocating the establishment of an Asian monetary fund to strengthen financial cooperation with neighboring countries, and advocating the establishment of a global fund for the development of energy and setting-up fund, for grain security.

19.5 Finance supports the "going global" strategy

The "going global" strategy is an extremely important strategical decision made by the Central Committee of the Chinese Communist Party and the State Council, according to changes in the domestic and international situations. The significance of financially supporting the "going global" strategy can be summed up in the following aspects:

(1) For the need of guaranteeing the security of the national economy and foreign exchange reserves.
(2) For the need of helping enterprises absorb surplus production capacity and promoting the adjustment and upgrading of China's structure of industries.
(3) For the need of advancing the growth of the national economy with the development of trade by investment.
(4) For the need of cultivating multinational firms to boost China's international competitive power.
(5) For the need of developing China's finance itself. Implementation of the "going global" strategy calls for the joint advancement of the enterprise community and the finance community, so as to strengthen China's overall economic and financial competitive edge and maintain national interest and security.

There is a preliminary effect on finances supporting the "going global" strategy. A diversified pattern has been formed for the rapid development of direct overseas investment, the main bodies of the structure of investment, diversification of industries, venues for investment, and investment modes. In 2008, China's direct overseas investment amounted to as much as US$52.15 billion, an all-time high since the government began to carry out its "going global" strategy at the end of 1990s. China's overseas investment is becoming a new force in the international investment field.

At the same time, we are clearly aware that there are deficiencies in our financial service system and its functions, even failing to provide enough support to the "going global" strategy. To begin with, a complete financial support system for carrying out a "going global" strategy has not yet been formed, thus failing to provide investing enterprises with adequate support. Also, the development of China-owned overseas financial institutions is slow and their service efficiency is low; they are not able to provide overseas enterprises with timely and effective service. Next, financial institutions, more often than not, tend to "fight the battle single-handedly", thus failing to form a synergy in order to support enterprises wishing to "go global". Subsequently, the degree of internationalization in domestic banks is low and their financial services fail to keep pace with the development of the "going global" strategy. Lastly, the level of cooperation with international guarantor organizations is low and fails to meet the need for international investment insurance.

Against the background of the current international financial crisis, quite a number of countries are aware of the urgency to cooperate with China in an unprecedented manner and they attach more importance to drawing on China's experience in development, as well as China's position and role globally, and depend more heavily on China's domestic market, technology, and especially China's advantage in capital in particular. This has provided China's expansion of deeper international cooperation with more space for development. During the international financial crisis that was brought about by the American sub-prime crisis in financial institutions of the United States and European countries, it appeared that a number of countries had trouble in even taking care of themselves. Undoubtedly, this has brought unprecedented historical opportunities for China. Time and tide wait for no man. We must make full use of the situation and make great efforts in these aspects. The current situation requires us to fortify our awareness to be sure of seizing the opportunity. Therefore, we should seize the opportunity, advance in a unified and coordinated way, be pragmatic, highlight the key issues, and display finance's function of "moving a weight of 500 kg with a weight of 4 ounces", centering around national energy sources and resource strategies, accelerating the expansion of international financial business, continuing to display the role of financial cooperation and its driving force, working in active coordination with China-invested enterprises, and with relevant governmental departments, in formulation and implementation of a "road map" for the overall strategy, performing well a "combined boxing" strategy, advancing cooperation in various fields through financial cooperation to realize a new big-leap-forward, promoting "two resources, two markets, and two overall situations" in order to lay down a solid foundation for China's long-term peace and stability, economic development, and a guarantee of energy resource security and grain security, to contribute to the realization of the goals of China's financial diplomacy.

19.6 Development-oriented finance actively supports the strategy of "going global"

As a development financial institution of the government, China Development Bank actively enforces the intentions of the government, conscientiously works in coordination with the national strategy of "going global", and persists in "seizing the situation, grasping every new opportunity, looking to the future, highlighting key issues, and mastering regular patterns". With the strategy for national development and security in mind, the Bank is making great efforts to expand international cooperation. Through diversified financial measures such as comprehensive credit lines, syndicated loans, currency swapping, and gross settlements, the Bank backs up qualified domestic enterprises with strength in "going global", conducts mutual-beneficial cooperation in fields of energy development, people's livelihood and other areas and by utilizing the markets and resources at home and abroad to support the rapid development of domestic economy. In supporting the "going global" strategy, China Development Bank persists in taking the late Premier Zhou Enlai as an example, learning from him and his spirit, and endeavors to do many more things that have a far-reaching, historic meaning.

To go out and to be rooted abroad, in order to establish a highly reliable and mutually dependent relationship with cooperative partners and regions, China Development Bank has put forward the policy of "sending charcoal in snowy weather, making preparations for possible projects, looking to the future, striving for mutual benefits, and win–win results" and has formed a set of guidelines for routine work — planning first, achieving a common understanding among higher-level management, advancing cooperation on financing issues, establishing cooperation platforms, persisting in market operation, and controlling risks. The five working principles are as follows: persisting in mutual benefits and win–win results, doing what is appropriate in light of local conditions; persisting with the advantage by complementing each other, bringing into play systematic synergy of governmental cooperation, financial cooperation, and enterprise cooperation, continuing in market-oriented operation and administrating cooperation in various ways insisting on planning first and stressing the importance of prior good planning for all fields and other projects, continuing in pragmatism and high efficiency to provide our cooperative partners with individualized services.

In supporting "going global", China Development Bank begins its work according to the law of finance and has preliminarily formed a set of strategic thinking as follows:

(1) *Justice first; profit second*: the credit relationship thus established is a long relationship.
(2) *More giving than taking*: the credit relationship thus established is a sincere relationship. No short-term gains are sought after. Continued support for "going global" will not be given up just because, during the initial stage, operation is both time- and effort-consuming and the return is low.
(3) *Resources exchange*: a mutually-beneficial credit relationship needs to be established. This is not only expected to overcome capital- and technology-related difficulties for partner but also to guarantee a long-term, stable supply of resources from abroad for China. A foundational credit relationship is to be established. Persistence in planning first means that, while making overall plans for China's global operation, China helps cooperative partners formulate their plans for development. We should actively be conducting exchanges and training and strengthening mutual understanding with cooperating nations.
(4) *Diversified service*: a flexible credit relationship is to be established. According to the characteristics and needs of the various

projects, relatively flexible forms, commercial modes of rational structure, and credit structure will be adopted to provide a diversified financial service.

(5) *Underlining key issues and developing credit relationships with the Third World*: China Development Bank has inherited and carried forward the theory of "three worlds" and set great store in it by utilizing traditional favorable factors to conduct the development of financial cooperation with countries in Asia, Africa, and Latin America in order to develop a credit relationship with the Third World.

19.7 Summary

Financial diplomacy is a product of the in-depth development of economic globalization and an important tool to pursue national interests. As international economic intrinsic links have been enhanced in the process of economic globalization, cooperation and development have thus become the purposes and themes of China's "go global" strategy in the new era. Thus, development-oriented financial institute, in line with the principles of "joint development, seeking common ground while reserving differences, and mutual benefit", have dynamically cooperated with the international community, particularly with developing countries in infrastructure construction, and prepared development plans together to promote each other's development (Figure 19.1).

Based on the overall situation of national development strategies, development-oriented financial institutes have comprehensively considered multiple factors like agricultural projects, resources exploration, infrastructure construction, and social bottlenecks according to the rules and characteristics of the financial work, adhered to the principles of "placing justice before benefits, giving before taking, swap of resources and providing comprehensive support, and diversified services", and initially formed a set of strategic thoughts and effective measures to energetically support domestic enterprises to "go global", invest abroad, and achieve mutual benefits.

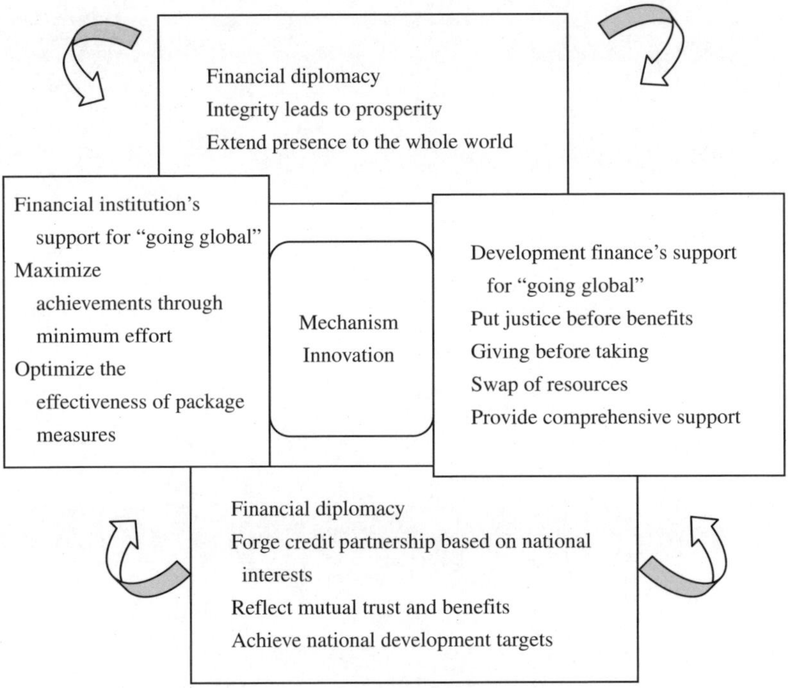

Figure 19.1: Financial diplomacy.

As of September 2010, CDB had dispatched 141 working groups to other parts of the world, established a new international business system, and developed into an international development-oriented finance institution with Chinese characteristics.

Chapter 20

Properly Handle Five Relations to Ensure the Stable and Rapid Economic Development of China

The global recession brought about by the US financial crisis has been the most serious international event since World War II. The causes are related to various factors: the over consumption in the Europe and the United States, the irrational international financial system set up after World War II, the lack of effective demand in the international market, the loopholes in international financial regulation, and the fervent pursuit of short-term leverage incomes of some enterprises. In response to the international financial crisis and China's unbalanced and unsustainable economic development, China should draw on the experience and learn from the lessons both at home and abroad, establish a long-term, effective mechanism to guard against financial risks, and properly handle five relations to ensure the stable and rapid economic development of China.

20.1 The relation between emergency response and mid- and long-term development

In the process of economic and social development, China will inevitably encounter some unexpected events and thus should have mental preparation and measures for emergency to properly solve the pressing problems and create favorable conditions for mid- and long-term development. As to natural disasters like the massive earthquake in Wenchuan, Sichuan Province, China should have contingency measures for such unavoidable events; as to major incidents in the changing economic environment like the successive bankruptcy of SMEs affected by the international financial crisis, China should provide basic living allowances for the employees of such enterprises; as to the competition and game on the international market, China needs a high-level strategic planning for any tricks our rivals may play. Among the abundant problems faced by China, the most critical issue is employment; without employment, there will be no demand, consequently no market and no potential for business expansion. Thus, development-oriented financial institute, as a vital tool of the government, should focus on creating jobs in its policy and funding arrangements. Meanwhile, development-oriented financial institute should be well aware that some issues such as the structure and development mode are fundamental and deep-rooted, that is, restructuring and development paradigm shift will take tremendous efforts. It is imperative for development-oriented financial institute to help the government integrate considerations of emergency and mid- and long-term development, turn immediate emergency measures into mid- and long-term development mechanism, and seek for the new thoughts of changing crisis into opportunity. Accordingly, efforts should be launched to (i) promote the building of emergency response mechanism with financing operations, including further improving the national catastrophe insurance system and the unemployment insurance system; (ii) strengthen analysis on the dynamics of economic and social environment, optimize planning, and improve the level of international development strategies; (iii) energetically support the development and entrepreneurship of SMEs; (iv) intensify the construction of infrastructure, basic industries and pillar industries, and resolutely promote the technological, product, and industrial upgrading; (v) increase the basic social security system, and give priority to helping the most needy urban and rural population. In a word, dealing with the relation between emergency and mid- and long-term development by starting from improving the mechanisms can avoid sharp economic ups and downs.

20.2 The relation between the domestic market and the international market

The domestic market has always been the foothold of development of China's economy. Development-oriented financial institutes should intensify efforts to establish the virtuous cycle of domestic market and expand domestic demand and supply. Generally, big economies are based on the domestic market. As China boasts a vast market of 1.3 billion population and enjoys huge market space with respect to urbanization, industrial development, residents' consumption, and ecological and environmental protection, China's development needs to rely on the domestic market and its own capital accumulation, so it has been absolutely wise of the central government to consider expanding domestic demand as the footing of economic growth. In the meantime, development-oriented financial institute should recognize that combining the expansion of domestic demand and the expansion of external demand is an integral part of the strategic plan for national prosperity. With the development of economic globalization, the organic link between different economies is increasingly close, and so is the intrinsic link between China's development and that of its counterparts in the world. China is unlikely to attain sustainable economic growth and modernization by just relying on its own internal needs; instead, it should intensify exchanges with the international market and rely on both internal and external demand to achieve rapid economic growth. After over 30 years of reform and opening up, China's economic development has been increasingly dependent on international markets, and the dependence on foreign trade mounted from 9.7% in 1978 to 58.25% in 2009. In an open economy, domestic and international markets promote each other. The expansion of international markets and the increase of exports can give impetus to the domestic business investment, improve the employment rate, and raise personal income, thereby increasing the domestic investment and consumer demand; in turn, the increase of domestic investment and consumer demand will drive the imports and raise the income of foreign residents, thus further boosting international demands for products and services. Currently, China's economy is characterized by its robust export of various products and its dependence on the import of energy and mineral raw materials like oil, gas, and mineral resources. Therefore, China should give full consideration to the background of economic globalization while developing its domestic market. In international cooperation, in addition to focusing on energy and mineral resources,

China should also highlight agricultural cooperation and may forge partnership with some developing countries rich in agricultural resources. Such cooperation can create conditions for Chinese agriculture to "go global" and establish a buffer zone for China's food security on the one hand and on the other hand, help alleviate local food shortage and consolidate the ties between both sides. China should make long-term plan in this regard to ensure the benefit of the nation and future generations. The international financial crisis has attenuated the US-centric global power, and it has also brought opportunities to the expansion of globalization featuring multi-polar development. One case in point is that the Latin American countries, once regarded as the backyard of the US, have successively turned to China for financing support. This provided a rare opportunity for China to promote the independent globalization. Against this backdrop, development-oriented financial institute should effectively implement the central government's proactive opening up strategy, seize the opportunity to expand their international presence, and energetically strengthen international cooperation to lay a solid foundation for long-term prosperity. Given that underlying the current dwindling international market are numerous opportunities, it is advisable for development-oriented financial institute to energetically open up overseas markets and expand external demand amidst the shrinking of traditional external markets.

20.3 The relation between real economy and virtual economy

Real economy refers to all the production, distribution, exchange, and consumption processes associated with ordinary goods or services and also the realization process of use value and value of goods. Real economy includes sectors like agriculture, industry, transportation, construction, commerce, and post and telecommunications. Virtual economy refers to all the production, distribution, exchange, and consumption processes associated with monetary commodities and the realization process of use value and value, including the banking sector, securities, insurance, capital markets, money markets, and foreign exchange markets. Real economy and virtual economy are like two sides of a coin. On the one hand, real economy is the foundation of virtual economy. The following are the characteristics of real economy:

(1) Real economy provides the material basis for the development of virtual economy. The emergence and development of virtual economy must be based on the material conditions of real economy. Otherwise, the virtual economy would be like a tree without roots.
(2) Real economy always puts forward higher requirements for virtual economy and promotes it to keep growing.
(3) Real economy is an indication of the development level of virtual economy, and also the starting and ending points of it.

On the other hand, virtual economy is relatively independent, having its own law of development and exerting reaction to real economy. The following are the characteristics of virtual economy:

(1) Virtual economy affects the external environment of real economy, including the total funds of the society, financing, circulatory status, and so on.
(2) Virtual economy gives impetus to the development of real economy because the prerequisite for the normal development of real economy is that there must be adequate funds and a variety of convenient, fast financial instruments.
(3) The development of virtual economy restricts the development degree of real economy. Historically, the stages of virtual economy development, including the capitalization of idle money, the socialization of interest-bearing capital, the marketization of securities, the internationalization of financial markets, and the integration of international finance, have reflected the development level of the real economy.

To properly deal with the relation between real economy and virtual economy, it is necessary to comply with four principles:

(i) give equal importance to both of them; (ii) make overall plans and give full consideration to the macro planning, strategic layout, and other aspects of the two economies; (iii) seek for balanced development in terms of both the speed and the scale of development; and (iv) allow them to have their own operating mode, conduct code, inherent requirements, and service objects and form coherent macro- and micro-management mechanisms. To withstand the recession, US needs to make efforts simultaneously in both real economy and virtual economy and promote their coordinated development.

20.4 The relation between financial innovation and regulation

The financial crisis in 2008 originated from the US subprime mortgage derivatives. The fact that subprime mortgage is an innovative financial product has aroused doubts about financial innovation, which requires that development-oriented finance must handle the relationship between financial innovation and financial regulation in an appropriate manner. Summarizing the lessons learned from the crisis, China needs to further improve financial supervision and must not give up development-oriented finance, or get stuck in financial innovation for fear of running risks. Without innovation, the diverse financing needs are unlikely to be satisfied and the competitiveness of financial institutions is also about to be damaged. Financial innovation, whereas it itself complies with the law of financial development, reveals the cause of US subprime crisis: there were too many innovative products of the subprime mortgage derivatives targeted at ordinary people and there was no necessary financial regulation. We must learn a lesson from this to avoid such problems. Based on analysis of the cause and propagation mechanism of the US subprime crisis, there are four points worthy of our attention: (i) financial innovation should be conducive to economic development, and cannot be completely separated from the real economy for self-loop; (ii) financial innovation should comply with the law of economic development to avoid excessive expansion of financial assets and over virtualization of the economy; (iii) financial innovation should cater to different groups with customized products and services rather than render the same product or service to all people; and (iv) financial innovation should strictly comply with industry standards and the code of conduct and be kept in order to ensure financial stability and healthy economic development. In short, financial innovation must be escorted by appropriate financial regulation, which is capable of not only keeping things under control but also protecting the innovative vitality. This is a superb art to allow financial innovation and regulation to promote each other. On the one hand, financial regulation boosts financial innovation. To improve competitiveness and efficiency, financial institutions have always sought for innovative financial products, a process beneficial to economic advance. On the other hand, financial innovation propels the constant adjustment of financial regulation. Innovation exacerbates the uncertainty of financial activities and increases the difficulty in financial regulation, forcing regulatory authorities to continually seek for more effective management approaches and constantly transform the financial regulatory system. To properly handle the relation between financial innovation and financial regulation, financial institutions must make financial innovation under the premise of serving the needs of the economy, steer the innovation of financial system, financial mechanism and financial products to promote the development of real economy and improve the core competitiveness of the industry, and pool efforts in financing expansion and risk diversification to provide stronger financial support for economic growth. Meanwhile, financial regulatory authorities must adapt to the changes and trends of the industry, formulate innovation-friendly indicators and measures, build financial regulation emergency system, and strengthen monitoring over the security of the financial system so as to ensure its steady operations. Since China's reform and opening up, the transformation of the financial sector has made remarkable achievements; but development-oriented financial institute should be well aware that China's financial innovation is at the primary stage, innovative financial products still fail to meet the needs of the rapid economic and social development, and the financial system is not strong enough to support the grand modernization drive. Thus, development-oriented financial institute should intensify the efforts in financial innovation.

20.5 The relation between the structural reform and development of policy-oriented finance

The reform and development of CDB, a policy-oriented financial institute as generally believed, has received wide attention from both at home and abroad.

(1) *The reform and development of CDB has reflected the strategic requirements of mid- and long-term development of the state.* CDB has continuously deepened reform throughout the exploration, and always shared a common fate with China's economic development and the reform and opening up. In 1994, the State Council approved the establishment of CDB, indicating that China's financial reform has entered a substantial stage. Since 1998, CDB has constantly deepened its reform, realized the government's targets in a market-based approach, and achieved satisfactory results, which have in turn created favorable conditions for further deepening the reform. Under new circumstances, the restructuring and transformation of CDB is an active exploration to refine the modern financial system with Chinese characteristics. Against the backdrop of economic downturn and with little domestic and foreign experience to draw on, CDB needs to sum up experience and lessons through its own practice of reform. Having actively adapted to the changing situation at home and abroad and focused on the fundamental requirement of ensuring financial security and economic security and serving the country's mid- and long-term development, CDB has proposed the principle of "four changes and four non-changes" based on opportune study on new situations and new measures. The "four changes" refers to the diversification of ownership structure, the modernization of governance structure, the marketization of management, and operation and the diversification of service functions; and the "four non-changes" means that its state-owned nature, fundamental functions, market positioning, and cooperative mode will remain unchanged. After the reform, CDB will remain as a state-owned bank to provide services

for the country's mid- and long-term development and as a bond bank and wholesale bank mainly engaged in mid- and long-term investment and financing in basic facilities, basic industries, and pillar industries. It will continue to abide by the theory and practice of development-oriented finance and cooperate with the government and enterprises in a market-oriented manner. Practice has proved that upholding the principle of "four changes and four non-changes" is conducive to the smooth transition of CDB, the continuity of existing businesses, and the prevention or resolution of difficulties and problems arising from the transition.

(2) *The reform and development of CDB has reflected the requirement of financial ecological diversity*. At the primary stage of socialism, China faces arduous tasks of mid- and long-term infrastructure construction, which are mainly reflected in the following aspects: the large gap between urban and rural areas and the imbalance of regional development; the irrational industrial structure, weak agricultural foundation, restricted energy security, and the extensive growth mode featuring high input, high consumption, high pollution, and low efficiency; the backward innovation capacities among the 49 major countries around the world, lagging behind Brazil, India, and other developing countries; the need to accelerate the development of urbanization in the next 30 years as more than 500 million farmers will move to the cities. Resolving these widely concerned difficult issues requires long-term, stable, and tremendous financing support. According to preliminary estimates, the funding gap will amount up to RMB281.5 trillion in the next three decades. There is no doubt that the government finance can play a leading role, but only relying on this is far from enough; commercial banks are indispensable, but the governance structure and for-profit purpose of commercial banks determine that they cannot provide large long-term credit to meet the financing needs of some basic industries and balance regional development. Investments in the mid- and long-term construction and hotspot social fields, where commercial banks are generally unwilling and unsuitable to engage in, usually involve enormous capitals, long period, and uncertain returns. Moreover, the still backward market system and the financial market incapable of

meeting the need of rapid, sustained growth remain as the Achilles' heel of China's mid- and long-term development. Unbalanced development determines China's financial ecological diversity and calls for the long-term function of development-oriented finance. It has turned out that under the government support and by issuing financial bonds on state credit to raise funds, CDB has, on the one hand, concentrated the short-term, dispersed money in the financial system and effectively mitigated the systemic risks of financial markets; on the other hand, it has increased investment in basic facilities, basic industries, and pillar industries and hotspot social areas and expanded the multiplier effect and acceleration effect of bond investment. Furthermore, it has promoted the effective implementation of industry development policies. Through market-oriented operations, CDB has realized the targets set by the government, promoted market development by financing, and helped overcome the investment and financing difficulties in the fields of mid-and long-term development and social hotspots.

(3) *The reform and development of CDB has embodied the requirements of China's "go global" strategy*. The financial crisis has intensified the adjustment of global economic pattern, propelled the reform of the international financial system, and promoted the development of emerging industries. Countries worldwide have re-examined the relationship between the government and the market, especially the US-led major advanced economies, which have not only increased policy and funding support for new energy, high technology, and intellectual development but also strengthened the government's financial management and intensified the role of policy-oriented finance and the intervention of state credit. It can be said that in many countries, the governments have been expanding the scope of functions and started to play a more positive role: (i) strengthening macro control to ensure macroeconomic stability; (ii) establishing market rules, correcting the market deviation, and maintaining the economic order; (iii) regulating social distribution and arranging for social security; and (iv) reinforcing international cooperation to jointly cope with global issues. The initiatives taken by the international community — actively adjusting government functions and

giving full play to the role of policy-oriented finance to gain a favorable edge in the competition in the 21st century, are inspiring and worth our consideration.

Given the complex domestic and international situation, China should draw on both the domestic and international experience, adhere to the government-led market economy, strengthen the functions of development-oriented finance in stabilizing the thriving market and boosting the sluggish market, and particularly give further play to the professional and commercial role of development-oriented finance in the international competition as China is accelerating the "go global" strategy. Under the leadership of the State Council and relevant departments and backed by the elaborate organization of the party committee of CDB, the great efforts of all workers and the strong support and active participation of the society, the reform of the CDB will definitely build a corporate governance structure that meets international norms and will further improve its management, expand the functions of investment and financing services, enhance the ability to support the state's mid- and long -term development strategy, and make further contribution to boosting economic and social development.

20.6 Summary

Affected by the global financial crisis, China's economy may face the thorniest condition in the next decades, which is primarily reflected in the following aspects: the increasing socioeconomic uncertainties and the deteriorating export environment may further enlarge the losses caused by the financial crisis; the existing contingency measures are difficult to come into play in a short time and the GDP growth rate may drop sharply; the efficiency of most enterprises is not optimistic, which may exert significant impact on the income of urban and rural residents; the RMB is derogatory at home and appreciating abroad and the people may suffer growing pressures owing to the high price, the falling stock market and real estate as well as the declining effective purchasing power; social contradictions may be more prominent and a growing number of unexpected

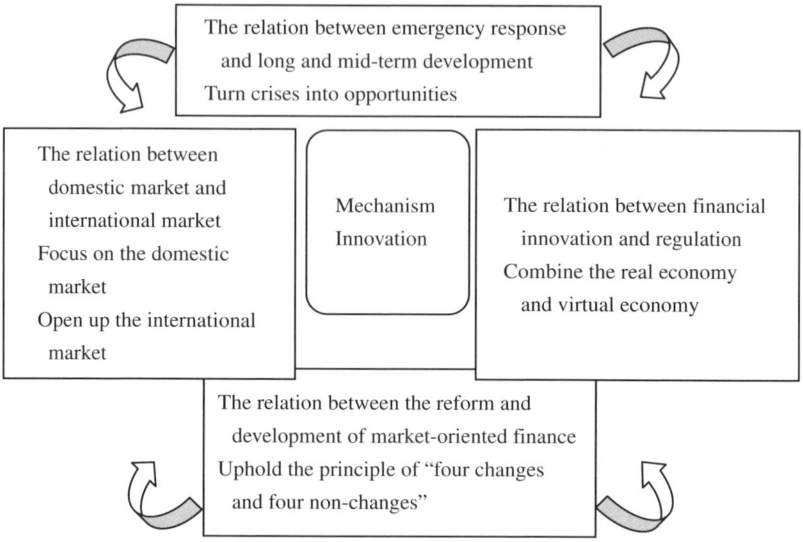

Figure 20.1: Properly handle five relations.

events are likely to happen (Figure 20.1). Accordingly, the key to ensuring China's stable and rapid economic development is to properly deal with the aforesaid five relations and prepare for long-term plight by taking the following measures:

(1) *Accelerate the establishment of subsistence food supply system.* Based on the existing subsistence allowances, food and clothing vouchers can be directly distributed to the most destitute urban and rural populations. Funds and food will come from government budget and donations from enterprises and the society, and will be managed by local governments and the communities designated by the civil affairs department. Voucher holders may get food from the specified store or specialty store. Based on preliminary estimates, the government may spend RMB10 billion each year to guide social resources and attract business products and national material reserves and circulation products, which will benefit 20 million of the most needy people and create 700,000 new jobs. The US has adopted such an approach since the Great Depression in the 1930s. China may consider establishing a similar system when appropriate according

to its specific situations, which can not only enrich the social security system and strengthen the social safety network but also contribute directly to the domestic consumption.

(2) *Step up the establishment of the Stock Market Stabilization Fund.* The proposed RMB20 billion fund, a policy-oriented fund targeted at retail investors short of market knowledge, will be established by the policy-oriented financial institutes. The Fund will acquire the shares retail investors are ready to sell when the stock market is experiencing long-term, sharp fluctuations, and will allow them to buy back their shares based on a certain percentage of the price when the market becomes stable. Thus, the Fund will be conducive to the steady development of the stock market and also the improvement of the capital market broker system.

(3) *Step up the improvement of the National Innovation Fund system.* Innovation is the best way to reduce the negative impact of the economic cycle. The country may consider allotting RMB20 billion to build the national re-guarantee company and another RMB20 billion to expand the existing national guidance fund for the high-tech industry. Such guidance fund and guarantee system can help solve the contradiction between fiscal technology investment and the commercial finance, enhance the demonstration and amplification effect of government funds in supporting technological innovation and industrialization, promote industry upgrading, improve production efficiency and product quality, adjust product structure, accelerate the building of the national innovation system, and thus enhance China's core competitiveness.

(4) *Accelerate the establishment of the National Land Fund.* On the national level, we should analyze the whole process of land property formation and analyze the corresponding rights of national ownership at different levels (central, local, collective, and individual) and at different stages (transfer, development, construction, lease, mortgage, etc.) to further clarify the respective property boundary, establish the local constraint mechanism based on national land ownership, urge the local government to establish the localization management mechanism featuring standardized operations and

intensive development under the guidance of the central policy, and develop the value transfer mechanism of rural land contract rights. By leveraging the Land Fund to concentrate the ownership values and market-based operations of the national land, we can achieve effective regulation of both land and finance, reasonably guide urban and rural construction, and enhance the self-circulation and growth of the land assets to realize the sustainable use of land and the harmonious and coordinated development of urban and rural economy.

(5) *Speed up the construction of the Shanghai World Financial Center (SWFC)*. The development strategy of the SWFC needs to be further improved to form a pattern in which Beijing, Bohai New Area, and Chongqing light around Shanghai, so that Shanghai can develop into the financial information center, currency exchange center, and securities trading center in Asia and highlight Chinese characteristics amidst the adjustment of the international financial pattern.

(6) *Further improve the international economic development strategy*. We need to develop the "go global" strategy of "keeping in a low profile and getting involved actively; setting foothold in Asia and tending toward the world; offering timely help and achieving mutual benefits; extending presence and focusing on long-term growth" and the mid- and long-term strategy of "slow export growth and tremendous overseas production" while innovating the respective management systems of increment and stock. Specifically, we can shift the current foreign exchange settlement system to the filing system, allow enterprises to directly retain a portion of needed foreign currency, and provide opportunities for the people to independently use foreign exchange; on the other hand, we can gradually expand the international influence of RMB by encouraging currency exchange in RMB with surrounding countries; actively promote the establishment of Northeast Asia Bank and the Asian Monetary Fund to strengthen financial cooperation with our neighbors and encourage qualified enterprises to set up overseas resource and production bases and opportunely acquire strategic stake. Efforts must be made to elaborately design China's version of the international financial governance program and actively get involved in the preparation of

global planning and standards to reflect the interest demands of our country and the aspirations of developing countries.

In short, China should concentrate on "maintaining growth, expanding domestic demand, adjusting structure, boosting employment, improving quality, conserving resources, building mechanisms, and increasing confidence" in the next stage, look for an advanced conduction mechanism between policy and micro activities, prevent reckless leaps in the name of saving the economy, abandon prestige projects in excuse of stimulating the economy, avoid the vicious cycle that may arise from investment expansion or the missing of the golden opportunity for international presence because of over-cautiousness.

Bibliography

Alfred D. Chandler, JR. 1990. *Scale and Scope — The Dynamics of Industrial Capitalism*, The Belknap Press of Harvard University Press, Cambridge, Massachusetts, London, England.

Balcerowize Leszek, 1995. *Socialism, Capitalism, Transformation,* Budapest, Central European University Press.

Chen Yuan, 2013. Aligning State and Market-China's Approach to Development Finance, Beijing, Foreign Languages Press.

China & World Economy, 21(2), March–April, 2013, Beijing, Institute of World Economics and Politics Chinese Academy of Social Sciences.

China Economic Quarterly, 6(1), 2006, Peking University Press.

China Modernization Research Center, China Modernization Research Report, 2007, Beijing, Peking University Press.

David M. Bachman, 2002. *Chen Yun,* First Chinese Edition, Beijing, Chinese Bibliography Press.

De Rivero, Osealdo, 1980. *New Economics Order and International Development Law*, Oxford Pergamon Press.

Deng Yingtao, 2011. *New Energy Revolution and Development Path*, Hong Kong, Strong Wind Press.

Dong Guoliang, 2012. *Urban Pattern Science — The Theory and Method to Solve Urban Diseases Fundamentally*, Beijing Science Press.

Drew Fudenberg and Jean Tirole, 2002. *Game Theory*, Beijing, China Renmin University Press.

Ezra F. Vogel, 2013. *The Era of Deng Xiaoping*, Beijing, SDX Joint Publishing Company.

Frederic S. Mishkin, 2005. *The Economics of Money, Banking, and Financial Markets,* Sixth Edition, Beijing, China Renmin University Press.

Gao Jian, 2009. *Debt Capital Markets in China*, Beijing, Economics Science Press.

Globalization and Modernization: The Strategic Choice of China's Moderation in the Context of Globalization, 2009, Beijing, Science Press.

Harvey S. Rosen, 2003. *Public Finance*, Sixth Edition, Beijing, China Renmin University Press.

Henry Kissinger, 2012. *On China*, Beijing, China CITIC Press.

Hungdah Chiu and Shao-chuan Leng, 1984. *China Seventy Years After the 1911 Hsin-hai Revolution,* Charlottesville University Press of Virginia.

Jarald Greenberg and Robert A. Baron, 2000. *Behavior in Organizations: Understanding and Managing the Human Side of Work,* Seventh Edition, USA. Prentice Hall, Upper Saddle River, New Jersey 07458.

Jiang Hong, 2012. *An Outline of World Economy — Research on Typical and Atypical Path of Development*, Beijing, China Renmin University Press.

Karl Marx, 1975. *Capital,* First Chinese Version, Beijing, People Press.

Lin Yifu, 2012. *New Structural Economics — A Framework for Rethinking Development and Policy*, Beijing, Peking University Press.

Liu Junjie, 2005. *Development of County Economy and Construction of Small Towns,* Beijing, Social Sciences Academic Press (China).

Liu Shouying and Luo Dan, 2004. *Can China Feed Itself: Chinese Scholars on China's Food Issue,* Beijing, Foreign Languages Press.

Mao Tse-Tung, 1965. *Selected Work of MAO TSE-TUNG,* First Edition, Beijing, Foreign Languages Press.

Meng Xiansheng and Wu Fangze, 2006. *The War of Great Strategy — The Energy Way,* Beijing, China Youth Press.

Michel Crouhy, Dan Galai and Robert Mark, 2005. *Risk Management*, Beijing, China Economy Press.

N. Gregory Mankiw and William Scarth, 1995. *Macroeconomics,* Canadian Edition, New York, Worth Publishers.

N. Gregory Mankiw, 2005. *Macroeconomics,* Fifth Edition, Beijing, China Renmin University Press.

Paul Arthur Berkman, 2002. *Science Into Policy: Global Lessons from Antarctica,* Academic Press, Adivion of Harcourt, Inc.

The Journal of World Economy No. 4 (2013). Beijing, China World Economics Association, Institute of World Economics and Politics Chinese Academy of Social Sciences.

World Economics and Politics No. 3 (2013). Beijing, Editorial Department of the Journal of World Economics and Politics.

Zou Lixing, 2009. *Development-Oriented Finance and Economy in China-A Historical Review and Prognostic Assessment*, USA, Bloomington, Indiana.

Zou Lixing, 2009. *Lessons from Development of US: Mechanism of Financial Imperialism*, Changsha, Hunan University Press.

Zvi Bodie, Alex Kane, and Alan J. Marcus, 2005. *Investment,* Sixth Edition, International Edition, McGraw Hill.

Epilogue

I had the honor to work at the China Development Bank after I returned in 2003 from my studies in the United States. I participated in the practice of development-oriented finance and respected the banner of development-oriented finance. I had originally planned to organize some people for an in-depth study of the principles of development-oriented finance and China's development economics. But I later found I had no conditions and ability to organize such a study. So I switched my limited energy to the research on the ideological basis, theoretical contents, operating mechanisms, and innovative development of development-oriented finance. The aim was to learn and publicize development-oriented finance. This research work ended in September 2010 with a preliminary draft, and I was greatly encouraged by Mr Jiang Zhenhua, former vice chairman of the Standing Committee of the National People's Congress, who wrote the foreword after going through the draft. As both the timing and contents needed further consideration, the draft was kept from publishing. But in the recent global financial crisis, development-oriented finance further demonstrated its unique roles. Accordingly, I felt it was the right time to present this preliminary report to readers, humbly hoping to attract further discussions, advance the theoretical and practical studies of development-oriented finance and China's modern economic and financial systems and promote the healthy and sustainable development of the Chinese economy and the world economy at large. In the course of this research, I have received support and guidance from leaders, care and help from co-workers and friends, and understanding and support from family members. I owe gratitude to them all. If this research is somewhat fruitful, it is a result of collective effort. But the errors and omissions belong to myself.

I am firmly convinced that the theory and practice of China's development-oriented finance is a banner of scientific development and also an important force to solve the financing bottleneck of the modernization drive. It is a great cause, which also serves the interests of the whole world. Proceeding from a new historical starting point and looking forward to the future, development-oriented finance has a long and tedious journey to cover. Under the leadership of the State Council and relevant departments and with the meticulous organization of the CDB party committee, the enterprising efforts of all CDB employees and the strong support from all walks of life, CDB will certainly advance development-oriented finance to a new height and make greater contributions to China's modernization drive.

Lixing Zou
November, 2013

Name and Subject Index